MICROSTATION 95

FUNDAMENTALS

Nancy A. Olson

New Riders

New Riders Publishing Indianapolis, Indiana

MicroStation 95 Fundamentals

By Nancy A. Olson

Published by:
New Riders Publishing
201 West 103rd Street
Indianapolis, IN 46290 USA

Copyright © 1996 by New Riders Publishing

Printed in the United States of America 1 2 3 4 5 6 7 8 9 0

Library of Congress Cataloging-in-Publication Data

```
Olson, Nancy A., 1960-
    MicroStation 95 Fundamentals.
        p.   cm.
    ISBN 1-56205-607-7
    1. Computer-aided design.  2. MicroStation.
TA174.047 1996
620'.0042'02866369--dc20        96-7073
                                CIP
```

Warning and Disclaimer

This book is designed to provide information about the MicroStation program. Every effort has been made to make this book as complete and as accurate as possible, but no warranty or fitness is implied.

The information is provided on an "as is" basis. The author and New Riders Publishing shall have neither liability nor responsibility to any person or entity with respect to any loss or damages arising from the information contained in this book or from the use of the disks or programs that may accompany it.

Publisher	Don Fowley
Publishing Manager	David Dwyer
Marketing Manager	Mary Foote
Managing Editor	Carla Hall

Product Development Specialist
Alicia Buckley

Development Editor
John Kane

Project Editor
Laura Frey

Copy Editor
Phil Worthington

Technical Editor
Jim Gearhard

Associate Marketing Manager
Tamara Apple

Acquisitions Coordinator
Stacey Beheler

Publisher's Assistant
Karen Opal

Cover Designers
Anne Jones,
Aren Howell

Cover Production
Aren Howell

Book Designer
Anne Jones

Production Manager
Kelly Dobbs

Production Team Supervisor
Laurie Casey

Graphics Image Specialists
Stephen Adams, Sonja Hart,
Clint Lahnen, Laura
Robbins, Todd Wente

Production Analysts
Jason Hand
Bobbi Satterfield

Production Team
Heather Butler,
Angela Calvert
Terrie Deemer,
Tricia Flodder,
Aleata Howard,
Scott Tullis,
Christine Tyner,
Karen Walsh

Indexer
Cheryl Dietsch

About the Author

Nancy A. Olson is currently employed as a senior systems analyst in the Information Services Division/Geographical Information Systems for the City of Milwaukee, Wisconsin. Nancy earned bachelor degrees in Geography and Anthropology from the University of Wisconsin-Milwaukee. During her 12 years in the industry, she has worked in production and training on IGDS, MicroStation, Unix system administration, and database management. In addition, she has experience in programming in the Unix shell, writing User Commands, programming in MDL, and supporting MicroStation users.

Nancy has broad experience as a trainer and freelance writer. Her training repertoire includes an introductory course in MicroStation 2D and courses in advanced MicroStation topics such as interface configuration, workflow considerations, productivity tips and hints, writing User Commands, and using Edit Graphics Utility and Network File Systems (NFS). These courses are offered through her company, Technical Directions. Nancy frequently speaks at The MicroStation Community (TMC) Forums held around the country and is an interim board member of TMC. She also has spoken at the AEC show, the Intergraph Graphic Users Group conferences and at the University of Wisconsin-Milwaukee Center for Continuing Engineering Education. She holds a position on the *MicroStation Manager* magazine's advisory board and is a technical editor. Nancy's other writings include articles in *MicroStation Manager* magazine, the *MicroStation Bible*, and *Inside MicroStation 5*.

Trademark Acknowledgments

Dedication

I dedicate this book to Greg (DC), for his unending support, encouragement, and enthusiasm. I truly hope that I can provide the same to you in your upcoming endeavors and that this book does as well as I know you will do.

Acknowledgments

I would like to thank several people for their assistance with this book: Bentley Systems for providing answers to my questions and problems; the editorial staff at New Riders for their efficiency and patience with my work; and finally to all my friends and family for their understanding during this project.

Contents at a Glance

Part 1: Understanding MicroStation

1. Getting Started
2. Taking MicroStation for a Test Drive
3. Building a Solid Foundation

Part 2: Learning How to Draw in 2D

4. Setting Up a Drawing File and Workspace
5. Placing Simple 2D Elements
6. Viewing a Drawing
7. Drawing with Accuracy
8. Placing More 2D Elements
9. Manipulating 2D Elements
10. Modifying 2D Elements
11. Advanced 2D Element Placement

Part 3: Putting on the Final Touches

12. Applying Patterns and Fills
13. Placing Dimensions
14. Working with Text
15. Plotting Your Drawing

Part 4: Sharpening Your Skills

16. Building and Placing Standard Symbols
17. Boosting Your Performance
18. Referencing Other Drawings
19. Changing the Way MicroStation Looks
20. Creating Drawing Standards

Table of Contents

Introduction   1
    How This Book Is Organized   3
    Following the Book's Conventions and Exercises   4
    New Riders Publishing   6

Part 1: Understanding MicroStation   9

1 Getting Started   11
    Understanding MicroStation Input Methods   12
    Using Input Devices   13
    Starting MicroStation   16
    Using the MicroStation GUI   19
    Getting Help   35
    Summary   36

2 Taking MicroStation for a Test Drive   37
    Starting Your First Design   38
    Setting Up the Screen   39
    Drawing on Grid Paper   41
    Drawing Lines   45
    Placing Blocks   50
    Moving Elements   52
    Copying Elements   55
    Deleting Elements   57
    Undoing a Deletion   58
    Ending a Design Session   59
    Finishing a File   61
    Summary   61

3 Building a Solid Foundation   63
    Understanding MicroStation Levels   64
    Understanding the Design Plane   79
    Introducing the Coordinate System   80
    Defining Working Units   80
    Setting Your Working Units   84
    Saving Your Work   86
    Summary   87

Part 2: Learning How to Draw in 2D   89

4   Setting Up a Drawing File and Workspace   91
Understanding MicroStation Workspaces and Interfaces   92
Other Functions of the MicroStation Manager Dialog Box   95
Creating a New Design File   97
Opening a Design File   102
Ending a Design Session   103
Opening a Design File When Entering MicroStation   108
Performing File Maintenance from MicroStation   108
Summary   113

5   Placing Simple 2D Elements   115
Tool Settings   116
Placing Lines   117
Active Element Symbology   125
Changing the Active Symbology   126
Placing Shapes and Polygons   131
Summary   142

6   Viewing a Drawing   143
Manipulating the View   145
Repainting the Display   147
Changing the Contents of the View   148
Controlling What You See   158
Saving Your View Settings   165
Summary   168

7   Drawing with Accuracy   169
Working with Tentative Points   170
Drawing on Grid Paper   178
Using Other Locks for Accuracy   182
Controlling the Coordinate Data Format   185
Using AccuDraw   187
Checking Accuracy   196
Protecting Elements from Change   206
Summary   206

8   Placing More 2D Elements   207
Placing Circles   208
Placing Ellipses   215
Placing Arcs and Partial Ellipses   217
Modifying Arcs and Partial Ellipses   222

Modifying Arcs, Circles, and Ellipses with the
Element Selection Tool   224
Rounding Corners   228
Using Arrays   233
Summary   238

9   Manipulating 2D Elements   **239**
Deleting Elements   240
Undo and Redo   242
Manipulating Multiple Elements at One Time   244
Copying Elements   262
Moving Elements   264
Parallel Command   266
Scaling Elements   268
Rotating and Spinning Elements   270
Mirroring Elements   272
Summary   274

10   Modifying 2D Elements   **275**
Changing or Modifying Lines and Shapes   276
Extending Lines   281
Deleting a Portion of Specified Elements   283
Inserting and Deleting Vertices   293
Changing How Elements Look   296
Selecting Elements by Attributes   300
Changing Elements by Element Information   305
Summary   306

11   Advanced 2D Element Placement   **307**
Exploring Custom Line Styles   308
Placing Stream Curves   319
Using Points   321
Summary   323

Part 3: Putting on the Final Touches   **325**

12   Applying Patterns and Fills   **327**
Patterning an Area   329
Patterning Areas Containing Holes   338
Patterning Linear Elements   345
Showing Pattern Attributes   346
Matching Pattern Attributes   346
Turning Off Pattern Display   347

Defining and Filling Complex Elements   348
Summary   352

13   Placing Dimensions   355
Understanding Dimensioning in MicroStation   356
Associating Dimensions   358
Dimensioning Lengths   359
Dimensioning Arcs and Angles   364
Dimensioning Diameters and Radii   369
Creating and Using Dimension Components Groups   373
Choosing the Settings   373
Changing the Way Existing Dimensions Look   380
Summary   381

14   Working with Text   383
Placing Text   384
Choosing and Changing Text Settings   386
Using Text Placement Options   392
Editing Text   395
Replacing Text   397
Copying and Incrementing Text   399
Matching Text in the Drawing   400
Using Advanced Text Placement Types and Features   402
Creating and Using Glossaries   408
Summary   411

15   Plotting Your Drawing   413
Creating Your First Plot   414
Understanding the Plotting Process   417
Plotting Full-Scale Drawings   419
Using the Plot Settings Box   420
Plot Resymbolization with Pen Tables   423
Saving the Configuration   428
Summary   428

Part 4: Sharpening Your Skills   429

16   Building and Placing Standard Symbols   431
Understanding Cell Libraries   433
Building Your First Cell   437
Using Your First Cell   443
Using Other Special-Purpose Cell Commands   446

Working with Cells 448
Using Shared Cells 452
Cell Selector 454
Summary 455

17 Boosting Your Performance   457
Defining a Workspace 458
Understanding Configuration Variables 459
Working with Function Keys 465
Setting Up and Modifying Seed Files 473
Changing Button Assignments 474
Attaching Menus 475
Macros 476
Summary 478

18 Referencing Other Drawings   479
Benefits of Using Reference Files 481
Attaching a Border File 484
Breaking the Reference Connection 494
Lining Up the Files 496
Keeping the Reference File Information Fresh 497
How MicroStation Finds the Reference Files 499
Summary 500

19 Changing the Way MicroStation Looks   501
Examining the Workspace Components 502
Setting User Preferences 503
Configuring the User Interface 514
Summary 520

20 Creating Drawing Standards   521
Approaching Drawing Standards 522
Using Standards for Design and Directory Names 523
Sharing Files 526
Establishing Working Units 528
Defining Design-File Features 530
Utilizing Cells, Shared Cells, and Symbols 538
Using Reference Files 541
Archiving and Backups 542
Summary 542

Index   543

INTRODUCTION

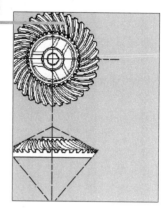

*W*elcome to MicroStation 95 Fundamentals. *This book is intended to introduce CAD users and professionals to MicroStation 95. Whether you are new to MicroStation or a user of past versions of the package,* MicroStation 95 Fundamentals' *explanations and exercises will help you efficiently use MicroStation.*

If you own Version 5, you will be excited to learn about MicroStation's enhancements and will want to implement the new features described in this book as quickly as possible. Throw away your custom palettes and start using the Cell Selector utility. Rethink those scripts, function keys, and user commands that set element symbology—record a macro. MicroStation 95 Fundamentals *is your guide to learning, understanding, and using the new features and functionality present in MicroStation. Some of the new features are described in the following list.*

◆ **The improved GUI.** The graphical user interface (GUI) of MicroStation is changed to conform to many of the windows-based standards. Docking tool boxes and familiar icons are now in MicroStation.

◆ **"SmartLine" tool.** Think of the SmartLine tool as a way to create a complex element that contains lines and arcs. Both lines and arcs can be drawn individually but the SmartLine tool joins the individual elements as they are placed to create a single complex element.

◆ **AccuDraw.** You can use AccuDraw for precision input when you place or modify elements. Basically, every data point entered on-screen can be accurately placed with the features found in AccuDraw.

◆ **Plot Resymbolization.** MicroStation gives you the ability to resymbolize elements at plot time. You can change the color, style, or weight of elements as they are plotted to create different effects with the same design and reference files, which means no more copies of the design file for plotting purposes.

◆ **Improved methods for customizing your interface.** Configuration tools included in MicroStation enable you to modify the pull-down menus, the tools on the tool boxes, and to create your own custom tool boxes. These configuration tools create a binary-portable resource file so that you can build the new menus on one platform and then transfer them without worry to any other computer platform running MicroStation.

◆ **BASIC Macros.** Record and play features enable the nonprogrammer types to create automated routines to improve productivity.

◆ **Cell Selector Utility.** This utility creates a custom tool box quickly and easily from all the symbols or cells in one or multiple cell libraries. What used to take hours to create is now available in only seconds.

MicroStation 95 Fundamentals was written with both the new and experienced MicroStation user in mind. New users need no previous experience with MicroStation before reading this book, and can expect to have a thorough understanding of MicroStation tools and techniques by the time they reach the end of *MicroStation 95 Fundamentals*. Even if you have worked with earlier versions of MicroStation, you will find *MicroStation 95 Fundamentals* a valuable learning tool when exploring the new features and functionality of MicroStation.

How This Book Is Organized

MicroStation 95 Fundamentals divides MicroStation's commands, concepts, and functionality into easy-to-understand chapters. In the beginning chapters, you learn MicroStation concepts and how to set up and create design files. Next, master how to place, manipulate, and modify 2D elements. Then you place standard symbols, dimensions, and text. You also learn to plot the final product. Later in *MicroStation 95 Fundamentals*, you discover how to customize MicroStation to suit your individual needs.

Part One: Understanding MicroStation

Part One instructs you on how exercises are set up in this book. You will learn about the basic components of MicroStation's graphical user interface (GUI) and the components of your design files by putting them to use in the exercises. After completing Part One, with the basic concepts out of the way, you are ready to move on to placing and editing elements.

Part Two: Learning How to Draw in 2D

Part Two of *MicroStation 95 Fundamentals* takes you through the steps necessary to set up a design file. You learn how to place elements such as lines, circles, arcs, shapes, and other complex element types. Tips are included on advanced viewing techniques, how to draw with accuracy, and how to manipulate and modify the graphics elements. Part Two also deals with placing some of MicroStation's more complex element types, such as custom line styles.

Part Three: Putting on the Final Touches

With most of the hard work done, Part Three takes you through adding the finishing touches. You learn to create and place patterns, dimension the objects you have drawn, place and edit text, and plot your design file.

Part Four: Sharpening Your Skills

Part Four of *MicroStation 95 Fundamentals* deals with increasing your efficiency and sharpening your drawing skills. Part Four covers four areas of advanced drawing techniques: how to create standard symbols or cells, use MicroStation's reference file capability, change MicroStation's look and feel, and create drawing standards.

With this last part of *MicroStation 95 Fundamentals* under your belt, you are well on your way to becoming a MicroStation expert.

Following the Book's Conventions and Exercises

For the most part, the conventions put to use in *MicroStation 95 Fundamentals* are the same ones found in the MicroStation documentation that comes with the software. Other conventions used deserve a closer look.

Exercises

A sample exercise follows to explain how all the exercises in this book are presented. The exercises are generally followed by one or more illustrations (see fig. I.1). The illustrations are screenshots captured during the actual exercise and should assist you in performing the exercise steps. Exercises are arranged in two columns. The left column displays the screen prompts and instructions for you to follow. The right column displays information on what should happen after you perform the instructions. The bubble numbers in the exercise refer to the input points given in the illustration.

SAMPLE EXERCISE

Continue from the preceding exercise with the INTRO.DGN design file open.

Choose **T**ools, *then* **M**ain, *then* **L**inear Elements	Displays Linear Elements tool box
Choose Place Line	Activates the Place Line command
Enter first point	
Pick a point at ①	Anchors line end point
Enter end point	
Pick a point at ②	Places first line

Turn on Angle	Displays black button
Enter **45**	Activates Angle field and enter 45
Pick a point at ③	Places second line

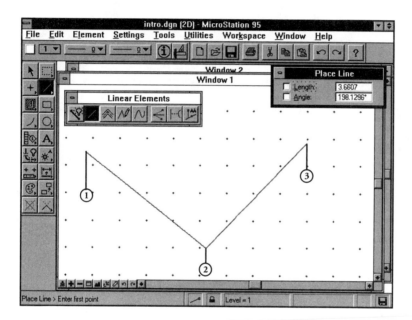

Figure I.1

Sample exercise illustration.

Click the reset button

All the exercises in the book are set up like the previous sample exercise.

Other instructions in the exercise can include values that are entered from the keyboard. The exercises indicate typed keyboard input as bold text. In the sample exercise, the Angle field should be activated by clicking in the field—a flashing line shows the input point. Delete the contents of the field and enter the value specified in the instructions.

Notes, Tips, and Warnings

MicroStation 95 Fundamentals gives you tips on how to be more efficient, warnings to help you avoid trouble, and notes for valuable advice.

Note   *Notes* typically complement the general discussion or set off instructions about a particular topic. Notes give you additional thoughts about the subject, or they might restate some valuable piece of information you need to remember. Notes also tell you how to avoid problems and give you possible remedies for the error messages that crop up from time to time.

Tip   *Tips* give you the benefit of the author's experience. Tips might tell you how to conserve system resources or how to make your computer run faster. Tips can give you shortcuts or clue you in on other drawing tools or operations that could save you valuable time.

Warning   Think of *warnings* as raising a red flag. Warnings tell you when danger is approaching. Until you are completely familiar with how MicroStation works, you might find that some operations are more volatile than others. Warnings signal when danger is near, describe the necessary cautions you should take, and explain any treatment needed to recover from a possible mishap.

New Riders Publishing

The staff of New Riders Publishing is committed to bringing you the very best in computer reference material. Each New Riders book is the result of months of work by authors and staff who research and refine the information contained within its covers.

As part of this commitment to you, the NRP reader, New Riders invites your input. Please let us know if you enjoy this book, if you have trouble with the information and examples presented, or if you have a suggestion for the next edition.

Please note, though: New Riders staff cannot serve as a technical resource for MicroStation 95 or for questions about software- or hardware-related problems. Please refer to the documentation that accompanies MicroStation 95 or to the application's Help systems.

If you have a question or comment about any New Riders book, there are several ways to contact New Riders Publishing. We will respond to as many readers as we can. Your name, address, or phone number will never become part of a mailing list or be used for any purpose other than to help us continue to bring you the best books possible. You can write us at the following address:

New Riders Publishing
Attn: Publisher
201 W. 103rd Street
Indianapolis, IN 46290

If you prefer, you can fax New Riders Publishing at (317) 581-4670.

You also can send electronic mail to New Riders at the following Internet address:

ddwyer@newriders.mcp.com

NRP is an imprint of Macmillan Computer Publishing. To obtain a catalog or information, or to purchase any Macmillan Computer Publishing book, call (800) 428-5331.

Thank you for selecting *MicroStation 95 Fundamentals*!

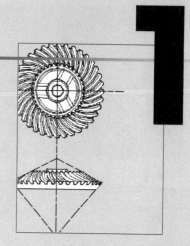

Understanding MicroStation

CHAPTER

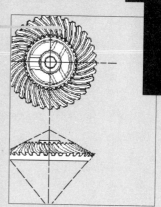

Getting Started

*T*he MicroStation environment, or graphical user interface (GUI), is one of the friendliest on the market. Make no mistake, however; MicroStation is a powerful application that offers many options and features. Chapter 2 gives you a quick tour of MicroStation, but first, you need an understanding of the basics: what the input options are, where the tools and commands are located, and how to move around in the GUI. With a little practice, you will find that it's a very productive environment.

At the time of this writing, MicroStation runs on 15 different operating systems and platforms. This book concentrates on running MicroStation on the Windows 3.1/DOS platform. The documentation that ships with MicroStation should have adequate instructions for loading and launching MicroStation for your platform. Although platforms and operating systems vary, MicroStation functionality should be the same on any platform.

This chapter covers the following topics:

- Understanding MicroStation input methods

- Using and arrangement of buttons on your cursor or mouse

- Starting MicroStation

- Using the MicroStation GUI

- Using the pull-down menus

- Using the tool frames and boxes

- Manipulating the view windows

- Getting help in MicroStation

Understanding MicroStation Input Methods

In MicroStation, as with many programs that offer a graphical user interface, your input device has several different button actions. MicroStation has three types of mouse/cursor input: *data points*, *resets*, and *tentative points*. A fourth, less common, input method applies only to the tablet menu: *command points*.

Data Points

You use the data point most often for input in MicroStation. To issue a data point, you move the cursor to the appropriate point and click the left mouse button. The left mouse button (the data button) is most often used to interact with MicroStation's interface.

Reset

You use the right mouse button (the reset button) on the input device to terminate commands and to dismiss pull-down menus. If you get stuck or just want to stop what you're doing, right-clicking usually does the trick.

During some commands, right-clicking once just backs you up a step. The *Note*
dimensioning commands, for example, might require multiple resets to terminate the command. Reading the Status Bar can help you determine whether
you've successfully terminated the command.

Tentative Points

You use the tentative point to locate or snap to elements for precision input. To pick
a tentative point, you move the cursor to the appropriate point and click the
Tentative button. Chapter 7, "Drawing with Accuracy," covers the tentative point
thoroughly. The default mouse button setting for the tentative button is the 1 and 2
button pressed simultaneously. If you have a 3-button mouse you can customize the
button assignment and make the tentative point be the middle button.

Command Points

The Command button is used only on systems configured with a tablet, tablet menu,
and tablet cursor, to activate commands from the tablet menu.

Using Input Devices

MicroStation, like other CAD programs, enables you to use a mouse or a tablet menu
and cursor for entering points into the drawing. Note that MicroStation refers to a
tablet menu input device or puck as a *cursor*. This book calls it a *tablet cursor* to
differentiate it from the various on-screen cursors. The variety of mice and tablet
cursor styles are plentiful; 2-button mice, 3-button mice, 4-button cursors, 12-button
cursors, and 16-button cursors. MicroStation comes with default settings for both
the mouse and tablet cursor.

The MicroStation documentation calls the screen cursor a pointer. This book, as   *Note*
well as most modern software that includes a GUI, however, calls it a *cursor*.
(See the section "The Screen Cursor," later in this chapter.)

To avoid confusion, this book calls the digitizer tablet puck or cursor a *tablet
cursor*.

Default Settings for Mice

The default configuration for MicroStation PC is for a 2-button mouse. Refer to table 1.1 for details.

You can change the default button settings in MicroStation by choosing **B**utton Assignments from the Wor**k**spaces pull-down menu.

 Note   The term "Left Button - Right Button Chord" in the Button Assignment dialog box means that you must hit the left and right buttons simultaneously.

Table 1.1
Mouse Assignments for DOS or Windows (2-Button Mouse)

Button Number	Action
1 (left)	data button
2 (right)	reset button
1 + 2 (together)	tentative button

 Tip   If you have a 3-button mouse, you might want to change the button assignment for the tentative button from the 1 and 2 chord setting to the "middle button," which would be easier to use.

Default Settings for Tablet Cursors

Using a tablet menu with a tablet cursor adds another button option to the list. You must choose commands from the tablet menu with a command button. See table 1.2 for the defaults on tablet cursor button assignments.

Table 1.2

Tablet Cursor Assignments for DOS (12-Button Cursor)

Button Number	Action
1	data button
2	command button
3	tentative button
4	reset button

You can program the additional buttons on the 12- and 16-button cursors for quick access to commands and key-ins.   *Note*

Using Buttons in the Exercises

MicroStation offers more functions than the number of buttons on a mouse, so it assigns several functions to each button. Table 1.3 lists and describes the standard button actions (and the terms used for them throughout the book). All actions listed are demonstrated in this chapter. Review the table and use it as a reference.

Table 1.3

Button Actions and Exercises

Exercise Instruction	Button Procedure
Click	Press and release a button quickly (refers to the data button unless otherwise specified)
Pick a data point	Click on a point or enter a data point
Double-click	Click twice in quick succession
Press and hold	Press the data button and hold it down
Drag	Press the data button while the cursor is on an item, hold it down, and move the cursor on the screen, then release the button
Click on	Click the data button while the cursor is on an item
Click in	Click the data button while the cursor is in a window or a box

Starting MicroStation

You can start MicroStation in a number of ways, varying with the operating system. In DOS, for example, you enter MicroStation from the command line, while in Windows 3.1, Windows NT, or Windows 95, you double-click on an icon. A copyright and license screen appears briefly while MicroStation loads the design file.

Note Your prompt indicating the drive letter might differ from C:\. If so, substitute the drive letter on your system whenever you see C: in this book.

ENTERING MICROSTATION FROM WINDOWS 3.1

Double-click on MicroStation Program Group	Opens window and displays MicroStation icon (see fig. 1.1)
Double-click on the MicroStation icon	Opens MicroStation window
Click on the Maximize button (in upper-right corner of the MicroStation window)	Fills screen and opens the MicroStation Manager dialog box inside (see fig. 1.2)

Figure 1.1

The Windows MicroStation 95 Program Group.

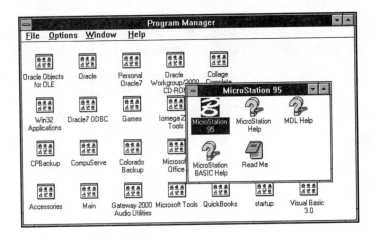

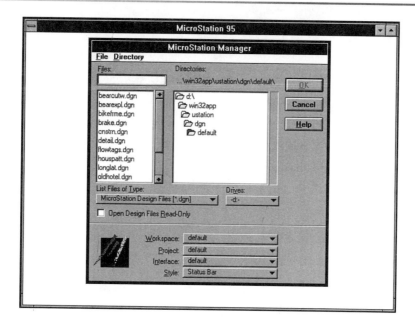

Figure 1.2

The MicroStation Manager dialog box.

Choosing **C**ancel in the MicroStation Manager dialog box closes MicroStation.   ***Warning***

As you proceed through the chapters in this book, you can practice the commands in MicroStation in your own design files. The exercises in this book are designed with the assumption that you enter MicroStation using the default workspace, default interface, and with status bar style. In addition, you should use the default SEED2D.DGN design file for each design file you create throughout the book. Chapter 4 covers the purpose of the seed file. For the time being, create your first design file as indicated in the following exercise.

SETTING A WORKSPACE AND CREATING A DESIGN FILE

Choose default *for the* **W**orkspace *in the MicroStation Manager box (see fig. 1.2)*

Choose default *for the* **In**terface *(see fig. 1.2)*

Choose Status Bar *for the* **S**tyle *(see fig. 1.2)*

Choose **N**ew *from the* **F**ile *pull-down menu*   Create Design File dialog box appears

Verify that the directory shown is the ...\dgn\default directory (see fig. 1.3)

Continues

Verify that the seed file displayed is ...\default\seed\seed2d.dgn (see fig. 1.3)

Enter **CHAP01.DGN** in the Files: field (see fig. 1.3)

Choose **O**K	Creates Design File and closes dialog box
In the Files *list, double-click* CHAP01.DGN	Opens design file and displays MicroStation Status Bar, view 1, view 2, and Main tool frame (see fig. 1.4)

Figure 1.3

Creating your first design file.

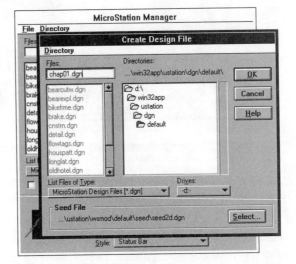

Figure 1.4

Your first look at MicroStation.

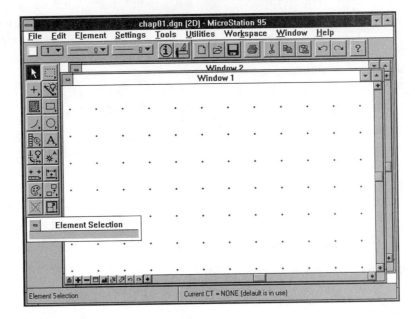

Now that you have created and entered your first design file read further for information about the MicroStation graphical user interface (GUI).

Using the MicroStation GUI

You use the graphical user interface to interact with the MicroStation program. The primary components of the GUI are the Status Bar and the Application Window pull-down menus, the dialog and settings boxes, the tool frames and boxes, the views into the design file, and the cursor.

The Status Bar and the Application Window

The Application Window and the Status Bar are the key players in MicroStation's GUI. The Application Window contains a title bar across the top of the window that indicates the name of the file and the pull-down menus. The Status Bar contains the prompts and several shortcuts to common MicroStation settings.

Reading the Status Bar

One purpose of the Status Bar is to prompt you through commands and give you information on active settings, symbology, status, and errors. The Status Bar has five fields for these purposes (see fig. 1.4).

- ◆ The first field displays the active command name and displays instructions concerning what to do next during a command. It prompts you, for example, to Enter first vertex, Enter first point, Identify an Element, and so on. Watch this field as you use MicroStation and as you do the exercises in this book.

- ◆ The second field displays the active snap lock and provides a quick way to change snap settings by clicking on the field.

- ◆ The third field displays the active lock setting and provides an easy way to change it by clicking on the field.

- ◆ The fourth field displays the active level setting and lets you set the active level by clicking on the field.

- ◆ The last field displays the element type and level during the manipulation and modification commands.

The Pull-Down Menus

The pull-down menus in the Application Window give you access to all of MicroStation's commands, settings and dialog boxes, and functions. You have two options to activate a pull-down menu: using the cursor or using the hot keys, or mnemonics, from the keyboard.

To open a pull-down menu with your cursor, place the arrow on the pull-down menu name and click the data button. The pull-down menu appears and waits for you to choose a menu item. Move the cursor to the item desired and click the data button again.

Note

Another way to choose items from the pull-down menus requires a click-hold-and-drag operation. To identify a pull-down menu from the Application Window, press and hold down the data button on the menu name, then drag to the item on the pull-down you want to activate. Release the button to activate the command. This method was the only one available in versions before MicroStation Version 5.0.

Choose a menu selection technique that works best for you.

To use the keyboard to open a pull-down menu, press the Alt key and type the character that appears underlined in the pull-down menu name. Press Alt+F, for example, to issue the File pull-down menu. After you activate the pull-down menu, you can type the underlined character in any menu item name to select that item. These underlined characters sometimes are called *keyboard shortcuts*, *mnemonics*, or *hot keys* in this book.

Tip

Before keyboard shortcuts can function, the Application Window must be active, with the title bar bold or highlighted. Using keyboard shortcuts with the Application Window inactive generates beeps or produces other unexpected results. Pressing the Esc key activates the Application Window.

The following list briefly describes each of the pull-down menus. This book covers each individual menu item in detail in the appropriate chapter(s).

♦ The File pull-down menu provides items you can use to manipulate your design file. Chapter 4 covers these items in detail.

♦ The Edit pull-down menu provides items you can use to edit elements in your design file. Chapter 9 covers these items in detail.

◆ The Element pull-down menu provides items for setting element defaults, such as color, line weight, text size, dimensions, and so on. Chapters 5 and 10 cover these items in detail.

◆ The Settings pull-down menu provides items you can use to set defaults for your active design file. Chapters 3 and 7 cover these items in detail.

◆ The Tools pull-down menu provides items you can use to activate the tool boxes and frames. Chapter 2 covers these items in detail.

◆ The Utilities pull-down menu provides miscellaneous items you can use to activate a key-in field and execute external programs. Chapter 20 covers these items in detail.

◆ The Workspace pull-down menu provides items you can use to set environment defaults, perform user interface customization, make button assignments, and so on. Chapter 19 covers these items in detail.

◆ The Window pull-down menu provides items you can use to manipulate the views of your active design file. Chapter 6 covers these items in detail.

◆ The Help pull-down menu provides items you can use to retrieve context-sensitive help. This chapter covers these items in detail.

An arrow that appears to the right of an item on the pull-down menu indicates an item that opens a submenu. Choosing Main from the Tools menu, for example, opens a submenu (see fig. 1.5).

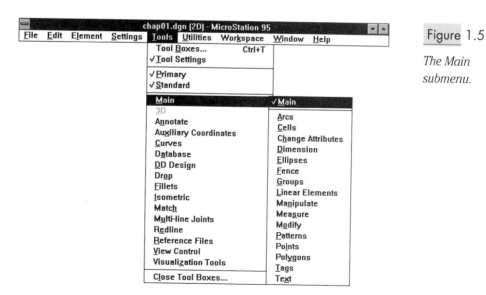

Figure 1.5

The Main submenu.

To choose an item from the submenu, you can use your cursor or you can type the hot key character for that item. To dismiss the submenu, choose a different item from the pull-down menu or press Esc. To dismiss the entire pull-down menu, press Esc again, and the pull-down menu is dismissed.

Another shortcut to commands is the keyboard accelerator. Keyboard accelerators, when available, appear next to the item on the pull-down menu. The keyboard accelerators use the Control key to bypass the pull-down menus altogether and activate a command directly. Key-ins for accelerators are shown on the pull-down menu. Press Ctrl+O, for example, to activate the **O**pen item from the **F**ile pull-down menu.

Menu items that appear grayed out, or dimmed, aren't available for selection. Some commands require that you meet special conditions before they can function. The **3**D item in the **T**ools pull-down, for example, becomes available only when the active design file is a 3D file.

Dialog and Settings Boxes

Some of the items on the pull-down menus activate dialog and settings boxes. The Save **A**s item on the **F**ile pull-down menu, for example, opens the Save Design As dialog box (see fig. 1.6). Notice that this box contains buttons labeled **O**K, Cancel, and **H**elp. You close the dialog box by choosing **O**K or Cancel before proceeding with your design. If you attempt to do something outside a dialog box while it's open, MicroStation beeps. Dialog boxes require that you respond before you continue your drawing, whereas settings boxes enable you to alternate between drawing and using them to make settings.

Figure 1.6

The Save Design As dialog box.

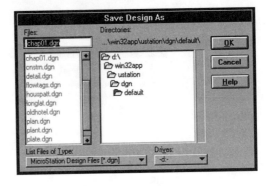

An ellipsis (...) following an item's name in a pull-down menu indicates that choosing the item opens a dialog box.

Note

Choosing **A**ttributes from the El**e**ment pull-down menu, for example, opens the Element Attributes settings box (see fig. 1.7). The main differences between dialog and settings boxes are that settings boxes don't have **O**K or Cancel buttons, and they let you continue working in a design session while they remain on-screen. To close a settings box click on the menu button (the button with a minus sign in it) in the upper left corner. A pull-down menu is displayed, from which you can choose **C**lose. A quicker way is to double-click on the menu button.

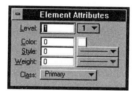

Figure 1.7

The Element Attributes settings box.

Some dialog and settings boxes have their own pull-down menus. The Reference Files settings box, for example, offers three pull-down menus: **T**ools, **S**ettings, and **D**isplay (see fig. 1.8).

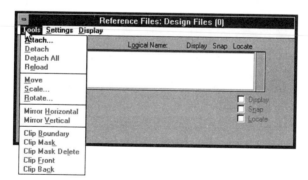

Figure 1.8

The Reference Files settings box, showing pull-down menus.

You can use the hot keys for pull-down menus inside settings and dialog boxes, but only when the box is active (highlighted).

Note

Dialog and settings boxes can contain key-in fields, lists, buttons, and on/off toggle items (see fig. 1.9). Again, you can manipulate these choices using the cursor or the keyboard. A dotted outline indicates the active item in the box, as one surrounds Length in figure 1.9.

Figure 1.9

Options of a dialog or settings box.

To change the value in a key-in field, activate the field by clicking in it, and enter the new value or text. To replace the contents of the field either double-click on the field or press and drag across the characters to highlight it. To do the same from the keyboard, press Tab until the key-in field is the active field, and enter the new text.

You can execute a button by clicking on it or by pressing Enter when the dotted outline surrounds it.

Note   You also can press the Tab key to cycle through the fields and buttons in settings and dialog boxes to make them the defaults.

To turn the toggle on or off, click on it or press Enter when the toggle is active.

Note   The **O**K button appears in a dialog box with a thicker border surrounding it, as in the Save As dialog box, to indicate that it is the default button (see fig. 1.6). Pressing Enter while an item in the dialog box is active acts the same as clicking on the **O**K button, which executes the dialog box. Pressing Enter with the Cancel button active, however, acts like clicking on the Cancel button, which executes the Cancel function.

The next exercise demonstrates the two methods for activating pull-down menus. To illustrate the **C**lose tool boxes command, you step through opening two tool boxes.

ACTIVATING PULL-DOWN MENUS WITH THE CURSOR AND KEYBOARD

Continue from the preceding exercise with the CHAP01.DGN design file open.

Choose **T**ools	Opens **T**ools pull-down menu
Choose **R**eference Files	Opens the Reference Files tool box
Press Alt+T	Activates **T**ools pull-down menu
Type **m**	Activates **M**ain pull-down menu
Type **l**	Activates the Linear Elements tool box

You now should have two or more tool boxes open.

Choose **T**ools	Opens Tools pull-down menu
Choose C**l**ose Tool Boxes	Opens the Close Tool Boxes dialog box with the Close Undocked toggle on.
Click on **O**K *or press Enter*	Closes all undocked tool boxes

Tool Frames and Boxes

Tool frames and boxes contain icons that represent the drawing tools, which you use to issue various commands. After you learn to recognize the tools, they are very efficient (see fig. 1.10). You can quickly glance at a tool frame or box and click on an icon to issue a command. The icons were introduced with the GUI in MicroStation 4.0 and have been a great success.

A *tool frame* is a special tool box, in that you can use it to issue commands or to call up other tool boxes. You can use the Main tool frame, for example, to pick the Place SmartLine command or to tear off the Linear Elements tool box.

Note

Figure 1.10

*The Main tool
frame.*

Moving Tool Frames and Boxes

Tool boxes take up space on-screen, so you might need to move them around to
work more efficiently. When you move your cursor to the title bar or any edge of a
tool box, it changes into an arrow (see fig. 1.11). While the cursor appears as an
arrow, you can use it to move the tool frame or box. If you click and hold on the tool
box title bar, you can then drag the tool box to a new location. When you have the
tool box where you want it, release the button.

Figure 1.11

The Move cursor.

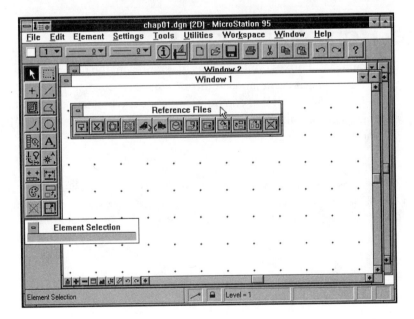

Now, try moving a tool box in the following exercise.

MOVING TOOL FRAMES AND BOXES

Continue from the preceding exercise, using the CHAP01.DGN design file.

*Choose **T**ools*   Opens **T**ools pull-down menu

*Choose **R**eference Files*   Opens the Reference Files tool box

Move your cursor to the title bar of   Displays arrow cursor
the Reference Files tool box

Press and hold the data button and   Moves outline of Reference Files
move the cursor on the screen   tool box

Release the data button   Drops Reference Files tool box at new location
                                                  (see fig. 1.12)

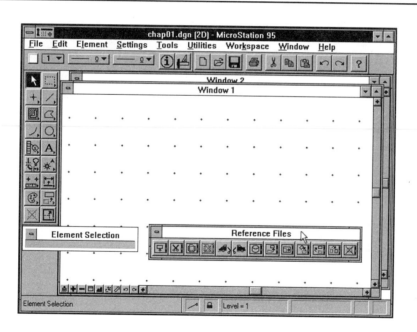

Figure 1.12

The Reference Files tool box moved.

Docking Tool Boxes

A new feature introduced in MicroStation is the capability to dock tool boxes. As the recent exercises have illustrated, moving tool boxes around can cover a portion of your view. When you dock a tool box, it becomes part of the MicroStation Application window and doesn't lay on top of your view.

 Note

> You can dock tool boxes and frames to any edge (top, bottom, left, or right) of your Application Window. Notice that the view size automatically adjusts to accommodate the docked tool box.

To dock a tool box, move the tool box to any edge of the Application Window and release the data button. After you successfully dock the tool box, its title bar disappears. The title bar only appears in undocked tool frames and boxes.

In the next exercise, you activate a tool box and dock it on the right side of the Application Window.

DOCKING A TOOL BOX

Continue from the preceding exercise, using the CHAP01.DGN design file.

Move your cursor to the title bar of the Reference Files tool box	Displays arrow cursor
Press and hold the data button while moving the cursor to the right edge of the Application Window	Moves outline of Reference Files tool box
Release the data button	Docks the Reference Files tool box (see fig. 1.13)

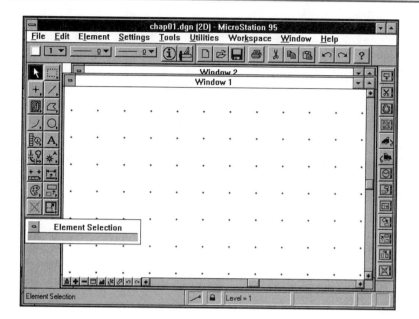

Figure 1.13

The Reference Files tool box docked.

Undocking Tool Boxes

To undock a tool box, you reverse the docking operation. You just grab the tool box on its edge from the docked position and drag it back into the view or window.

To close or remove an individual docked tool box, either undock the tool box and follow one of the procedures provided in the next section or choose the tool box name from the **T**ools pull-down menu in the Application Window. To close or remove all the docked tool boxes, choose C**l**ose Tool Boxes from the **T**ools pull-down menu.

Note

Closing Tool Boxes

You can close tool boxes from the title bar by clicking on the menu button (the button with a minus sign in it) in the upper left corner. A pull-down menu appears, from which you can choose **C**lose (see fig. 1.14). A quicker way to close a tool box is to double-click on its menu button, which closes it immediately.

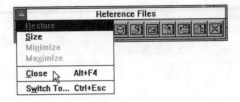

Figure 1.14

The Tool Box functions.

Note   If you remove a docked tool box by choosing the tool box name in the **T**ools pull-down menu and then activate it again later, it returns in its former docked position.

Try closing the Reference Files tool box in the following exercise.

CLOSING A TOOL BOX

Continue from the preceding exercise, using the CHAP01.DGN design file.

Click on the window menu button in the upper left corner of the Reference Files tool box	Pop-up menu appears
*Choose **C**lose*	Closes Reference Files tool box

Note   You can use the same procedure to close settings boxes and views, each of which has a similar window menu and button in its upper left corner.

Warning   Closing the Application Window in this fashion produces an Alert box warning: This will exit MicroStation 95. Choose **O**K to exit, or choose Cancel and return to your MicroStation session.

MicroStation Tools

To choose a tool from a tool box, just click the data button on the tool icon. Choosing the tool highlights it, indicating that it activated the command. To choose a command from the tablet menu, just click on the Command button.

CHOOSING COMMANDS FROM THE MAIN TOOL FRAME

Continue from the preceding exercise, using the CHAP01.DGN design.

*Move your cursor to the tool in the
upper-right corner of the Main tool box*

Click on the tool   Activates Place Fence command, highlights
                                          icon, and displays command name in Status Bar

*Move your cursor to the tool
below Place Fence*

Click on the tool   Activates Place SmartLine command,
                                          highlights icon, and displays command name
                                          in Status Bar (see fig. 1.15)

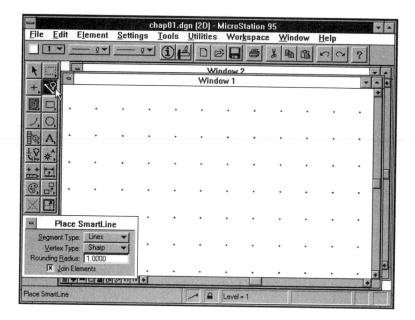

Figure 1.15

*The Place
SmartLine
command active.*

Tool Boxes

The icons you see on the main tool frame are only the tip of the iceberg. Small arrows in the lower right corners of the icons indicate that tool boxes are available. To open a tool box from a frame, press and hold the data button on one of these tools. Move your cursor to the SmartLine tool, for example, and press and hold (see fig. 1.16).

Figure 1.16

*The Linear
Element tool box.*

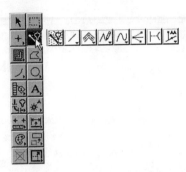

Drag your cursor to highlight one of the other icons that appear (see fig. 1.17), and release the button to issue that command. The tool box disappears, and the main frame now displays the tool you have chosen (see fig. 1.18). The tool you select remains on the main tool frame until you select a different one from the tool box. Also notice that the active command name in the Status Bar changes.

Figure 1.17

*Highlighting a
new tool on a tool
frame.*

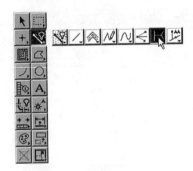

Figure 1.18

*The new
command
activate.*

Activate some fence commands in the next exercise.

CHOOSING A COMMAND FROM THE TOOL BOX

Continue from the preceding exercise, using the CHAP01.DGN design file.

Move your cursor to the icon in the upper right corner of the Main tool frame	
Press and hold the data button	Opens the Fence tool box
Move your cursor to a different icon, then release the button	Activates the command you selected

Views

A *view* is a window into your design file. Chapter 6, "Viewing a Drawing," offers details concerning how to manipulate your design in a view. For now, this section presents a short discussion of the mechanics of views and the GUI.

The title bar, across the top of the view, identifies the name of the view or the view number. Eight views are possible in MicroStation. The window menu button in the upper left corner should seem familiar—clicking on it closes a view the same way you can click on one to close a tool box.

You can use the two buttons in the upper right corner to manipulate the view. Clicking on the first button, a down arrow, minimizes the view to an icon (see fig. 1.19). Double-clicking on the icon returns the view to its former size.

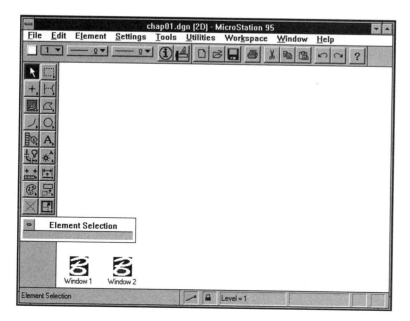

Figure 1.19

The icon view.

Clicking on the second button, an up or up/down arrow, stores the previous size or maximizes the view. If the icon appears as an up arrow, clicking on it maximizes the view. If the icon appears as an up/down arrow, clicking on it returns it to the size of its most recent previous view.

 Note   If tool boxes are docked, the Maximize button on the Application Window is smart enough not to open the view under them.

You also can resize the view in the X (horizontal), Y (vertical), or both (diagonal) directions. Moving the cursor to the outer edge of the view changes it to a double-headed arrow. If your cursor is on the top or bottom edge of a view, it changes to an up/down arrow, and on the left or right edge of a view, it changes to a left/right arrow. If your cursor is in any of the four corners, it changes to a diagonal, double-headed arrow. While your cursor appears as any of these arrows, you can press the data button, hold it, and drag the view to a new size. An outline of the view appears as you move the cursor, and the view assumes the shape of the outline when you release the data button.

RESIZING A VIEW

Continue from the preceding exercise, using the CHAP01.DGN design file with view 1 open.

Click on the Minimize button	Reduces the view to an icon square (see fig. 1.19)
Double-click on the icon	Returns the view to previous size
Move the cursor to one of the view edges	Displays the double-headed arrow cursor
Press the data button and drag the edge to new location, then release	Lines appear to show the new view location
Click on the Maximize button	Enlarges the view to fill the screen
Click on the Maximize button	Returns the view to previous size

The Screen Cursor

The screen cursor, commonly referred to as the cursor in the MicroStation GUI, takes on different forms. The cursor appears differently on-screen depending on what you're doing or where it is. When you choose a placement command, for example, the cursor appears as a +, but after you start the command, the cursor changes to an × (see fig. 1.20).

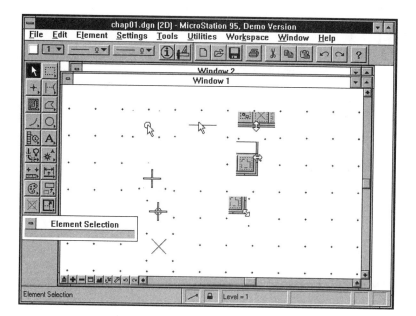

Figure 1.20

MicroStation cursor types.

Getting Help

MicroStation offers extensive on-line help; you can activate **H**elp from the Application Window pull-down (see fig. 1.21). Help looks different depending on what operating system you use. Review your delivered documentation on the specifics of using Help in MicroStation.

Choose **H**ow to Use Help from the **H**elp pull-down menu to find more information on the Help utility.

Note

Figure 1.21

The Help pull-down menu.

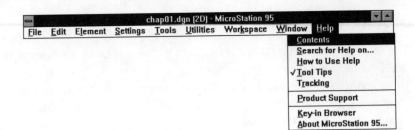

Summary

This chapter presented a great deal of essential information about the MicroStation graphical user interface (GUI). To learn and use MicroStation effectively, you need to be comfortable with the features discussed in this chapter.

C H A P T E R

Taking MicroStation for a Test Drive

*T*his chapter puts you in the driver's seat and gives you a chance to take MicroStation for a test drive. The first MicroStation drawing you construct is a simple 12' × 10' office floorplan. You don't have to be an architect, however, to benefit from the exercises in this chapter. The settings, tools, and techniques apply to any type of drawing.

First, you create a new design file and call it CHAP02.DGN. After you lay out the office perimeter, you use some basic drawing tools and techniques to draw a few desks and bookcases. To place the furniture in the office space, you get your first crack at using the Move, Copy, Delete, and Undo operations.

Note
The purpose of this chapter is to give you an initial feel for the way you work with MicroStation, not to cover the use of any commands in-depth. Therefore, the commands you use in this chapter are explained fully in later chapters.

If you learn no other operation in this chapter, learn Undo. Undo is an invaluable tool. Undo "undoes" what you really didn't want to do. Undo can "undelete" elements you delete by mistake (with a few caveats).

This chapter concludes by teaching you the proper techniques for closing a design file and ending a design session. Ending a design session is just as important as setting up a design file.

In this chapter, you learn how to do the following:

♦ Set up the screen

♦ Draw on grid paper

♦ Draw lines

♦ Place basic 2D lines and shapes

♦ Fit an entire design file in a view

♦ Move, copy, and delete elements

♦ Recover deleted elements

♦ End a design session properly

Starting Your First Design

To begin your first design, you must execute MicroStation and create a design file. You have already done this in Chapter 1, so look back to the section entitled "Starting MicroStation" if you need some help or review of this procedure.

Setting Up the Screen

Before you begin the office floorplan, you need to set up the way MicroStation appears on-screen. The next few exercises take you through opening two important tool sets, the **M**ain tool frame and the Primary and Standard tool boxes.

A good habit to develop is to dock the **M**ain tool frame open on the display screen at all times; doing so saves you time and energy. The **M**ain tool frame contains most of the drawing tools, such as the Place tools; the Move, Copy, Modify, and Delete tools; the Text and Cell tools; and so forth. The **M**ain frame appears on the left with the 18 default icons that appear when you first open it.

Opening Tool Frames and Boxes

Open the **M**ain tool frame by choosing **T**ools, **M**ain, **M**ain (see fig. 2.1) from the submenu. Likewise, to complete your setup, choose **P**rimary and **S**tandard from the Tools menu. Your design file probably came up with these two boxes open, because it's the standard configuration, but someone else might have used the machine you're using, or you might have inadvertently removed them.

Choosing **M**ain, then **M**ain again from the Tools pull-down menu will cause the Main tool frame to vanish if it is currently open. Just reselect the menu option to bring it back. A check mark in front of the menu item in the pull-down menu indicates the item is already open.

MicroStation stores the names of your open tool boxes and their arrangement on-screen in the workspace, which lets several people who need to use the same PC or workstation arrange the menus to their own liking in their own workspace. See Chapter 19 for more information about workspaces and how to customize them.

Tip

In the following exercises, you open both the **M**ain tool frame and the **P**rimary and **S**tandard tool boxes, if they're not open in your MicroStation session.

OPENING THE MAIN FRAME

Create a new drawing called CHAP02.DGN.

Choose Tools, Main, Main *(see fig. 2.1)*	Opens the Main tool frame, or closes it if it was open
Choose Tools, Primary	Opens the Primary tool box, or closes it if it was open
Choose Tools, Standard	Opens the Standard tool box, or closes it if it was open

Figure 2.1

Opening the tools you'll need for production.

Now that you've set up the tools you need, you can begin drawing. At this point, however, drawing in MicroStation is like freehand drawing on a drafting table. In manual drafting, you use T-squares, triangles, grid paper, and other devices to draw accurately. CAD drafting offers its own set of accuracy tools. Two important accuracy tools are the display grid and grid lock; using them is equivalent to drawing on grid paper.

Drawing on Grid Paper

MicroStation comes equipped with a display grid and a grid lock. Turning on this display grid helps you visualize distances when drawing, much like when you use graph paper. The display grid consists of crosses and dots, arrayed at specific distances that you can adjust. This grid is perfect for performing schematic drawings, such as process drawings, instrumentation drawings, flow diagrams, or charts. With grid lock turned on, the screen cursor only locks on to the grid points (crosses, dots). This means you can draw perfectly straight lines at 45° and right angles.

Note

If you can't see the grid dots, don't be alarmed. MicroStation doesn't display the dots when you try to display an area that's too large. The dots do not appear when the display would be so dense with dots that they would no longer be of value.

In this chapter, you create an office floorplan using the display grid and grid lock. Chapter 7, "Drawing with Accuracy," shows you more completely how to use these features, and covers other accuracy matters in greater detail as well.

First, you need to turn on the drawing setting, or lock, to force the drawing cursor to lock on to those grid points.

Introducing Locks

MicroStation 95 Fundamentals introduces many new locks and their uses. *Locks* are settings that determine the way MicroStation reacts when it interprets your input. If you turn on Level Lock, for example, MicroStation lets you select and change only elements on the active level. Normally, you would have Level Lock turned off so you can select or modify any element on any level in the design file. Another lock, Snap Lock, helps you grab onto specific element points such as a midpoint, end point, or center of a circle. If you turn off Snap Lock, you cannot snap or grab onto existing elements. Grid Lock works in conjunction with the display grid.

Locking the Cursor to the Grid

If you have the grid displayed, accuracy requires a method of locking the drawing cursor to the grid when placing input points. You accomplish this by turning on **G**rid Lock. After you turn on **G**rid Lock, the cursor locks onto the grid points (dots) and grid references (crosses). Drawing straight lines and right or 45-degree angles becomes a breeze with Grid Lock active.

You can turn the view attribute, display grid, on or off in any selected view. **G**rid Lock is more akin to a placement setting; it affects element placement, not view display. Grid Lock is either on in all views or off in all views; it can't be on in one view and off in another view at the same time.

Note   If you turn on Grid Lock but not the display grid, input points still lock onto the grid.

In the following exercise, you activate **G**rid Lock by choosing the Lock icon in the status bar (see fig. 2.2), and then turning on the **G**rid Lock button.

Figure 2.2

Turning on Grid Lock.

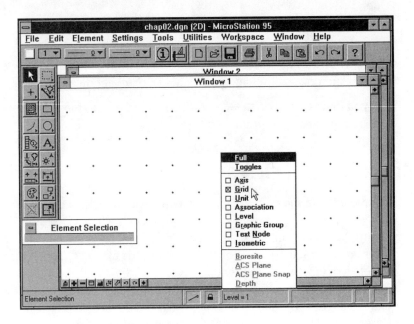

TURNING ON GRID LOCK

Continue from the preceding exercise, using the CHAP02.DGN design file.

Click on the Lock *icon in the status bar (refer to figure 2.2)*	Opens Lock settings box
Click in the **G**rid Lock *toggle button*	Turns Grid lock on and dismisses settings box

MicroStation doesn't automatically save the grid settings when you exit. You must use Sa**v**e Settings to save these settings in the design file. Otherwise, when you reopen the drawing, the grid and grid lock settings no longer are in effect.

Warning

Saving the Settings

Think of drawing on a drafting table. During the drawing process, you might lay out the locations and scales of various details on a sheet, or perhaps select graph paper on which to letter. Think of the sheet size, the color and hardness of the pencils, the straightedges and templates, and even the size of the graph paper as drawing settings. MicroStation has drawing, or active, settings also. Whether the grid is displayed or hidden and whether Grid Lock is turned on are examples of active settings. The number of views you have open, their position on the display screen, and how far you might be zoomed in or zoomed out in certain views, also are examples of active settings.

You might change some settings only once during an entire design session; for example, you might want to attach a different cell library or reference file to the current drawing. These attachments remain until you open another design file or exit MicroStation. When you reopen the design file, however, you have to make the attachments again, unless you use Sa**v**e Settings. When you attach a new cell library or reference file and you want it to stay attached, use Sa**v**e Settings after you make the attachment.

You change certain active settings often during a design session, including such settings as the drawing color, line weight, and active drawing level. During a typical design session, you also change the view orientations by zooming in or out or by windowing the views many times. Saving these active settings each time you change them wouldn't make sense. Save these active settings only at the end of a drawing session (for example, before a break, lunch, or at the end of the day).

When you choose Sa**v**e Settings, MicroStation records the active setting's values, such as grid display (on or off), grid lock (on or off), active drawing level, active color, and so on. It also notes open views and their orientation. MicroStation then writes this information in the header of the design file. The next time you open the file, MicroStation writes this header information back into memory and establishes the active drawing settings.

Saving active settings has nothing to do with saving the elements you have drawn.

Sa<u>v</u>e Settings saves all views, all view attributes, current locks, all active and applied level symbologies, and so on. In some offices, it might be determined that the CADD project leader should save settings in order to maintain consistency within the project. For your information, this book will identify all settings that are saved with Sa<u>v</u>e Settings.

 Note MicroStation, by default, doesn't work the way most computer programs work. In the word processing world, for example, you have to save what you write as you work or it's gone. MicroStation, however, continually saves what you draw. This feature is user customizable and Chapter 19 discusses how to change it.

In the next exercise, you use the fabled Sa<u>v</u>e Settings option (see fig. 2.3). The status bar displays `Settings Saved` after MicroStation completes the operation.

CHOOSING SAVE SETTINGS FROM THE FILE PULL-DOWN MENU

Continue from the preceding exercise, using the CHAP02.DGN design file.

Choose <u>F</u>ile, Sa<u>v</u>e Settings   Saves the current active drawing settings in the design file header

Figure 2.3

Choosing Save Settings from the File pull-down menu to save your active design file settings.

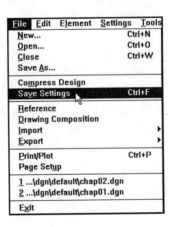

 Tip The keyboard accelerator for Sa<u>v</u>e Settings is Ctrl+F.

Now that you have established a means of drawing accurately, you can begin drawing an office plan.

Drawing Lines

In the next exercise, you place the first office wall with the Place Line tool. The Place Line tool creates a line based on two input points. The first input point defines the start of the line, and the second input point determines the line's end point. After you place the second input point, the Place Line tool assumes that you want to draw a second line. To do so, continue placing input points. When you finish placing lines, either click the reset button (right mouse button) or choose another tool.

Each line you draw is a separate graphic element. If you want several lines to act as one element rather than as a series of separate line segments, use the Place SmartLine tool.

Note

Selecting a Tool

The Main tool frame has 18 icons. MicroStation certainly has more than 18 drawing tools. Attached to each icon (except the Select Element icon in the upper left corner and the Delete Element icon in the lower right corner) are tool boxes. A *tool box* is a secondary set of tools called from a parent, or frame.

One of the parent frames in MicroStation is the Main tool frame. MicroStation offers a few other frames, such as 3D tools and Dimension Driven Design.

Each tool box contains a group of drawing tools that perform similar operations. You find different text placement tools in the Text tool box, for instance, and you find tools you use to draw lines in the Linear Elements tool box. The next exercise uses the Place Line.

You can tell which icons have tool boxes by the filled-in arrow symbol (>) in the lower right corner of the icon.

Tip

To select a tool that is displayed on the Main tool frame, simply click on the icon.

To select a tool other than the default icon from a tool box, you first put the cursor over the tool. Pressing and holding the data button down on that tool causes the child tool box to appear. As you move the cursor over the different tools, the command name changes on the status bar. When you reach the tool you want to use (Place Line is the second tool on the tool box), release the data button to select that drawing tool.

Note

After you choose the Place Line tool, look at the Main tool frame on the display screen. The Place SmartLine tool no longer is the default icon on the Main tool frame.

Each time you choose a tool from a child tool box, that tool becomes the default icon on the Main tool frame. As you switch drawing files during a session, these new icon defaults remain in force.

When you exit, MicroStation discards the modified Main frame. The next time you start MicroStation the Main tool frame appears with its 18 original default icons.

In the following exercise, you draw the first wall by choosing the Place Line tool and then placing two input points using the cursor.

Each cross on the display grid represents one master unit (let's call them feet (')). The 10' × 12' office has four walls. You place the first point in the lower left corner of the view, then count over 10 crosses and place a second input point to create the first wall. Follow the exercise and see figure 2.5 to place the first office wall. Notice how the input points *jump to* (a commonly used phrase for "lock on") the grid dots.

PLACING THE FIRST WALL

Click and hold on the SmartLine tool	Opens child tool box
Release the data point when the cursor is on the Place Line tool (see fig. 2.4)	Activates the Place Line tool
`Enter first point` *Pick first input point at ① (see fig. 2.5)*	Defines wall's starting point
`Enter end point` *Pick second input point at ② (10 crosses from first point)*	Defines wall's endpoint and draws line
`Enter end point`	Prepares for another line

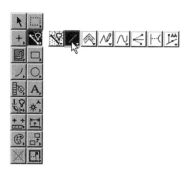

Figure 2.4

*Choosing the
Place Line tool.*

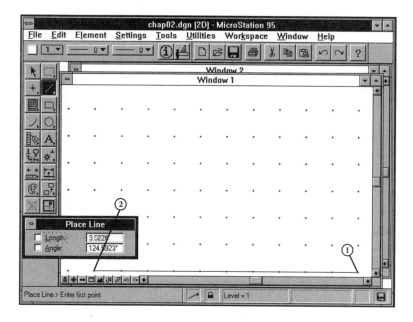

Figure 2.5

*Placing the first
wall.*

You construct the three remaining walls of the office with the constraint feature in
the Tool Settings box, instead of building the walls by counting cross-hairs with the
cursor.

Continuing the Office Perimeter with Constraints

The Tool Settings box contains the constraints for each command. It appears when
you select a command and always displays the command name in its title bar (see
fig. 2.6). You can finish lines you started using the Place Line tool by entering values

in the Tool Settings box. Two values appear for the Place Line tool: **L**ength and **A**ngle constraints. When you place a line with constraint, you can enter a length, an angle, or both to define the line.

In the case of this office, the dimensions are 10' by 12'. You can use working units, decimals, or fractions for the length value. To set a length constraint, enable the **L**ength check box and enter a value in the text box.

Figure 2.6

The Tool Settings box with the Place Line constraints.

 Tip   To enter a fraction, remember to place a space between the whole number and the fraction (for example, **3 1/2**).

The second constraint is the **A**ngle option, which you use to determine direction. MicroStation measures direction in degrees counterclockwise from the horizontal axis (usually parallel with the bottom edge of the display screen). The direction from left to right across the display screen is 0°. Going from the bottom of the screen to the top is 90°. Going right to left is 180° and going top to bottom is 270° (see fig. 2.7).

Figure 2.7

Screen directions in degrees.

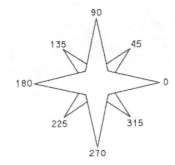

In this next exercise, the Place Line tool still is active from placing the first office wall. You use the constraints to complete the last three walls of the office perimeter in the following exercise. Figure 2.11 shows how the finished office perimeter should look.

In the following exercise, you continue placing the lines that represent the walls of the room.

PLACING LINES WITH CONSTRAINTS

The Place Line tool should still be running from the last exercise; if not, choose it now. The prompt line should read Enter end point; if not, pick the last end point of the previous line.

Enter end point   Prompts for input

Click in the Tool Settings box and
enable the **L***ength constraint*

Enter **12**

Choose a point at ① *(see fig. 2.8)*   Draws a line 12'

Choose the Fit View icon in the   Changes the view extents to display
View Control bar ②   all elements in the file

Click the Reset button   Exits Fit View command and returns to
                                                    the Place Line command

Enter **10** *in the* **L***ength constraint*

Choose a point at ③   Draws a line 10'

Toggle off the **L***ength constraint*

Toggle on the **A***ngle constraint*

Enter **270** *in the* **A***ngle constraint*

Pick a point at ④   Draws last wall

Toggle off the **A***ngle constraint*

Click the Reset button   Resets Place Line command and is ready for
                                                    another operation

Enter first point

*Completed room
outline.*

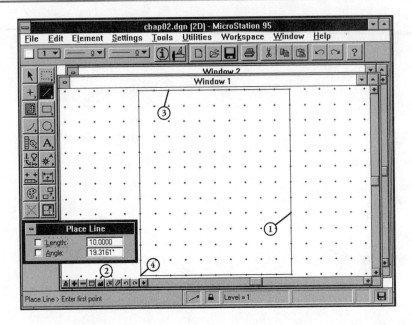

In the previous exercise, you were instructed to fit the design into your view or window. This was necessary because the 12' wall was drawn outside the view area. Many commands, collectively known as *view controls*, possess the capability to display different portions of your design on the computer screen as you draw.

MicroStation offers a variety of view controls. You can become acquainted with how they work by working through the exercises in this book. Fit View enables you to see the big picture. Fit View centers and displays the entire design file in a view.

Placing Blocks

During the next few exercises, you use the Place Block tool to create furniture. The new office plan calls for two desks, one for you and one for Fred. Each desk is 3' × 5'.

Place Block requires two input points, which define the opposite corners of the shape or block. You encounter several other shape drawing tools later. After you place the first corner, move the cursor away from that point. Notice how MicroStation dynamically drags the desk shape. This feature makes sizing the shape easier before placement.

In the next exercise, you choose the drawing tool first and pick the two input points that define the opposite corners of the 3' × 5' desk (your desk). Figure 2.13 illustrates defining the desk shape for you and Fred. The office plan calls for some bookcases for storage. As long as Place Block is active, now also is a good time to draw a 1' × 3' bookcase (see fig. 2.9). A later exercise uses Copy Element to create several more bookcases.

PLACING FURNITURE WITH PLACE BLOCK

Choose Place Block *from the Main tool frame*

`Enter first point` *Pick a point at* ① *(see fig. 2.9) and move the cursor*   Picks first desk corner and the desk shape appears

`Enter opposite corner` *Pick another point at* ②, *5 crosses down and 3 to the left of* ①   Picks second desk corner and places desk

Now draw a second desk for Fred.

`Enter first point` *Pick a point at* ③ *(see fig. 2.9)*   Picks first desk corner

`Enter opposite corner` *Pick another point at* ④   Picks second desk corner and places desk

As long as the Place Block tool is active, make one bookcase. You use Copy Element to add more bookcases in a later exercise.

`Enter first point` *Pick a point at* ⑤ *(see fig. 2.9)*   Picks first bookcase corner

`Enter opposite corner` *Pick another point at* ⑥   Picks second corner and places the bookcase

---

Figure 2.9

Drawing the desks and bookcase.

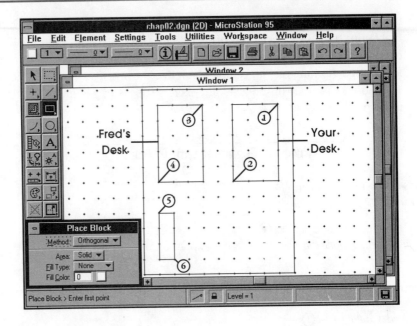

Moving Elements

Maybe positioning Fred's desk along the same wall as yours was not the best idea—not much room for the bookcases. Moving Fred's desk to the opposite wall might do the trick. In the next exercise, you use Move Element to move Fred's desk across the room.

Sometimes, you might want to move some element from one place to another, in this case, Fred's desk. Other times, you want to leave the original object where it is and make a copy of it.

Moving an element is a two-step process. First, after you choose the Move Element tool, you identify the element you want to move using a data point, which becomes the first point of the move displacement. Next, you drag the element to its new location and pick a second input point to identify the element's final position. Chapter 9, "Manipulating 2D Elements," examines Move Element in detail. For now, just follow the directions. The screen cursor shows the position of Move Element on the Main tool frame in figure 2.10.

Before you move Fred's desk, take a look at a second way to select tools from tool boxes.

Figure 2.10

Move Element command on the Main Tool Frame.

Tearing Off a Menu Tool box

If you intend to use several of the commands from one of the tool boxes off the Main frame, you can tear it off for quick access to each command. You tear off the tool box by clicking and dragging it into the design area. As you move the cursor, an outline rectangle remains visible to represent the tool box. Release the button after you position the outline to place the tool box.

> The outline rectangle that appears as you move your cursor away from the main tool frame varies in size based on the tool box.

Note

In the following exercise, you tear off the Manipulate Element tool box and use the Move tool to move Fred's desk to the other side of the office. Figure 2.11 shows Fred's desk in its new location.

MOVING FRED'S DESK INTO POSITION

Continue from the preceding exercise, using the CHAP02.DGN design file.

Tear off the Manipulate tool box

Choose the Move Element *tool from the Manipulate tool box*

`Identify element` *Pick the desk at* ① *(see fig. 2.11)*

Selects the desk and sets base point of move displacement

`Accept/Reject (select next input)` *Pick a second point at* ②

Places the desk (see fig. 2.11)

Continues

`Accept/Reject (select next input)`	Prompts for another point
Click the Reset button	Accepts location and readies tool for another operation

`Identify element`

Moving Fred's desk with Move Element.

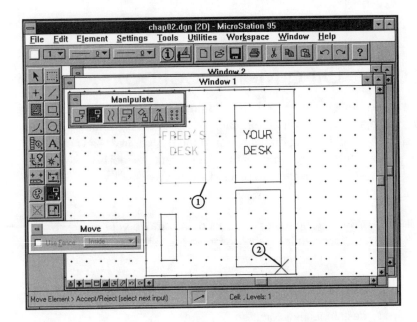

Tip

In the preceding exercise, you clicked the Reset button to interrupt the Move Element command. If you hadn't done so, the desk shape would have remained attached to the cursor, ready for you to move the desk somewhere else. Drawing tools work this way—you can use them repeatedly. MicroStation offers a user preference called Single Click, which determines how tools are selected when you press the data button. MicroStation offers two ways of selecting a tool: *locked* and *single-shot*. When you make a locked tool selection, the tool repeats until you reset or select another tool. A single-shot tool selection prevents repetition of the tool; after one iteration, the default tool is selected.

The default for the Single Click preference is locked selections.

The new location for Fred's desk looks perfect. Now work through the next exercise to copy some bookcases for storage. You used Place Block to draw the first bookcase. You use the much anticipated Copy Element command to place the remaining bookcases in the office.

Copying Elements

Copy Element works much the same way as Move Element, except that it leaves the original in place. Use Copy Element when you want to copy a single element, multiple elements, or a complex cell or symbol. You can copy an element over the top of the original or copy something to a new location. The copy process requires two input points.

You can identify multiple elements by defining a selection set. Chapter 9, "Manipulating 2D Elements," covers selection sets in detail.   *Tip*

First, you use a data point to identify the element you want to copy, which becomes the first point of the copy displacement, that is, the point on the element from which you are copying. Next, you drag a copy of the element to a new location before giving a second input point to place the copy. Chapter 9 discusses Copy Element in detail. Copy Element is the first tool on the Manipulate Element tool box (see fig. 2.12). Figure 2.13 shows adding bookcases to the office space.

Figure 2.12

Choosing Copy Element from the Main tool frame.

COPYING BOOKCASES

Continue from the preceding exercise, using the CHAP02.DGN design file.

Choose Copy Element *from the Manipulate tool box (see fig. 2.12)*

Continues

`Identify Element` *Pick the bookcase at ① (see fig. 2.13)*	Selects the bookcase and sets the base point of displacement
`Accept/Reject (select next input)` *Pick a second input point at ②*	Places a second bookcase

Even as you have created a new bookcase using Copy Element, notice how a bookcase outline still is attached to the cursor. Continue placing Data points and place one more bookcase next to the second bookcase.

`Accept/Reject (select next input)` *Pick a third input point at ③ (see fig. 2.13)*	Places a third bookcase
`Accept/Reject (select next input)` *Click the Reset button*	Accepts copy and interrupts Copy Element tool
`Identify Element`	

Close the Manipulate Element tool box

Figure 2.13

Using Copy Element to create multiple bookcases.

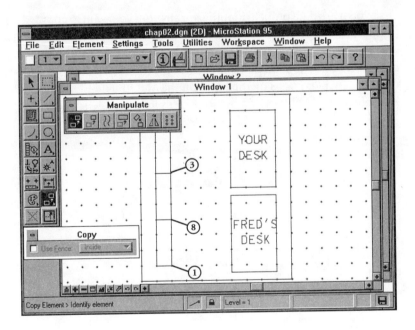

Deleting Elements

One drawing tool that gains instant popularity among new users is the Delete Element tool. The Delete tool is found on the Main tool frame—the lower left icon with the red X. Think of the Delete Element tool as your drafting eraser.

Deleting in MicroStation takes two steps. First, after you choose the Delete tool, you pick the element you want to remove. MicroStation highlights the element and asks `Accept/Reject (select next input)`. Rather than just delete the element in question, MicroStation uses this prompt to ask, "Are you really sure this is the element you want to delete?" With only one line on the display screen, it is easy to pick the line that should be removed. However, envision a drawing so dense with lines, circles, arcs, text, and dimensions that you need to be a "sharpshooter" to hit the right element for deletion. That is why MicroStation asks the question, "Accept/Reject?" If you realize you've highlighted the wrong element, just click on the Reset button to reject the element, and then try again to pick the correct element.

To recap, deleting elements takes two picks with the cursor or mouse: one pick to identify the element and a second pick to confirm the element's deletion. You don't have to pick the second point (the accept point) on the element; just pick any point in any open view away from any element.

Figure 2.14 shows picking Fred's desk for removal.

REMOVING A DESK WITH THE DELETE ELEMENT TOOL

Continue from the preceding exercise, using the CHAP02.DGN design file.

Choose the Delete Element *tool from the Main tool frame*

`Identify Element` *Pick the desk at* ①   Identifies the desk for removal
(see fig. 2.14)

The next prompt asks for confirmation. You don't have to pick the desk again; just pick any point.

`Accept/Reject (select next input)`   Erases the desk
Pick a confirmation point at ②
(see fig. 2.14)

`Identify Element`   Readies tool for another operation

What if you delete the wrong element? Then you can learn about Undo, which reverses most operations, including the deletion process.

Figure 2.14

Deleting Fred's desk.

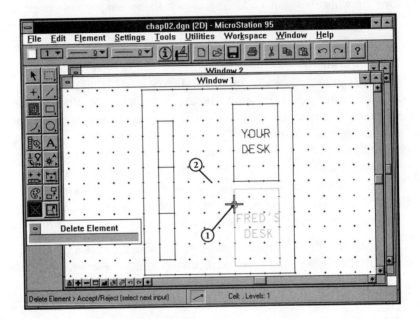

Undoing a Deletion

Undo reverses or "undoes" the last drawing operation. The operation might have involved copying a circle, placing some text, or deleting an element. Chapter 9 talks more about Undo, its options, and Undo's buddy, Redo.

Undo keeps track of the last drawing operation. Open the **E**dit pull-down menu and notice that Undo echoes the last drawing operation. In this case, the last operation involved Delete Element. The Undo selection on the **E**dit menu now reads **U**ndo delete element. This tells you that if you select Undo, it will reverse the last operation, which was Delete Element.

Now use Undo to recover Fred's desk. Maybe you were hasty in moving Fred's stuff out of the office. To recover the deleted desk, issue the Undo command by choosing **E**dit, **U**ndo (see fig. 2.15).

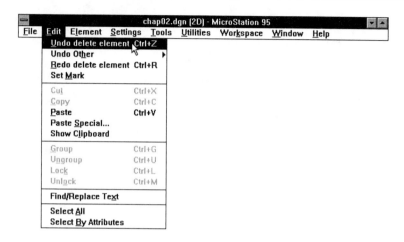

Figure 2.15

Choosing Undo delete element.

The shortcut key for Undo is Ctrl+Z.

Tip

Ending a Design Session

Ending a design session correctly is as important as setting up the file when you begin drawing. When you delete an element, MicroStation hides it from view, but keeps it in the design file. To end a drawing session correctly, you should remove the deleted elements and possibly save the active drawing settings. After you complete those two operations, you can close the active drawing and call up another file, or exit MicroStation.

Earlier in this chapter, the process of saving the settings was discussed. Save Settings saves the active drawing settings as well as the view positions on the display screen and their orientations in the active design file. Exiting MicroStation or switching to a different design file should include three actions:

♦ Use Compress Design to remove all the deleted elements from the design file.

♦ Use Save Settings to store any active setting changes that were made during the design session in the active design file.

♦ Either exit MicroStation or choose a new design file in which to work.

Removing Deleted Elements from the Design File

You cannot see a deleted element and it doesn't plot, but the deleted elements remain part of the design file until you get rid of them. Deleted elements take up valuable disk space. You use Compress Design to remove deleted elements from a design file. Because the compress operation removes the deleted elements, the design file takes up less file space. Because the design file is smaller, MicroStation can locate and display the remaining active elements more quickly.

You should try to develop a habit of compressing the design file each time you end the drawing session or during a session after you delete large numbers of elements. You activate Compress Design by choosing File, Compress Design (see fig. 2.16). The message File Compressed appears on the status bar after MicroStation completes the compress operation.

Tip   You cannot undelete elements after you use Compress Design, nor after you switch drawing files or exit MicroStation.

Figure 2.16

Choosing Compress Design from the File pull-down menu.

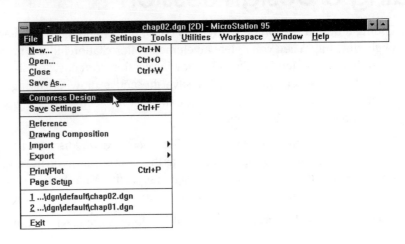

Finishing a File

You might decide to take one of two avenues after you finish a particular design file. If you need to work on another drawing, you could close the current design file and open a new second file. Otherwise, you might close the active drawing and exit MicroStation altogether. Choose File, Exit to close MicroStation.

To close the current drawing and open a second file, choose File, Close. Choosing Close automatically opens the MicroStation Manager dialog box, from which you can choose a second file.

Summary

Congratulations! You made it through the first design session. This chapter was written to give you a feeling for MicroStation. Now you can continue through the book for details on the commands covered in this chapter and much, much more.

Building a Solid Foundation

*T*he foundation of every drawing or design is the design file itself. This chapter discusses two important features of every design file: levels and working units. The concept of levels, common to many CAD packages, enables you to create a productive, organized arrangement of the data in your design file. Working units *provide a means to define the precision and accuracy of your design file. You must understand these concepts to function effectively in MicroStation. In conjunction with working units, other important concepts and terminology are discussed in the chapter, including the design plane and the coordinate system. This chapter covers the following topics:*

♦ *Understanding MicroStation levels*

♦ *Understanding the design plane*

♦ *Introducing the coordinate system*

♦ *Setting working units*

♦ *Saving your work*

Understanding MicroStation Levels

Many CAD programs include some type of level concept, be it called *levels*, *overlays*, *layers*, or something else. In the manual method of drawing, you use overlays or transparencies to draw different features. Each overlay has specific features assigned to it, such as streets, building outlines, or property outlines (see fig. 3.1). When you put different combinations of these transparencies together, you can create different variations of the total design. An electronic-design file is no different; MicroStation's levels are equivalent to manual drawings' transparencies.

Figure 3.1 shows effective use of levels. Each level contains features such as streets, buildings, and property lines. You create a product from these three levels by displaying them together.

Figure 3.1

An illustration of levels.

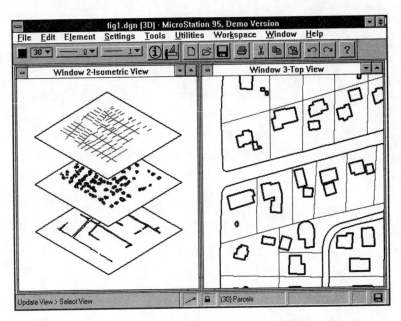

MicroStation lets you have up to 63 levels (sometimes called overlays or layers in other CAD programs) in each design file. You can turn each level on or off as you please. You can display and plot one level, all 63 levels, or any combination of levels to create a specific view or drawing.

Advantages of Using Levels

Levels give you the flexibility to create different design products. Levels also assist in the design process and organize the design data.

One of the biggest advantages of using multiple levels is the creation of different design products. On a facility map, for example, you might have features that represent water mains, water services, hydrants, manholes, and the like. If you put each of these water-facility features on a different level, you could easily plot or view several map products for different purposes. A map of the water-main network would be helpful as a wall map. A hydrant map could quickly be produced for the water hydrant inspectors. The list of possibilities is almost endless.

Levels also assist you in the design process. If the design file is dense and cluttered with different types of data, you can turn off levels that aren't immediately necessary. Doing so doesn't delete the data, it just hides them. You can turn the different types of data back on when you need them.

Levels also enable you to organize your data. If the data is spread among different levels, you easily can change or manipulate portions of the data. You also can use levels to take a quick check of the design for missing data by viewing one level at a time.

The Active Level

Each time you place an element in a design file, you place it on one of the 63 levels. The level on which you place the element is called the *active level*.

You can quickly determine the active level by looking at the Status Bar. The Status Bar displays the level as `Level=levelnumber`. In figure 3.2, for example, the active level is 59.

Figure 3.2

Level=59 indicates the active level.

The Status Bar has many different functions. If you don't see the `Level=`, click on the Status Bar to activate the display.

Tip

Changing the Active Level

You can change your active level at any time. To change the active level, click on the Level= in the Status Bar, which opens the Set Active Level dialog box (see fig. 3.3). Click on the level number you want to become the active level and choose the **O**K button or simply double-click on the desired level number.

Figure 3.3

The Set Active Level dialog box.

 Note   Later in this chapter, in the section "Named Levels," you learn how to name levels. Rather than remember the number of the level that contains streets, you can display and activate the street level by name.

In the following exercise, you use the Set Active Level dialog box to activate a new level for drawing.

Changing the Active Level

Create a design file called CHAP03.DGN.

Click on the Level= *in the Status Bar*	Opens the Set Active Level dialog box
Click on number 20	Activates level 20
Choose **O**K	Applies the new active level of 20 and displays Level=20 in the Status Bar

---

Now, level 20 is the active level. The default reaction of changing the active level is level 1 becomes a displayed level. The section "Display Levels," in this chapter, offers more information about levels that are on but are not the active level.

Placing Elements on the Active Level

Each element you place is located on the active level. When you place an element in the following exercise, you are placing it on the active level, which you set as 20 in the previous exercise.

PLACING ELEMENTS ON THE ACTIVE LEVEL

Continue from the preceding exercise with the CHAP03.DGN design file.

Choose the Place SmartLine *tool by clicking at* ① *(see fig. 3.4)*	Activates the Place SmartLine command
Pick a point at ②	Starts line
Pick a point at ③	Completes line
Click the Reset button	

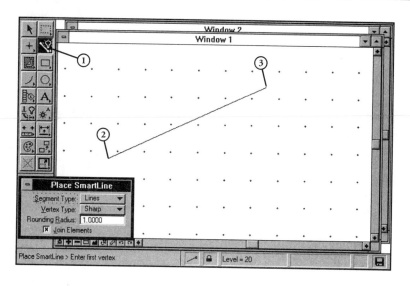

Figure 3.4

Placing an element on the active level, 20.

Display Levels

You can have only one level active at a time, but you can display any combination of levels on-screen. You can choose the display levels by using the View Levels settings box. To activate this settings box, choose **S**ettings, **L**evel, **D**isplay from the pull-down menu.

The View Levels settings box (see fig. 3.5) shows the numbers 1 through 63, which represent all the levels in your file. The number highlighted with the black circle indicates the active level. Level numbers displayed with black squares are on (displayed). Levels without highlighted numbers are off and not displayed.

Figure 3.5

The View Levels settings box.

You can double-click on a new level number in the View Levels settings box to change the active level. The black circle appears on the new number, and the former active level appears with a black square. Notice that the `Level=` statement in the Status Bar changes to reflect the new active level. Until you change the active level again, every element you place, you place on this level.

 Tip   Remember, View Levels is a settings box, so you can display it on-screen while you draw. You might want to keep it up on-screen for quick access. Also note that the View Levels settings box can be moved partially off-screen for more room.

MicroStation offers the capability to display eight views of your drawing on-screen. You can display a different combination of levels in each of the eight views. Eight views are only practical if you have two display monitors.

The design file of a floor plan, for example, would have many different components: dimensioning, annotations, and interior walls and doors. You could display all or some of these levels in each of the four views (see fig. 3.6).

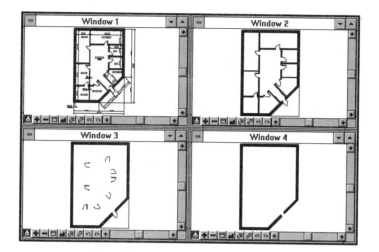

Figure 3.6

Different display levels in four views.

In figure 3.6, the view labeled "Window 1" in the title bar shows the entire design and all its levels. The view labeled "Window 2" displays everything but the text. The view labeled "Window 3" displays only the exterior walls and doors. The view labeled "Window 4" displays only the exterior walls of the floor plan.

The active level is always displayed. You cannot turn off the active level the way you can turn off other display levels.

Chapter 6, "Viewing a Drawing," discusses multiple views and how to use them.

Note

Controlling Display Levels from the Settings Box

The View Levels settings box highlights levels that are displayed with black boxes. If you click on a level that is displayed, the black box disappears indicating that MicroStation will turn off the display of that level when you press the **A**pply button. You must choose the **A**pply button to make the level changes effective. If you don't choose the **A**pply button before you remove the settings box, no changes take place.

Tip   You can turn on a block of levels from the View Levels settings box by pressing the Shift key, and then clicking and dragging in a diagonal direction from one corner of the block to the other corner.

Try changing your active level and turning off the level display in the next exercise.

TURNING DISPLAY LEVELS ON OR OFF WITH THE VIEW LEVELS SETTINGS BOX

Continue from the preceding exercise, using the CHAP03.DGN design file.

Choose Settings, Level, Display	Opens the View Levels settings box
Double-click on number 1	Level 1 becomes the active level
Place another line, as in the previous exercise	
Click on level number 20 in the View Levels settings box	Removes black square from number 20
Choose Apply	Turns off level 20 (the first line) in view 1 (see fig. 3.7)

Figure 3.7

Displaying level 20 turned off.

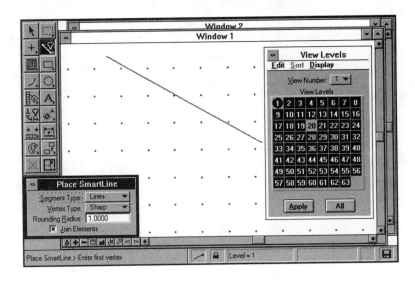

Turning Off the Display for the Active Level

The following rules govern the active level:

♦ Your active level is always displayed; you cannot turn off display of the active level.

♦ You must always have an active level.

You placed the last line in the previous exercise on level 1. To turn off the display for the active level, such as level 1, you must first make another level active. Try this in the next exercise.

TURNING OFF THE ACTIVE LEVEL

Continue from the preceding exercise, using the CHAP03.DGN design file.

Double-click on number 2 *in the* View Levels *dialog box*	Displays a circle (active level) around number 2 and a square around (on) number 1
Click on level number 1 *in the* View Levels *settings box*	Removes black square from number 1
Choose **A**pply	Removes the line place on level 1 from the display (see fig. 3.8)

The elements still exist, they just aren't displayed in the view.

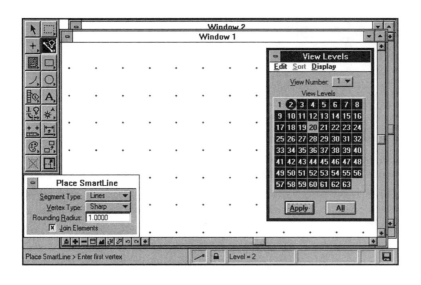

Figure 3.8

Displaying level 2 active and level 1 turned off.

Level Dos and Don'ts

Levels are extremely important in any CAD file because they provide flexibility. Drawing on just one level isn't an effective use of the design file, or of CAD.

Determine the levels for each type of feature in your design before you start drawing your first element. Try to determine all possible uses or plots for your design. If you create a base for other disciplines, you should consider their needs as well as your own. If your floor plan is going to be used as a base for the plumbing and electrical wiring of the structure, for example, consider the requirements of each of those disciplines.

A base map is another example of the flexibility that levels give to a design file. The base map could contain streets, alleys, curbs, lot lines, lot dimensions, and so on. Later, you could use the same base map to add the water and sewer infrastructure. No modification of the design file would be required if all the features were on different levels; each discipline could use only the relevant levels. The water department could use the base map for their purposes and display only some of the data. If streets and alleys were on the same level, however, the water infrastructure group would be forced to display streets and alleys despite being interested only in the streets.

Sixty-three levels should enable you to split up your drawing features into the smallest common denominator. The file in the preceding base map example could be created using streets on one level and alleys on another, for example, thus providing the flexibility to turn off alleys when necessary.

Named Levels

If you find it difficult to remember which components of your drawings go on what levels, try using named levels. *Named levels* enable you to assign names and descriptions to levels or to a group of levels. You can then turn levels on and off by using the name rather than the number.

You assign names to a level in the Level Names dialog box (see fig. 3.9). To activate the dialog box, choose **S**ettings, **L**evel, **N**ames. You also can get the Level Names from the View Levels settings box. Choose **D**isplay, then Level Names from the View Levels settings box pull-down menus.

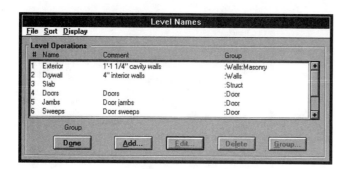

Figure 3.9

The Level Names dialog box.

In the following exercises, you use a design file delivered with MicroStation titled FLOOR.DGN and a previously defined set of named levels to explore the use of named levels. A set of named levels is called a *level structure*.

After you design the file, open an existing level structure by choosing **F**ile, **O**pen in the Level Names dialog box.

OPENING AN EXISTING LEVEL STRUCTURE

Choose **F***ile,* **O***pen*	Opens the Open Design File dialog box
Double-click on the ustation *directory*	Changes the directory list
Double-click on the dgn *directory*	
Double-click on the learning *directory*	Lists designs to choose from in the **Fi**les list (see fig. 3.10)
Double-click on the file FLOOR.DGN	Activates and opens the FLOOR.DGN file (see fig. 3.10)
Choose **S***ettings,* **L***evel,* **N***ames*	Opens the Level Names dialog box

If a level structure is not already attached, do the following:

Choose **F***ile,* **O***pen from the Level* **N***ames dialog box*	Issues the Open Level Structure dialog box
Change to the \ustation\data *directory and double-click on the file* FLOOR.LVL	Selects FLOOR.LVL, closes the Open Level Structure dialog box, and attaches the level structure

Figure 3.10

*Opening the
FLOOR.DGN
design file.*

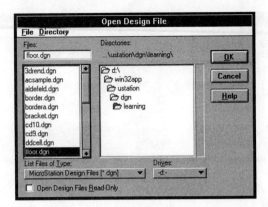

Tip You get the same results as the preceding exercise by choosing **E**dit, **D**efine Names in the View Levels settings box.

The attached existing level structure has four level name groups. These name groups appear on the right side of the Level Names dialog box (refer to figure 3.9). Each level name is assigned to a single level. A group can contain many level names or levels. The Door group, for example, contains level names: Doors, Jambs, and Sweeps (see fig. 3.11). If you want to display only the level name groups, choose Group Operations from the **D**isplay pull-down menu in the Level Names dialog box (see fig. 3.11).

DISPLAYING LEVEL NAME GROUPS OR THEIR CONTENTS

Continue from the preceding exercise, using the FLOOR.DGN design file and Level Names dialog box.

Choose **D**isplay, *then* Group Operations

Pick a point on Door   Shows the levels of the Door group (see fig. 3.11)

Level name groups can contain levels, more groups, or both. As an example, look at the level name group Walls. A + appears next to the name, indicating an additional group inside the Walls group. A single-click on the group Walls shows you the level contained in this group. If you double-click on the group Walls, another group is displayed in the Group list box called Masonry.

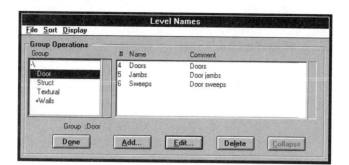

Figure 3.11

The Door name level group and its contents.

Note

If you set the Level Names dialog box display to Level Operations, you see multiple groups displayed in the group column, separated by colons. The level name Exterior, for example, is in the group Walls:Masonry (refer to figure 3.9).

To create a new named level, choose **A**dd in the Level Names dialog box. The Level Name subdialog box appears (see fig. 3.12). Enter the number of the level you are naming in the **N**umber field, the name of the level in the Na**m**e field, and, optionally, a comment describing the level contents in the **C**omment field.

Tip

Level names can be up to 16 characters long, but keep them as short as possible for easy access. If you follow this strategy, however, make sure to use the **C**omments section to elaborate on the level contents.

In the following exercise, you add a level name. You must change the current Group Operations display to add a level name. With Group Operations display on, you can manipulate (create and delete) only groups.

CREATING A NEW LEVEL NAME

Continue from the preceding exercise, using the FLOOR.DGN design file.

Choose **D**isplay, *then* Level Operations   Displays all named levels

Choose **A**dd   Issues the Level Name subdialog box (see fig. 3.12)

Type **20** *and press Tab*   Enters level number

Continues

Type your name and press Tab	Enters name
Type a comment like `PracticeLesson 3`	
Choose **O**K *or hit Enter*	Closes the Level Name subdialog box and displays a named level defined for number 20 (see fig. 3.13)

Figure 3.12

The Level Name subdialog box.

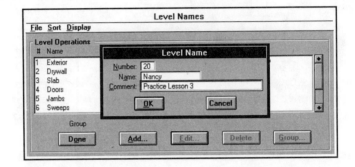

Figure 3.13

Named level defined for level 20.

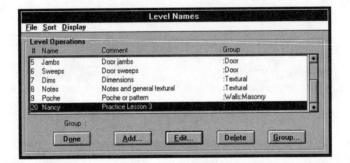

To add the named level to an existing group, choose the **G**roup button while the level name is highlighted. This opens the Select Target Group dialog box. Pick the group to which you want to move or copy the level name and choose **G**roup.

Warning If you add or delete level names, be sure to save the level structure before you exit the design file. If you do not save, the named level disappears when you exit and reenter MicroStation. Choose **F**ile, **S**ave in the Level Names dialog box to open the Save Level Structure subdialog box. Click on **O**K to save the level structure with the same name, or enter a new name and then click on **O**K.

Using Level Names

To use your named levels, choose Level Names or Level Groups from the **D**isplay pull-down menu in the View Levels settings box.

The display of Level Names in the View Levels settings box shows each level name and the views that currently have that level display on (refer to figure 3.13). Figure 3.14, for example, indicates that the level named Exterior currently is being displayed in all eight views.

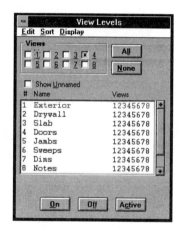

Figure 3.14

Level names displayed in the View Levels settings box.

To turn a named level on or off, choose the level in the list box and click the appropriate toggle button in the Views area. The level name display for each view indicated is turned on or off.

Try using named levels in the next exercise, but first turn off the views labeled Window 2, Window 3, and Window 4. Then maximize view 1 and choose Fit View to see the floor plan.

TURNING OFF NAMED LEVELS

Continue from the previous exercise, using the FLOOR.DGN design file and the View Levels settings box.

Close views 2, 3, *and* 4

Maximize view 1   Maximizes the view on the display area

Fit View   Displays all elements in the view

Continues

Choose **D**isplay, *then* Level Names

Toggle on view 1

Toggle off views 2, 3, 4, 5, 6, 7, 8
(see fig. 3.15)

Choose Drywall *from list box*	Highlights level named Drywall
Choose O**ff**	Turns off level Drywall in view 1 only

Now in the next exercise, change the display to Level Groups and turn the display off for all three levels that contain door data.

Figure 3.15

Drywall level off in views 1 and 4.

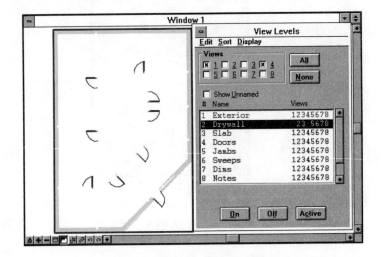

TURNING OFF NAMED GROUPS

Continue from the previous exercise, using the FLOOR.DGN design file and the View Levels settings box.

Choose **D**isplay, *then* Level Groups

Choose Door *from the* Group *list box*	Highlights level group Door, and displays the three levels it contains
Choose O**ff** *from the* Group *section*	Turns the Door group off in the selected view (see fig. 3.16)

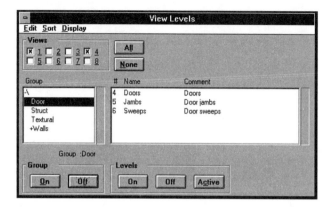

Figure 3.16

Level groups displayed in the View Levels settings box.

The active level displayed on the Status Bar indicates the level name and the level number in parentheses. Choose the active level in the View Levels settings box by highlighting the level name, then choosing the A**c**tive button, or by double-clicking on the name in the list box.

Note

Display Level Settings

MicroStation remembers the levels displayed in each view if you choose **F**ile, Sa**v**e Settings. If you set up the display levels in your view and exit MicroStation without using Sa**v**e Settings, you lose your setup of the view's display levels.

Display levels are only one of the settings MicroStation saves when you use the Sa**v**e Settings option. Throughout this book, you are introduced to more settings saved using this command.

Note

Understanding the Design Plane

The *design plane* is the total available drawing area in your design file. You can think of the design plane as a gigantic square sheet of grid paper. The grid is made up of 4,294,967,295 squares across and 4,294,967,295 squares up (see fig. 3.17). These numbers reflect the total number of available units or UORs (Units of Resolution).

Figure 3.17

The design plane.

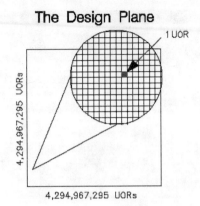

Introducing the Coordinate System

Your design file uses a Cartesian coordinate system in which coordinate values are expressed in x (horizontal) and y (vertical) positions. The point known as 0,0 is called the *global origin*. Usually, the global origin point is located in the center of the design plane, which gives you both positive and negative coordinates (see fig. 3.18). You can change this global origin, but most applications should have sufficient area in any plane.

Figure 3.18

The global origin.

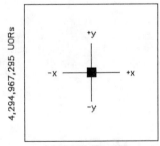

Defining Working Units

An architect, for example, will want to work in the units of feet and inches; therefore, a door opening in the design file is placed, dimensioned, and measured to reflect three feet.

You draw in full-size units, and the file is scaled when you plot. For example, a plotted sheet size could be 24 inches, but the border in the design file could measure one mile or perhaps 24 feet. You can define the scale as 1 foot = 1 inch or 1 mile = 24 inches when you plot the drawing.

Components of Working Units

Working units are composed of master units, subunits, and positional units. Master units are made up of subunits, and subunits are made up of positional units. The master unit is your largest unit of measure, and the positional unit is your smallest unit.

Master Units

A *master unit* is always defined as 1 and cannot be changed. The only change you can make to the master unit is its label. A master unit can represent 1 mile to a global mapper, 1 foot to an architect, or 1 inch to a mechanical draftsman.

Subunits and positional units are where your working units start to take shape and your definition of master units starts to make sense.

Subunits

A *subunit* is defined as the number of units in a master unit. Using the preceding examples, a mapper using 1 mile as a master unit would define 1,760 subunits per master unit, and would name the subunits yards; an architect using 1 foot as a master unit would define 12 subunits per master unit and would name the subunits inches; and a mechanical drafter using 1 inch as a master unit would probably define the subunits as 1/10 of an inch.

Positional Units

Positional units are the smallest components of working units and are defined as the number of units in a subunit. In the architectural example, a positional unit might be 8,000, making the working units 1 master unit = 12 subunits and 1 subunit = 8,000 positional units. In the mechanical example, 1 master unit or inch = 10 subunits or 1/10 of an inch and 1 subunit or 1/10 of an inch = 1,000 positional units or 1/1,000 of an inch.

> **Note**   Working units usually are expressed as master unit:subunits:positional units; for example, 1:12:8,000.
>
> Also, common abbreviations include "mu" for master unit, "su" for subunits, and "pu" for positional units, or "mu:su:pu."

Effects on the Design Area

You have more than four billion UORs on the design plane. If you did not define any working units or if you had 1 master unit = 1 subunit = 1 positional unit, then the design area would be 4 billion squares, or 4 billion master units in the x and y directions. Because the UORs are the smallest possible addressable points in the file, the positional units organize the UORs into subunits, and the subunits are combined to give you a master unit. When you put more positional units in a subunit or more subunits in a master unit, you get greater precision but the size of the design area decreases.

Look at the architectural example again with the working units of 1:12:8,000 in reference to the design area (see fig. 3.19). The UORs on the design plane get divided by the number of positional units to give you a total number of subunits on the design plane. Four billion UORs—8,000 positional units gives you 536,870 subunits or inches available on the design plane. Now, if you take every 12 inches or every 12 subunits and call them a master unit, you have 536,870 divided by 12 = 44,739 by 44,739 feet available on the design plane. Your design plane stays the same size, but the grid squares are divided up.

Figure 3.19

The design plane reflecting working units of 1:12:8,000.

The Design Plane

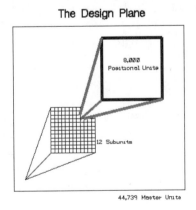

Don't worry; you're not going to run out of drawing space in the design area. Your design plane is 4 billion UORs square for a reason! Suppose you were drawing a map of the United States. The distance from San Francisco to New York is more than 3,000 miles. You could define your working units as miles, yards, and feet, and your total design area would still be 804,300 square miles. With those working units, you would have enough design area to draw the entire planet (the distance around the equator is only 25,000 miles!).

Defined Accuracy and Precision

Positional units along with subunits define the precision of the design. If you define your working units as 1:1:1, the precision of your design is 1 master unit. With these working units defined, the precision of the design is the number of UORs in a master unit or the number of positional units times the number of subunits (see fig. 3.20).

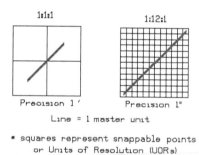

Figure 3.20

Element precision and accuracy.

In the preceding architectural example, the working units are 1:12:8,000, which means that the precision of the file is 12 × 8,000 or 1/96,000 of a foot. In essence, the precision of your file is 1/1,000 of 1/8 inch. Indeed, the precision of your design would far exceed the precision to which the carpenter and construction team could build.

Consider the U.S. map example described previously. The precision of the file would be 1,760 yards × 3 feet, which means that you would have 5,280 addressable points or UORs in one master unit. At that map scale, you could draw the entire United States in one design file, showing building footprints for every house and business to a measurable degree of accuracy of 1 foot. That is some file!

Of course, you would never want to create such a huge file, but this example illustrates the point. You have plenty of design area to work in, with even an excess of accuracy. You wouldn't design a bridge to 1/10,000 of an inch, but you would need that kind of accuracy and precision to design a computer chip.

Setting Your Working Units

Working units define the units of measure, the precision of the file, and the size of the design area. MicroStation uses the working unit concept to enable you to draw in real coordinates or in the units of measure that best fit your application.

Working units are defined and stored in each design file. When the design file is created, it gets default working units from the seed file. Chapter 17, "Boosting Your Performance," provides more information about seed files.

To review or change the active working units, choose **S**ettings, **D**esign File. The Design File Settings dialog box appears (see fig. 3.21).

Figure 3.21

The Design File Settings dialog box.

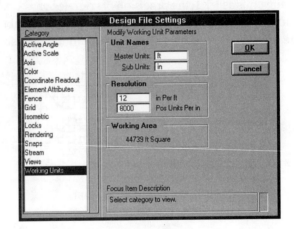

Choose Working Units from the bottom of the **C**ategory list. The first section of the Working Units dialog box, Unit Names, defines the unit names. Enter two characters in the **M**aster Units and **S**ub Units fields to specify the master units and subunits. The names are for display purposes only; you encounter these names in the measurement commands. The names can be any characters, so try changing "ft" to ' and "in" to ". When MicroStation reads out and displays data on the screen, it reads 23' 2" instead of "23ft 2in."

The second section of the dialog box, Resolution, is the important part. This section does not have a field for master units because a master unit is always one. The subunits and positional units are the units you need to define. Notice that the area to the right of each field defines the field with the name you have entered in the Unit Names section of the dialog box. In this example, the subunit definition reads in Per ft or " Per '; the positional unit definition reads Pos Units Per in or Pos Units Per ".

As you change your subunits and positional units, notice that the third section of the dialog box, entitled Working Area, changes.

If you choose **OK** after making a change, an Alert box appears, bearing the following message:

```
Changing your Working Units will change the size of existing elements.
```

If elements exist in the design file when you change the working units, the elements' position to the UORs does not change (see fig. 3.22). In your floor plan, for example, the north wall measured 42 feet with the working units defined as 1:12:8,000. If you make a simple change to the positional unit to one-tenth of an inch (1:12:10), the same north wall would measure 33,600 feet.

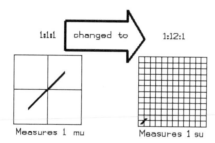

Measures 1 mu   Measures 1 su

* squares represent snappable points
or Units of Resolution (UORs)

Figure 3.22

Effects of changing your working units.

Review the working units in your design file in the following exercise.

CHANGING YOUR WORKING UNITS

Continue from the preceding exercise, using the FLOOR.DGN design file.

*Choose **S**ettings, Design File*	Opens the Design File Settings dialog box
Choose Working Units from the Category List	
*Double-click in the **M**aster Units field and type **ft**, and then press Tab*	Sets master unit name "ft" for feet
*Type **tn** in the **S**ub Units field and press Tab*	Sets subunit name to "tn" for tenths
*Choose **O**K*	Closes the Design File Settings dialog box

Tip   If you need to switch between Metric and English working units, try setting your English working units to 1:10:2,540 and your metric working units to 1:10:1,000. These working units convert back and forth nicely because there are 2.54 centimeters per inch.

Saving Your Work

MicroStation, unlike most PC programs on the market, doesn't force you to save your work during or even at the end of your design session. It automatically saves your work throughout your design session, with the default settings.

Tip   You can choose **F**ile, Save **A**s to take a snapshot of the file before you start major changes or before you start a "what-if" scenario.

If you don't want MicroStation automatically saving your changes, you can turn off this feature by choosing Wor**k**space, **P**reference to open the Preferences dialog box. Choose Operations from the **C**ategory list. On the right side of the dialog box, disable the **I**mmediately Save Design Changes option (see fig. 3.23). If you turn off this feature, MicroStation prompts you to save your changes when you exit the design file.

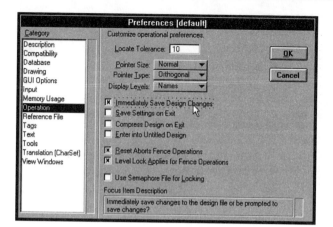

Figure 3.23

Changing the default saving preference.

Summary

Levels are easy to understand and important in any design process. If you set up a level definition (what elements go on what level), specify as many features on different levels as possible. MicroStation has 63 levels available in each design file, so use them.

Working units might sound difficult at first, but all you really need to do is determine the measurement in which you would like to draw and measure, and the precision of the file. Set your working units and stick to them.

You can learn more about working units in the discussions on seed files in Chapter 4, "Setting up a Drawing File and Workspace," and Chapter 17, "Boosting Your Performance."

PART 2

Learning How to Draw in 2D

CHAPTER

Setting Up a Drawing File and Workspace

*T*he manual method of creating a drawing is as straightforward as collecting the tools you need to complete the job. Setting up a design file requires much the same preparation in an electronic file. In MicroStation, you get the tools you need and the design session defaults by choosing the workspace, you get the working units and precision from a seed file, and you get the drawing area you need by creating the file.

This chapter introduces you to four functions you need to know about MicroStation: different ways to start MicroStation, how to create new design files, different ways to access design files, and finally, how to exit MicroStation. For good measure, it also covers such topics as naming conventions and standards, typical errors, and file-manipulation commands.

In this chapter, you learn about the following:

♦ Understanding MicroStation workspaces and interfaces

♦ Working with the MicroStation Manager dialog box

♦ Creating a new design file

♦ Opening a design file

♦ Closing a design file

♦ Exiting MicroStation

♦ Changing the workspace for MicroStation

♦ Performing file and directory maintenance in MicroStation

Understanding MicroStation Workspaces and Interfaces

A workspace is a collection of data and definitions specific to that particular discipline or application. The module or discipline configuration defines settings and defaults for directories and variables to use while you are in that particular workspace. The name (and location) of the default seed file while you use the mapping workspace, for example, is \ustation\wsmod\mapping\seed\map2d.dgn. If you use the workspace entitled default, the seed file and its location are defined as \ustation\wsmod\default\seed\seed2d.dgn. You can always select a different file or directory, but the workspace gives you a starting point. Later, you learn how and where to modify these settings to meet your personal needs.

Note   The defined seed file is used in the process of creating new design files. Seed files contain design file defaults.

Note   The workspace you use for the exercises in this book is named *default*. All the exercises you encounter in this book assume you're working in the default workspace.

Other workspaces delivered using MicroStation are arch, archacad, autocad, civil, default, learning, mapping, maprev, mde, mechdrf, and mechnew.

See table 4.1 for a brief description of the available workspaces in MicroStation.

Table 4.1

Workspaces Delivered with MicroStation

Workspace Name	Application or Purpose
arch	Architectural applications
archacad	Architectural AutoCAD users
autocad	Familiar environment for AutoCAD users
civil	Civil application
default	Generic application, all tools available
learning	New user environment
mapping	Mapping application
maprev	Mapping review only applications
mde	MDL development environment
mechdrft	Mechanical drafting applications
mechnew	Mechanical new user

The interface you select, in some cases, narrows the tools and menus down to what makes sense for the particular application. The learning workspace, for example, provides the commonly used tools among all applications.

> **Tip**
> Although the interface might not include tools for every command, every command is still accessible by entering its name in the key-in field. See Chapter 17, "Boosting Your Performance" for more information about the key-in field or Chapter 19, "Changing the Way MicroStation Looks" for more information about modifying the user interface.

See table 4.2 for a brief description of the available interfaces in MicroStation.

Table 4.2
Interfaces Delivered with MicroStation

Interface Name	Application or Purpose
arch	Architectural applications
autocad	Familiar environment for AutoCAD users
civil	Civil application
default	Generic application, all tools available
mapping	Mapping application
mde	MDL development environment
mechdrft	Mechanical drafting applications
newuser	Beginner's application
v40	Displays menu and configuration similar to MicroStation Version 4.0
v50	Displays menu and configuration similar to MicroStation Version 5.0

Each time you select a workspace, it selects a default interface. If you select the learning workspace, for example, the interface automatically becomes new user. You can change the interface after choosing the workspace if you want something other than the default for that workspace. See table 4.3 for the workspace and default interface.

Table 4.3
Workspaces and Their Default Interfaces

Workspace Name	Default Interface
arch	arch
archacad	autocad
autocad	autocad
civil	civil
default	default
learning	newuser

Workspace Name	Default Interface
mapping	mapping
maprev	none
mde	mde
mechdrft	mechdrft
mechnew	newuser

If you want an interface selection other than the one the workspace chose for you, choose the interface after you choose the workspace.

MicroStation remembers the last workspace and interface used the last time it executed on your machine. Make sure to verify the workspace and interface selected before you enter a design file.

You can activate a specific workspace from the command line or from a program item in Windows by adding **-wu*workspace name*** to the command line. For example, ustation -wulearning would activate MicroStation and the learning workspace regardless of the last workspace selection.

Tip

Other Functions of the MicroStation Manager Dialog Box

The MicroStation Manager dialog box enables you to do file maintenance, select a directory, or begin a design session by choosing a design file. The MicroStation Manager dialog box is the first thing you see when you enter MicroStation or when you close an existing design session.

The **F**ile pull-down menu of the MicroStation Manager dialog box includes options you can use to create **N**ew design files, **C**opy a design file, **R**ename a design file, **D**elete a design file, get **I**nfo such as size and date last modified, **M**erge two or more design files, and **C**ompress a design file (see fig. 4.1). Also, notice that the **F**ile pull-down menu displays the last four design files you have used in the current workspace, which gives you a quick way to recall previous design files. The E**x**it item stops MicroStation and returns you to the operating system prompt.

Figure 4.1

The MicroStation Manager File pull-down menu.

The **D**irectory pull-down menu includes options that let you create a **N**ew directory, **C**opy a directory, Co**m**press all design files in a directory, **S**elect Configuration Variable, select the Current **W**ork Directory, or select any of the four previous directories you have been working in (see fig. 4.2). The following exercise shows you how to switch directories.

SWITCHING DIRECTORIES

Choose **D***irectory, then* **S***elect* Configuration Variable	Lists the variables defined in MicroStation for this workspace
Scroll down the list and select MS_SEEDFILES	Highlights selection
Choose **O**K	Displays MicroStation Manager dialog box, with seed directory set by configuration variable
Choose **D***irectory, then* **1**	Sets directory back to the previous directory

---

Note

If you use the keyboard mnemonics (hot keys) to activate the pull-down menus and their commands, notice that the previous design file and directory are listed with the numbers one through four. Just enter the number to select the item from the keyboard.

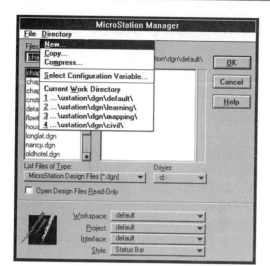

Figure 4.2

*The MicroStation
Manager Directory
pull-down menu.*

Creating a New Design File

To create a new design file, choose **F**ile, **N**ew in the MicroStation Manager dialog
box, which opens the Create Design File dialog box (see fig. 4.3).

Figure 4.3

*The Create Design
File dialog box.*

You need to consider two things before you create a design file: the destination or
the directory in which you place the new file, and the seed file or the defaults to be
applied to the file.

Specifying the Directory

The default destination directory appears below the Directories: field in the Create Design File dialog box. You should verify that the destination directory is correct before you create the design file; if it is not, change the default directory before you go any further.

A directory structure is hierarchical in nature. The top of the directory structure in DOS or Windows is the drive itself. Directories are used as a means to organize your hard drive and the data it contains. You can place your files inside a directory, or you can create a directory within a directory to further organize your data. The term *directory path* refers to the absolute location of the file from the root or hard drive level. The c:\ustation\dgn directory path, for example, indicates that you are pointing to the dgn directory, which is located in the ustation directory on the C hard drive.

Defining a New Directory

The directory path you see in the Directories field of the Create Design File dialog box is the last directory used. You can change it by selecting another drive or directory from the listing.

Double-click on any of the open folder icons to move to that level in the directory path. As an example, if your directory list is c:\ustation\dgn\default and you select the dgn folder in the listing by double-clicking on it, your new directory path becomes c:\ustation\dgn. To add a subdirectory to the path, double-click on an icon that appears as a closed folder in the listing. To choose the directory called learning, for example, double-click on the folder in the list.

Tip Directory and file lists can become long and cumbersome to scroll through. A shortcut to scrolling through the list is to activate the list by clicking on it or pressing Tab until the outline appears around the list, and then typing the first character of the directory name. The listing jumps to the first directory starting with that character. Keep hitting the character until you have selected the appropriate folder or file.

Selecting a Seed File

You must specify a seed file when you create a new design file. A *seed file* typically is an empty design file that contains design file defaults for working units, views, and file settings, such as active level. In essence, the seed file is copied during creation of a design file and renamed to the file name you specify.

MicroStation comes delivered with some seed files appropriate for different applications. MicroStation has several different seed files for architectural, civil, default, mapping, and mechanical drafting applications, for example. These seed files are located in the DOS directory path \ustation\msmod*application*\seed.

Chapter 17, "Boosting Your Performance," covers details about how and why you would create your own seed files.

Tip

When you create a file, the seed file determines whether the file is two-dimensional or three-dimensional. Most seed files indicate the dimension in the name. The standard architectural 2D and 3D seed files are SDARCH2D.DGN and SDARCH3D.DGN.

Another standard naming convention to help you identify a seed file involves whether it is defined with metric or English working units. A seed file with an "m" as the last character generally means that file is defined with metric working units. The file MECHDET.DGN is the delivered seed file for mechanical details defined with English working units. The file MECHDETM.DGN is the delivered seed file for mechanical details defined with metric working units.

To specify a seed file other than the one shown in the Seed File field at the bottom of the Create Design File dialog box, choose the **S**eed button. The Select Seed File dialog box appears (see fig. 4.4), which looks and acts much like the previous Create Design File dialog box.

Choose a seed file by double-clicking on the file name or selecting the file name and clicking on **O**K. The Select Seed File dialog box then closes, and the file name is displayed in the Seed File field in the Create Design File dialog box.

Note

You can use any design file as a seed file. If you choose a file that contains elements, the new file contains the same elements. Remember that creating a design file simply copies a seed file and renames it to create your new design file. You could choose CHAP03.DGN, used in the last chapter, as your seed file.

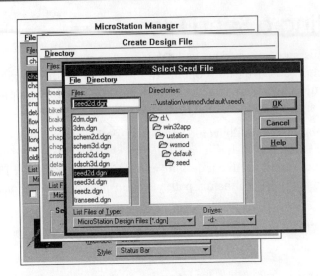

Figure 4.4

*The Select Seed
File dialog box.*

Specifying Design File Names

The last step of creating your new design file is to type the name of your file in the Files key-in field. All design file names in MicroStation contain a name, a period, and a three-character extension. If you don't enter an extension, MicroStation automatically defines it as DGN. The extension of the file helps you later to isolate design files from other files and also helps you identify the file's purpose. In MicroStation, for example, a backup file might have a .BAK extension.

Tip   You can enter **filename.ext** or enter only the file name, and MicroStation adds the default DGN extension for you.

The default DGN isn't a required file extension. It might be helpful to use custom extensions to help you identify the type of design a file contains. A mapping or utility application, for example, might have multiple files associated with one geographic area. One file might contain the landbase and have the extension of BAS, another might contain the water infrastructure and have the extension of WAT, and yet another might contain the sewer infrastructure and have the extension of SEW. The file names in this example would have all the same names with different extensions expressing the type of design they contain.

Another good example of this type of naming convention might be an architectural application, in which one file would be the floorplan of a building, another would be the heating and cooling, and yet another the electrical wiring. All these files could use the project number as the file name and have different extensions indicating the discipline or purpose.

Make your file names meaningful. Files like WATER.DGN or AUGUST16.DGN could be meaningless months from now. Consider how the old manual method labels and organizes the paper drawings. You do not have to reintroduce bad practices, but you might get some ideas about how the manual methods keep things organized (or unorganized, as the case may be).

Tip

The rules regarding which characters are valid and how long a file name can be depend on the operating system on which you run MicroStation. In DOS and in Windows 3.1, the maximum number of characters for a file name is eight characters, a dot or period, and a three-character extension. If you enter a file name longer than eight characters, MicroStation uses only the first eight characters plus the extension to create the file.

Unix, on the other hand, has a maximum of 14 characters in a file name, including the extension. The Unix operating system does not require file extensions, and will truncate the file name at the 14th character. As an example, if you attempt to create a file with the file name 12345678901234.DGN, the result is a file with the name 12345678901234 and no extension. Another difference between Unix and DOS is that Unix is a case-sensitive operating system and DOS is not, meaning that the Unix computer treats a capital "A" as a different character than a lowercase "a," whereas DOS treats them as the same character.

If you have several different machines on your network, you should consider all the systems for file-naming limitations. If you have DOS and Unix machines on the same network, for example, keep to the eight-character maximum file name to be compatible with both machines. Also, to be compatible with DOS, use only lowercase characters in Unix.

Tip

In the following exercise, you create a new design file.

CREATING A NEW DESIGN FILE

Choose default for the **W**orkspace *in the MicroStation Manager dialog box*	Automatically selects default interface
Choose Status Bar *for the* **S**tyle	
Choose **F**ile, **N**ew	Opens the Create Design File dialog box
Verify that the directory shown is the ...ustation\dgn\default directory	
Verify that the seed file displayed is ...ustation\wsmod\default\seed\seed2d.dgn	
Enter **CHAP04.DGN** in the F**i**les: key-in field	
Choose **O**K	Creates Design File and closes the Create Design File dialog box

Note　If the design file already exists in the destination directory, MicroStation informs you with an Alert box, and prompts you to overwrite the existing file or Cancel.

Tip　You also can use your operating system to copy the seed file to create your design file.

Opening a Design File

To open a design file from the MicroStation Manager dialog box, type its name in the **N**ame field, choose an existing file name by double-clicking on the name in the F**i**les listing, or select the file to highlight it. Then choose **O**K.

When you create a design file from the MicroStation Manager box, it becomes the selected file, so you can just click on **O**K or press Enter to open the design file.

Tip　The files shown in the F**i**les field depend on the value defined in the List File by **T**ype pop-down field. To view all the files in the directory, choose the pop-up field and choose **A**ll Files (***.***). To view only DGN files, choose **M**icroStation Design Files (***.DGN**) in the pop-up field.

If you get the Alert box shown in figure 4.5, you have a corrupted file.   *Warning*

If you choose **O**K, MicroStation attempts to repair the file. You should *always* make a copy of the file *before* attempting to repair the file in this fashion. MicroStation attempts to repair it, but often cuts off a portion of the design file, leaving you with some missing elements. This result might be better than starting your design from scratch, but another option available to you is the Edit Graphics Utility (EdG).

The EdG utility enables you to edit a graphics file in a nongraphics command-line interface. This utility is not for the lighthearted beginner, but it is available, and is delivered with MicroStation. The documentation goes into some detail about fixing corrupted files with the EDG utility.

Figure 4.5

The Alert box for corrupted files.

Ending a Design Session

Two good habits you should get into when you close a design file are saving the settings and compressing the design.

Most PC applications require that you save your work periodically or at least   *Note* when you exit the file. Unless you change the delivered settings, MicroStation does not require either. As you modify, add, or delete elements, the file is kept current on the hard drive without any user intervention. You do not have to remember to save your work because MicroStation saves it for you.

The File design command, which you issue by choosing **F**ile, Sa**v**e Settings, saves a number of parameters. Chapter 2 discusses the process of saving settings, as well. View configurations and values you change in the setting boxes during the design session are saved and stored to the design file by this menu item. MicroStation saves these types of file-specific settings to what is called the *design file header*. When you return to the file, MicroStation reads the design file header and displays the file the same way you left it. Choose **F**ile, Sa**v**e Settings to save the current design file settings.

Tip Use the keyboard accelerator for easy access to the Sa**v**e Settings item on the **F**ile pull-down menu by pressing Ctrl+F.

Design compression, mentioned briefly in Chapter 2, compresses all the deleted elements from the file. Your design file grows each time you place an element, but it does not shrink when you delete elements. Deleting an element marks it for deletion, but leaves the element in your file. When MicroStation reads the file, it displays only the active elements and skips over the "deleted" elements. You might wonder why those deleted files are still there, though. The deleted elements are useful for commands such as Undo and Redo. After you complete a design or make many changes, compressing those deleted elements out of the design file is a good idea. You can delete the excess baggage to get a smaller, more efficient design file (and a faster MicroStation).

Tip If you encounter a problem or aren't sure of changes you have made, you might want to hold off on compressing your file—compressing the design makes any changes permanent and unrecoverable.

If you accidentally delete all the elements in the file, and the Undo command does not bring them all back, for example, do not compress your design. You can use the Edit Graphics Utility (EdG) to recover deleted elements, or you might have in-house MicroStation support staff who can help you retrieve the deleted elements.

Storing the Settings

Some of the MicroStation settings are stored as part of your design file, and others are stored with the MicroStation workspace. The active level and the level displays, for example, are stored with the design file, which is the reason you can open different design files and get different looks—each design file has its own settings.

On the other hand, menus and palettes that are open when you exit MicroStation are stored with the MicroStation workspace, so when you start MicroStation again you get the same look and feel. Chapter 19 covers more details about creating a user workspace. For now, just be aware that the way you leave MicroStation is the way you will see it the next time you enter the program.

Entering Another Design File

The design file that is open is referred to as the *active* design file. MicroStation allows only one file to be active at a time. When you open a new design file, the current design file is closed.

If you want to open a different design file, you can use the Open Design File dialog box (see fig. 4.6). You access the Open Design File dialog box by clicking on the Open File icon in the Standard toolbox, by pressing Ctrl+O, or by choosing **F**ile, **O**pen. Many of the same features in the MicroStation Manager dialog box are available from this dialog box. The **F**ile pull-down menu enables you to access the last four files, and the **D**irectory pull-down menu enables you to quickly change the directory path to previously selected paths.

Figure 4.6

The Open Design File dialog box.

You can type the name in the F**i**les field, and press Enter; double-click on the file in the F**i**les list; or highlight the design file, and click on **O**K. After you choose a file, the dialog box disappears, the currently active design file closes, and the new file opens.

Remember to save your settings and compress your active design file before you open a new design file.

Note

You can create new design files that have all the same options from the **F**ile pull-down menu in the MicroStation Application Window while you are in a graphics design session. Choose **F**ile, **N**ew, or click on the New File icon in the Standard tool box (see fig. 4.7), to open the Create Design File dialog box.

Figure 4.7

*Clicking on the
New File icon
opens the Create
Design File dialog
box.*

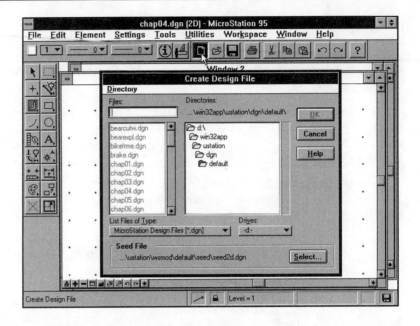

    Tip

The only difference between creating a design file while in a design session
versus creating a design file while in the MicroStation Manager dialog box is
that the new file automatically opens after you create it during the design
session.

A quick way to reopen a design file that you have recently opened is to choose it
from the **F**ile pull-down menu. Choose the **F**ile pull-down menu, and select the file
or type the number found at the bottom of the menu. File names appear with the
complete path or with a ...\, indicating that the complete directory path was too long
to be displayed (see fig. 4.8).

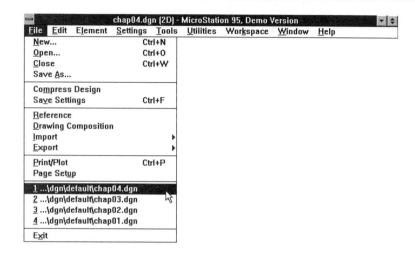

Figure 4.8

The File pull-down menu for quick access to the last four design files.

Closing a Design File

You can close the active design file and return to the MicroStation Manager dialog box by choosing **File, Close** (or by pressing Ctrl+W). The active file and all tools or commands disappear, and the MicroStation Manager dialog box appears.

Use **Close** only if you need to do file maintenance such as file delete, file rename, or file copy. Otherwise, to open another file, use **Open**, which is faster.   *Note*

Exiting MicroStation

To exit MicroStation altogether, choose **File, Exit** from the pull-down menu. The design file closes and MicroStation exits, returning you to the DOS or Unix command line, or to the Windows Program Manager.

Pressing Alt+F4 or double-clicking on the minus sign in the upper left corner of the Application Window also exits MicroStation. When the alert box appears, choose **OK** to close and exit MicroStation or Cancel to return to MicroStation.   *Tip*

Opening a Design File When Entering MicroStation

Another alternative is available at the command line to simultaneously enter MicroStation and open an existing file. You can bypass the MicroStation Manager box altogether by including the file name in the command line, such as:

```
ustation -wudefault chap04
```

 Note   If you work in MicroStation under Microsoft Windows, you must use the MicroStation Manager dialog box to open design files or add the file name to the Program Item.

The extension DGN is not required in the preceding example. MicroStation assumes a DGN extension if you do not indicate a specific extension.

Enter the file name and the complete path if the file is not located in your current directory. If you do not enter the directory path, and MicroStation cannot find the file in the present working directory, an Alert dialog box appears.

Choose **O**K, and the MicroStation Manager dialog box appears, or choose Cancel and return to the operating system prompt.

Performing File Maintenance from MicroStation

The MicroStation Manager dialog box provides you with a means to do file and directory maintenance without exiting MicroStation.

File Maintenance

Each of the three file-manipulation selections (**C**opy, **R**ename, and **D**elete) requires you to select the file in the F**i**les list first.

Choosing **F**ile, **C**opy from the MicroStation Manager dialog box opens the Copy File dialog box (see fig. 4.9). The default values for the **F**rom and **T**o fields copy the selected file to the same directory with the same file name and a BAK extension. You can change the file name and extension and enter a new path for the file.

Figure 4.9

The Copy File dialog box.

Choosing **F**ile, **R**ename opens the Rename File dialog box (see fig. 4.10), and prompts you to enter the new file name for the selected file in the **T**o field. You can also enter a directory with the file name in the **T**o field to rename and move the file at the same time.

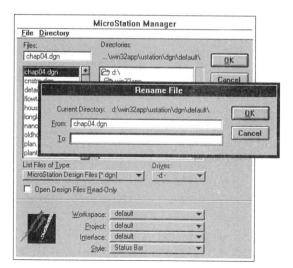

Figure 4.10

The Rename File dialog box.

Choosing **F**ile, **D**elete opens an Alert dialog box (see fig. 4.11) asking you to choose the **O**K or Cancel button to confirm the requested deletion.

Figure 4.11

*The Delete Files
Alert box.*

Choosing **F**ile, **I**nfo opens a File Information dialog box (see fig. 4.12) showing the absolute or full path where the file is located, the size, and the date and time the file was last opened or modified.

Figure 4.12

*The File
Information dialog
box.*

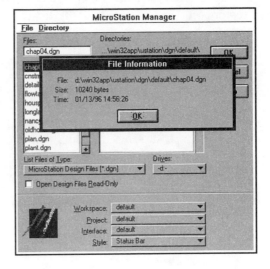

Choosing File, Merge opens a Merge dialog box (see fig. 4.13). Choose the Select button in the bottom section titled Merge Into: to define the file you want to contain the merged files.

Figure 4.13

The Merge dialog box.

Then choose the Select button in the section titled Files to Merge to open the Select Files to Merge dialog box (see fig. 4.14). Pick each file and choose the Add button. After you select all the files you want to merge, choose the Done button. The Merge dialog box then appears, displaying files you have selected. Choose the Merge button to merge the files together, or choose Cancel.

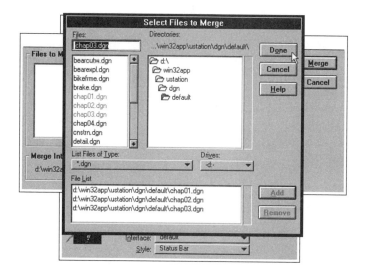

Figure 4.14

The Select Files to Merge dialog box.

Choosing **F**ile, C**o**mpress performs a compress design on the selected file.

Directory Maintenance

Three directory-manipulation features are available in the **D**irectory pull-down menu of the MicroStation Manager dialog box: **N**ew, **C**opy, and Co**m**press.

Choosing **D**irectory, **N**ew opens a Make Directory dialog box (see fig. 4.15), asking you to enter a **D**ir name. The directory is created within the current directory displayed above the field.

Figure 4.15

The Make Directory dialog box.

Choosing **D**irectory, **C**opy opens a Copy Directory dialog box (see fig. 4.16). The Current Directory shown in the dialog box is copied to the value specified in the **D**ir field. By default, the dialog box displays the current working directory in the **D**ir field, or the directory you were in when you executed MicroStation.

Warning   Copy a directory and you copy all the files in the directory! So take care with this command.

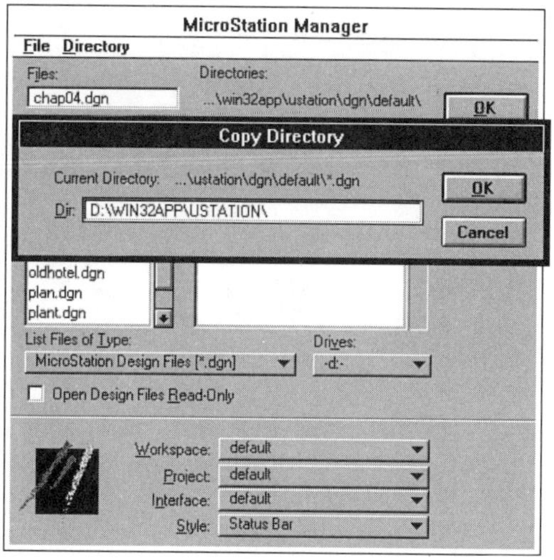

Figure 4.16

The Copy Directory dialog box.

Choosing **D**irectory, Co**m**press compresses all the files in the directory you are currently displaying in the MicroStation Manager dialog box. An alert box will display the number of files and the directory; choose **O**K to continue or Cancel to return to the MicroStation Manager dialog box.

Summary

Now you know the ins and outs of MicroStation. You have seen several methods of getting in and out of the MicroStation program and your design files. You should have a basic understanding of workspaces and interfaces, both what they do for you and how to select them. Look for more details on interfaces and workspaces in later chapters.

Placing Simple 2D Elements

*A*ll maps, electrical schematics, mechanical designs, or architectural floor plans are composed of simple elements. The framework of every drawing consists of lines and shapes. The lines in your design file could represent streets, electrical wiring, the teeth of a gear, or a wall in an architectural floor plan. The shapes in your design file could represent building outlines, a resistor, a bolt, or a bookcase. This chapter covers placing simple lines and shapes, elements you use in all applications.

MicroStation offers several different ways to place lines and shapes in your design file. All the methods of element placement discussed in this chapter have merit. Some of the line and shape commands provide you with constraints that enable efficient and precise placement. Constraints enable you to place an element's endpoints or vertices at a specific length or angle at the time of placement.

In this chapter, you learn about the following:

♦ Placing lines

♦ Using the Tool Settings window constraints

♦ Finding the commands

♦ Understanding element symbology

♦ Changing the active symbology

♦ Placing shapes and polygons

Chapter 8 covers placing circles, arcs, and ellipses.

Tool Settings

The Tool Settings window changes dynamically to show you the constraints and settings available for the active command. Unmodified, the default workspace opens the Tool Settings box whenever you open a design file. If your workspace doesn't open the Tool Settings box for you when you enter a design file, choose **T**ool, **T**ool Settings or just pick a command off the Main tool frame to open the Tool Settings box. The settings box displays the name of the active command in its title bar at all times and the constraints and settings for that command (see fig. 5.1).

Figure 5.1

The Tool Settings window with Place Line as the active command.

If you aren't sure whether the Tool Setting box is open, choose the **T**ool pull-down menu from the Application Window and look for a check mark before **T**ool Settings. If you find a check mark, you know the Tool Settings box is open, so dismiss the pull-down menu by clicking a data point off the menu or by pressing Esc.

Tip

Placing Lines

The two primary commands for placing simple lines are Place Line and Place SmartLine. First, tear the Linear Elements tool box off the Main frame, as indicated (see fig. 5.2), or retrieve the tool box from the pull-down menus by choosing **T**ools, **M**ain, **L**inear Elements. The Place Line command places a single linear element with two endpoints. The Place SmartLine command places a multisegment linear element with 2 to 101 points or vertices.

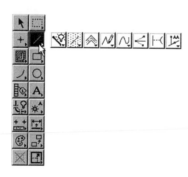

Figure 5.2

The Linear Elements tool box.

You can't visually distinguish the difference between placing a series of segments with Place Line and Place SmartLine; however, Place Line creates multiple elements, and Place SmartLine creates a single element with multiple segments.

Note

The exercises in the first half of this chapter demonstrate the Line and SmartLine commands. Each line exercise builds a north arrow (see fig. 5.3).

Figure 5.3

*The completed
north arrow.*

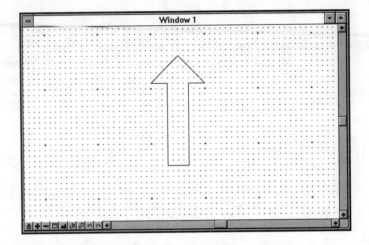

The Place Line Command

Placing a line using the Place Line command entails picking a start point and an endpoint. You can continue placing lines from the last point by picking additional points. You can place additional lines, each with the previous endpoint as its start point, as shown in the following exercise.

PLACING LINES

Create a design file called CHAP05.DGN.

*Tear off the Linear Elements tool box
from the Main frame*

Zoom in once   Displays the dots of the grid

*Choose the Place Line tool from the
Linear Elements tool box*

Enter first point *Pick point at* ①   Anchors line endpoint
(see fig. 5.4)

Enter end point *Pick point at* ②   Completes line

Enter end point *Pick point at* ③   Places next line

Enter end point *Pick point at* ④

Continue picking points ⑤ *through*
⑧ *(see fig. 5.4)*

Enter end point *Click the*
Reset button

Enter first point

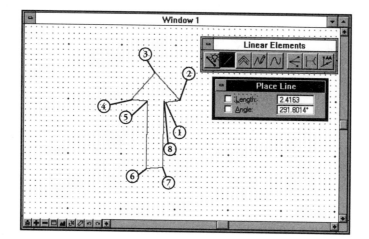

Figure 5.4

Placing lines.

> You might have experienced some difficulty making a nice-looking north arrow in the previous exercise. One solution would have been to turn grid lock on, but that wasn't the point of this exercise. Read on to learn how to place the lines more accurately.

Note

Placement Constraints

The Place Line command is one of the tools in MicroStation that has constraints available to help you place lines more efficiently. The constraints provide a quick and easy way to define the length and/or angle of the element. Constraints are set by the options found in the Tool settings box.

The **L**ength constraint, if turned on, places a line of a specified length. The first point picked anchors the line. The second point defines the angle, and the line is drawn at the angle constrained to the preset length.

Try placing your north arrow again, but this time, with constraints in the next two exercises.

PLACING LINES WITH LENGTH CONSTRAINT

Continue from the preceding exercise with the CHAP05.DGN design file and the Linear Elements tool box open. Delete the previous arrow.

Choose the Place Line tool from the Linear Elements tool box

*Turn on the **L**ength button in the Tool Settings box*	Activates length constraint
Enter **1.5** *in the **L**ength field*	Sets 1.5 as preset length
Enter first point *Pick point at* ① *(see fig. 5.5)*	Anchors line endpoint, and displays 1.5-unit line at cursor

Move the cursor and see how the angle changes but the length remains constant.

Enter end point *Pick point at* ②	Defines angle of line and places the line

Place Line is ready to draw another length-constrained line.

Enter **.3** *in the **L**ength field*	
Press Tab or Enter	Sets .3 as preset length
Enter end point *Pick point at* ③	Defines angle of line and places the line
*Turn off **L**ength*	Deactivates length constraint

Figure 5.5

Placing a line with a Length constraint.

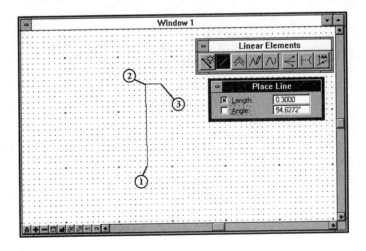

The **A**ngle constraint, turned on, enables you to place a line only at the angle defined. Again, the first point you pick anchors the line. The second point defines the length. Because the angle is constrained, the second point defines the length by projecting the point to the line at 135 degrees.

PLACING LINES WITH ANGLE CONSTRAINT

Continue from the preceding exercise with the CHAP05.DGN design file and the Line command in progress.

Turn on the **A**ngle *button*	Activates angle constraint
Click in the **A**ngle *field and delete the contents*	
Enter **135** *in the* **A**ngle *field*	Sets 135 as preset angle

Move the cursor and see how the length changes, with a constant 135° angle.

`Enter end point` *Pick point at* ① *(refer to figure 5.5)*	Defines length of line and places the line at 135°
Enter **225** *in the* **A**ngle *field*	Sets 225 as preset angle
Press Tab or Enter	
`Enter end point` *Pick point at* ② *(see fig. 5.6)*	Defines length of line and places the line at 225°
`Enter end point` *Click the Reset button*	
Turn off **A**ngle	Deactivates angle constraint

Delete your second attempt at drawing a north arrow.

The Place Line command changes slightly with the **L**ength and **A**ngle constraints both on. These constraints alter the traditional placement of the line because MicroStation requires only one point to place the line at the defined length and angle.

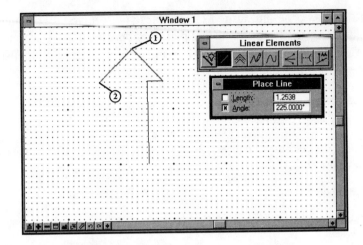

Figure 5.6

Placing a line with
Angle constraint.

The Place SmartLine Command

The Place SmartLine command places a set of continuous lines, called a *line string*, when the constraint segment type is set to lines. A group of individual lines might look the same as a line string, but the advantage is that a line string is one element. You can place three individual lines in a Z pattern, for example, or you can place one line string. The advantage a line string bestows is that when you want to delete, move, or modify the lines later, you have only one element to manipulate, not three individual lines.

Warning   Make sure the **J**oin Element toggle button in the Tool Settings box is on. If not, the SmartLine tool places individual lines rather than a line string.

You use the SmartLine tool and pick points or vertices in the view to place a line string. Then you click the Reset button to terminate. In the next exercise, you use SmartLine tool to place a line string for your north arrow and turn on Grid Lock.

PLACING A SMARTLINE

Continue from the preceding exercise with the CHAP05.DGN design file and the Linear Elements tool box open.

Choose the Place SmartLine tool
from the Linear Elements tool box

Verify that the **S**egment Type *is Line*

Verify that the **V**ertex Type *is Sharp*

Verify that the toggle **J**oin Elements *is enabled*

Choose **G**rid *from the Lock icon pop-up
menu in the Status Bar*

Enter first point *Pick point at* ①   Anchors line endpoint

Enter end point *Pick point at* ②   Completes line segment

Enter end point *Pick point at* ③   Places next segment

Enter end point *Pick points* ④
through ⑧ *(see fig. 5.7)*

Enter end point *Click the*   Accepts line string and resets command
Reset button

Enter first point

Choose the Delete Element tool

Select the line string   The whole arrow highlights

Click a reset   Arrow remains

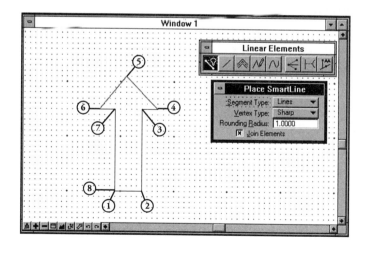

Figure 5.7

*Placing a line
string.*

Notice that when you identify the line string, the whole arrow highlights and would be deleted in one operation—that's the difference between the earlier north arrows placed using lines and this one placed using a line string.

 Note

The Place SmartLine tool has the same length and angle constraints as the Place Line tool when using the AccuDraw features. Chapter 7, "Drawing with Accuracy," discusses AccuDraw.

 Note

The maximum number of points for a line string is 101. If you exceed the 101-point maximum, you create a *complex chain*, which is a special element type that groups together linear elements, such as line strings, to form one element. Chapter 12 discusses complex chains.

The SmartLine tool offers several different constraint options, which makes it very versatile. The discussion here is about linear elements, which calls for a look at the Lines, Segment Type for the SmartLine tool. Chapter 8, "Placing More 2D Elements," discusses the Arc Segment type.

The **V**ertex Type in the Tool Settings box changes the way the SmartLine tool places and interrupts the points you place. The first option, Sharp, creates a line string, as demonstrated in the previous exercise. Other Vertex Types are **R**ounded and **C**hamfered.

If you choose **R**ounded for the **V**ertex Type, the next constraint is Rounding **R**adius, which tells SmartLine to automatically round the corner of the lines (see fig. 5.8). If you choose **C**hamfered for the **V**ertex Type, the next constraint reads Chamfer **O**ffset. See figure 5.9 for a example of the chamfer setting.

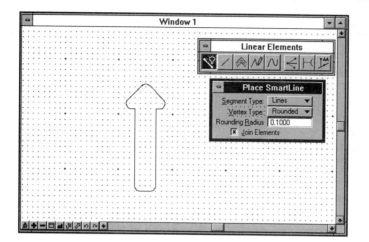

Figure 5.8

North arrow with rounded corners.

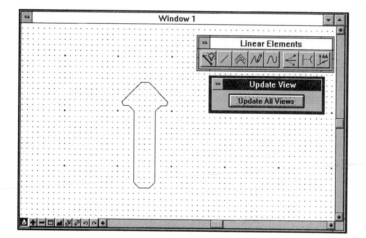

Figure 5.9

North arrow with chamfered corners.

Active Element Symbology

The term *active symbology* refers to the active settings for level, color, weight, and line style. MicroStation applies the active symbology to any new elements you create, and displays it at all times in the Primary tool box.

The Primary tool box generally is docked in the upper left corner immediately below the pull-down menus. If you don't see the Primary tool box, you can activate it by choosing **T**ools, **P**rimary.

Note You can dock the Primary tool box on any side of your view, but for the purposes of this book, the exercises assume that you haven't changed the default interface, which docks the Primary and Standard tool boxes under the Application Window.

Changing the Active Symbology

You can change the active symbology any time you want, even during a placement command. The active symbology settings affects only the element you are about to place, not the existing elements. You can change each of the active symbology settings independently; for example, level 25 can have elements of different weights, colors, and line styles.

Changing Symbology from the Primary Tool Box

You can change the active color, level, line style, and line weight from the Primary tool box.

To change the active color, choose the color box in the docked primary tool box and the color palette appears (see fig. 5.10). Notice that the current active color appears larger and with the color number. You can set the color by positioning the cursor and clicking on it. The new active color displays in the box.

Figure 5.10

*Changing the
active color.*

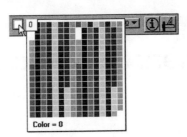

Note The next item in the Primary tool box is another way to change the active level. Choose the item with a data point and a pop-up selection appears (see fig. 5.11).

Figure 5.11

Changing the active level.

To change the active line style, choose the Active Line Style list box in the Primary tool box (see fig. 5.12). You can choose any of the eight default line styles from the list box. The numbers (0–7) correspond to the eight default types (see table 5.1). The **C**ustom and **E**dit line style options are covered in Chapter 11, "Advanced 2D Element Placement."

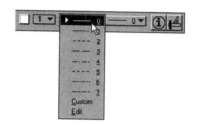

Figure 5.12

Changing the active line style.

The active line style is marked with an arrow in the list box.

Note

Table 5.1

Line Codes and Styles

LC #	Description
0	Solid
1	Dotted
2	Medium dashed
3	Long dashed
4	Dot dashed
5	Short dashed
6	Dash dot dot
7	Long dash, short dash

To change the line weight, choose the Active Line Weight list box, from which you can choose the available weights (0–15) (see fig. 5.13).

Figure 5.13

*Changing the
active line weight.*

Changing Symbology with the Element Attribute Settings Box

You also can use the Element Attributes settings box to change and display the active symbology. To open this settings box, choose E**l**ement, **A**ttributes in the pull-down menu. The settings box displays the active **L**evel, **C**olor, **S**tyle, **W**eight, and Element Cl**a**ss input fields (see fig. 5.14), as well as the current color, line style, and line weight in the text boxes to the right of their input fields.

Figure 5.14

*The Element
Attributes settings
box.*

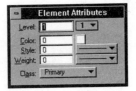

You can change the symbology by entering a new number in the appropriate field. In the case of color, style, and weight, you can choose the **C**olor, **S**tyle, or **W**eight settings for a visual selection. The pop-up menus are identical to those on the E**l**ement pull-down menu.

In the following exercise, you change color, style, and weight using the three methods described earlier.

CHANGING ACTIVE SYMBOLOGY

Continue from the preceding exercise with the CHAP05.DGN design file open.

Choose **E***lement, then* **A***ttributes*	Displays the Element Attributes settings box
Click on the box displaying the color in the color palette, then pick a new color	Updates the color number in field and displays new color
Choose the Place Line tool and pick two points at ① *and* ② *(see fig. 5.15)*	Displays line with new color
Choose the Active Line Style list box and pick a dashed line style	Changes active line code
Pick a point at ③ *in view 1*	Begins drawing line in dashed style
Choose the Active Line Weight list box then **9**	Changes active line weight to 9
Enter next vertex or reset to complete Pick a point at ④	Completes line with weight of 9
Click the Reset button	
Close the Element Attributes settings box and the Linear Elements tool box	

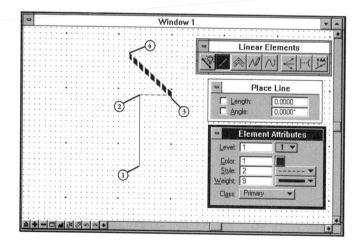

Figure 5.15

Changing the active symbology.

Determining Element Class

A setting for Element Class appears on the Element Attributes settings box and warrants some explaining. The element class is either **P**rimary or **C**onstruction. Generally, you should draw your elements in primary class with a few exceptions.

Construction class elements (see fig. 5.16) have a special property that enables you to place elements that you use as drawing aids. A construction element or drawing aid might be a parallel line or an extension of a center line in a mechanical design. You draw the element with the **C**lass attribute set to **C**onstruction. Immediately after you place the construction element, you should reset the **C**lass attribute to **P**rimary.

Figure 5.16

View 1 with construction elements, View 2 without.

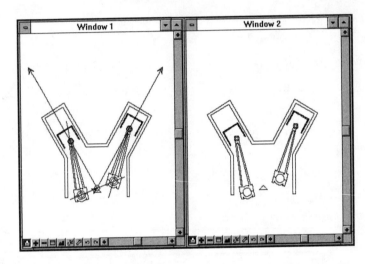

You can use the View Attributes settings box to turn off the construction element display from each view. Activate the View Attributes settings box by choosing **S**ettings, then **V**iew Attributes.

Turn off Construction display in the View Attributes settings box before you plot to plot the primary class elements only. You can leave these elements in the design file for future modifications without affecting the final plot.

 Warning

If you use construction class elements, don't forget to change the class setting back to primary before you continue to place elements. If you forget, elements that should be displayed will disappear when you turn off construction element display. You can change construction elements to primary elements and vice versa using the Change Element Attributes command (discussed in Chapter 10).

Placing Shapes and Polygons

A *shape* in MicroStation is a closed element that encloses an area. You can fill shapes with a color or pattern them. The Polygons tool box contains tools for the four shape commands: Place Block, Place Shape, Place Orthogonal Shape, and Place Polygon (see fig. 5.17). You can tear the Shape tool box off the Main frame (see fig. 5.18) or activate it by choosing **T**ools, **M**ain, Pol**y**gons.

Figure 5.17

The Polygons tool box.

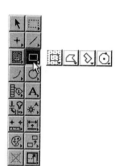

Figure 5.18

The Polygons tool box.

The next half of this chapter is devoted to placing shapes and polygons. In the following exercises, you build a flowchart resembling the one shown in figure 5.19. Before you begin, clear the views of elements placed so far. You can delete them or change the levels displayed. Remember: You can't turn off the display of the active level; you must make a different level active first.

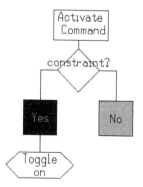

Figure 5.19

The completed flowchart.

The Place Block and Rotated Block Commands

The first tool on the Polygons tool box, Place Block, has four options: **M**ethod, A**r**ea, **F**ill Type, and Fill **C**olor.

Method Orthogonal Block

An orthogonal block is a rectangle or a square that you always place at a right angle to the X and Y axis. The command requires you to pick two opposite diagonal points to define the rectangle. You pick the first point, which anchors the corner of the block, and then a rectangle appears on the screen as you move the cursor around. Pick the second point to define the opposite diagonal corner and MicroStation places the block (see fig. 5.20).

PLACING AN ORTHOGONAL BLOCK

Continue from the preceding exercise with the CHAP05.DGN design file open.

Tear off the Polygons tool box

Activate line weight 1 from the
Primary tool box

Activate line style 0 or solid
from the Primary tool box

Choose the Place Block tool from the
Polygons tool box

Verify **M**ethod *is set*
to **O**rthogonal

`Enter first point` *Pick point*   Anchors corner of block
at ① *(see fig. 5.20)*

Move the cursor and see it drag a rectangle.

`Enter opposite corner`   Completes command and draws block
Pick point at ①

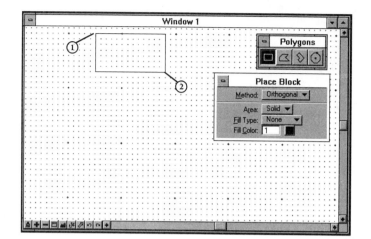

Figure 5.20

*Placing an
orthogonal block.*

Orthogonal blocks are placed at a right angle to the view, not to the drawing. If a view has been rotated, an orthogonal block is placed at a right angle to the view. See Chapter 6 for more information on view rotation.   ***Note***

Type Rotated Block

A *rotated block* is a rectangle or a square that you can place at any angle. The command requires you to pick three points—the first to anchor the block, the second to define the rotation angle, and the third to define the opposite diagonal corner to complete the block (see fig. 5.21).

Because placing the second point is like shooting in the dark, you might consider placing an angle constraint construction line as a guide for the angle of the base before you place the rotated block. Chapter 7 includes a discussion of alternatives for precise placement of the second point.   ***Tip***

PLACING A ROTATED BLOCK

Continue from the preceding exercise with the CHAP5.DGN design file and the Polygons tool box open.

*Choose the Place Block tool from
the Polygons tool box*

Continues

*Choose **M**ethod and select **R**otated*

`Enter first base point` *Pick point at ① (see fig. 5.21)*	Anchors corner of block
`Enter second base point` *Pick point at ②*	Defines angle of block
`Enter diagonal point` *Pick point at ③*	Completes command and draws block

Figure 5.21

Placing a rotated block.

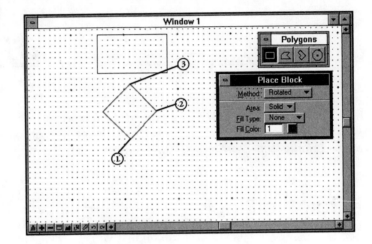

Area Solid and Hole

Solid and **H**ole Area modes define how or if you can pattern the element. Because hole elements are the exception rather than the rule in most designs, you should always work in Solid mode. You can't pattern hole elements. You can turn on the Area Hole mode to place an element inside another element that you intend to leave unpatterned. Figure 5.22 shows a patterned (crosshatched) rotated block that was placed in Solid mode and a smaller orthogonal block inside that was placed in Hole mode. Chapter 12 covers patterning.

Figure 5.22

A crosshatched rotated block with an orthogonal block hole.

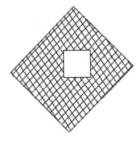

Fill Type: None, Opaque, or Outlined

You have three options for fill. You can choose not to fill the shape with color (none), fill the shape with the same color as the outline shape (opaque), or fill the shape with a different color than the color of the outlined shape (outlined), as shown in figure 5.23.

> If filled elements don't appear filled on-screen, check the attributes of the view. *Tip*
> Choose **S**ettings, **V**iew Attributes to verify that Fill is on.

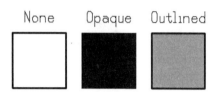

None   Opaque   Outlined

Figure 5.23

Fill options.

In the following exercise, you place a block filled with the same color as in the outlined shape.

PLACING A FILLED BLOCK

Continue from the preceding exercise with the CHAP05.DGN design file and the Polygons tool box open and the Place Block tool selected.

Choose **M**ethod *and select*
Orthogonal

Choose **F**ill Type *and select*
Opaque

`Enter first point` *Pick*   Anchors corner of block
a point at ① *(see fig. 5.24)*

`Enter opposite corner`   Completes block, filled with solid color
Pick a point at ②

Figure 5.24

Figure 5.24

*Placing a filled
block.*

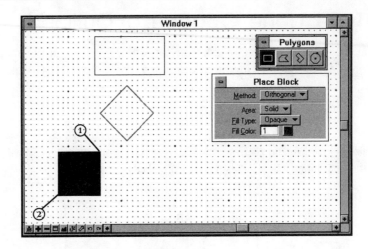

Fill Color

Fill color displays the color number in the field and the color in a small box to the
right. If you want to change the fill color, you can enter the color number in the field
or visually choose the color by activating the color palette.

Changing the fill color when the **M**ethod is set to **N**one or **O**paque changes the
active symbology. If you select Out**l**ined for the **M**ethod, the fill color doesn't modify
the active color or the outline—it fills the shape with the specified color.

To activate the color palette, click on the box displaying the color. To select a new
color, position the cursor over the color you want and press a data point. If you
successfully choose a new color, the field and color box updates after you release
the Data button.

In the following exercise, you place a block filled with a different color than the
outline of the shape.

PLACING AN OUTLINED FILLED BLOCK

Continue from the preceding exercise with the CHAP5.DGN design file and the Polygons tool
box open and the Place Block tool selected.

Choose **F**ill Type *and select* Out**l**ined	Activates Fill Color option
Click on the color button	Displays color palette
Pick a new color	

`Enter first point` *Pick a point at* ① *(see fig. 5.25)*	Anchors corner of block
`Enter opposite corner` *Pick a point at* ②	Completes block with different fill color

Choose **F**ill Type *and select* **N**one

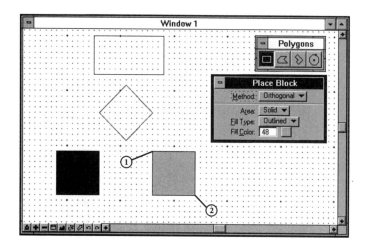

Figure 5.25

Placing an outlined block.

The Place Shape Command

The second tool on the Polygons tool box is Place Shape (see fig. 5.26). The Place Shape command requires between 3 and 101 points.

When you choose the Place Shape tool, the Tool Settings box has the same constraints as the Place Block tool with one exception, the **C**lose Element button. Remember that the definition of a shape is a closed element. As you pick the points to define the shape, you must close the shape before you exit the command or choose a new command. Otherwise, MicroStation discards the shape. To close the shape, pick the last point close to the same location as the first point or choose **C**lose Element from the Tool settings box.

PLACING A SHAPE

Continue from the preceding exercise with the CHAP05.DGN design file and the Polygons tool box open.

Choose the Place Shape tool from the Polygons tool box

Continues

Choose **F**ill Type *and select* None

`Enter first point` *Pick point at* ① *(see fig. 5.26)*	Anchors first point of shape
`Enter end point` *Pick point at* ②	Displays first side of shape
`Enter end point` *Pick point at* ③	Displays second side of shape
`Enter end point` *Pick point at* ④	Displays third side of shape
`Enter end point` *Pick point at* ⑤	Displays fourth side of shape
`Enter end point` *Pick point at* ⑥	Displays fifth side of shape
`Enter end point` *Pick point near* ①	Displays fourth side of shape and closes shape

`Enter first point`

Figure 5.26

Placing a shape.

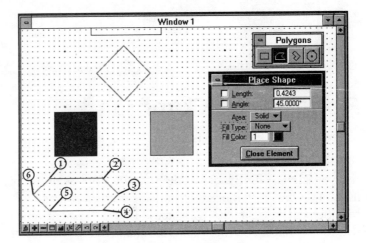

Constraints are provided with the Place Shape command, much like the Place Line command covered earlier in this chapter. You can place each point of the shape with the assistance of the constraints. You can turn constraints on or off during shape placement. For example, you could have been placed the shape in the previous exercise with two 1.0 length constraints for the top and bottom lines and 45,135,225,315 degree angle constraint to make the sides.

> You cannot use length and angle constraint at the same time with the Place Shape command.

Note

The Place Orthogonal Shape Command

The third tool on the Polygons tool box is Place Orthogonal Shape. An orthogonal shape is defined with 3 to 101 points. You place all segments of the shape at orthogonal angles to the previous segment. Pick the first two points (see points 1 and 2 in fig. 5.27), for example, to define the starting angle. MicroStation places any segments you place from then on at a right angle to the segment you just placed.

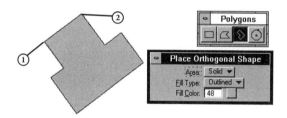

Figure 5.27

Placing an orthogonal shape.

Orthogonal shapes are a great way to place building or house footprints on a map or site plan. In keeping with all the shape commands, the last point you pick must be on the first point to close the shape.

The Place Polygon Command

The polygon commands enable you to place regular polygons, and shapes that have at least three sides of equal length. The fourth tool on the Polygons tool box is Place Polygon. Depending on the setting of its **M**ethod option (**I**nscribed, **C**ircumscribed, or By **E**dge), it issues the Place Inscribed Polygon, Place Circumscribed Polygon, or Place Polygon by Edge command. The other options for this tool are number of **E**dges, **R**adius, A**r**ea, **F**ill Type, and Fill **C**olor. This section discusses the settings unique to polygons: **M**ethod, number of **E**dges, and **R**adius. See the section of this chapter on Place Rotated Block for a discussion of A**r**ea, **F**ill Type, and Fill **C**olor.

Polygon Types

The **T**ype option setting refers to the relationship of the polygon to the points picked. You can choose one of three methods of placement: **I**nscribed, **C**ircumscribed, or By **E**dge. Before placing the polygon, you must first enter a value for the number of **E**dges or sides in your polygon.

Note   The following descriptions of polygon placement assume that no radius value has been entered (a radius setting of 0:0:0). The polygon radius setting is discussed after this Polygon Method section.

♦ **Inscribed polygon.** The Place Inscribed Polygon command requires two points to define an imaginary circle, within which the polygon is inscribed. With the inscribed polygon, the vertices of the polygon are on the circle (see fig. 5.28). One point places the center of the polygon (see point 1 in fig. 5.29), and the second point sets the vertex or corner point of the polygon (see point 2 in fig. 5.29). The second point you pick defines the radius and angle of the polygon, from which the length of the sides is derived. In figure 5.28, the dotted circle represents a radius of 4.

Figure 5.28

The difference between inscribed and circumscribed polygons.

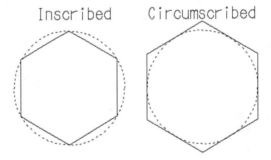

Figure 5.29

Placing an inscribed polygon.

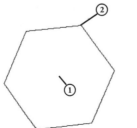

♦ **Circumscribed polygon.** The Place Circumscribed Polygon command also requires two points to define an imaginary circle, about which the polygon is circumscribed. The midpoints of the sides of the polygon are tangent to the circle. The first point (point 1 in fig. 5.30) picks the center of the polygon, and the second point (point 2 in fig. 5.30) sets the midpoint of one of the polygon sides. The second point picked defines the radius and angle of the polygon, from which the length of the sides is derived.

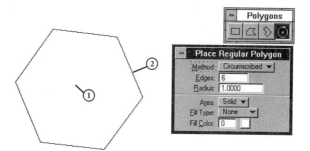

Figure 5.30

Placing a circumscribed polygon.

♦ **Polygon by edge.** The Place Polygon by Edge command also requires two points, but neither point is the center of the polygon. The two points define the length and angle of one side of the polygon (see point 1 and point 2 in fig. 5.31), from which the radius and center point are derived. The polygon sides are drawn in a clockwise direction from these two points.

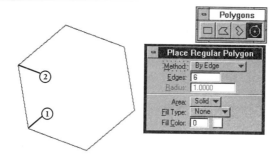

Figure 5.31

Placing a polygon by edge.

Polygon Radius

The **R**adius option setting forces the polygon to the size specified. This setting affects only the placement of inscribed and circumscribed polygons. With a preset radius, both types are placed with one point in the center of the polygon and a second point that defines the angle, but not the radius. Note that the same radius value for the two different polygon types will result in different size polygons because one is circumscribed around and the other is inscribed within the imaginary circle defined by the radius.

Summary

The commands covered in this chapter should get you well on your way to creating your first design in MicroStation. Remember that shapes are closed elements that have area. Later chapters in this book cover filling shapes with patterns and measuring them. Although you can color, pattern and measure areas not bounded by a shape element, using shapes where appropriate is an effective way to use MicroStation.

CHAPTER 6

Viewing a Drawing

*T**his chapter demonstrates how to manipulate MicroStation's views with a set of view controls and attribute settings. These view controls and settings determine not only what you see on the display screen but also how the graphics are displayed in those views. Set Grid, for instance, turns a display grid on or off in a view. Copy View copies what you see in one view to a second destination view. Zoom In takes you in for a closer look. Zoom Out enables you to move back incrementally.*

Each one of MicroStation's eight views can be manipulated independently. View 1 might have a view of the entire design file; for example, a subdivision. View 2 might have a perspective of a particular section of the drawing, perhaps an entire street in the subdivision. View 3 might have an extreme close-up, maybe a street intersection.

This chapter starts by showing you where the view controls are located on the user interface. It teaches you how to manipulate, resize, and repaint MicroStation's views. Then you learn how to change the perspective of what you see in the views and how to control that display. Next, you learn how to work in multiple views and how to save and recall view display information. The chapter ends with ways to use views to be more efficient.

In this chapter, you learn about the following:

♦ Finding the view control tools and settings

♦ Manipulating a view

♦ Resizing a view

♦ Repainting the display

♦ Changing the contents of the view

♦ Controlling what you see

♦ Saving your view settings

MicroStation's view controls and settings determine what you see in a view and how that information appears on-screen. The View Attributes settings box (see fig. 6.1) determines the characteristics or attributes of the graphics displayed in a particular view. The View Control tool box (see fig. 6.2) and the individual window or view icons contain the most common view manipulation tools, and the **W**indow pull-down menu (see fig. 6.3) contains the bulk of the view control operations.

Figure 6.1

The View Attributes settings box.

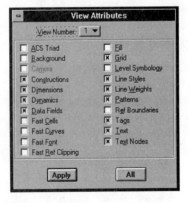

Figure 6.2

The View icons and View Control tool box.

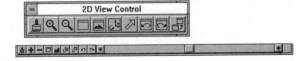

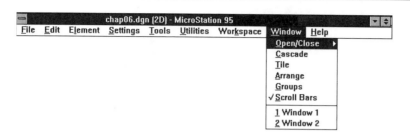

Figure 6.3

The View pull-down menu.

Manipulating the View

By now, you probably have taken a peek and even used a few of MicroStation's view controls, such as Update View, Fit Active Design, Zoom In, and Zoom Out.

Even though many of MicroStation's view controls and settings are dispersed throughout this book, you can find all of them in this chapter. Think of this chapter as your view control reference guide.

View On and Off

You can open or close views by choosing **W**indow, **O**pen/Close from the pull-down menus in the MicroStation Application Window (see fig. 6.4). Options 1 through 8 represent the possible views. (You can have eight views open at any one time.) You can have all eight views open on a single display screen, or if you use two display screens, you could use the eight views across both screens. Each time you open a drawing, the views that were active the last time the save settings command was invoked are the same views that open.

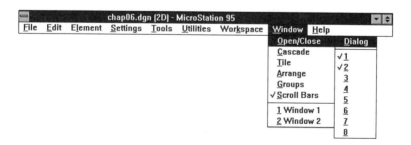

Figure 6.4

Choosing Open/ Close from the View pull-down menu.

If you need to open and close views frequently during a design session, you might want to use the View Open/Close settings box (see fig. 6.5). This settings box, accessed at the top of the **O**pen/Close submenu, enables you to open or close a view by clicking on the appropriate view check button.

Figure 6.5

*The View Open/
Close settings
box.*

Tip   You also can close a view by double-clicking on the window menu button located in the upper left corner of a view.

Other Window Menu Commands

Other items in the Window menu enable you to view open windows differently. The following list briefly describes these items.

- **Cascade**. Choosing **W**indow, **C**ascade resizes all open views and arranges them in view number order, as shown in figure 6.6.

Figure 6.6

Cascading views.

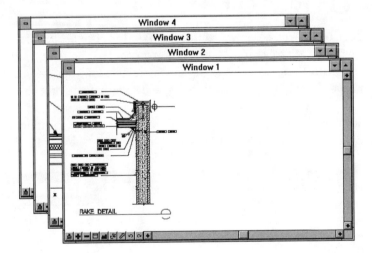

- **Tile**. Choosing **W**indow, **T**ile resizes all views on the display screen so that all view sizes are equal. If you have three views open, MicroStation resizes the three views so that they take up equal space on the display screen (see fig. 6.7).

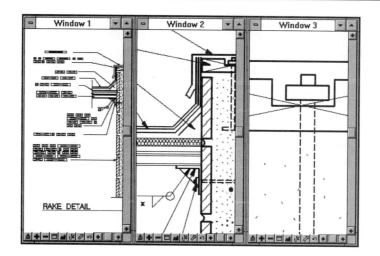

Figure 6.7

Three tiled views.

♦ **Arrange**. Choosing **W**indow, **A**rrange resizes the views to make them visible and to best use the screen area.

Repainting the Display

You can use the Update command to repaint or update the computer's display screen. This command doesn't update the elements in the design file; MicroStation does that automatically as you draw the elements (unless you change this setting). Update just repaints the screen to give you a better look at your work. You can access the Update View tool from the View Control tool box and from the bottom left corner of each view.

If you choose the Update command from the scroll bars in the window, MicroStation updates view immediately. If you choose the Update command from the View Control tool box, the Status Bar prompts `Select View`. Keep in mind as you select the view control tools from the tool box that MicroStation has no way of knowing which view you want to update. Pick a data point in the view to complete the operation.

The Tool settings box contains an Update All Views button when you select the Update View icon or tool. Choose that button to update all currently displayed views.

Tip   If you click the reset (right mouse) button during an update, your design appears incomplete—not all the elements are visible. Choose the Update command again and wait for the Status Bar to flash the `Display Complete` message.

Changing the Contents of the View

MicroStation comes with a variety of view control tools to help you choose new view orientations. Fit enables you to fit all the elements of your file in a view. Zoom In and Zoom Out enable you to move closer in or farther back in a view. Window Area enables you to pick an area to display in the view. You also can swap display screens, rotate views, and even undo a view operation.

Look at the Fit view control first, and then read the other view controls included in this section.

Seeing the Big Picture

The Fit view controls have four variations defined in the Tool settings box. Fit A<u>c</u>tive fits the entire active drawing in a view. Fit **A**ll brings the active drawing and any attached reference files into view. Fit **R**eference redefines the view area to fit only the attached reference files. Fit Ra<u>s</u>ter brings any raster files into the view.

Note   Fit requires one data point to pick the view you want to "fit" if you choose the command from the View Control tool box.

The next exercise takes you through the process of using Fit Active design. First, use an existing design file delivered with MicroStation and save a copy of the file as CHAP06.DGN.

FITTING A VIEW

Open the design file CD9.DGN, found in the ustation\dgn\learning directory.

Choose **F**ile, *then* Save **A**s   Opens the File Save As dialog box

Change the directory back to dgn\default

Type **CHAP06.DGN,** *and click on* <u>O</u>K	Copies CD9.DGN dgn\default directory as CHAP06.DGN and opens it
Choose <u>W</u>indow, <u>O</u>pen/Close *then* **3**	Turns view 3 off
Choose <u>W</u>indow, <u>O</u>pen/Close *then* **4**	Turns view 4 off
Choose <u>W</u>indow, <u>T</u>ile	Tiles view 1 and 2 (see fig. 6.8)
Choose Fit View from the scroll bar of view 1	Brings entire drawing into view (see fig. 6.8)

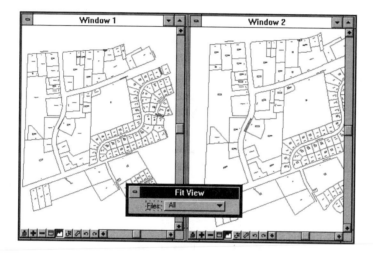

Figure 6.8

Fitting view 1.

If you ever lose your place in the design file, use Fit to bring the entire drawing into view. Sometimes you fit the view and you can see only a few small dots. This means you have elements in the drawing that are quite far apart. Zoom in on the dots, and either move the graphics together or delete what you don't need.

Tip

Using the Zoom Commands

Zoom In enables you to move in for a close look. Zoom Out enables you to step back and see more. You can find both Zoom In and Zoom Out on the scroll bar in each view and in the View Control tool box.

The Zoom In command requires a point in the view. After selecting the command, move the cursor into the view, notice the rectangle that appears on your cursor is the shape of the view and defines the new area to be displayed (see fig. 6.9). Select a point in the view that will become the center of the zoomed-in view (see fig. 6.10).

Figure 6.9

Zoom In rectangle.

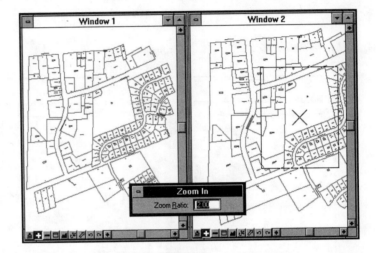

Figure 6.10

Zooming in on view 2.

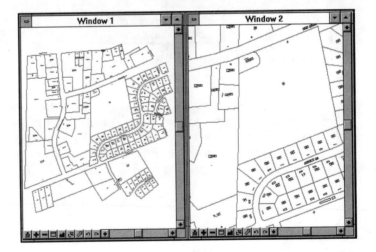

The Zoom Out command doesn't require a point in the view if you choose the command from the scroll bar. The command immediately zooms out the view, maintaining the center point of the view. If you want to continue to zoom out, choose the icon again from the scroll bar to maintain the center point or give a point on-screen from which to zoom out. The point given in the view becomes the new center point (see fig. 6.11).

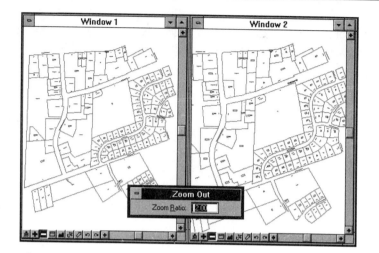

Figure 6.11

Zooming out in view 2.

Click the Reset button to reset the tool after you finish using the zoom commands.

Note

When zooming in, you eventually reach what is called a *minimum window*, meaning you can move in no closer. If you zoom back out, you reach what is called *maximum window*, meaning you can move back no farther.

The default zoom factor is 2, which means that the objects appear half their size with every zoom out and double their size with every zoom in. If you would like to zoom in or out faster, try entering **4** in the Tool settings dialog box for the command to zoom in by a factor of 4.

Window Area

Window Area enables you to select a certain area of the drawing sheet you want to display in the view. In the subdivision example, you might need to work on Elderberry Drive (lower right corner of the subdivision). You could zoom in several times, but you might not get exactly what you want. Windowing may be a more efficient way to get the area extents that you need.

Window Area is found on the scroll bars or on the View Control tool box. The Window Area command requires two data points to define a rectangular shape around the new work area.

Note   Notice that after you give the first point, the cursor shows a box, the same shape as the view, to assist you in getting just the right area.

Try defining a new window area in the following exercise.

Using Window Area

Continue from the last exercise, with CHAP06.DGN still open.

Choose the Window Area icon from the scroll bar in view 2

`Define first corner point` *Pick a point at* ① *(see fig. 6.12)*   Shows rectangle of window area

`Define opposite corner point` *Pick a point at* ②   Adjusts view 2 with a new window area (see fig. 6.13)

Click the Reset button to reset the view control

`Display complete`

Figure 6.12

Picking the window area corners.

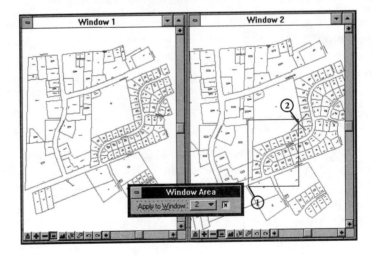

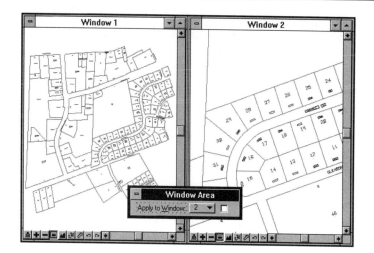

Figure 6.13

Showing new window area in view 2.

Panning

Window Area has gotten you to the right street in the subdivision. Now suppose Lot 24 really needs your attention. You could work with Lot 24 shifted to the left, or you could use the scroll bars or panning to center Lot 24 in the view.

Zoom In, Zoom Out, and Window Area all have their place as view controls in MicroStation. Sometimes these controls suit the situation perfectly. If you want to take a closer look at something, use Zoom In.

The scroll bars in each view or window enable you to shift a view's display. The scroll bars allow you to move the window area to the right, left, up, and down. Click the arrows in the scroll bar to shift the area in that direction. Click in the gray area between the arrow and the scroll box to move a frame in that direction.

Panning enables you to shift the view's display in much the same way as you slide a drawing sheet on a drafting board. When you want to work on a new area of the sheet, you shift the paper a little and retape it.

Panning in a View

Panning can be a very productive method of moving around in a design file. Normally, you use the window and zoom controls to set the view so you can see just enough of the drawing to work in. Then you pan to shift the design file to a new work area.

You can use one of two methods to pan in a design file. One method involves using the Pan View command from the scroll bar or the View Control tool box. Choose the command and pick a point in the view and an arrow appears on your cursor. The second point you provide defines the distance you want to move. Move down the street of your design file by defining the arrow in the opposite direction you want to move.

The other method of panning is a more interactive way to move around in your design file. You activate dynamic panning by pressing the Shift key on the keyboard and then by clicking the left mouse button (the data button) slowly in the direction you want to move. The display starts to shift as you move the pointer in any direction on the screen. The farther you move the pointer away from the initial location at which you placed the input point, the faster the display shifts. Release the mouse button when you are satisfied with the view's location. You can release the Shift key as soon as the panning process starts.

In the next exercise, you put Lot 24 in the center of your view.

PANNING

Continue from the preceding exercise, with view 2 as shown in figure 6.13.

Choose Pan View from the
scroll bar (see fig. 6.14)

`Select view` *Pick a point at* ①   Arrow is displayed and rubberbanding on
(see fig. 6.14)   your cursor

`Define amount of panning` *Pick a point*   Adjusts view to new area (see fig. 6.15)
at ②

Click the Reset button to exit the view control

Now experiment with the interactive method of panning. Try moving down the streets—and don't run off!

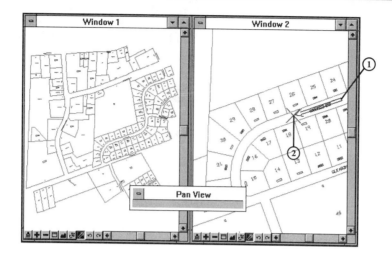

Figure 6.14

Picking the panning distance.

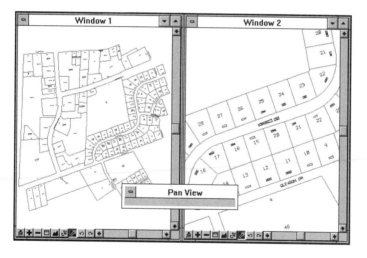

Figure 6.15

A better look at Lot 24 in view 2.

Undoing a View Operation

View Previous and View Next are two view controls that enable you to undo a view operation. Suppose you have a view windowed to just the right perspective. Maybe you are working on the right side of the drawing sheet. You pan or move over to the left side, to the notes section, to make an annotation. Now you want to get back to that exact view orientation you were at on the right side. Choose the View Previous icon to negate the last view operation by clicking anywhere in the view. Choosing View Previous and picking a data point three times in the view negates the last three view operations. Choose View Next and a data point in the view to negate the last View Previous operation. In this example, View Previous and View Next can quickly move you back and forth from the notes section to the drawing.

Follow this example: You zoom in to position 1. Then you zoom in farther to position 2. Choosing View Previous would take you back to position 1. If you choose View Next after choosing View Previous, you are taken back to position 2 again. In other words, you can choose View Next only after you use View Previous.

Rotating What You See

Typically, you think of rotating three-dimensional views. But you can also rotate a two-dimensional view. You can rotate each view independently. To rotate a view, you choose the Rotate View icon from the View Control tool box or from the scroll bar in the view.

View rotation options include By **2** Points and **U**nrotated, found in the Tool settings box. Choose **2** Points and the command Rotate View by 2 Points is activated and prompts you to identify two points in the view to define the rotation angle. The view that will be rotated is defined by the first point picked.

Try rotating the design file view by two points in the following exercise.

 Note

To orient a view to its original position, select **U**nrotated from the Tool settings box and select the view.

ROTATING A VIEW

Continue from the preceding exercise with CHAP06.DGN still open.

Choose View Rotate *icon*	Activates the Rotate View command (see fig. 6.16)
Define first point *Pick point at* ① *(see fig. 6.16)*	Displays a box representing the new view and a line to help you determine the new X axis
Define X axis of view *Pick point at* ②	Rotates the view (see fig. 6.17)
Display Complete	

Choose Unrotate *from the Tool settings box*

Pick a point in view 1   View 1 changes back to 0 degree rotation

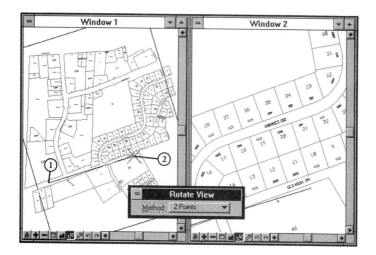

Figure 6.16

Rotating View 1.

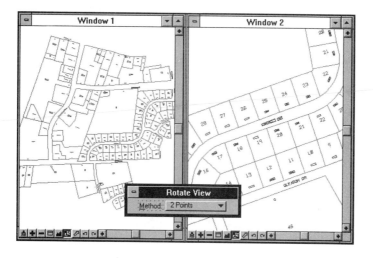

Figure 6.17

View 1 rotated.

The CHAP06.DGN file remains unchanged so far. The exercises you have done have modified only the file's view orientation. To view the file the way it was before the exercises, close the design file and reopen it. Don't choose Save Settings before you close; otherwise, the view changes are saved to the design file.

Controlling What You See

This section deals with changing how the graphics are represented on the display screen. View attributes determine what is displayed and how it is seen in a view. If you turn off the Dimensions view attribute, for example, dimension elements are hidden from view. If you turn on the Fill view attribute, closed elements that have the fill attribute display with color appear filled.

Attaching different color tables is another way to affect how elements appear in views. Color tables are attached to a design file, not to a view. You can attach color tables during or after the design process. Attaching a color table doesn't affect the color with which the element was created, only its display color.

The last item discussed in this section is level symbology display. You can use the level symbology display feature to assign a display color, style, and weight to elements on a particular level in the design file. Placing only center lines on level 2, for example, might be a standard in your office. For display purposes, you could change all the elements on level 2 to green, dashed, with a weight of 4.

The next section looks at the view attribute settings, and then discusses color tables and level symbology.

View Attributes Settings Box

The View Attributes settings box (see fig. 6.18) enables you to set various view characteristics. These characteristics determine not only what you see in a view but also how that information is displayed. For instance, with pattern display turned off, patterns no longer display in that view. The information still remains in the design file; it is just not displayed.

Figure 6.18

The View Attributes settings box.

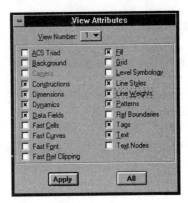

To open the View Attributes settings box, choose **S**ettings, **V**iew Attributes in the MicroStation Application Window. You can set view attributes independently in each view. Because MicroStation enables you to plot what you see on the computer's display screen, the way you set the view attributes affects the hardcopy plot.

Table 6.2 includes all the view attribute settings.

Table 6.2

View Attribute Settings

Setting	Resulting Action
A**C**S Triad	Turns on or off the display of a coordinate triad representing the active auxiliary coordinate system.
Background	Causes a background image to be displayed behind a view.
Ca**m**era	Turns the view camera on or off (available only in 3D design files).
Con**s**truction	Turns on or off the display of construction-class elements.
D**i**mensions	Turns on or off the display of dimension elements.
Dy**n**amics	Turns on or off the dynamic display or update of elements as they are changed.
Data Fields	Turns on or off the display of data fields.
Fast **C**ells	With Fast Cells turned on, cells display as rectangles.
Fast C**u**rves	With Fast Curves turned on, curve elements display as line segments.
Fast F**o**nt	With Fast Font turned on, all text displays in the default fast font.
Fast **R**ef Clipping	Changes the clipping boundary to a block shape.
Fill	With Fill turned on, closed elements appear filled with color if they have the filled attribute turned on.
Grid	Turns the display grid on or off.
Level Symbology	Turns level symbology display on or off.
Line St**y**les	Turns line style display on or off.
Line **W**eights	Turns line weight display on or off.

Continues

Table 6.2, CONTINUED
View Attribute Settings

Setting	Resulting Action
Patterns	Turns on or off the display area and linear pattern elements.
R**e**f Boundaries	With Ref Boundaries turned on, clipping boundaries display as dashed lines.
Ta**g**s	Turns the display of tag data text on or off.
Text	Turns the display of text on or off.
Te**x**t Nodes	Turns the display of text nodes on or off.

Working with Color Tables

Color tables are attached to design files. If MicroStation cannot find the color table attached to the design file, MicroStation uses a default color table located in the \USTATION\DATA directory. The graphics card in your computer or workstation determines the number of colors and the range of color shades displayed on the computer screen.

You open the Color Table dialog box by choosing **S**ettings, **C**olor Table from the pull-down menu. The color palette has cubes that range from 0, the first color cube in the upper left corner, to 255, the last color cube in the lower right corner (see fig. 6.19).

The following sections show how to copy a color, modify a color, and save and attach a new color table to a design file.

Figure 6.19

The Color Table settings box.

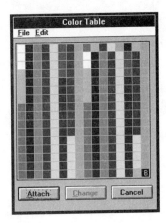

Copying a Color

To copy a color on the color palette, first pick the color you want to copy, then select the destination color you want to change. Perform these steps to copy a color on the color palette:

1. Click on the color you want to copy. You might want to copy the color assigned to color 47 to color number 3, for example.

2. Choose **E**dit, **C**opy Color from the Color Table dialog box pull-down menu.

3. Click on the color you want to change, in this example, color number 3.

4. Choose **E**dit, **P**aste Color from the Color Table dialog box pull-down menu. Color number 3 assumes the new color.

To see the color change in the active design file, you must choose **A**ttach or **F**ile, then Save **A**s from the Color Table dialog box pull-down menu. (Choosing Save **A**s opens the Save Color Table dialog box.) Save the changed color table under a new name. Color tables normally have the file extension TBL and are located in the \ustation\data directory.

Note

You lose the changes you make to a color table after you exit the design file if you don't use the Save **A**s option to save those changes. Choosing **A**ttach only temporarily changes the color for this design session. Be careful to check with your administrator before changing standard color tables.

Warning

Modifying a Color

You modify a color on the color palette by double-clicking on the color you want to change. Double-clicking on a color opens the Modify Color dialog box (see fig. 6.20), which enables you to choose a color name from the Named Colors list box; change the percentage of red, green, or blue (0–255) assigned to the color; or change the color's hue, saturation, or value (red, green, and blue values, or cyan, magenta, and yellow values). The dialog box shows you the color as you adjust the settings. After you set the color, click on **O**K.

Figure 6.20

*The Modify Color 1
dialog box.*

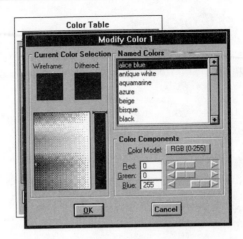

 Note To see the color change in the active design file, you must either choose **A**ttach or choose **F**ile, then Save **A**s from the Color Table dialog box pull-down menu.

Attaching a New Color Table

You can attach different color tables to the active design file during a design session. You can attach only one color table to a design file at any one time. Color tables change only the display of the elements in a design file; they don't change the color attribute of the element in the design file itself. MicroStation doesn't store a specific color with an element—just a color number. Therefore, if an element attribute for color is number 3, the element might display as blue with one color table attached and as green (or whatever color is defined as 3) with another color table attached. The following steps attach a color table:

1. Choose **S**ettings, **C**olor Table, to open the Color Table dialog box.

2. Choose **F**ile, **O**pen from the Color Table dialog box pull-down menu, to open the Open Color Table dialog box (see fig. 6.21).

3. Either enter the file name of the new color table, or move the slider bar in the **F**iles list box until you see the file you want and then click on it and choose **O**K.

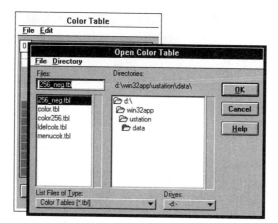

Figure 6.21

The Open Color Table dialog box.

Altering an Element's Display

MicroStation comes equipped with a level symbology feature. You assign symbology to levels in much the same way you assign symbology to elements. Level symbology includes color, line style, and line weight. Element symbology includes these items plus others. If you turn on level symbology display in a view, it overrides the element symbology display in that view.

Suppose, for example, you set the level symbology for level 4 to the color yellow, a line style of medium dashed, and a line weight of 1. With level symbology turned on, any element on level 4 takes on the new symbology, regardless of how the element exists in the active design file.

You might create a level symbology table for personal reasons. You might have a hard time differentiating between two colors or line weights. You can use a level symbology table to change the display of those hard-to-differentiate colors or line weights without affecting the department standards in the least. While you view the file, the line weights are thicker. After you finish working with the file, turn off level symbology display. The next person opening the file sees the element's display symbology, not the level symbology display.

Figure 6.22 shows a level symbology display table. Activate the check boxes to change color, style, and weight. This table shows levels 1 and 2 set to 2, solid line, and weight 1. Level 3 is set to 3, solid line, and weight 1. Level 4's color is set to 4, medium dashed, and weight 1.

Figure 6.22

*The Level
Symbology
settings box.*

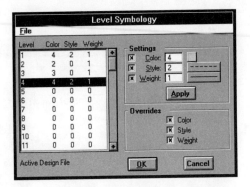

First, set up a level symbology display table. Then activate the level symbology display by turning on the **L**evel Symbology check button in the View Attributes settings box. You can turn the level symbology display on and off in each view separately.

In the next exercise, you change the color display of the property lines in the subdivision. MicroStation's default color table displays the rights-of-way elements on level 40 as color 8 or gray. Go through this exercise, changing elements on level 40, from gray to green by means of the level symbology table.

USING A LEVEL SYMBOLOGY TABLE

Continue from the last exercise, with CHAP06.DGN still open.

Choose **S**ettings, **L**evel *then* **S**ymbology	Opens the Level Symbology settings box (see fig. 6.22)
Move the slider bar to level 40 and pick the line	Highlights level line
Turn on **C**olor	
Enter **2** *in field*	
Choose **A**pply, *then choose* **O**K	Changes color for level 2, then closes dialog box
Choose **S**ettings, **V**iew **A**ttributes	Opens the View Attributes settings box
Turn on **L**evel Symbology, *choose* **A**pply	Changes parcel outlines from gray to green
Turn off **L**evel Symbology, *choose* **A**pply	Changes parcel outlines back to gray
Close View Attributes settings box	

Keep in mind that if you turn on the level symbology display, it might affect the way elements plot, regardless of how the elements really exist in the active design file.

Note

Changing the level symbology table or turning on the display for level symbology changes an active view setting. Remember to save settings before you switch design files or end the design session. If you want to save the view attributes.

Level symbology information is stored in the design file, not in an external table or resource file. If you want to have all the files for a particular project use level symbology display, think about the following options. You could set the symbology in your seed file. Then each time you create a design file for the project, the level symbology would be set up for you. If you already have a set of design files and you want to use symbology display, you have at least two choices. You could open each file and set the table, but that might be tedious and time-consuming, depending on the number of files. You also could choose **F**ile, **I**mport from the Level Symbology dialog box and identify a file that has the correctly defined level symbology to copy.

Saving Your View Settings

Saving a view's setting is much like taking a snapshot and saving it for reference later. When you save a view, you don't copy the elements in that view to another location in the design file; you only save the view's display coordinates.

The next few exercises walk you through the process of saving, recalling, and deleting saved views.

Saving a Named View

Saving a view takes three actions: you open the Saved Views settings box (see fig. 6.23), enter a name of the view and a description if appropriate, and then pick the view you want to save. The name of a saved view can be 6 characters; its description can be up to 24 characters in length.

Figure 6.23

*The Saved Views
settings box.*

SAVING A NAMED VIEW

Continue from the preceding exercise with CHAP06.DGN still open. Choose Zoom In from the View Control tool box, and pick the intersection of Beaverton and Gleason in view 1 (the intersection at the bottom of the subdivision and toward the right).

*Choose **U**tilities, then* Saved **V**iew   Opens the Saved Views settings box

*Enter **bg** in the **N**ame: input box*

*Enter **Beaverton & Gleason** in the
Description: input box (see fig. 6.24)*

Set Source View *to* **1**, *then choose **S**ave*

    View saved

Figure 6.24

*Saving the view of
the intersection at
Beaverton and
Gleason.*

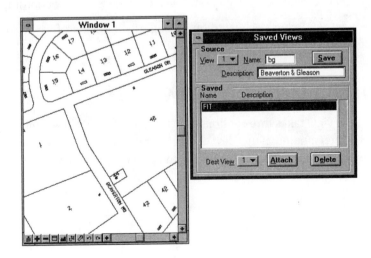

You also can attach a saved view as a reference file. Check out how to use reference files in Chapter 18, "Referencing Other Drawings." **Note**

Recalling a Named View

You recall a named view by opening the Saved Views settings box, picking the destination view, and choosing **A**ttach. You can place the named view in one view or in multiple views.

In the following exercise, you recall the saved view that you created in the preceding exercise.

RECALLING A NAMED VIEW

Continue from the preceding exercise with CHAP06.DGN and the Saved Views settings box still open.

Choose Fit *from the Saved Views settings box*

`Select view` *Pick view 1*   Shows entire subdivision

Choose **A**ttach   Recalls the named view FIT and updates view 1

Choose BG *from the Saved Views settings box*

`Select view` *Pick view 1*

Choose **A**ttach   Recalls the named view BG and updates View 1 (see fig. 6.24)

Notice how the name on view 1's title bar changes from "Window 1" to "Window 1-BG" after attaching the named view. This is a good way to note that you are working with a named view. **Tip**

Deleting a Named View

Deleting a named view is fairly simple. You open the Saved Views settings box, choose the view for deletion, and click on D**e**lete.

DELETING A NAMED VIEW

Continue from the preceding exercise with CHAP06.DGN and the Saved Views settings box still open. The named view, BG, is still highlighted in the settings box.

Choose Delete   Erases the BG entry from the settings box

`BG deleted`

Close the Saved Views settings box.

Tip   Think about saving views named "title" for the title block, "border" for the drawing border, "revblk" for the revision block, and "notes" for the notes section. Now attach these saved views to function keys for quick recall. See Chapter 17, "Boosting Your Performance," for more details on function keys.

Summary

Now that you have finished this chapter, you are well on your way to becoming a view expert. A good percentage of your design time is spent moving around in the views and redisplaying the graphics. Many view commands are available in MicroStation to make it easy and efficient to see what you want.

CHAPTER 7

Drawing with Accuracy

O *ne of the biggest advantages of using a computer for drawing is the accuracy you can attain with relatively little effort. If you have "done time" on a drafting board with pen and ink, you know the effort it takes to draw a straight line at the correct angle and length. With the automated tools of MicroStation, the effort of placing lines and other elements at a predetermined angle, scale, and length is minimized, and the accuracy can be greatly enhanced.*

The precision of your file or drawing is defined by the working units. If you are a mapper, you probably measure or place features on your map in feet, tenths of a foot, and hundredths or even thousandths of a foot. For other applications, such as mechanical and electrical work, millimeters and centimeters might be more appropriate units of measure. Regardless of units, using the proper techniques and controls in MicroStation ensures great accuracy.

You can achieve accuracy in different ways for different circumstances. This chapter introduces you to the concept of the tentative point and methods of snapping to existing elements to provide accuracy between elements. Then you explore other methods for attaining accuracy through the use of grids and precision placement. You also discover how to check the accuracy of existing elements with the measurement tools supplied with MicroStation.

In this chapter, you learn the following:

♦ Using the tentative point to snap to existing elements

♦ Drawing and setting up a grid

♦ Using the axis and unit locks

♦ Controlling the coordinate data format

♦ Using AccuDraw

♦ Checking accuracy

♦ Protecting elements from change

Working with Tentative Points

The first level of accuracy in a design file is the *tentative point*, which you use in conjunction with snap locks. The tentative point enables you to snap to or "grab" existing elements in your file by a particular point. After you snap to an element, you can use that point to start a new element, move the old element, or start a measurement from that point; in other words, treat a tentative point like a data point. A variety of tentative point snap lock options are provided to quickly attach to an end point, a midpoint, a center, and so on.

On a PC with a two-button mouse, the tentative point is activated by pressing both buttons at the same time; called a *two-button chord*. On a PC with a three-button mouse, the tentative point is generally activated as the center button. If you have a tablet with a cursor, the third button should be defined to activate the tentative point. After you press the tentative point button, a crosshair appears on your view twice the size of the normal cursor.

To set or review the cursor or mouse buttons from the Workspace pull-down menu, choose **B**utton Assignments.

Note

Snap Lock

You can snap to elements in different places depending on the element type and the snap lock setting. You can turn snap lock on or off from the Locks settings box or the Lock Toggles settings box. From the **S**ettings menu, choose Loc**k**s, and then choose **F**ull to open the Locks settings box or **T**oggle to open the Lock Toggles settings box (see fig. 7.1). You also can open these two settings boxes from the status bar by clicking on the Lock icon then choosing **F**ull or **T**oggle from the pop-up menu (see fig. 7.2). You can use either of these settings boxes to set several locks, including snap lock. If snap lock is off, your tentative points will not snap to or highlight existing elements.

When you turn snap lock on, Locks=SN appears in the right-hand field of the MicroStation status bar.

Note

Figure 7.1

*Use the Locks and
Lock Toggles
settings boxes to
set several locks,
including snap
lock.*

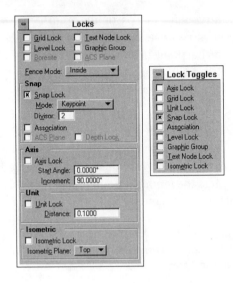

Figure 7.2

*You also can
access Lock
settings boxes
from the status
bar.*

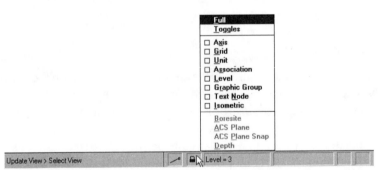

When snap lock is on, if you place your cursor close to an element and pick the
tentative point, the cursor snaps to a point on the nearest element, and the element
snapped to highlights with the active highlight color.

Tip   You can change your highlight color by choosing **D**esign File from the **S**ettings
menu. Choose Color from the Category list on the left side of the dialog box.
Choose a new highlight color from the pop-up field labeled Element Highlight
color.

If you pick a data point after picking a tentative point, the tentative point location
is accepted as the input point.

When snap lock is on, the tentative point provides an accurate way to snap to and select or identify an element. To place a line starting at the exact center of a circle, for example, you can snap to the center with the tentative point and begin your line. First choose the Place Line command and position your cursor close to the center of the circle. Issue a tentative point (thereby highlighting the circle). Then pick a data point to accept the tentative point location. Your line end point is anchored to the circle center. Try this in the following exercise.

USING A TENTATIVE POINT TO SNAP

Create a file titled CHAP07.DGN.

Choose **S**ettings, *then* Lo**ck**s, *then* **T**oggles, *and make sure snap lock is on (highlighted or checked)*	Displays the Lock Toggles settings box
Close the Lock Toggles *settings box*	
Choose the Place Circle *tool*	
`Identify Center Point` *Pick a point in the view*	Defines center point
`Identify Point on Circle` *Pick a point*	Defines a point on the diameter of the circle and places it in the file
Choose the Place Line *tool*	
`Enter first point` *Pick a tentative point near the circle's center (see fig. 7.3)*	Snaps a double-size cursor to the center and highlights the circle
If the circle does not highlight, pick the tentative point again.	
Pick a data point ① *(see fig. 7.3)*	Accepts the tentative point and anchors the line end point
`Enter end point` *Pick a data point* ① *(see fig. 7.4)*	Completes the line
Choose the Reset button	Resets (is ready for new first point)

Figure 7.3

Snapping to the center of the circle snaps a double-size cursor to the center and highlights the circle.

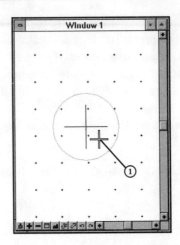

Figure 7.4

Enter an end point to complete the line.

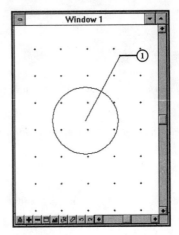

Snap Lock Modes

The snap mode setting determines how the tentative snap lock snaps to elements. You can change the snap mode in the Locks settings box (see fig. 7.5) or by using the Snap Modes pop-up menu from the status bar (see fig. 7.6). Another option is to display the Snap Mode tool box (see fig. 7.7). Choose Button Bar from the pop-up menu in the status bar as seen in figure 7.6.

Figure 7.5

You can change snap modes in the Locks settings box.

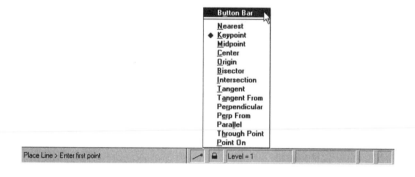

Figure 7.6

You also can change snap modes by choosing the Snap Mode button from the status bar to open the Button Bar menu.

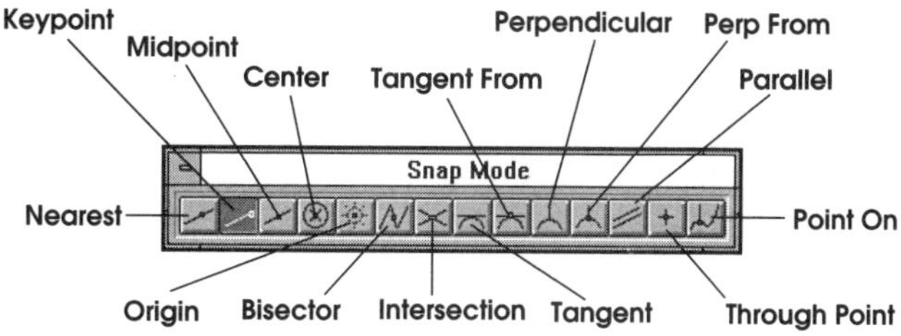

Figure 7.7

Choose Button Bar from the pop-up menu in the status bar to display the Snap Mode tool box.

The Snap Mode pop-up menu and the button bar offer a temporary snap mode: after you select the snap mode desired and use it to issue a data point, the snap mode changes back to the one previously set. If you generally work with the keypoint snap lock on, for example, you can easily change the snap mode to center for a quick snap without returning to the menu or button bar to reset the keypoint before continuing your work.

Note The status bar displays the active snap mode setting with an icon in the middle of the bar.

You can permanently activate a snap mode setting with the pop-up menu or the button bar. To do so, press Shift and then choose the mode from the pop-up menu or double-click on the button bar.

The pop-up menu shows the active permanent mode with a diamond shape. If a temporary selection has been made, the temporary lock is denoted with a diamond and the permanent lock setting is shown with a square. The button bar denotes a permanent snap mode with a dotted gray shade.

 Tip You can open the snap mode pop-up menu at your cursor in the current view by holding down Shift and then picking a tentative point. Close the pop-up menu by resetting or picking a snap mode.

Table 7.1 describes the different modes.

Table 7.1
Snap Mode Settings

Mode	Description
Nearest	Snaps to nearest point on an element
Keypoint	Snaps to original input point along an element or at increments between, see snap divisor section
Midpoint	Snaps to only the midpoint of an element or segment of an element
Center	Snaps to centroid point of an element (line or shape)
Origin	Snaps to cell origins
Bisector	Snaps to a midpoint of an entire element

Mode	Description
Intersection	Snaps to a point at the intersection of two elements
Tangent	Forces a point to be tangent along an element
Tangent From	Forces a new element to be tangent at this point
Perpendicular	Forces a point to be perpendicular along an element
Perp From	Forces a new element to be perpendicular at this point
Parallel	Forces a point to be parallel with a snapped element
Through Point	Forces an element to pass through the tentative point
Point On	Forces a point onto the element chosen by the tentative point

Experiment with two of the snap modes in the following exercise.

SNAPPING WITH OTHER MODES

Continue from the preceding exercise with the CHAP07.DGN design file open.

Choose Button Bar *from the Snap Mode pop-up menu*	Activates button bar tool box
Choose the Midpoint snap button (refer to figure 7.7)	Activates Midpoint snap
Pick a tentative point near the line placed in previous exercise	Highlights line and snaps to midpoint of line
Choose the Keypoint snap button	Activates Keypoint snap
Pick a tentative point near the end of the line placed in previous exercise	Highlights line and snaps to end point of line

Snap Lock Divisor

The snap lock divisor is used with the Keypoint snap lock mode. The Keypoint snap lock forces the tentative point to the native keypoints of an element. A divisor setting of 1 indicates that the keypoint snap lock snaps only to the points defined as the native keypoints of the element (see table 7.2).

Table 7.2
Native Keypoints of Elements (Divisor set to 1)

Element Type	Native Keypoints
Arcs	Center, end points, and points on x/y axis if present
Circles	Center and each quadrant
Lines	Two end points
Line strings	Each vertex
Shapes	Each vertex or corner point

Changing the divisor alters the number of snap points between the native keypoints. Setting the snap divisor to 3, for example, effectively divides the line into three equal parts, giving you four snap points on the line. You change the keypoint divisor in the Full Lock setting box by choosing **S**ettings, Loc**k**s, then **F**ull.

Snap locks are an important part of being productive with MicroStation, so be sure to experiment with the different snap locks.

Drawing on Grid Paper

Chapter 2, "Taking MicroStation for a Test Drive," introduced you to the grid concept. This section gives you the details on displaying, using, and setting up a grid.

Displaying a Grid

Grid displays are view-independent. You can display a grid on all views or only on selected views. Activate the View Attributes settings box by choosing **V**iew Attributes from the **S**ettings menu (see fig. 7.8). To turn on the grid display in one or more specific views, first choose a view number on the top of the View Attributes settings box, turn on the **G**rid toggle button, and then choose Apply. Repeat this for each view in which you want to display the grid. To turn on the grid in all views, turn on the **G**rid button, then select the All button.

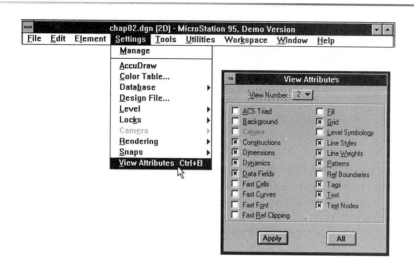

Figure 7.8

You can display a grid on select views.

You might need to change view attributes many times throughout a design session. A quick way to do this is to use the keyboard accelerator Ctrl+B to invoke the View Attributes settings box. Or you can pick the window menu button (the minus sign in the upper left corner) of any window or view, then choose View Attributes.

Tip

In the next exercise try turning the grid display on and off in view 2.

DISPLAYING A GRID

Continue from the preceding exercise with the CHAP07.DGN design file open.

Choose **S**ettings, *then* **V**iew, *or press Ctrl+B*	Displays the View Attributes, Attributes settings box
Choose **V**iew Number 2	Displays the view attribute settings for view 2
Click on the Window 2 title bar	Places view 2 in front of view 1

Zoom in until you can see both grid crosses and grid dots.

Turn off the **G**rid *toggle button*	
Choose Apply	Grid crosses disappear from view 2

Continues

*Turn on the **G**rid toggle button*

Choose Apply   Displays grid in view 2

Close the View Attributes settings box.

Using a Grid

You can use grid displays for reference only or with grid lock, as a form of precision input. As reference only, the grid provides quick reference to the size of elements and features in the design file. If your grid reflects crosses at every master unit, for example, you can easily determine a rough estimate of line length using the grid crosses and dots.

You also can use the grid as a form of precision input, using grid lock to force elements to the grid. Grid lock forces all data points or input points to the nearest grid dot. In an electrical schematic application in which elements are placed in a strict vertical and horizontal pattern, the grid display and grid lock can enable speedy and accurate diagram creation.

You can turn grid lock on and off in several different ways. Grid lock appears in the Full Lock and Lock Toggles settings boxes, and in the lock pop-up menu in the status bar.

Tip   Whenever you change the status of a lock, the MicroStation status bar displays the current lock settings in the upper left field. Locks=GR,SN indicates that grid lock and snap lock are on.

Defining and Changing a Grid

You can display a grid at any scale or size. You must determine two factors to display a grid: the distance between each grid dot and the number of grid dots between grid crosses. To establish these settings, choose **D**esign File from the **S**ettings menu to open the Design File Settings dialog box (see fig. 7.9). Then select Grid from the **C**ategory list.

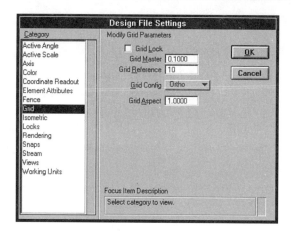

Figure 7.9

To display a grid, you must determine the distance between each grid dot and the number of grid dots between grid crosses.

To interpret the value in this dialog box, you must know the working units defined in your file. What is defined as a master unit, a subunit, or a positional unit? The design file has the following working units: 1 master unit=1 cm, 1 subunit=1/10 of a cm or 1 mm, and 1 positional unit=1/1000 of a cm. With this information and figure 7.9, you can evaluate the grid settings. The Grid Master value in the Design File Settings dialog box determines the distance between grid dots. The current setting is 1 subunit or 1 mm, making the distance between grid dots 1 mm. The Grid **R**eference value in the dialog box reflects the number of dots between grid crosses. The setting is 10, which makes the distance between grid crosses 10 × 1 mm or 1 cm.

The Grid Configuration setting is defined as orthogonal for grids that are at right angles along the x and y axes. Other selections for grid configurations include isometric with grid dots at a 30° angle and offset, which displays every other row halfway between the previous row. The Grid Aspect ratio (y/x) setting enables you to define a nonproportional grid. An aspect ratio of 2.0000, for example, produces a grid with grid dots every 2 mm in the y direction and every 1 mm in the x direction. This changes the distance between grid crosses to 1 cm in the x direction by 2 cm in the y direction.

CHANGING THE GRID

Continue from the preceding exercise with the CHAP07.DGN design file open.

Choose the Lock icon on the status bar

Displays the Lock Toggles pop-up menu

Continues

Choose **G**rid	Activates grid lock
Choose Place Block *on the Main tool frame*	
Pick two points on the grid in view 2	
Choose **S**ettings, *then* **D**esign File	Opens the Design File dialog box
Choose Grid *from the* **C**ategory *list*	Displays the current grid settings

Now change the grid settings and note the changes in grid display. The block has not changed size; only the distance between the dots and the number of grid crosses have changed.

Change Grid **R**eference *to* 5	Displays five grid dots between crosses
Change Grid **M**aster *to* .2	Sets the distance between dots to .2, which displays dots every 2 subunits and grid crosses every 5 grid dots
Choose **O**K	Makes changes to the grid display and closes the Design File Settings dialog box

Change the settings back to .1 (1 subunit between grid dots) and 10 grid dots between crosses, and close the Design File Settings dialog box by choosing OK.

Tip   You also can enter :2 for 2 subunits. This shortcut is available in all dialog boxes that represent master unit coordinates of 0:2:0.

Using Other Locks for Accuracy

Now that you know how to set up and draw on a grid, two other locks can help you increase your accuracy: *axis lock* and *unit lock*. Unit lock and axis lock enable you to quickly place a point at a precise length or angle. You can configure both these locks to suit your individual needs using the Locks settings box (see fig. 7.10). After you configure these locks, turn them on or off from the Lock Toggles settings box or from the status bar.

Figure 7.10

The axis lock and unit lock can help you increase your accuracy.

Axis Lock

A**x**is Lock forces all input or data points to the nearest point at the angle defined as the axis increment. If A**x**is Lock is on and the increment is set to 45 degrees, for example, the element placement commands place points only at 45-degree increments from the first point given.

In the next exercise, use A**x**is Lock to draw a representation of a staircase (see fig. 7.11). Set the axis lock increment to 90 to quickly place simple lines at 90 degrees from the previous point. Do not worry about even length risers and treads; the next section covers that with **U**nit Lock.

WORKING WITH AXIS LOCK

Continue from the preceding exercise with the CHAP07.DGN design file open.

Choose **S***ettings, then* Loc**k**s *then* **F***ull*	Displays the Locks settings box
Turn on A**x**is Lock	
Change **In***crement to* 90	Sets axis lock to horizontal and vertical only
Choose the Place SmartLine tool	

Place the staircase as shown in figure 7.11.

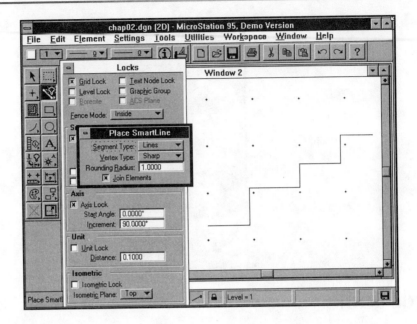

Figure 7.11

*You can create a
staircase in profile
using Axis Lock.*

Unit Lock

You might have had difficulty drawing the staircase in the last exercise with even risers and treads. You can change the grid and then use grid lock to make the staircase more accurate, or you can use the unit lock feature as a quick alternative. Unit Lock forces all data points the defined distance from the last point.

In the following exercise, you draw another representation of a staircase with the aid of both A**x**is and **U**nit Lock (see fig. 7.12).

WORKING WITH UNIT LOCK

Continue from the preceding exercise with the CHAP07.DGN design file open.

In the Locks settings box, turn on
Unit Lock

Change **D***istance to* 1

Choose the Place SmartLine *tool
from the Main tool frame*

Place the staircase as shown in figure 7.12.

Turn off **U**nit Lock

Turn off Ax̲is Lock

Close the Full Lock Settings box

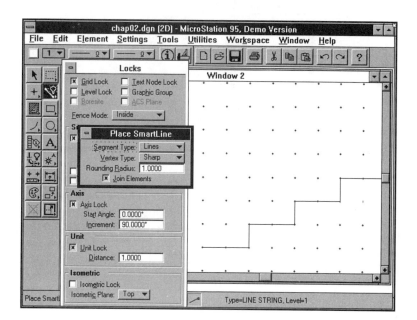

Figure 7.12

You also can use Unit Lock to create another similar staircase in profile.

> You also can use Ax̲is and U̲nit Lock in conjunction with element manipulation commands to make precision available with commands such as Move, Copy, Modify, Extend, and so on.

Tip

Controlling the Coordinate Data Format

You can customize the way you input precision data and the way that measurements are displayed by using the Coordinate Readout category of the Design File Settings dialog box (see fig. 7.13). Here you can establish settings for the format of coordinate data and angle data with a great deal of flexibility.

Figure 7.13

The Coordinate Readout settings enable you to customize the way you input precision data and the way that measurements are displayed.

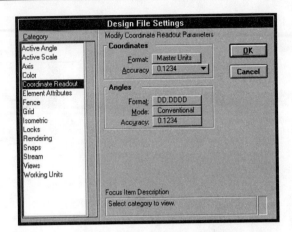

The top portion of the Coordinate Readout settings box is devoted to the interpretation of the coordinate format and accuracy values. The coordinate data **F**ormat options are Master Units, Subunits, and Working Units. The **A**ccuracy setting defines the display for the number of digits past the decimal point or the fraction to be used for data readout. The **A**ccuracy setting only affects the readout if the format is Master Units or Subunits. Table 7.3 demonstrates the differences between these three formats with the **A**ccuracy set to 0.1234.

Table 7.3

Coordinate Data Formats

Format	Readout	Example
Master units	Master units.subunits and positional units	422.0281
Subunits	Master units: subunits.positional units	422:0.2810
Working units	Master units: subunits:positional units	422:0:281

The bottom portion of the Coordinate Readout settings box is devoted to the interpretation of the angle format, mode, and accuracy values. The angle format options are degrees with decimal point accuracy; and degrees, minutes, and seconds. Three angle mode options are available: conventional, azimuth, and bearing (see fig. 7.14).

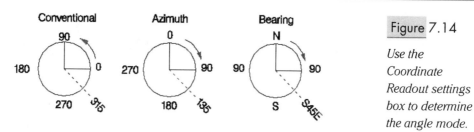

Figure 7.14

Use the Coordinate Readout settings box to determine the angle mode.

Table 7.4 demonstrates the differences between the three angle formats with the accuracy set to 0.1 on a horizontal line.

Table 7.4

Coordinate Angle Formats

Format	Readout	Example
Conventional	0° is set to horizontal (left-right)	90°
Azimuth	0° is set to vertical or north	360°
Bearing	0° is set to vertical or north	N0°W

Using AccuDraw

AccuDraw is a command to allow you precision input when you place or modify elements. Basically, every data point entered on-screen can be accurately placed with the features found in AccuDraw. To start AccuDraw, select the AccuDraw icon from the Primary tool box (see fig. 7.15) to open the AccuDraw settings box.

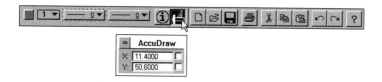

Figure 7.15

AccuDraw is a helpful tool for precision input when you place or modify elements.

Note AccuDraw has different effects depending on the tool selected. Future chapters cover the element placement and modification features of AccuDraw.

Note Unlike most settings boxes, the AccuDraw settings box can be docked.

Precision Input

When AccuDraw is active, a compass is displayed on your cursor. The compass represents one of the two different coordinate systems available in AccuDraw. The square compass in figure 7.16 is displayed when AccuDraw is in the rectangular coordinate system, and the round compass in figure 7.17 is displayed for the polar coordinate system. You can use each compass to enter a value to precision place a point. When the rectangular coordinate system is active, you enter x,y coordinates. When the polar coordinate system is active, you enter the coordinates as distance/angle. One of the compasses is displayed on your cursor after you choose your first point when using any of the element placement commands. To switch between the two coordinate systems, press the spacebar on the keyboard.

 7.16

The square compass is displayed when AccuDraw is in the rectangular coordinate system.

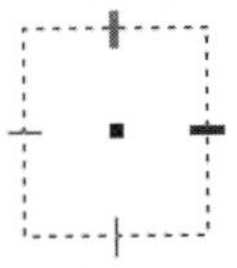

Figure 7.17

The round compass is displayed for the polar coordinate system.

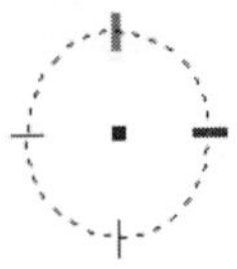

You can change between coordinate systems at any time while using a command by pressing a spacebar.

Tip

Notice that each compass differentiates the positive axes with a thicker line. In your design file you will also notice the compass displays positive x in red and positive y in green.

Another important function of the compass involves the positive axes. As you place a SmartLine, the compass moves to each new data point and displays at the angle defined by the last two points. Figure 7.18 shows a line placed at approximately 20 degrees, for example. Notice the compass moves to the last data point and has the same 20-degree orientation. Entering a positive y value at this point places another line at a right angle to the previous line or an angle of approximately 115 degrees. To return a compass to the orientation of the view with traditional positive x and y values, enter the letter V. The compass rotates as shown in figure 7.19.

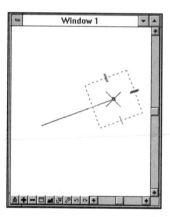

Figure 7.18

As you place a SmartLine, the compass moves to each new data point and displays at the angle defined by the last two points.

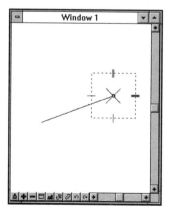

Figure 7.19

Enter the letter V to return a compass to the orientation of the view with traditional positive x and y values.

Rectangular Coordinate System

The rectangular coordinate system enables you to precision place a point with x,y data from a known point. The new point is placed an x distance and y distance from the last data point or compass origin.

 Note

You do not have to activate the field in the AccuDraw settings box if you move your cursor in the direction (axis) you want to enter the value. As you move, the appropriate field becomes active in the settings box.

Neither does AccuDraw require you to highlight the field to replace; you are already in replace mode.

Polar Coordinate System

The polar coordinate system provides angle and distance precision placement.

 Note

In the polar coordinate system, you must activate the Angle field by choosing it in the AccuDraw settings box, pressing a tab, or pressing the down arrow on your keyboard.

The angle is set in terms of degrees; or degrees, minutes, and seconds, depending on the settings in the Coordinate Readout category of the Design File Settings dialog box.

The following exercise demonstrates the AccuDraw placement methods with both rectangular and polar coordinate systems. In the exercise, you place a widget with accuracy (see fig. 7.20).

Figure 7.20

You can use AccuDraw to accurately place a widget.

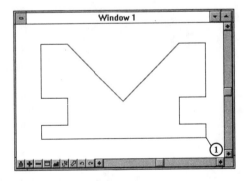

| If you misplace a point, you can press Ctrl+Z to undo it. | *Tip* |

PLACING ELEMENTS WITH ACCUDRAW

Continue from the preceding exercise with the CHAP07.DGN design file open.

Select the Place SmartLine *tool*

Activate AccuDraw

| *Pick a point at* ① *(refer to figure 7.20)* | Anchors first point |

Verify that the rectangular coordinate system is active. If not, press the spacebar.

| *Move the cursor up, away from the first point* | Activates the y field in the AccuDraw settings box |

Type **.5**

| *Pick a point in Y direction to accept* | Places first line segment straight up |

| *Move the cursor left, away from the last point* | Activates the x field in the AccuDraw settings box |

Type **1**

| *Pick a point to accept* | Places next line segment to the left |

| *Move the cursor up, until you see a horizontal line capping the line segment* | Horizontal line represents a line of the same length as previous input |

| *Pick a point to accept* | Places next line segment up |

| *Move the cursor right, until you see a horizontal line capping the line segment* | Horizontal line represents a line of the same length as previous input |

| *Pick a point to accept* | Places next line segment |

| *Move the cursor up, away from the last point* | Activates the y field in the AccuDraw settings box |

Continues

Type **2**	
Pick a point to accept	Places next line segment up
Move the cursor left, away from the last point	Activates the x field in the AccuDraw settings box
Type **1**	
Pick a point to accept	Places next line segment to the left
Press the spacebar on the keyboard	Switches to the polar coordinate system
Type **3**	
Press the Tab key	Activates Angle field
Type **45**	Enters angle
Pick a point to accept	Places next line segment at 45 degrees
Move the cursor up and left until you see a horizontal line capping the line segment	Horizontal line represents a line of the same length as previous input
Pick a point to accept	Places next line segment at 135 degrees
Press the spacebar on the keyboard	Switches to the rectangular coordinate system
Type **V**	Rotates the coordinates compass
Move the cursor left, away from the last point	Activates the x field in the AccuDraw settings box
Type **1**	
Pick a point to accept	Places next line segment to the left
Move the cursor down, away from the last point	Activates the y field in the AccuDraw settings box
Type **2**	
Pick a point to accept	Places next line segment down

Move the cursor right, away from the last point	Activates the x field in the AccuDraw settings box
Type **1**	
Pick a point to accept	Places next line segment
Move the cursor down until you see a horizontal line capping the line segment	Horizontal line represents a line the same length as previous input
Pick a point to accept	Places next line segment
Move the cursor left, until you see a horizontal line capping the line segment	Horizontal line represents a line the same length as previous input
Pick a point to accept	Places next line segment
Move the cursor down, away from the last point	Activates the y field in the AccuDraw settings box
Type **.5**	
Pick a point to accept	Places next line segment
Move the cursor right, away from the last point	Activates the x field in the AccuDraw settings box
Type **6.2426**	
Pick a point to accept	Places next line segment—closes widget
Pick a Reset	

Using Tentative Points with AccuDraw

All AccuDraw key-ins are performed from the compass origin, as shown in the preceding exercise. You can use a tentative point to change the origin of the compass or move the compass to a new location. After the compass is moved, any AccuDraw values keyed in are measured from the new compass. The next exercise, for example, uses a midpoint snap and redefines the compass origin to place a hole in the widget as shown in figure 7.21.

Figure 7.21

*You can use a
midpoint snap
and redefine the
compass origin to
precision place a
hole in a widget.*

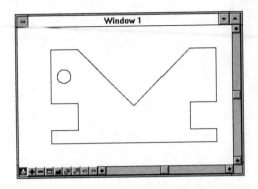

PLACING ELEMENTS WITH TENTATIVE POINTS AND ACCUDRAW

Select the Place Circle tool	Displays tool settings for circle tool
Choose the Center Method of placement (see fig. 7.22)	
Set the constraint Diameter to .5	
Choose the Midpoint snap lock from the status bar	
`Tentative point` *at* ① *(refer to figure 7.22)*	
Type **O**	Changes the origin point
Move the cursor right, away from the compass	Activates x field in the AccuDraw settings box
Type **.5**	
Type **O**	Moves compass .5 units from last point (see fig. 7.23)
Choose a data point with circle in center of compass	Places circle

Try to place the hole on the other side of the widget. When you are finished, type **Q** to close AccuDraw. The AccuDraw settings box must be the active box (have the focus), or typing Q will give you unexpected results.

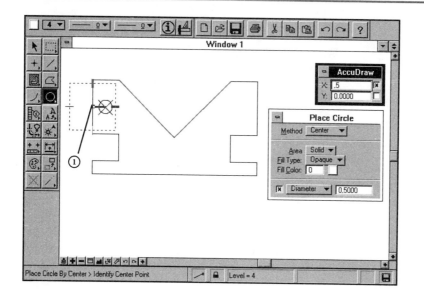

Figure 7.22

You can use tentative points to redefine a compass origin.

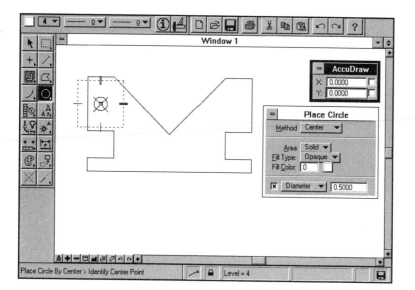

Figure 7.23

*Move the compass away from the last point and type **O** to change a compass origin.*

AccuDraw has a wide range of features and functionality. To view all the AccuDraw shortcuts type a question mark (?) when the AccuDraw settings box is active. The AccuDraw Shortcuts settings box appears (see fig. 7.24).

Figure 7.24

You can discover all of AccuDraw's shortcuts by typing a question mark when the AccuDraw settings box is open.

Checking Accuracy

To verify the accuracy of elements, MicroStation provides measurement commands. The measurement commands include Measure Distance, Measure Radius, Measure Angle Between Lines, Measure Length, Measure Area, and Measure Volume. You can access these commands from the Main tool frame (see fig. 7.25).

Figure 7.25

Measurement commands enable you to verify the accuracy of elements.

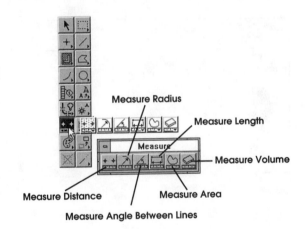

Measure Distance

The Measure Distance command has four options for measuring distance: Between Points, Along Element, Perpendicular, and Minimum Between. When the Measure Distance icon is highlighted in the Measure tool box, a Distance button appears in the Tool settings box. The current option is displayed on the button. Choosing Distance or clicking on the button opens a list of the following four measuring methods:

♦ **Between Points.** This option issues the Measure Distance Between Points command. Pick any two points in the view, and MicroStation displays the distance between those points in the status bar. This command does not require an element, so you can measure under any circumstance. You can, for example, verify the distance between grid crosses with two points. Additional data points continue the measurement from the first point given; a reset prompts you to enter the start point again.

♦ **Along Element.** This option issues the Measure Distance Along Element command. This command requires you to select a point on an element, and a second point displays the distance along the element. The difference between this command and the Between Points command is that this command measures the distance along the path of the element, not the shortest distance between the points. Additional data points continue the measurement from the first point given; a reset prompts you to identify an element again.

♦ **Perpendicular.** This option issues the Measure Perpendicular Distance From Element command. This command requires you to identify an element from which to construct a perpendicular measurement. You select the element, and a temporary element appears indicating the perpendicular line of measurement. The perpendicular line appears only for the duration of the command. It saves you the effort of placing a perpendicular element for the measurement alone.

♦ **Minimum Between.** This option issues the Measure Minimum Distance Between Elements command, which requires you to identify two elements to measure. MicroStation analyzes each element and determines the minimum distance between them. The distance is displayed in the status bar while the minimum distance path is shown in the view with a temporary line displayed with the highlight color. As soon as you pick another data point or click the Reset button, the temporary line disappears.

The following four exercises use the elements you placed in the previous exercises that represent a staircase. They sample the four measurement commands described in the preceding list.

MEASURING DISTANCE BETWEEN POINTS

Continue from the preceding exercise with the CHAP07.DGN design file open.

Tear off the Measure tool box

Continues

Choose the Measure Distance command and make sure the Between Points option is current	Issues the Measure Distance Between Points command
Enter start point Pick the point at ① (see fig. 7.26)	
Define distance to measure Pick a point at ②	

Note that in figure 7.26, the dashed line represents the path of measurement.

Define distance to measure Click the Reset button	Prompts for new start point

The measurement is displayed in the status bar.

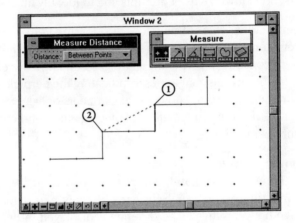

Figure 7.26

Using the Measure Distance Between Points command.

MEASURING THE DISTANCE ALONG AN ELEMENT

Continue from the preceding exercise with the CHAP07.DGN design file open.

Set the Measure Distance option to Along Element	Issues the Measure Distance Along Element command
Identify Element at first point Pick a point at ① (see fig. 7.27)	
Enter end point Pick a point at ②	

Note that in figure 7.27, the dashed line represents the path of measurement along the element, but does not appear on your screen.

`Measure more pnts/Reset to reselect`
Click the Reset button

The measurement is displayed in the status bar.

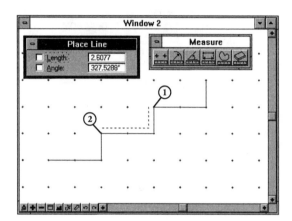

Figure 7.27

The dashed line represents the path of measurement along the element.

Before continuing with the next two exercises, place a line representing a handrail to measure perpendicular and minimum distances.

MEASURING PERPENDICULAR DISTANCE

Continue from the preceding exercise with the CHAP07.DGN design file and the Measuring tool box open.

Set the Measure Distance option to   Issues the Measure
Perpendicular   Perpendicular Distance From
                                     Element command

`Enter first point `*Pick a point*
at ① (see fig. 7.28)

`Enter end point `*Pick a point*
at ②

In figure 7.28, the dashed line represents the path of measurement.

Continues

```
Measure more pnts/Reset
to reselect Click on the Reset
button
```

The measurement is displayed in the status bar.

Figure 7.28

*Measure
perpendicular
distance from stair
profile to handrail.*

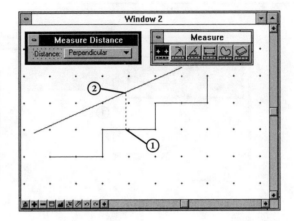

MEASURING THE MINIMUM DISTANCE BETWEEN ELEMENTS

Continue from the preceding exercise with the CHAP07.DGN design file and the Measuring tool box open.

*Set the Measure Distance option to
Minimum Between*

Issues the Measure Minimum
Distance Between Elements
command

```
Identify first element Pick
a point at ① (see fig. 7.29)
```

```
Accept, Identify 2nd element/
Reject Pick a point at ②
```

```
Accept, Initiate min dist
calculation Pick a point
```

In figure 7.29, the dashed line represents the path of measurement, showing the shortest path between the two elements. This measurement might be different in your drawing.

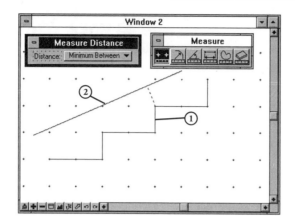

Figure 7.29

The dashed line represents the path of measurement, showing the shortest path between two elements.

Measure Radius

Use the Measure Radius command (see fig. 7.30) to measure the radius of circles and arcs. The command also measures the major and minor axes of ellipses, half ellipses, and quarter ellipses. If a circle or arc is identified, the command displays Radius= in the status bar. If an ellipse is identified, the command displays Major: Minor: in the status bar.

Figure 7.30

Use the Measure Radius command to measure the radius of circles and arcs and the major and minor axes of ellipses, half ellipses, and quarter ellipses.

Measure Angle

The Measure Angle command (see fig. 7.31) measures the angle between two elements, such as lines, line strings, or shapes. If the two elements you select do not connect in the view, an intersection point is calculated to serve as a point for the measurement.

Figure 7.31

*The Measure
Angle command
measures the
angle between
two elements,
such as lines, line
strings, shapes, or
multilines.*

Measure Length

The Measure Length command has many functions. First, the command measures
the length of a linear element simply by selecting the element. The tolerance setting
in the tool settings box (see fig. 7.32) controls the level of accuracy when measuring
a curve or mass properties. A small number in the tolerance field results in a better
measurement of the curve and requires more processing time. A large number
in the tolerance field results in an approximation of the curve's points when
measuring.

Figure 7.32

*The tolerance
setting of Measure
Length command
controls the
degree of the
measurement's
accuracy.*

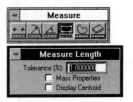

The difference between the Measure Length command and the Measure Distance
Along Element command is that the former measures the entire element, whereas
the second prompts you to identify two points along the element to measure.

The Mass Properties option in the tool settings box provides more information about
the element's measurements (see fig. 7.33). Open the Display pull-down menu to
reveal options that provide a total mass properties report (see fig. 7.34). The Radii
Of Gyration option in the Display pull-down menu produces a temporary element
in the centroid of the element measured.

Figure 7.33

The Mass Properties box provides additional information about the element's measurements.

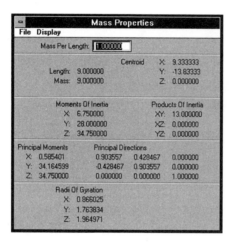

Figure 7.34

The Mass Properties report including details about moments and products of inertia, principal moments, and radii of gyration.

You can save the contents of the Mass Properties box as an ASCII text file by choosing File, **S**ave from the pull-down menu in the Mass Properties window.

Measure Area

The Measure Area command enables you to measure the area of any closed shape. Method options include Element, Fence, Intersection, Union, Difference, Flood, and Points (see fig. 7.35). Choose the **M**ethod button to display the current method or select a different method. The same options for tolerance and mass properties of the Measure Length command are available with this command.

Figure 7.35

You can measure the area of any closed shape with the Measure Area command.

The following list describes the Measure Area command method options:

♦ **Element.** This option requires you to identify an element and then accept the element to initiate the measurement. The status bar displays the area and perimeter of the element, for example, A=9.0000 SQ cm, P=12.0000.

♦ **Fence.** If a fence is present, this menu item is available. The Fence option does not require any input from the user and quickly displays the area and perimeter of the fence in the status bar. The Place Fence command is discussed in Chapter 9, "Manipulating 2D Elements."

♦ **Intersection.** This option measures the area and perimeter of the intersection or the common area that both elements occupy (see fig. 7.36).

Figure 7.36

Use the Measure Intersection option to measure the intersection of two elements.

♦ **Union.** This option measures the area and perimeter of the union of two elements or the total area of both elements (see fig. 7.37).

♦ **Difference.** This option measures the area and perimeter of the difference of two elements (see fig. 7.38). The element you select first is measured, then the area the second element occupies is subtracted.

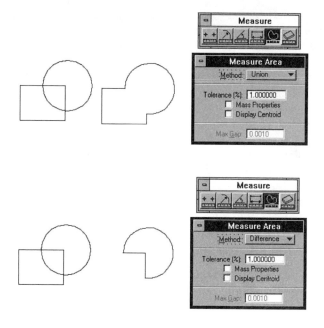

Figure 7.37

Use the Measure Union option to measure the union of two elements.

Figure 7.38

Use the Measure Difference option to measure the area and perimeter of the difference of two elements.

♦ **Flood.** This option measures area and perimeter without requiring shapes. The area defined by a group of elements such as arcs and lines, for example, can be measured with the Flood option. Pick a point inside the area, and MicroStation automatically calculates the path. The Max Gap field in the tool settings box helps determine the path by defining the distance MicroStation will search to connect the element or generate a path.

With the Flood option, a large file with many elements takes a long time to process.

Warning

♦ **Points.** This option measures an area that you define by points—no elements are required. The command prompts you to place the vertices for a temporary shape. After you pick the vertices, click the Reset button, and the area and perimeter display in the status bar.

Protecting Elements from Change

After you place elements and verify them as accurate, you can lock them to make sure they are not changed accidentally. Locked elements cannot be modified or deleted without being unlocked first.

You lock elements by first selecting the arrow in the top left corner of the Main tool frame. This arrow is the *Element Selection tool*. Pick the element you want to lock with the Element Selection tool and then choose **E**dit, Loc**k**.

Note

> Some commands, such as Delete Element, do not identify locked elements nor tell you that the element is locked. If you try to modify such an element, MicroStation displays Element not found in the status bar.

You can unlock elements by highlighting them with the element selection tool and choosing **E**dit, Unl**o**ck.

Summary

Features like snapping and AccuDraw contribute a productive design session. Refer to this chapter as you complete exercises that instruct you to snap or use AccuDraw. Because these topics are diverse and broad in scope, both tentative points and AccuDraw are discussed throughout the remaining chapters of this book.

CHAPTER 8

Placing More 2D Elements

C ircles, ellipses, and arcs are three element types you need to place for every discipline. This chapter discusses the commands you use to place these element types. If you remember from your high school geometry class, a circle is a closed, single curved line of which every point is an equal distance from the center point, an ellipse is a circular shape that has two different axis values, and an arc is a portion of a circle. Actually, in MicroStation, a circle is stored as an ellipse element in which the major and minor axes are equal.

In addition to teaching you how to place circle, ellipse, and arc elements in your design, this chapter discusses some of MicroStation's Modify Arc commands. It also takes a closer look into the Element Selection tool and some advanced commands that place fillets and arrays. The discussion of these features shows you the options and the power available in MicroStation.

Hope you haven't forgotten about levels, because you use level displays and change the active level throughout the exercises in this chapter. You also practice using snap locks to snap to these bits of geometry. If you need help, review Chapter 7, "Drawing with Accuracy."

In this chapter, you learn about the following:

♦ Using the Place Circle and Place Ellipse commands

♦ Using the Place Arc and the Partial Ellipse commands

♦ Using the Modify Arc commands

♦ Using the Element Selection tool for modifying arcs, circles, and ellipses

♦ Rounding corners using the fillet commands and SmartLines

♦ Placing multiple copies of an element in a rectangular or circular pattern using the Array commands

Placing Circles

You find the tools for the Place Circle and Place Ellipse commands on the Main tool frame (see fig. 8.1). You can tear off the Ellipses tool box from the Main tool frame, or you can choose **M**ain, **E**llipses to open this tool box from the **T**ools pull-down menu. The first tool on the Ellipses tool box represents the Place Circle commands. The second and last tool on the tool box represent the commands to place ellipses.

Figure 8.1

Ellipses tool box on the Main tool frame.

Although the tool box has only two icons, several different methods are available for placing circles and ellipses. The Place Circle command places a circle by one of three methods. The tool settings box displays the **C**enter, **E**dge, and **D**iameter in the Method pop-up menu (see fig. 8.2).

Figure 8.2

The Circle tool and its methods.

Place Circle By Center Method

The Place Circle By Center command places a circle by using two points. The first point defines the center of the circle, and the second point on the circle's edge defines the radius of the circle.

PLACING A CIRCLE

Create a design file called CHAP08.DGN.

Tear off the Ellipses tool box

Choose the Place Circle tool

Verify the Method is set to Center

Identify Center Point *Pick point at* ① *(see fig. 8.3)* — Anchors center point of circle

Identify Point on Circle *Pick point at* ② — Places circle

Identify Center Point

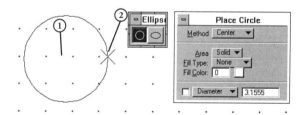

Figure 8.3

Placing a circle by center.

The Place Circle By Center command has two constraints available, located at the bottom of the tool settings box. The constraints provide a **D**iameter or **R**adius choice from the pop-up menu. If you select the **D**iameter or **R**adius constraint, the command requires only one point at the center to place the circle; the size of the circle is determined by the constraint setting.

You can place concentric circles easily using the Place Circle By Center command. In the following exercise, you practice placing two concentric circles using the **R**adius constraint. After you place the first circle, you use Center snap mode to place the larger circle.

PLACING A CIRCLE WITH THE DIAMETER AND RADIUS CONSTRAINT

Continue from the preceding exercise with the CHAP08.DGN design file open.

Make level 4 the active level,
and turn off level 1

Choose the Place Circle tool

Turn on the **D***iameter constraint toggle button*

Enter **2** *in the* **D***iameter constraint field*

`Identify Center Point` *Move*   Places circle
cursor into design area, and pick
point

Click on **D***iameter and select* **R***adius*
from the pop-up menu

`Identify Center Point` *Change*
the **R***adius constraint field to* 2

Pick the snap icon in the Status Bar   Displays snap pop-up menu

Choose **C***enter*   Activates single-shot center snap mode

Pick a tentative point near center   Highlights circle
of first circle

If the circle didn't highlight, repeat the last couple steps. Choose Center snap from the Status Bar and attempt to snap with the tentative point to the circle center again.

Pick any point to accept tentative snap   Places circle (see fig. 8.4)

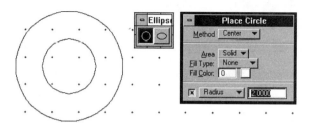

Figure 8.4

*Placing concentric
circles by center
using the Diameter
and Radius
constraints.*

Notice that the Place Circle By Center tool also offers settings for A**r**ea, **F**ill Type, and Fill **C**olor. The discussion in Chapter 5 of the Place Shape commands includes settings exactly like these. Review Chapter 5, "Placing Simple 2D Elements," for details about filling shapes with colors.

> You must turn on Fill in the View Attributes settings box before elements will appear filled on-screen. To activate the View Attributes settings box, choose **V**iew Attributes from the **S**ettings pull-down menu or from the view pull-down in the upper left corner of each view.

Note

Place Circle By Edge Method

The Place Circle By Edge command requires three points. The first two points define points on the edge of the circle; the third point defines the radius and places the circle in your design file. In the following exercise, you use the edge method to place a circle inside the two lines (see fig. 8.5). To place the circle in the next exercise, activate the tangent snap mode by holding down the Shift key and choosing **T**angent from the snaps pop-up menu in the Status Bar.

> The closer to a straight line that the points lie on, the larger the radius of the circle.

Tip

PLACING A CIRCLE BY EDGE

Continue from the preceding exercise with the CHAP08.DGN design file open.

Make level 5 the active level, and turn off the display for level 4

Circles placed in previous exercise disappear from the view

Continues

Place two lines (see fig. 8.5)

Turn off the Radius constraint

*Choose the Place Circle By Edge
tool*

*Hold down the Shift key and choose
Tangent from the Status Bar Snap Mode pop-up
menu*

`Identify Point on Circle` *Pick a tentative point on the first line*	Highlights the line
`Accept tentative` *Pick any point*	Accepts tentative point
`Identify Point on Circle` *Pick a tentative point on other line*	
`Accept tentative` *Pick any point*	Accepts tentative point
`Identify Point on Circle` *Pick point at* ①	Places circle
`Identify Point on Circle`	

Figure 8.5

*Placing a circle by
edge.*

Turning on the **R**adius constraint for the Place Circle By Edge command makes the constraint define the radius and the command requires you to enter only two points. The first point defines the edge of the circle, and the second point defines the orientation. In the next exercise, you place a circle by edge with the **R**adius constraint (see fig. 8.6).

PLACING A CIRCLE BY EDGE WITH THE RADIUS CONSTRAINT

Continue from the preceding exercise with the CHAP08.DGN design file open.

Choose the Place Circle By Edge tool

*Turn on the **R**adius constraint, and
enter **1** in the **R**adius constraint
field (see fig. 8.6)*

`Identify Point on Circle` *Pick a*   Accepts tentative point
tentative point on vertical line

`Accept tentative` *Pick any point*   Displays circle

`Identify Point on Circle` *Pick*   Places circle
point at ①

`Identify Point on Circle`

*Turn off the **R**adius constraint*

*Hold down the Shift key and choose
Keypoint from Status Bar snap pop-up menu*

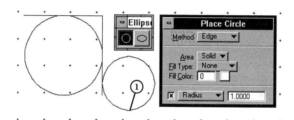

Figure 8.6

*Placing a circle by
edge with the
Radius constraint.*

Place Circle By Diameter Method

The Place Circle By Diameter command is a simple two-point command, and has
no constraints available. The first input point anchors the circle edge, and the
second input point defines the diameter and the rotation of the circle. A *diameter*
is defined as a straight line that passes through the center of the circle. Figure 8.7
illustrates this command by showing two circles that have the same first points and
different second points.

In the following exercise, you place a circle using the Place Circle By Diameter
command. You first place a line, then you place a circle (see fig. 8.8).

Figure 8.7

*Defining diameter
and orientation by
the second input
point.*

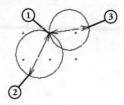

PLACING A CIRCLE BY DIAMETER

Continue from the preceding exercise with the CHAP08.DGN design file open.

*Make level 6 the active level, and
turn off the display for level 5*

Select the Place Line tool

*Place one line at approximately a
140° angle*

*Turn off **A**ngle constraint*

Choose the Place Circle By Diameter tool

`Enter first point on diameter` *Pick a tentative point near the endpoint of the line*	Highlights line
Pick any point	Accepts highlighted element
`Enter second point on diameter` *Pick a tentative point on second line*	
Pick any point to accept tentative point	Places circle
`Enter first point on diameter`	

Figure 8.8

*Placing a circle by
diameter.*

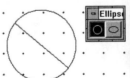

Placing Ellipses

The geometric shape called a circle is an *ellipse* that has X and Y axes of different lengths. The long axis is called the *major axis*, and the shorter one is called the *minor axis*. In MicroStation, the axes are defined by a *primary radius* and a *secondary radius* (see fig. 8.9).

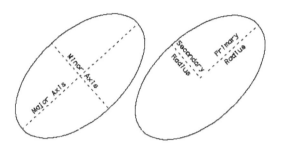

Figure 8.9

Ellipse definition.

Place Ellipse By Center and Edge

Three points are required to place an ellipse with the Place Ellipse By Center and Edge command (with no defined constraints). The first input point defines the center of the ellipse, the second point defines the primary radius and the rotation of the ellipse, and the third point defines a point on the secondary radius. As a drawing aid, the Place Ellipse By Center and Edge command places a temporary point to represent the center and a dotted line to represent the primary axis.

You can define any one or all three constraints in the Ellipses tool box to create an ellipse with more precision. The input requirements of the Place Ellipse By Center and Edge command change, depending on the constraints applied. If you turn on the **P**rimary radius constraint, the command prompts you for the center point and the secondary radius; the second point defines the secondary radius as well as the rotation. If you turn on the **P**rimary and **S**econdary radius constraints, the command prompts you for the center of the ellipse and the rotation angle. Finally, if you turn on the **P**rimary, **S**econdary, and **R**otation constraints, the command prompts you only for the center of the ellipse.

Watch the prompts in the Status Bar—they tell you what point the command wants.

Tip

Place Ellipse By Edge Points

The Place Ellipse By Edge Points command requires three points and has the same constraints available as the Place Ellipse By Center and Edge command.

Watch the constraints in the tool settings box as you place the ellipse in the next exercise. After you pick the second point to define the primary radius, the **P**rimary and **R**otation constraints are turned on automatically.

PLACING AN ELLIPSE BY EDGE POINTS

Continue from the preceding exercise with the CHAP08.DGN design file open.

Make level 7 the active level, and
turn off the display for level 6

Draw three lines, as shown
in figure 8.10

Choose the Place Ellipse By Edge
Points tool

`Identify Point on Ellipse` *Pick a tentative point at* ① *(see fig. 8.10)*	Displays tentative point
Pick any point to accept tentative point	Displays temporary point
`Identify Point on Ellipse` *Pick a tentative point near the center line at* ②	Highlights center line
Pick any point to accept tentative point	Displays temporary point and ellipse
`Identify Point on Ellipse` *Pick a tentative point at* ③	Displays tentative point
Pick a point to accept tentative point (see fig. 8.10)	Places ellipse, and temporary points disappear

`Identify Point on Ellipse`

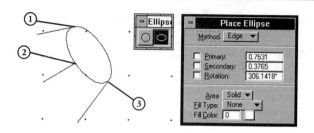

Figure 8.10

Placing an ellipse by edge points.

Placing Arcs and Partial Ellipses

You find the tools for the Place Arc and the Partial Ellipse commands on the Main tool frame (see fig. 8.11.)You can tear off the Arcs tool box from the Main tool frame or you can choose **M**ain, **A**rcs to open this tool box from the **T**ools pull-down menu.

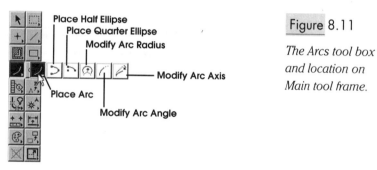

Figure 8.11

The Arcs tool box and location on Main tool frame.

The Arcs tool box contains two tools to place arcs, two tools to place half and quarter ellipses, and three tools to modify arcs.

Placing Arcs

Both Place Arc commands, Place Arc By Center and Place Arc By Edge, have three constraints: **R**adius, **S**tart Angle, and Sweep **A**ngle. Figure 8.12 illustrates each of these terms.

Figure 8.12

Figure 8.12

Arc features and definitions.

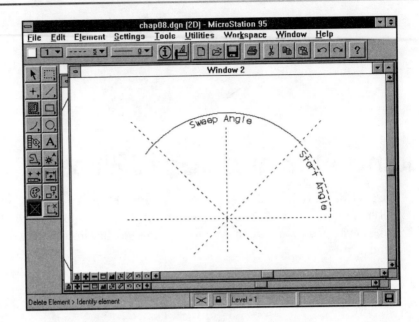

Place Arc By Center

The Place Arc By Center command prompts you for three points to place an arc. First, you pick the first endpoint for the arc. A temporary heavy black dot appears at the center point, and a temporary dashed line shows on your cursor. The second point defines the center point of the arc and the radius. The third point defines the sweep angle or length of the arc. After you finish the command, the center point dot and the temporary dashed lines disappear.

To clear the screen for the next several exercises, activate level 8 and turn off the display for all other levels. Begin by placing the elements shown in figure 8.13. Turn axis and grid lock on from the Status Bar pop-up lock menu, place linestrings with the SmartLine command or lines with the Place Line command. In the next exercise, you place a three-point arc to cap the lines.

Figure 8.13

Placing the line work for the next exercise.

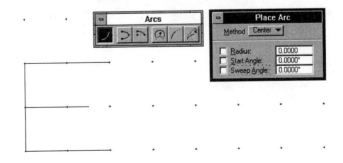

PLACING AN ARC BY CENTER

Continue from the preceding exercise with the CHAP08.DGN design file open and keypoint snap mode active.

Make level 8 the active level, and turn off the display for all other levels

Activate Axis and Grid lock from the Status Bar

Place the elements discussed above (see fig. 8.13)

Turn off Axis and Grid lock

Choose the Place Arc tool

Choose the Center Method

`Identify First Arc Endpoint` *Pick a tentative point near* ① *(see fig. 8.14)*	Highlights linestring
Pick a point to accept tentative location	Displays temporary point and circle as you move cursor
`Identify Arc Center` *Pick a tentative point near* ②	Highlights line
Pick a point to accept tentative location	Displays a temporary line and arc as you move cursor
`Identify Second Arc Endpoint` *Pick a tentative point near* ③	Highlights line string
Pick a point to accept tentative location	Places arc (temporary lines disappear)
`Identify Arc Center`	

Figure 8.14

*Placing an arc by
center.*

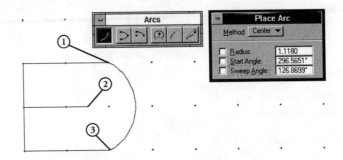

 Warning

You can place what looks like a circle with the Place Arc commands, but don't do it if you later need to fill or measure the area of the element. An arc and a circle have different definitions. A circle is defined as an ellipse element type, whereas an arc is defined as an arc element type. A circle can be filled with color because it's, by definition, a closed element. An arc isn't a closed element, no matter how close the endpoints are!

Place Arc By Edge

The Place Arc By Edge command also prompts you for three points to place an arc, but all three points are on the arc. After you pick two of the points on the arc's edge, the arc appears on the cursor. You can then experiment with the way the third point changes the radius, starting angle, and sweep angle.

PLACING AN ARC BY EDGE

Continue from the preceding exercise with the CHAP08.DGN design file open.

Choose the Place Arc *tool*

Choose the Edge Method

`Identify First Arc Endpoint` *Pick*   Highlights line
a tentative point near ①
(see fig. 8.15)

Pick a point   Displays temporary point

`Identify Point on Arc Radius` *Pick*   Highlights line
a tentative point near ②

Pick any point	Displays temporary arc
Move the cursor and watch the arc change.	
`Identify Second Arc Endpoint` *Pick a tentative point near* ③	Highlights line
Pick any point	Places arc (temporary points disappear)
`Identify First Arc Endpoint`	

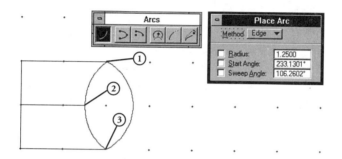

Figure 8.15

Placing an arc by edge.

Whether MicroStation draws a major (>180°) or a minor (<180°) arc depends on the location of and direction from which the cursor approaches the third point.

Tip

Placing Partial Ellipses

The Arcs tool box has two tools for placing partial ellipses (elliptical arcs). No constraints are available for the Place Half Ellipse command nor the Place Quarter Ellipse command.

Place Half Ellipse

The Place Half Ellipse command works similarly to Place Arc By Edge; it requires three points to place a half ellipse. The first point defines one endpoint of the half ellipse; the second point defines a point anywhere on the ellipse; and finally, the third point defines the other endpoint of the half ellipse (see fig. 8.16). The first and third points define either the major or minor axis of the ellipse.

Figure 8.16

Examples of a half ellipse and a quarter ellipse.

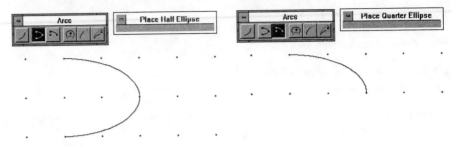

Place Quarter Ellipse

The Place Quarter Ellipse command requires three points to place a quarter ellipse. The first point defines one endpoint of the quarter ellipse, the second point defines the center, and the third point defines the other endpoint of the quarter ellipse (see fig. 8.16). One axis is from the first to second points, and the other axis is from the third to second points; which is the major axis and which is the minor axis depends on where the points are located.

Modifying Arcs and Partial Ellipses

The Arcs tool box has three tools for modifying arcs and partial ellipses. To understand the way these commands affect arcs and partial ellipses, you need to understand how the elements are stored in the design file.

MicroStation has approximately 88 element types. The arc element type (16) stores both arcs and partial ellipses. The type of data stored for both arcs and partial ellipses is identical. They store values for a primary axis, a secondary axis, a starting angle, a sweep angle, a center point, and a rotation angle. For an arc, the primary and secondary axis values are equal (that's the definition of an arc). A partial ellipse is stored as an arc element type with unequal major and minor axes.

Modify Arc Radius

The Modify Arc Radius command modifies the radius (axis) of an arc, leaving both endpoints where they are (see fig. 8.17). Pick an arc, and move the cursor to see this command's effects. After you're satisfied with the arc's new radius, click the Reset button.

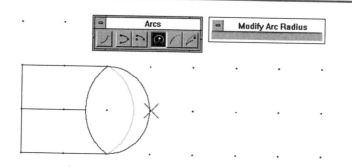

Figure 8.17

The Modify Arc Radius tool.

The Modify Arc Radius command doesn't work on arc elements that represent partial ellipses. The command is smart enough to know that an arc element that has different values stored for the primary and secondary axes doesn't have a constant radius.

The Modify Arc Radius command doesn't highlight a partial ellipse. The Status Bar displays the message Element not found until you identify a valid element for this command (that is, an arc with equal primary and secondary axes).

Note

Modify Arc Angle

The Modify Arc Angle command (see fig. 8.18) modifies the start point or the endpoint of an arc or partial ellipse; in other words, the command modifies the sweep angle of the arc element type. After you identify the arc or ellipse, pick the element close to the endpoint you want to modify. As you move the cursor, the arc drags. Pick a second point to temporarily place it, and press the Reset button after you're satisfied with its placement.

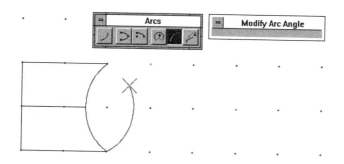

Figure 8.18

The Modify Arc Angle tool.

Modify Arc Axis

The Modify Arc Axis command modifies partial ellipses or arcs. If you use this command on a partial ellipse, you modify one axis at a time. Identify the ellipse near an axis to modify it. If you use this command on an arc, you effectively create a partial ellipse from your arc. An arc has equal primary and secondary axes; therefore, using the Modify Arc Axis command changes the length of one of the axes, thereby creating a partial ellipse. When you identify the arc, pick a point near the axis that you want modified (see fig. 8.19). Different arc sizes and definitions react differently to the Modify Arc Axis command.

Figure 8.19

The Modify Arc Axis tool.

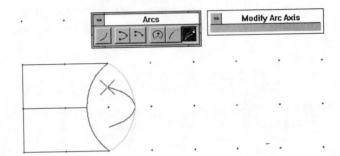

Modifying Arcs, Circles, and Ellipses with the Element Selection Tool

The Element Selection tool is used for many manipulation functions in MicroStation. This section introduces you to this tool in its capacity to modify arcs. Chapter 10 also discusses the Element Selection tool as it pertains to other element types.

The Element Selection tool is the arrow icon on the top left corner of the Main tool frame. You activate the Element Selection tool by clicking on the arrow. When you move back into the design area, you see that the cursor has changed to an arrow with a small circle at its point, similar to the one shown on the Main tool frame. If you pick an element while this tool is activated, the element shows its handles or vertices (see fig. 8.20) by highlighting them with small squares. To deselect the element, pick another element or a point in the design area in which there are no elements.

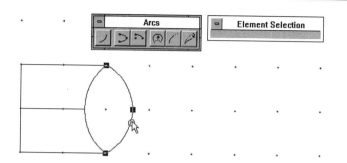

Figure 8.20

*The Element
Selection tool,
with an arc
selected.*

Modifying Arcs with the Element Selection Tool

To modify an arc angle with the Element Selection tool, press the Data button on one of the endpoint handles, drag the endpoint, and release it. The Element Selection tool modifies the angle just as the Modify Arc Angle command does.

> You can move the arc by pressing and dragging on any point that is not a handle.

Tip

To modify the radius of an arc with the Element Selection tool, press and drag on the handle showing the midpoint. The Element Selection tool modifies the radius (axes) without changing the sweep angle; in other words, the element endpoints are moved while the start and sweep angles stay the same.

In the next exercise, try using the Element Selection tool to modify existing arcs.

MODIFYING AN ARC ANGLE WITH THE ELEMENT SELECTION TOOL

Continue from the preceding exercise with the CHAP08.DGN design file open and the two previous arcs visible (or draw two arcs; see fig. 8.20).

Choose the Element Selection tool

Pick a point on the first arc   Displays handles of the arc (see fig. 8.20)

Press and drag one of the endpoints,   Changes arc angle (see fig. 8.21)
then release

Pick a point on the second arc	Displays handles of the arc
Press and drag the midpoint handle, then release	Changes arc radius and endpoints
Pick a point away from any elements	Deselects element and handles disappear

Figure 8.21

Arc angle modified with the Element Selection tool.

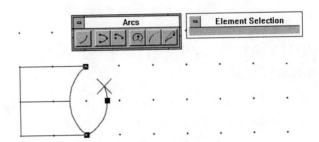

The Element Selection tool also modifies the start or sweep angles and the axes of a partial ellipse. Select the element with the Element Selection tool, and drag an endpoint to modify an angle; or drag the midpoint handle to modify or scale both axes (see fig. 8.22). The Element Selection tool modifies both axes, whereas the Modify Arc Axis command modifies only one axis at a time.

Figure 8.22

Modifying a partial ellipse.

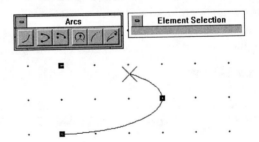

Modifying Circles and Ellipses with the Element Selection Tool

The Element Selection tool also modifies the axes of a circle or an ellipse. When you select a circle or an ellipse with the Element Selection tool, handles appear on the four axis points and on the four corners (see fig. 8.23). These handles define an imaginary box within which the circle or ellipse is inscribed. To modify one axis on the circle or ellipse, press and drag one of the handles that lie on the axis. To modify both axes, press and drag a corner handle.

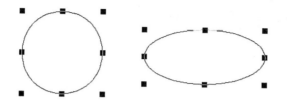

Figure 8.23

Handles of a circle and an ellipse.

Warning

Unless you use the following method, you will turn circles into ellipses.

You might not want to turn your circle into an ellipse. A circle and an ellipse are stored as the same element type (15); the distinguishing difference is that a circle has equal primary and secondary axes, whereas an ellipse doesn't. To modify a circle's radius and to keep the primary and secondary axes equal press and drag a corner handle with the cursor in a diagonal direction. With an ellipse, this scales both axes by the same factor.

In the following exercise, you use the Element Selection tool to modify a circle and an ellipse on level 9.

MODIFYING A CIRCLE AND AN ELLIPSE WITH THE ELEMENT SELECTION TOOL

Continue from the preceding exercise with the CHAP08.DGN design file open.

Make level 9 the active level, and turn off all other levels	
Place a circle and ellipse to modify	
Choose the Element Selection tool	Displays arrow and circle cursor
Select the ellipse	Displays handles of the ellipse
Press and drag the bottom middle handle, then release	Changes one axis of the ellipse
Drag the bottom left corner handle	Changes both axes as you drag
Select the circle	Displays handles of the circle
Drag one of the corner handles diagonally, away from the center	

Rounding Corners

You have two different approaches to rounding corners. One approach is to round the corners of lines and linestrings already placed in the design file using the fillet commands. The second approach involves placing the elements as a SmartLine and round the corners as you place the lines.

Fillet Commands

The Construct Circular Fillet command is a specialized arc-placement command. A *fillet* is an arc that is placed with a specific radius to round the corners at which two elements join. The arc is placed tangent to each element. Examples of applications in which you place fillets include rounding the corners of a street intersection, easing the edges of wood trim, filleting or radiusing a machine part, or rounding the corners of a gear.

Because the Circular Fillet commands require that you construct the fillet from existing elements (such as lines), they are considered to constitute an advanced form of element placement. You can open this tool box from the Tools pull-down menu by choosing Fillets (see fig. 8.24).

Figure 8.24

The Fillets tool box.

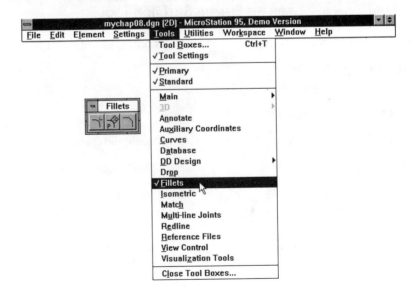

The first tool on the Fillets tool box issues the Construct Circular Fillet command. The Construct Circular Fillet command has two parameters associated with it: the **R**adius constraint and **T**runcate. The **T**runcate parameter controls the way in which the command treats the adjoining elements. The **T**runcate option menu displays three choices: **N**one, **B**oth, or **F**irst. If you choose **N**one, the adjoining elements are not modified (shortened) or extended to meet the arc. If you choose **B**oth, both elements are modified to meet the arc; if you choose **F**irst, only the first element selected is modified to meet the arc (see fig. 8.25).

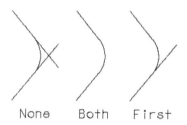

None   Both   First

Figure 8.25

Effects of the Truncate options.

In the following exercise, you create a street intersection (see fig. 8.26) and then fillet the intersection. Enter the radius in the **R**adius field, and select one of the choices from the **T**runcate option menu.

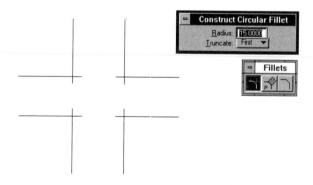

Figure 8.26

Streets to fillet.

PLACING FILLETS

Continue from the preceding exercise with the CHAP08.DGN design file open.

Make level 10 the active level, and turn off the display for all other levels

Continues

Turn on **G**rid *and* **A**xis *lock from the pop-up menu in the Status Bar*

Choose Place Line tool

Turn on the **L**ength *constraint*

Enter **50**

Turn on the **A**ngle *constraint*

Enter **0** *in* **A**ngle *field*

Place four lines, representing east/west street (see fig. 8.26)

Enter **90** *in* **A**ngle *field*

Place four lines representing north/south street (see fig. 8.26)

Choose Fit Design from the scroll bar in view 1

Turn off **A**xis *lock*

Choose **T**ools, **F**illets   Displays the Fillets tool box

Choose the Construct Circular Fillet tool

Turn on the **R**adius *constraint, clear the default value, and enter* **15**

Choose **N**one *from the* **T**runcate   Displays command name in the Status
option list   Bar as Circular Fillet (No Truncation)

Select first segment *Pick line at*   Highlights first line
① *(see fig. 8.27)*

Select second segment *Pick line*   Highlights second line and shows fillet
at ②

Accept-Initiate construction   Places fillet
Pick any point to accept placement

Choose **B**oth *from the* **T**runcate   Displays command name as Circular Fillet and
option list   Truncate Both

Select first segment *Pick line at* ③	Highlights first line
Select second segment *Pick line at* ④	Highlights second line and shows fillet with modified lines
Accept-Initiate construction *Pick point to accept placement*	Places fillet
*Choose **F**irst from the **T**runcate option list*	Displays command name as Circular Fillet and Truncate Single
Select first segment *Pick line at* ⑤	Highlights first line
Select second segment *Pick line at* ⑥	Highlights second line and shows fillet with modified first line
Accept-Initiate construction *Pick point to accept placement*	Places fillet
*Turn off **G**rid lock*	

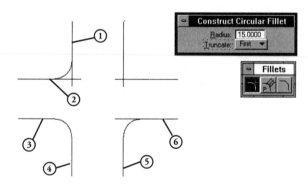

Figure 8.27

Fillets constructed.

Fillets are just a specialized way to place an arc. You can modify an arc placed using the Construct Circular Fillet tool by using any of the methods described previously: Modify Radius, Modify Angle, or Modify Axis.

Tip If you can't place the fillet between the lines with the radius you define, MicroStation displays the error message Illegal Definition in the Status Bar. Just change the radius and try the command again.

Other tools on the Fillets tool box for creating corners are the Construct Parabolic Fillet and Construct Chamfer tools. The Construct Parabolic Fillet tool is the second tool in the tool box. The command this tool issues depends on the **T**ype and T**r**uncate options you select on the tool box. The command places a curve element to round the corner.

Note Curve elements are different from arc elements. MicroStation calculates the curve from a series of points. You use the Modify Element command to modify a curve.

The Construct Chamfer command does not round the corner; it places a line element to construct a beveled edge. The options for this command are Distance **1** and Distance **2**. The first line selected is trimmed back from the intersecting point of the two lines, as defined by the Distance **1**. The second line selected is trimmed back from the intersecting point of the two lines as defined by the Distance **2**. A line element type is added to connect the two modified lines.

Tip If the chamfer is longer than the length of the lines, MicroStation displays the error message Illegal Definition in the Status Bar. Change the chamfer distance, and try the command again.

Place SmartLines with Arcs

An alternative to rounding the corners after you place the lines is to place the elements with rounded corners. Use the SmartLine tool to create linear elements with rounded or chamfered corners. Figure 8.28 was created with the SmartLine tool with **V**ertex Type set to **R**ounded and Rounding Radius set to 1.

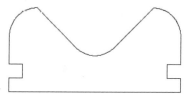

Figure 8.28

Widget with rounded corners placed with SmartLine.

The toggle button, Join Elements, in the tool settings box determines if SmartLine creates a complex element of all line segments and arcs. Turn the toggle off to create individual line segments and arcs.

Note

Using Arrays

Arrays enable you to copy an element or a group of elements multiple times in a rectangular or circular (polar) pattern. A *rectangular array* copies an element a specified number of times in the X and Y directions. A *polar array* copies an element a specified number of times around a point at a given angle.

You find the Array tool on the Manipulate tool box (see figs. 8.29). You can tear off the Manipulate tool box from the Main tool frame, or you can open this tool box from the **T**ools pull-down menu by choosing **M**ain, then Ma**n**ipulate.

Figure 8.29

The Array tool.

Rectangular Array

You use a rectangular array to place an element or a group of elements in a column and row pattern. The columns in your array reflect the number of times the element(s) is copied in the vertical, or Y direction in the Cartesian coordinate system. The rows in your array reflect the number of times the element(s) is copied in the horizontal, or X direction. The number of columns and rows and the spacing between them are defined in the tool settings box when the array command is selected (see fig. 8.30).

Figure 8.30

Rectangular Array tool settings box.

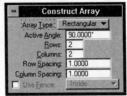

If you design the floor layout for a cafeteria, for example, you can place one table and use a rectangular array to place the other tables. In figure 8.31, the first table was placed in the lower left corner of the room and the Rectangular Array command was used to fill a room with tables (3 rows 12 master units apart and 5 columns 10 master units apart). Likewise, the four chairs were placed around the first table and were arrayed to fill the room with chairs. Incidentally, the chairs were grouped to easily array all four chairs in one operation. Later in the discussion about manipulating elements, you will learn how to group elements.

Figure 8.31

Cafeteria filled with tables and chairs with the rectangular array tool.

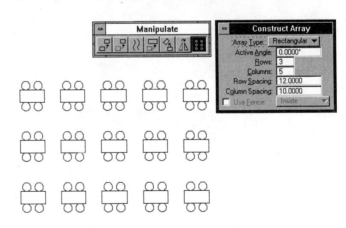

Polar Array

The Polar Array command enables you to copy an element or a group of elements a number of times at a given angle around a center point. To do a polar array, you specify the number of total items you want (including the existing element) and the delta angle between the items. See figure 8.32 for the tool settings of the polar array command.

Figure 8.32

Polar Array tool settings box.

To achieve a 360 degree array, divide the number of items into 360 for the delta angle.

Tip

You can rotate the element as it gets copied by turning on the **R**otate Items toggle button. If the toggle is off, the element is copied with its current orientation. The effects of this toggle button are shown in figure 8.33.

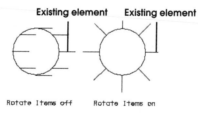

Figure 8.33

Effects of Rotate Items Toggle on polar arrays.

The Polar Array command prompts you to identify an element to copy; then it prompts you to accept the element and pick the array center point at the same time. The points you choose affect the way the command places the copies (see figs. 8.34 and 8.35).

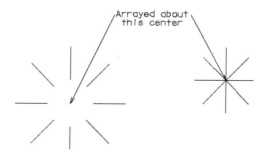

Figure 8.34

Effects of the center point.

Figure 8.35

*Effects of the
element selection
point.*

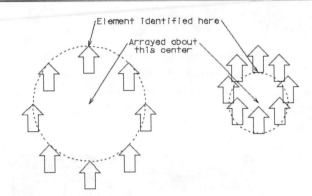

The first point identifies the element(s) and specifies the first endpoint of the array's radius and starting angle. If **R**otate Items is on, it also is the point about which the items are rotated as they are arrayed about the center point. The second point defines the center of the array and the second endpoint of the radius. See figures 8.35 and 8.36 for examples.

In the next exercise, you activate level 13, and turn off level 12 in your design file. Place a large circle and smaller one inside to represent a bolt hole in this machine part (see fig. 8.36). Use the Polar Array command to place bolt holes every 45 degrees around the circular part (see fig. 8.37).

Figure 8.36

*Starting the
mechanical
design.*

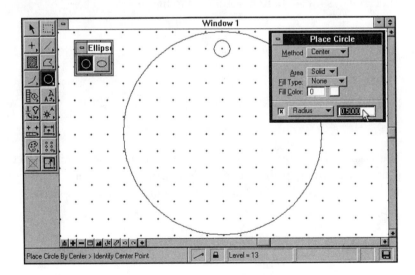

CREATING A POLAR ARRAY

Continue from the preceding exercise with the CHAP08.DGN design file open.

Make level 13 the active level, and turn off the display for all other levels	
Place a circle with a radius of 6	
Choose Fit View from the Status Bar	Fits the circle
Place a circle with a radius of .5 (refer to figure 8.36)	
Choose the Array tool	
Select Polar *from the* Array **T**ype *list*	
Enter **8** *in the* **I**tems *field*	
Enter **45** *in the* **D**elta Angle *field*	
Choose **C**enter *snap from the snap pop-up in the Status Bar while holding down the Shift key on the keyboard*	Activates center tentative
Identify element *Pick a tentative point near the center of the small bolt hole*	Highlights bolt hole
Pick any point to accept tentative location	
Accept, select center/Reject *Pick a tentative point near center of large circle*	
Pick any point to accept tentative location	Places seven bolt holes
Identify element	
Choose **K**eypoint *snap from the snap pop-up in the Status Bar while holding down the Shift key*	Activates center tentative

Figure 8.37

*Results of using
the Polar Array
command.*

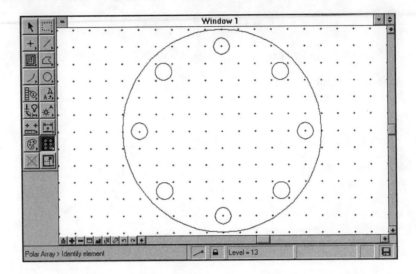

You can use arrays on a single element or on groups of elements. Chapter 9,
"Manipulating 2D Elements," discusses element grouping.

Summary

MicroStation offers many ways to place circles, ellipses, and arcs because there are
potentially many different situations when you design a drawing. If you don't know
the radius, for example, several commands can help you place circles or arcs
without defining one. As you learn MicroStation, you discover you usually have
more than one way to accomplish a task.

The specialty tools that have been discussed demonstrate MicroStation's versatility
and power. A good example is the Fillet command, which extends lines to arcs for
cleaning up an intersection and rounding the corners. You can place an arc at each
one of the corners with the Place Arc By Edge command and the **R**adius constraint;
however, this method takes four times longer, and you still have to clean up the
lines. Another alternative would be to use the SmartLine tool and create your
rounded corners as you place the linear elements. Likewise, the Array commands
represent a huge time savings for many applications.

CHAPTER 9

Manipulating 2D Elements

*T*he commands covered in this chapter are element manipulation commands: Delete, Copy, Move, Scale, Spin, Rotate, and Mirror. Each of these commands can be performed on a single element or a group of elements. Before the chapter goes into detail about each manipulation command, different methods of grouping elements are covered. As you experiment with each manipulation command, you can practice single-element manipulation and group manipulations.

In this chapter, you learn:

+ How to delete elements

+ How to use the Undo and Redo commands

+ How to manipulate multiple elements at one time

+ How to copy elements

+ How to move elements

+ How to scale elements

+ How to spin and rotate elements

+ How to mirror elements

This chapter covers manipulation commands as well as how to group elements for manipulation. The tools for the commands used in this chapter are located on the Main tool frame and several tool boxes. Two frequently used tools are also available on the Main tool frame: the Element Selection tool and the Delete Element tool.

In the discussion of grouping elements for manipulation, the Chain and Fence tool boxes are used. These tool boxes can be torn off the Main tool frame or opened with the pull-down menus.

In the last half of the chapter, the Manipulate tool box is discussed in its entirety.

 Tip   All the manipulation commands prompt you to identify an element, which is then highlighted. If your highlight color is not easily seen, such as a light gray highlight color on a white background, identifying elements might be difficult. You can change the color in which the element is highlighted by choosing **D**esign File from the **S**ettings pull-down menu. Choose Color from the **C**ategory list in the Design File Settings box and change the Element Highlight Color.

Deleting Elements

The Delete Element command was briefly discussed in Chapter 2, "Taking MicroStation for a Test Drive," and you probably have had plenty of opportunities to try this command since then. This section might point out some things you have not discovered on your own about deleting elements.

The Delete Element Command

The Delete Element tool is located on the Main tool frame. You cannot miss it because it is the only tool that appears in red. When you choose the Delete Element tool, the command prompts you to identify an element to delete. If you successfully pick an element, the element highlights and the command prompts you to accept and continue the delete process for the highlighted element or to reject it in order to pick a different element. To accept and delete the selection, you pick any other point.

Note

When you have an element identified or highlighted to delete, the MicroStation Status Bar displays the type and level of the element in the first field. This information can be extremely useful if you have any question as to which element is being manipulated.

Have you discovered that if you identify an element and give the accept point on another element, the command deletes the first element and highlights the second one? This technique saves time if you want to delete more than one element. Pick an accept point for the last element in the view away from the other elements or, if the drawing is crowded, on the same element.

Elements often share the same endpoints in a drawing. A line meets up with other lines or arcs, circles share the same center point, or lines meet a circle at the diameter. Elements that share points are highlighted in the order in which they were placed. This sometimes causes MicroStation to find a different element than the one you want. When you pick a point to identify an element and the first point you identify does not highlight the element you intended, then click the reset button and the next element placed in the file that shares the selected point is highlighted.

Note

The technique of resetting through elements is especially useful in design files that are dense with elements. You can reset as many times as necessary to get to the element you want. Of course, an alternative would be to snap or pick a tentative point to identify the element you want to manipulate. See Chapter 7 for more information about snap modes and the tentative point.

The Element Selection Tool

You have been exposed to some of the features of the Element Selection tool in Chapter 8, "Placing More 2D Elements." Another feature of the Element Selection tool is to identify elements for manipulation.

When you choose the Element Selection tool from the upper left corner of the Main tool frame and identify an element with the arrow cursor, handles appear on the element, indicating that it has been selected. To delete a selected element, you can choose the Delete Element command from the Main tool frame or press the Backspace or Delete key.

Other uses of the Element Selection tool are covered later in the chapter. See the section titled "Manipulating Multiple Elements at One Time."

Undo and Redo

If you make a mistake and delete an element you need, you can get it back without redrawing it. The Undo and Redo commands enable you to bring back the deleted element. The first section in the **E**dit pull-down menu contains the Undo and Redo commands.

Undo

The Undo command takes you back one operation or command, as if you never did that command. If you were to draw a circle and then delete it, for example, the Edit pull-down menu would display Undo Delete Element as the first option. So by choosing **E**dit, **U**ndo Delete Element, the circle you deleted would reappear. The status bar displays the message `<Delete Element> Undone`. If you want to undo the operation prior to that, choose **U**ndo again.

 *Warning*

Issuing the Compress Design command makes all changes in the design file permanent. You cannot undo any commands past the last design compression.

You can also undo all the changes you have made in a design session. The Undo All command undoes all the operations you have performed since you entered the design file or since the last design compression as long as it does not exceed the buffer. To issue the Undo All command, choose **E**dit, Undo Ot**h**er, **A**ll. This displays an Alert box with the message Do you really want to UNDO ALL CHANGES?. Choose **O**K to undo all the changes, or click on Cancel to clear the Alert box without making any changes.

The limit of the Undo command is determined by how much memory (KB) has been assigned to the undo buffer. For most situations, the default of 256 KB will be sufficient.

If the undo buffer is not large enough to store all your changes, selecting Undo All will undo only a portion of the changes.

You can change the undo buffer in the Memory Usage Category of the Preferences dialog box, which you can access by choosing **P**reference from the **W**orkspace pull-down menu. You must exit and restart MicroStation for the change to the buffer size to take effect.

Warning

Redo

The **R**edo command, as you might have guessed, will redo the effects of the Undo command. The **R**edo command can be activated by choosing it from the **E**dit pull-down or by using the Ctrl+R keyboard accelerator.

The **U**ndo and **R**edo commands in the **E**dit pull-down menu always display the command they will perform. For example, the item on the pull-down menu might say **U**ndo delete element, **U**ndo rectangular array, or **U**ndo place line.

Marking Your Place

Two other commands in the undo and redo family are Set **M**ark and **T**o Mark. You can think of the Set **M**ark command as putting a bookmark in a place you might like to go back to. Choose Set **M**ark from the **E**dit pull-down menu to place your bookmark, and use the **T**o Mark command under Undo Ot**h**er in the **E**dit menu to undo back to the bookmark.

These two commands can be useful for "what if" scenarios or if you know that you are about to do several operations that you might want to undo.

Manipulating Multiple Elements at One Time

Several methods, some permanent and some temporary, are available for grouping elements for manipulations. Before continuing with the manipulation tools, the methods of grouping elements are discussed so that you can use them to copy, move, scale, rotate, and mirror multiple elements at one time.

The first method uses the Element Selection tool to temporarily group many elements for manipulation. The **G**roup command used with the Element Selection tool can permanently group the elements in a design file or until you ungroup them.

Another method of grouping elements is Graphic Groups. Elements that have been assigned to a graphic group can be manipulated as a group or as individual elements depending on the setting of the Graphic Group lock. This is an old concept in MicroStation and it is used in some commands, such as patterning, to group elements together for easy manipulation.

Finally, the last method of grouping elements is the use of a fence. A *fence* is a temporary special-purpose shape that defines the elements for manipulating.

Note   The process of grouping linear elements into a complex shape is covered in Chapter 12. Complex elements give you another way to group elements together permanently.

Element Selection Sets

As you have seen, you can use the Element Selection tool to identify an element to delete or modify. The Element Selection tool can also be used to identify more than one element or a selection set for manipulation.

Earlier, this chapter explained how to use the Element Selection tool to identify an element and then delete it. What if you want to delete more than one element? You can select multiple elements by defining what is called a selection set. A selection set can be created with the Element Selection tool by picking additional elements individually or by defining a selection rectangle.

Tip

The Select **A**ll command found on the **E**dit pull-down menu can be used to put all the elements in your design file into a selection set.

The Select **A**ll command selects all the elements in the file, not just the elements that you see in the view.

Picking More Elements

To add other elements to a previously selected element with the Element Selection tool, hold down the Ctrl key and identify the element to add. Handles appear on each element you pick, indicating that it has been selected. Choose the Delete Element command from the Main tool frame, and all the selected elements on the selection set are deleted or hit the Backspace or Delete key on your keyboard to delete the elements.

You can also use the Ctrl key to deselect elements from the selection set. With the Ctrl key held down, deselect an element that is currently in the selection set by clicking on it again.

Note

If two elements that share the same handles are selected, the handle shared by the two elements is not displayed.

In the following exercise, try picking each element with the Ctrl key held down to add it to the selection set.

SELECTING MULTIPLE ELEMENTS WITH THE
ELEMENT SELECTION TOOL

Create a design file titled CHAP09.DGN.

Place the elements shown in figure 9.1

Choose the Element Selection tool

Continues

Pick the upper right box (see fig. 9.1)	Selects box and displays four corner handles
Press and hold the Ctrl key during the following steps	
Pick the lower left box	Selects box and displays four corner handles
Pick the lower left box again	Deselects box from selection set
Pick circle, then release the Ctrl key	Selects circle and displays eight handles
Press the Delete *command*	Circle and box on right are deleted
Choose **E**dit, *then* **U**ndo	

Figure 9.1

The selection set includes box and circle.

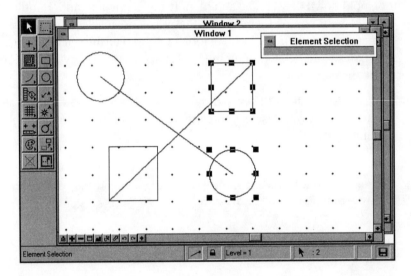

Note   Notice the arrow icon in the lower right corner of the Status Bar in figure 9.1. It indicates that a selection set is active and contains two elements.

Defining a Range for Selection

The Element Selection tool can also be used to select multiple elements with a selection rectangle. The Element Selection tool rectangle selects all the elements that fall completely inside or all the elements inside and touching the rectangle. Pick a point and drag in the view with the Element Selection tool and the temporary rectangle is shown on your screen. Drag the rectangle over the elements and when you release the data button, all elements completely contained inside the rectangle are selected.

In design files dense with elements, dragging a selection rectangle might get more elements than you want. For this reason, there is another feature to select elements inside the rectangle or any that touch the rectangle. Hold Ctrl+Shift down before you release the data button and all the elements partly inside or touching the rectangle are selected. This enables you to select multiple elements without entirely enclosing them in the selection rectangle.

When you use the rectangle function, be sure you pick the first corner point away from any elements or you will select an element instead of getting the rectangle.

After elements are selected, you can delete all the elements in one operation by choosing the Delete Element command or by pressing the Backspace or Delete key.

> You can lock an element or elements to prevent them from being moved or modified. To lock elements, select the elements with the Element Selection tool and choose Loc**k** from the **E**dit pull-down menu. If you attempt to modify a locked element with the Element Selection tool, MicroStation beeps and displays `Element is locked or in Reference file` in the Status Bar. If you attempt to modify a locked element with the Element Modification tools, the element will not highlight and `Element not found` is displayed in the Status Bar.
>
> To unlock elements, select the locked elements with the Element Selection tool and choose Unl**o**ck from the **E**dit pull-down menu.

Tip

In the next exercise, select the elements again but this time use the range selection feature.

Selecting a Range of Elements with the Element Selection Tool

Continue from the preceding exercise with the CHAP09.DGN design file open.

Choose the Element Selection tool

Press and hold at point ① *(see fig. 9.2), then drag toward* ②	Displays selection rectangle
Release the data button at ②	Selects and displays handles on all the elements inside the rectangle
Choose the Delete Element command	Deletes all elements
Choose **E***dit, then* **U***ndo delete element, or press Ctrl+Z*	Restores all elements

Figure 9.2

All the elements selected.

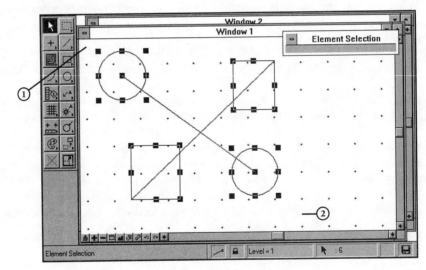

Note   If two elements share the same handles, as the boxes and line do in the preceding exercise, the handles will appear when only one of the elements is selected. If both elements are selected, no handles are displayed in the view.

Combining the two selection methods, the rectangle and the Ctrl+pick method, is a useful technique. Some design files can be quite dense, which makes it difficult to select elements with a rectangle, and time-consuming to select each element individually. Use the selection rectangle and then pick the elements that you want to add to or delete from the selection set while holding the Ctrl key down.

In the following exercise, you delete only the shapes and circles and leave the lines by combining the two selection methods.

SELECTING A RANGE OF ELEMENTS WITH THE ELEMENT SELECTION TOOL

Continue from the preceding exercise with the CHAP09.DGN design file open.

Choose the Element Selection tool

Press and hold at point ① *(see fig. 9.3), drag to ②,* *and release*	Selects and displays handles on all the elements inside the rectangle
Hold down the Ctrl key during the next two steps	
Pick a point at ③	Deselects line and its handles disappear
Pick a point on second line at ④, *then release the Ctrl key*	Displays handles on box corners, indicating that the line has been deselected
Choose Delete Element	Deletes shape and circle elements, leaving only lines
*Press Ctrl+Z, or choose **E**dit, then* ***U**ndo delete element*	

Figure 9.3

Deselecting lines from the selection set.

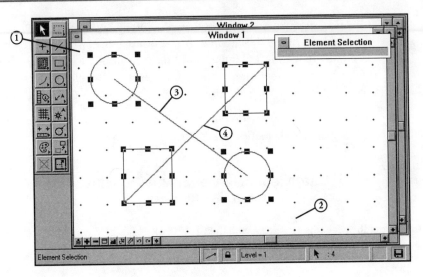

Deselecting Elements

To deselect a selection set, pick a point anywhere in the view away from any of the elements. Picking a point on an element deselects the current selection set and places the element in a new selection set.

Grouping

The selection sets described earlier are temporary. If you want to identify a different selection set, the first selection set is deselected. You can make a selection set permanent by choosing **G**roup from the **E**dit pull-down menu. The handles that appear for the group are no longer the element's individual handles, but eight handles showing you the outer extents of the group (see fig. 9.4). A group is permanently defined in the design file and is referred to as an orphan cell. You can exit MicroStation and reenter the design file, and the elements are still grouped together.

After elements have been grouped, they can only be manipulated as a group. Each time you select one of the elements in the group with any manipulation tool, you get the whole group. To manipulate the elements individually, you must ungroup the elements. To ungroup the elements, select the group with the Element Selection tool and choose U**n**group from the **E**dit pull-down menu.

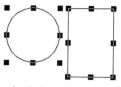
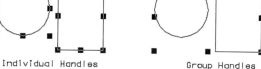

Individual Handles   Group Handles

Figure 9.4

Individual and group handles.

Group and **Un**group are only available in the **E**dit pull-down menu when a selection set is active.   *Note*

Try creating a group from a selection set in the following exercise.

GROUPING ELEMENTS WITH THE ELEMENT SELECTION TOOL

Continue from the preceding exercise with the CHAP09.DGN design file open.

Choose the Element Selection tool	
Pick the right box at ① *(see fig. 9.5)*	Selects box
Hold down the Ctrl key	
Pick bottom right circle at ②	Adds circle to selection set
Release the Ctrl key	
Choose **E**dit, *then* **G**roup	Displays eight handles that represent the extents of the group (see fig. 9.5)
Pick point away from elements	Deselects all elements
Pick one of the elements of the group	Redisplays handles for group
Choose Delete Element command	Deletes group
Choose **E**dit, *then* **U**ndo delete element	Restores group
Pick one of the elements of the group	Redisplays handles for group
Choose **E**dit, *then* **Un**group	Displays individual handles of box and circle

Figure 9.5

*Grouping the
shape and circle
elements.*

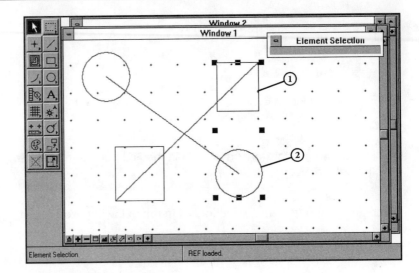

Graphic Groups

The graphic group concept is the grouping method that MicroStation uses in commands like patterning. Take a crosshatch pattern, for example: All the lines that make up the crosshatch are defined as a graphic group. The graphic group acts as a group or as individual elements, depending on the status of the Graphic Group lock. MicroStation creates graphic groups, and you can, too. If there are elements that you want to manipulate as a group, you can add and drop individual elements as you see fit.

Graphic Group differs from a selection set group in that you have the choice of manipulating the group or individual elements in the group based on the lock setting. Remember selection set groups can only be manipulated as groups.

Graphic groups can be manipulated with Copy, Move, Scale, and so on, in the same way as the delete operation demonstrated earlier.

Graphic Group Lock

The Graphic Group lock setting determines whether the group is manipulated as a whole or as individual pieces. You can turn Graphic Group lock on and off in the Lock Toggles settings box or the Lock settings box by choosing Locks from the Settings pull-down menu or by choosing the lock icon in the Status Bar. The effects of Graphic Group lock are illustrated in the following exercise.

Add to a Graphic Group

You can add elements to an existing graphic group, create new graphic groups, or drop elements from a graphic group. Tools for the Add to Graphic Group command and the Drop from Graphic Group command (see fig. 9.6) are located on the Main tool frame or on the Groups tool box.

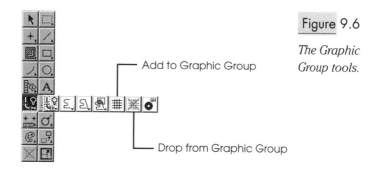

Add to Graphic Group

Drop from Graphic Group

Figure 9.6

The Graphic Group tools.

To add elements to a new or existing graphic group, identify the element or graphic group first and then each element you want to add. You are prompted to accept or reject each element you are adding. The Add to Graphic Group command functions like the Delete Element command in that you can give the accept point for one element and select the next element with the same data point.

Create a drawing of a desk, chair, and computer as shown in figure 9.7 for the next exercise on level 2. In the next exercise you will try the Graphic Group command by grouping the elements of the chair. Once grouped you will see the effects Graphic Group lock has on the chair.

CREATING AND MANIPULATING A GRAPHIC GROUP

Continue from the preceding exercise with the CHAP09.DGN design file open.

Set the active level to 2

Turn off the display for level 1

Clears the view of elements to begin this exercise

Place the elements shown in fig. 9.7

Choose the Add to Graphic Group command from the Main tool frame

Continues

`Identify element` *Pick one of the elements of the chair*	Highlights the element
`Add to existing group (Accept/ Reject)` *Pick a point on another element*	Highlights the element
Continue to select all the elements of the chair until the last element is highlighted.	
`Accept/Reject (select next input)` *Pick a point away from any other elements*	Adds the element to the graphic group
Choose Delete Element	
`Identify element` *Pick an element*	Highlights only one element
`Accept/Reject (select next input)` *Click the reset button*	
Choose Graphic Group lock from the Status Bar lock pop-up menu	
Choose Delete Element	
`Identify element` *Pick an element*	Highlights the graphic group
`Accept/Reject (select next input)` *Pick a point*	Deletes all the elements of the graphic group
Choose Edit, then Undo delete element	Chair is displayed

Figure 9.7

Graphic Group your office furniture.

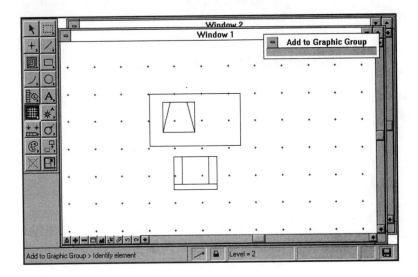

A quick way to create a graphic group would be to use the Element Selection tool. Select all the elements you want to group together with the Element Selection tool, create a group of the elements by choosing Group from the **Edit** pull-down menu. Select the Add to Graphic Group command and identify one of the elements you just grouped. Finally, choose Drop Complex, which drops the complex status on the elements. All the elements are assigned the graphic group number.

Tip

Drop from Graphic Group

When you drop elements from a graphic group, you select the group and all the elements are dropped. After a graphic group has been dropped, the elements can be manipulated separately regardless of the lock setting.

The Drop from Graphic Group command permanently drops the elements from the group in the design file. If you want to manipulate one element of a graphic group, turn off Graphic Group lock. Do not drop the elements from the graphic group needlessly. To get the group back could be tedious because you have to select each piece with the Add to Graphic Group command.

Warning

Fences

Fences are the last method of grouping elements for manipulation. A *fence* is a block or shape that temporarily groups the elements for manipulations. The fences give you effects similar to those of the Element selection tool rectangle, but they have more options.

The Place Fence tool (see fig. 9.8) can be found on the Main tool frame. Tear off the tools from the Main tool frame to activate the Fence tool box, or choose **F**ence from the pop-up menu by choosing **T**ools, then **M**ain.

Delete Fence Contents

Figure 9.8

Fence tools.

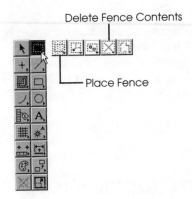

Place Fence

To use a fence for element manipulation, you must first define or place a fence. There are six different types of fences; see table 9.1 for a description of each.

Table 9.1

Fence Type Choices

Fence Type	Result
Block	Works just like the Place Block command—two opposite corners define the block
Shape	Similar to the Place Shape command in which a maximum of 101 points define the sides of the fence
Circle	Similar to the Place Circle—identify a center point and a point on the diameter
Element	Identify an existing element and a fence will be placed exactly on top
From **V**iew	Choose the view and a fence will be placed around the edge
From **D**esign File	Choose the active design, all attached files, or choose an element of a file to create a fence boundary of the elements in the view

Tip

When you are placing a fence with the shape type, the tool settings box includes a button that automatically closes a fence shape. Choose the **C**lose Fence button and MicroStation closes the fence shape you have started.

The elements that are affected by the fence manipulation depend on the **Fence** Mode selected in the tool settings box. Pick the Fence Mode pop-up field and see table 9.2 for a description of each choice. See figure 9.9 for a graphic representation of each fence mode. In figure 9.9, the heavy line represents the location of the fence. The thin dashed lines indicate what elements or what parts of the elements are effected during a manipulation command with the specified fence mode.

Table 9.2

Fence Mode Field Choices

Fence Mode	Effect
Inside	Elements entirely inside the fence are manipulated
Overlap	Elements inside or touching the fence outline are manipulated
Clip	Elements inside, or the portions of elements inside, the fence outline are manipulated
Void	Elements completely outside the fence are manipulated
Voi**d**-Overlap	Elements outside the fence or touching the fence outline are manipulated
Void-C**l**ip	Elements outside, or the portions of elements outside, the fence outline are manipulated

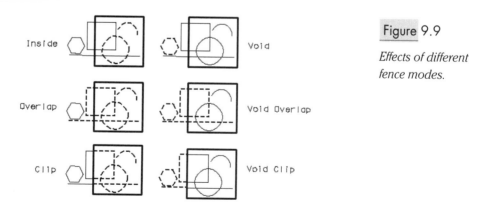

Figure 9.9

Effects of different fence modes.

Delete Fence Contents has its own tool on the Fence tool box so that you don't accidentally delete the contents of the fence when your intent is to delete one element. Choose the tool and MicroStation prompts you to delete the fence contents. One click anywhere on the screen deletes all the elements defined by the fence and fence mode setting.

 Warning

During a fence manipulation, if you click the reset button while the Status Bar is displaying Processing Fence Contents, the process will abort and only a portion of the fence contents will be manipulated. You can change this reset feature in the Operation Category of the Preferences dialog box. See Chapter 19 for more information.

Only one fence outline can be active at a time. To remove a fence, choose any of the Place Fence commands and the previous fence disappears.

In the next exercise, try placing a fence and deleting the fence contents.

DELETING FENCE CONTENTS

Continue from the preceding exercise with the CHAP09.DGN design file open.

Choose the Place Fence tool

*Choose **F**ence Type: **B**lock*

Enter first point *Pick point* ① (*see fig. 9.10*)   Starts fence block

Enter opposite corner *Pick point* ②   Places fence block

Choose Delete Fence Contents

Choose Fence **M**ode: **I**nside

Accept/Reject Fence Content   Deletes elements wholly contained within
Pick a point anywhere in the view   fence (see fig. 9.11)

*Choose **E**dit, then **U**ndo delete   Restores elements previously deleted
fence contents*

Choose **F**ence Mode: **O**verlap

`Accept/Reject Fence Contents` *Pick a point anywhere in the view*	Deletes elements within or overlapping fence—note desk was placed as a block element (see fig. 9.12)
Choose **E**dit, *then* **U**ndo delete fence contents	Restores elements previously deleted

Choose **F**ence Mode: **C**lip

`Accept/Reject Fence Contents` *Pick a point anywhere in the view*	Deletes elements and portions of elements within fence (see fig. 9.13)
Choose **E**dit, *then* **U**ndo delete fence contents	Restores elements previously deleted
Choose the Place Fence Block command	Removes fence outline

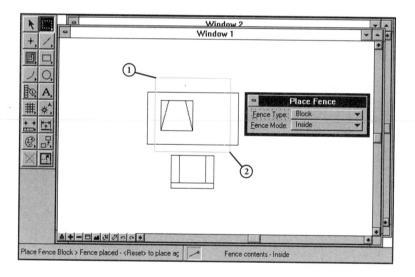

Figure 9.10

Placing the fence.

Figure 9.11

*Deleting with the
Inside Fence
Mode.*

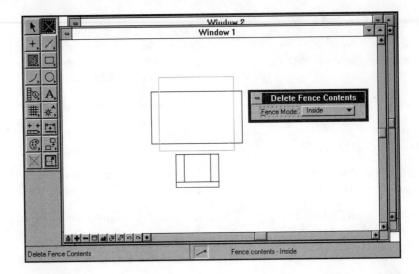

Figure 9.12

*Deleting with the
Overlap Fence
Mode.*

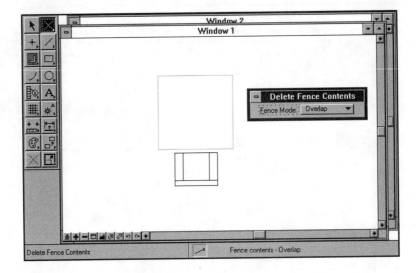

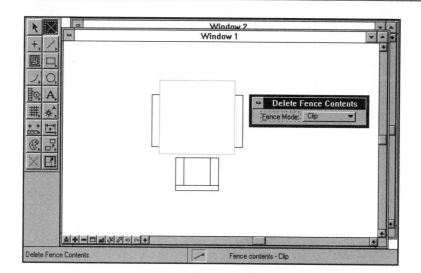

Figure 9.13

*Deleting with the
Clip Fence Mode.*

The undo buffer might not be big enough to undo some large fence manipulations. It is always a good idea to back up the file before doing massive changes on your design.

Warning

It is good practice not to leave any of the void fence modes active. If you choose one of the void fence modes to do element manipulation, you should always activate inside, overlap, or clip after you have completed the operation. Leaving a void fence mode active can have disastrous effects if you choose a fence manipulation command and do not check the mode setting.

For example, what if you fence a small area to delete and the void fence mode is active? All the elements outside the fence would be deleted. In a large design, the undo buffer might not be large enough to completely undo this operation, and elements would be lost.

If you find it difficult to select the elements you want with a fence, use the Element Selection tool to select the elements with a rectangle and Ctrl+pick any element you do not want in the selection set.

Copying Elements

The tool for the Copy Element command is the default on the Main tool frame and the first tool on the Manipulate tool box (see fig. 9.14). Open the Manipulate tool box for the remainder of this chapter by tearing it off the Main tool frame or by choosing the Ma**n**ipulate item on the **M**ain pop-up menu under **T**ools.

Figure 9.14

The Manipulate tool box.

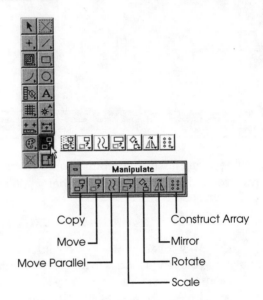

Copy

Move

Move Parallel

Construct Array

Mirror

Rotate

Scale

The Copy Element Command

Copy Element is the first tool on the Manipulate tool box. To copy one element, choose the tool and identify the element you want to copy. A copy of the element appears on the cursor. Pick a point to place the copy. Picking additional data points places additional copies. Clicking the reset button removes the element from your cursor and resets the command to begin again, prompting you to identify an element to copy.

Notice that the point you pick to identify an element to copy becomes the first point of the copy displacement used when the new element is placed. In the interest of saving time, identify the element at a point that has a logical relationship to the second point you will pick to place the copy. Otherwise, the copied element has to be moved later. For example, if you are copying a circle, you might identify the circle at its center so the copy can be placed by picking the new circle's center.

Tip

Remember the snap locks and how to use the tentative point discussed in earlier chapters? Now is the time to put these techniques to work for accurate selection and placement.

Try copying the chair in the following exercise. The chair is treated as one element with the copy command because it is a graphic group and the Graphic Group lock is on.

COPYING AN ELEMENT

Continue from the preceding exercise with the CHAP09.DGN design file open.

Tear off the Manipulate
tool box and choose Copy Element

`Identify Element` *Pick a*
point at ①   Highlights element of chair

`Accept/Reject (select next input)`   Places chair (see fig. 9.15)
Pick any point at ②

Click the reset button

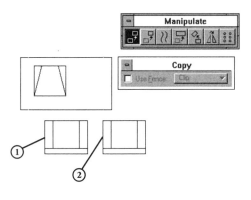

Figure 9.15

The copied chair.

Tip   You can use the same copy command to copy a single element, a selection set, a graphic group, or the contents of a fence. You can also use the **C**opy command to copy elements in a selection set and then paste the elements. Choose the Element Selection tool and identify the element(s), then choose **C**opy from the **E**dit pull-down menu. The elements are copied into a buffer and are ready to be pasted in. After you choose **P**aste from the **E**dit pull-down menu, the copied selection set appears in the view, move the new selection set to the desired location by pressing and dragging on any element, not on a handle.

You can also use **C**opy and **P**aste between files. Activate an element selection and choose **C**opy from the **E**dit pull-down menu. Open a new design file, and choose **P**aste from the **E**dit pull-down menu. The element selection appears on your cursor.

If you use the Element Selection tool to preselect elements, it allows only one iteration of the manipulation commands. After the manipulation, the Element Selection tool is reactivated. If you want multiple copies of multiple elements, consider using a fence instead of the Element Selection tool.

Moving Elements

The Move Element command is issued by the second tool on the Manipulate tool box. This command has the same features as the Copy Element command: you can move an element, a selection set, a graphic group, or the contents of a fence.

To use the Move Element command, identify the element or elements to move by picking a data point. The point you give to identify the element is the same point used to place the moved element. You can continue to pick points after you have selected the element to move it again and again. The selected element remains on your cursor until you click the reset button. In the next exercise, move the computer on the desk with a selection set.

Moving Elements with a Selection Set

Continue from the preceding exercise with the CHAP09.DGN design file open.

Choose the Element Selection tool

Press and drag the selection rectangle to   Displays handles on all elements on the table
include all the elements of the computer

Choose the Move Element tool

Identify element *Pick point* (see fig. 9.16)	Identifies the line and drags it with the cursor
Accept/Reject (select next input) *Pick point*	Moves the computer
Pick a point away from any elements to deselect the selection set	

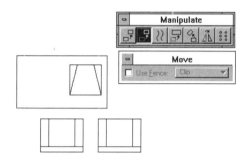

Figure 9.16

The moved computer.

In the next exercise, try placing a fence around the two chairs and moving them to better fit behind the desk.

Always check the fence mode setting before doing any fence manipulations, so there are no surprises. You can set the mode in any command that functions with a fence in the tool settings box.

Tip

MOVING ELEMENTS WITH A FENCE

Continue from the preceding exercise with the CHAP09.DGN design file open.

Choose Place Fence	
Choose Fence Type Block	
Pick two points to place fence around the two chairs	
Choose the Move Element tool	Displays Move Element in Status Bar
Turn on Use **F**ence	Displays Move Fence Contents in Status Bar
Set the mode to Inside	

Continues

Define origin *Pick point*	Picks up a fence point and displays fence outline on the cursor
Define distance *Pick point*	Moves all elements contained in fence block (see fig. 9.17)
Turn off Use **F**ence	
Choose Place Fence	Removes fence

Figure 9.17

*Moving the chairs
with a fence.*

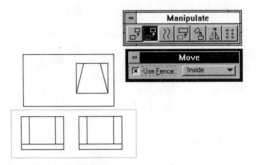

Tip The Element Selection tool has a built-in move function. You do not have to choose the Move Element command to move a selection set, although that method also works. To move elements in a selection set without selecting the Move command, drag an element of the selection set (but not on a handle). Dragging on a handle, remember, will modify the element.

Parallel Command

The next tool on the tool box is the Parallel command (see fig. 9.18). You can use this command to move an element parallel to the existing element or to copy an element parallel. If the **M**ake Copy button is on, the tool issues the Copy Parallel command; otherwise, it issues Move Parallel. In addition, you can enter a **D**istance constraint to move or copy parallel by a specified distance. After identifying the element to copy or move parallel, pick an accept point to define the direction or side to which to move or copy the element.

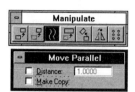

Figure 9.18

Clicking on the Parallel tool button in the Manipulate toolbox displays the Move Parallel dialog box.

The command name displayed in the Status Bar changes based on what constraints are set for the Parallel commands. With all the constraints off, the command name is Move Parallel by Distance. If the **M**ake Copy toggle is on, the command name is Copy Parallel by Distance. If the **D**istance toggle is on, the command name is Copy Parallel by Key-in.

> You cannot copy or move elements parallel using a fence or the selection set with this command. This type of manipulation can be accomplished using the Move Element or Copy Element command with AccuDraw.

Note

An example of using the Copy Parallel by Key-in Distance command is demonstrated in figures 9.19 and 9.20. Start by placing one line under Date (see fig. 9.19) and then copy parallel to complete the title block. The command Distance and Make Copy constraints are both turned on. The original element is identified at ① (see fig. 9.20) then, picking a data point ② above the original line made a copy under Project Name and additional data points ③ and ④ place lines below the original to complete the title block.

```
┌─────────────────────────────┐
│                             │
│    XYZ Company              │
│                             │
├─────────────────────────────┤
│ Project Name:               │
├─────────────────────────────┤
│ Date:                       │
├─────────────────────────────┤
│ Drawn By:                   │
├─────────────────────────────┤
│ Approved By:                │
└─────────────────────────────┘
```

Figure 9.19

An incomplete title block.

Figure 9.20

*The completed
title block.*

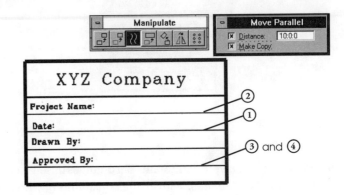

Figure 9.21

Scaling Elements

Occasionally, you might find that you placed an element at the incorrect size or that you need two copies of the element at different sizes. The Scale Element tool located on the Manipulate tool box can scale an original element, or it can scale a copy while leaving the original element in place (see fig. 9.21). You can also scale a single element, scale the contents of a fence, scale a selection set, or scale elements to be pasted into the design file.

*Clicking on the
Scale Element tool
button displays
the Scale dialog
box.*

The **X** Scale and **Y** Scale in the tool box indicate scale factors. You can double the size of an existing element by setting the **X** and **Y** Scale to 2. To scale down an element or a group of elements, use a decimal point value less than 1 in the **X** and **Y** Scale field, such as .5 to scale to half the size. You can scale an element proportionally or with different X and Y scales.

Tip

When the lock icon next to the scale fields is in the closed position, any value entered in the **X** or **Y** scale fields automatically changes the other to ensure proportional scaling.

When the lock is in the open position, you can enter different values for **X** Scale and **Y** Scale. Open or close the lock by clicking on the lock icon.

The point from which you identify the element or elements is the point from which it is scaled. So, as in the other manipulation commands, you want to pay particular attention to the point on the element you select, or you might need to move the element after you scale it. That just adds another step needlessly.

When you use fences and selection sets with the Scale command, the contents and the relative distance between elements are scaled. Fence and selection set scaling can be useful for scaling an entire drawing or creating a scaled-up copy for a blow-out or detail.

In the next exercise, create a loveseat for your office by scaling the chair. To do this, we will set an unproportional scale. The X scale will be 2 to increase the length of the seat and the Y scale will be 1 to maintain the cushion size. Graphic group lock should still be on from the previous exercises. If not, your chair will not copy and scale correctly in the following exercise.

SCALING AN ELEMENT

Continue from the preceding exercise with the CHAP09.DGN design file open.

Choose the Scale tool

*Pick **M**ethod Active **S**cale*

Pick the lock icon in the Tool Settings box　　　Lock opens

Enter 2 *in **X** Scale field*

*Verify **Y** Scale is 1*

*Pick Make **C**opy*　　　　　　　　　Toggle is on

Make sure that G**r**aphic Group lock is on in the pop-up menu from the Status Bar.

`Identify element` *Pick point (see fig. 9.22)*　　Highlights element of the chair at ①

`Enter origin point (point to scale about)`　Scales chair elements, copies, and positions
Pick point at ②　　　　　　　　　　loveseat

Click the reset button

Figure 9.22

*Creating a
loveseat by
scaling a chair.*

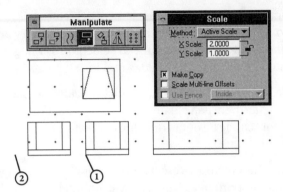

Rotating and Spinning Elements

The Rotate and Spin commands are both issued by the same tool in the Manipulate tool box (see fig. 9.23); which command is issued depends on the setting of the **M**ethod pop-up menu. If the Method is set to Active Angle the element(s) are rotated at the angle specified in the key-in field. If the Method is set to 2 points, after identifying the element(s) you are prompted to define a pivot point for a free-hand rotation, with no set angle. Spinning an element requires three data points: one to identify the element, one to pick a pivot point to rotate about, and one to define the rotation and place the element.

Figure 9.23

*Clicking on the
Rotate/Spin
Element tool
button displays
the Rotate dialog
box.*

Note   Remember that all of the manipulation commands, with the exception of the Parallel command, can be performed on an element, a graphic group, a selection set, or the contents of a fence.

SPINNING BY 2 POINTS

Continue from the preceding exercise with the CHAP09.DGN design file open.

Choose the Rotate/Spin tool

Choose **M**ethod **2** points

Identify Element *Pick point on the loveseat at* ① 　　　　 All the elements of the loveseat highlight because they are a graphic group and Graphic Group lock is on.

Enter Pivot point (point to rotate about) *Pick point at* ② *(see fig. 9.24)*

Enter point to define amount of rotation *Pick point at* ③ 　　　　 Places elements (see fig. 9.24)

Click the reset button

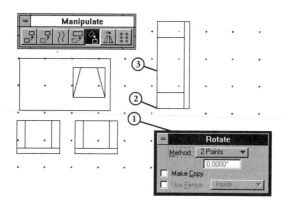

Figure 9.24

Spinning the loveseat.

Rotate an element or group of elements by choosing the Active **A**ngle **M**ethod. Rotating an element requires only two points: one to identify the element, and one to accept and place the element(s). Try rotating all the office furniture by 90 degrees with a fence in the next exercise.

Rotating Fence Contents

Continue from the preceding exercise with the CHAP09.DGN design file open.

Place a fence around all the furniture

Choose the Rotate/Spin tool

Choose Active **A**ngle *from the* **M**ethod *pop-up menu*

Enter **90** *in the field*

Pick Use **F**ence *toggle button*

Enter pivot point (point to rotate about) *Pick point at* ① *(see fig. 9.25)*	Rotates fence contents 90° about the point given

Click the reset button

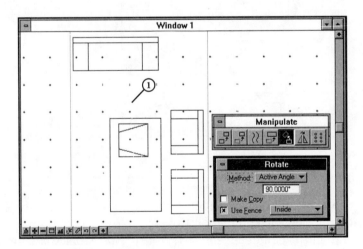

Figure 9.25

The rotated furniture.

Mirroring Elements

Several varieties of Mirror Element commands are issued by one tool in the Manipulate Tool Box (see fig. 9.26), depending on the Mirror **A**bout and pop-up menu setting.

Figure 9.26

Clicking on the Mirror Element tool button displays the Mirror dialog box.

You can mirror elements about a vertical line, a horizontal line, or a user-defined line. Either using a fence or a group or as individual elements. Use a fence in the following exercise to place additional chairs on the other side of the desk.

MIRRORING FENCE CONTENTS VERTICALLY

Continue from the preceding exercise with the CHAP09.DGN design file open.

Place a fence around the desk chairs

*Choose Mirror, set Mirror **A**bout to* Vertical, *and make sure* Use **F**ence *is on*

Issues Mirror Fence Cont About Vert (Orig.)

*Choose **M**ake Copy toggle*

`Accept/Reject Fence Contents` *Pick point at* ① *(see fig. 9.27)*

Mirrors fence contents

Click the reset button

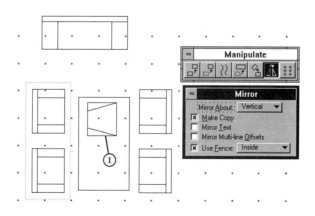

Figure 9.27

Mirroring the chairs about a vertical line.

Summary

You have learned a substantial number of commands for element and group manipulation. The element grouping methods make the manipulation commands even more versatile. Permanent groups can be made by grouping elements of a selection set or with Graphic Groups. Both of these methods are permanent, the difference being that a graphic group can be manipulated as a group or as individual elements depending on the graphic group lock setting. You will see more about graphic groups in future chapters, where MicroStation creates the groups for you. Finally, fences offer a variety of placement modes to "get what you want" on the fly and are not permanent in the design file.

MicroStation probably has fewer commands for placing elements than for manipulating and modifying existing elements. Remember that using the grouping tools in conjunction with the manipulation tools creates all kinds of possibilities.

Modifying 2D Elements

*T*his chapter explains and illustrates how you can modify existing elements in your design file. Often, elements placed on drawings or maps need to be changed after the designer or an engineer-in-charge looks at the plan.

You have seen most of the element placement commands and the manipulation commands in the previous chapters. Now the modification commands covered in this chapter enable you to change the geometry of those elements. You can modify linear elements (such as lines, line strings, and arcs) or closed shapes (such as blocks, circles, and ellipses). You can also modify an element's attributes or symbology, such as level, weight, color, and line style.

In this chapter, you learn

♦   *How to modify and change lines and shapes*

♦   *How to extend lines, modifying the line length while maintaining the angle*

♦   *How to delete part of an element*

♦   *How to insert and delete vertices on lines and shapes*

♦ How to change the attributes of an existing element or elements

♦ How to get information on an element to display and how to change the attributes

Note   Elements that have been chained or grouped together with the Complex Chain or Complex Shape commands can also be manipulated with the tools discussed in this chapter. See Chapter 12 for more details on complex elements.

Two tool boxes are discussed in this chapter: Modify and Change Attributes. Each tool box can be torn off the Main tool frame or opened from the Tools pull-down menu.

Changing or Modifying Lines and Shapes

MicroStation offers two ways for you to freely modify the endpoints or vertices of existing elements with no constraints. The Modify Element command enables you to pick any vertex or endpoint and move it to a new location to modify the element. Also, the Element Selection tool has its own built-in features for modifying vertices or handles.

The Modify Element Command

The tool for the Modify Element command can be chosen from the Main tool frame or from the Modify tool box (see fig. 10.1). You can open this tool box by tearing it off the Main palette or by choosing Modify from the Main submenu in the Tools pull-down menu.

The Modify Element command performs differently depending on the element type you are modifying. If you identify a circle, for example, the command modifies the radius. If you identify a line, the nearest endpoint is selected for a new location. The reaction of the command on some element types depends on where you identify the element. For example, if you pick a point on a block vertex, the block is modified and retains the right angles of the rectangle but if you choose the block on one side, it is turned into a parallelogram. Review table 10.1 to see how this command modifies each element type.

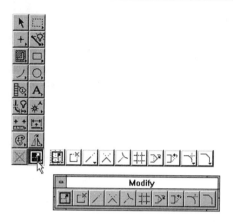

Figure 10.1

The Modify tool box.

Table 10.1

Modify Element Functions by Element Type

Element Type	Modify Element Command Action
Lines	Modifies nearest endpoint
Line strings	Modifies vertex or moves line segment
Blocks	Modifies size or changes to parallelogram
Shapes	Modifies vertex or moves shape side
Circles	Modifies radius
Ellipses	Modifies nearest axis
Arcs	Modifies radius and endpoints
Half ellipses	Modifies axis
Quarter ellipses	Modifies axis

Choose the Modify Element command from the tool box and pick a point to iden-tify the element. The closest vertex will be used by the command as the point to modify. To modify a line, for example, imagine a midpoint and identify a point anywhere on the half closest to the endpoint you want to modify. The command highlights the element and locates the nearest endpoint on the element. The vertex to be modified appears on your cursor; the element changes as you drag the cursor. Pick a point, and the changed element displays highlighted in the view.

The endpoint continues to be modified until you click the reset button. If you do not like the change you made, choose **U**ndo modify element from the **E**dit pull-down.

Tip   Throughout this chapter, and in your own work, be sure to utilize the tentative points to snap whenever appropriate. Snap, for example, to modify the endpoint of a line to join another element. If you snap you can be sure the elements meet at the same location, not short or overlapped.

Like the manipulation commands covered in the preceding chapter, all the modify commands display the element type and level selected in the Status Bar. You can use techniques for identifying elements in a dense file, such as resetting until the element you want highlights, with all the modification tools.

Create a design file called CHAP10.DGN and place a line, block, and an orthogonal shape as shown in figure 10.2. At the end of the chapter you will have a site plan that looks something like figure 10.25. In the next exercise, try modifying your first element, a line.

Figure 10.2

The basic design.

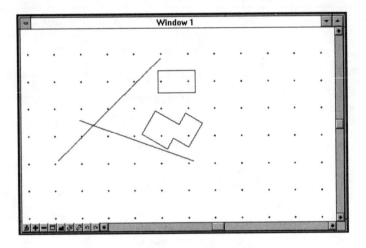

MODIFYING A LINE

Create a design titled CHAP10.DGN design file to be used for the exercises in this chapter.

Draw two lines, a block, and an orthogonal shape as shown in figure 10.2

Tear off the Modify tool box,
then choose the Modify Element *tool*

`Identify element` *Pick a point on the line near end* ①   Grabs nearest endpoint and drags line

`Accept/Reject (select next input)` *Pick a point at ② (see fig. 10.3)*	Places endpoint, but continues dragging
`Accept/Reject (select next input)` *Click the reset button*	Accepts new placement of line
`Identify element`	

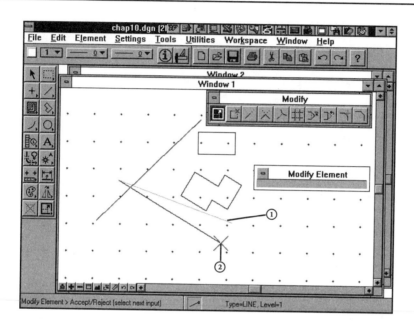

Figure 10.3

Modify line.

If you want to modify the endpoint of a line and maintain the current angle, use one of the Extend Line commands covered in the next section of this chapter.

Tip

A block is simply a shape element that happens to be orthogonal (all corners at 90°). The Modify Element command recognizes and maintains blocks as orthogonal shapes when you modify them by identifying a vertex, providing the Orthogonal toggle is on in the tool settings box. The proportions of other regular geometric shapes, such as polygons, are not maintained and are distorted by the Modify Element command. Try modifying the two blocks in the following exercise with the Orthogonal toggle on and off to see the different effects of the Modify Element command.

Modifying a Block

Continue from the preceding exercise with the CHAP10.DGN design file open.

Choose the Modify Element tool

`Identify element` *Pick a point near the top right corner of the rectangle* ① *(see fig. 10.4)*	Highlights and drags block

Verify that the Orthogonal constraint is on

`Accept/Reject (select next input)` *Pick a point* ②	Modifies block
`Accept/Reject (select next input)` *Click the reset button*	Accepts modification of block

Turn the Orthogonal constraint off

`Identify element` *Pick a point on the block vertex*	Highlights and drags vertex of block Note the orthogonal shape is not retained
`Accept/Reject (select next input)` *Click the reset button*	Rejects modification of block

Figure 10.4

Modify shapes.

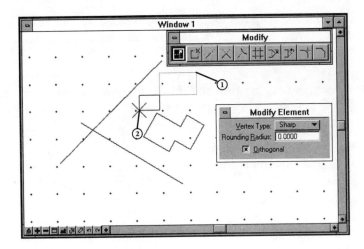

The Element Selection Tool

You can modify elements with the Element Selection tool by dragging on one of the handles of the selected element. The way the element is modified depends on the element you have selected and what handle you have picked. Some of the same rules of modification that apply to the Modify Element command also apply to the Element Selection tool. See the discussion of modifying arcs and circles with the Element Selection tool in Chapter 8.

One other difference between the Modify Element command and the Element Selection tool modification is the way the commands function on circles. When you modify a circle with the Modify Element command, you modify the radius. When you modify a circle with the Element Selection tool, you can modify the radius or one of the axes of the circle, creating an ellipse.

Try modifying the same elements as in the previous exercise, but this time, use the Element Selection tool. Identify each element and drag a handle to see how the element reacts.

Notice that modifying with the Element Selection tool requires that you click and hold on a handle to modify an element. Using this method of modification, you cannot snap to an element to precision place the modification.

Note

Extending Lines

There are four tools for extending lines on the Modify tool box (see fig. 10.5). The Extend Line commands modify the endpoint of a line while maintaining the angle of the line. The four commands enable you to extend an endpoint freehand or by a defined distance, extend two lines to form a corner, extend a line to intersect another element, and trim elements. None of these commands modify the angles of the lines.

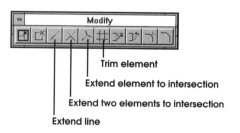

Figure 10.5

Extend tools.

You can use the Extend Line tool on the endpoints of a line or for the first and last line segments of a line string. The command requires two input points, one to identify the element, and the second to define the distance to shorten or lengthen the line segment. When you pick the line or line string, MicroStation finds the nearest vertex to modify. You can use the **D**istance constraint to extend or shorten a line segment by a specified value. Enter a positive number to extend the line segment or a negative number to shorten the line segment. If the **D**istance constraint is on, the second input point accepts or rejects the distance modification of the element.

Try extending the street line in the next exercise.

EXTENDING LINES

Continue from the preceding exercise with the CHAP10.DGN design file.

Choose the Extend Line tool

`Identify element` *Pick point* ①   Selects and drags endpoint,
(see fig. 10.6)   aligned with cursor

`Accept/Reject (select next input)`   Places new endpoint
Pick point ②

`Accept/Reject (select next input)`
Click the reset button

Figure 10.6

Extending a line.

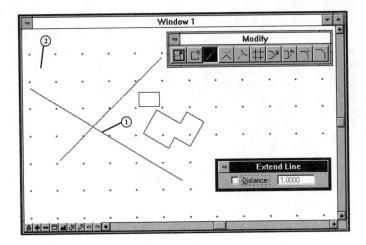

Before continuing with the extend commands, read about the Delete Part of Element command in the next section. This command will enable you to create a street outline that you can later clean up with the extending tools.

Deleting a Portion of Specified Elements

The logical progression of a design can often mean placing elements for construction and modifying those same elements later into the final product. You might, for example, place a circle with a defined radius for construction purposes and later break the circle into arc segments required for the final design with the delete part of element command.

> You can also remove parts of elements with the Clip Fence mode and Delete Fence Contents command. More information about fences can be found in Chapter 9.

Note

The Delete Part of Element Command

The Delete Part of Element command enables you to delete a portion of an element. The tool for this command is located on the Modify tool box. You can use this command on linear elements (lines, line strings, and arcs) or closed shapes (shapes and circles).

Delete Part of a Line or Line String

The Delete Part of Element command requires two points to break a line, a line string, or an arc. When this command is performed on linear elements, the result is two pieces or two elements. The first point identifies both the element and the starting point to delete from, and the second point indicates the end of the delete process (see fig. 10.7). Notice in figure 10.7 that the command deletes vertices from a line string if necessary.

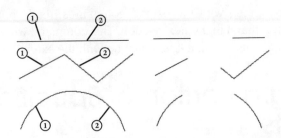

 Figure 10.7

*Examples of
deleting parts of a
linear element.*

In the next exercise, use the Parallel command to copy the street lines to represent street outlines and centerlines. Next, try the Delete Part of Element command to break the lines so you can clean up the intersections in future exercises.

Tip   The Parallel command is in the Manipulate tool box just above the Modify tools on the Main tool frame. It looks like two parallel lines.

DELETING PART OF A LINE

Continue from the preceding exercise with the CHAP10.DGN design file open.

Choose the Parallel command from the Main tool frame

*Turn on the **M**ake Copy toggle button*

Copy parallel both street lines (see fig. 10.8)

Choose Delete Part of Element

`Select start point for partial`   Breaks the line
`delete` *Pick point ① (see fig. 10.9)*

`Select end point for partial`   Completes command, creates
`delete` *Pick point ② (see fig. 10.9)*   opening, and results in two lines

*Continue with ③ through ⑥ as
shown in figure 10.9*

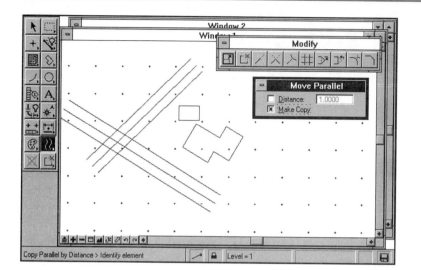

Figure 10.8

Parallel street outlines.

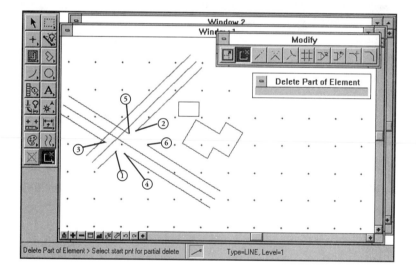

Figure 10.9

Breaking up the streets.

Delete Part of a Shape or Circle

The Delete Part of Element command requires three input points to delete part of a closed shape or circle. The first point identifies both the element and the point to start the delete process. The second point indicates the direction to delete, and the third point defines the end of the delete process. The command deletes part of an element between two vertices as well as deleting a vertex if necessary (see fig. 10.10).

Figure 10.10

Examples of deleting parts of closed elements.

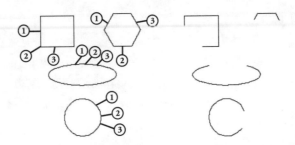

Deleting part of a closed shape or circle leaves you with an element of a different type. Deleting part of a shape changes the remaining portion into a line string. Deleting part of a circle or ellipse results in an element type of an arc for the portion remaining.

Note   Filled shapes and circles lose the fill attribute when you delete part of the element. You cannot fill a linear element such as a line string or arc. When you delete part of a closed element, the element type is changed and the fill attribute is gone. You can, however, combine linear elements to create and fill complex elements—see Chapter 12.

The Extend 2 Elements to Intersection Command

The Extend 2 Elements to Intersection tool can be used to extend or shorten two linear elements so that they meet. Valid elements for this command are lines, line strings, and arcs.

The command requires three input points: one to identify the first element to modify, one to identify the second element to modify, and a third point to accept the intersection that appears in the view.

Note   If no intersection is displayed in the view, the elements do not have paths that cross. The command gives no error message.

The point that you give to identify the first element determines the intersection and the way the elements are extended or shortened. Identify the elements on the portion of the element that you want to be used to create the intersection or the portion of the element you want to remain. Figure 10.11 demonstrates the various results of the Extend 2 Elements to Intersection command. The dashed lines indicate the elements that have been modified, and the bubbles show where the elements were picked. After you identify each element, the intersection is displayed. Accept the intersection with another point anywhere in the view or reset to try again.

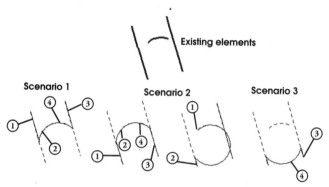

Figure 10.11

Different results based on different input points.

Now use the Extend 2 Elements to Intersection command to clean up the street intersection in the next exercise.

EXTENDING TWO LINES TO MEET

Continue from the preceding exercise with the CHAP10.DGN design file open.

Choose the Extend 2 Elements to Intersection tool

`Select first element for extension` *Pick point* ① *(see fig. 10.12)*	Highlights line
`Select element for intersection` *Pick point* ②	Extends both lines to meet
`Accept - Initiate intersection` *Pick any point* ③	Accepts modification
`Select first element for extension` *Pick point* ④	Highlights line
`Select element for intersection` *Pick point* ⑤	Extends both lines to meet
`Accept - Initiate intersection` *Pick point* ⑥	Accepts modification

Figure 10.12

Figure 10.12

*Cleaning up the
intersection.*

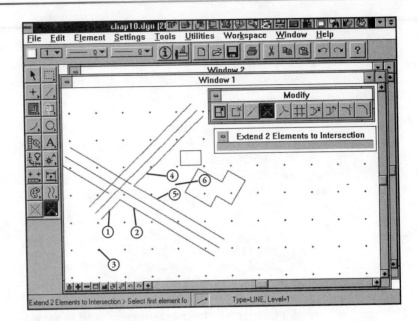

The Extend Element to Intersection Command

The Extend Element to Intersection command enables you to extend or shorten one linear element to an element of any type. You can, for example, extend an existing line to meet a shape, extend an arc to a circle, or extend a line to a line.

Again, the points you use to identify the elements determine the way the elements are modified. Figure 10.13 demonstrates the various results of the Extend Element to Intersection command. The dashed lines indicate the elements that have been modified.

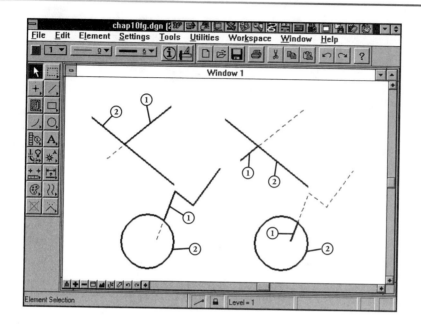

Figure 10.13

*Picking points that
work.*

EXTEND LINE TO INTERSECTION

Continue from the preceding exercise with the CHAP10.DGN design file open.

Choose Extend Element to Intersection

Select first element for extension *Pick point ① (see fig. 10.14)*	Highlights line
Select element for intersection *Pick point ②*	Highlights shape and extends line to meet
Accept - Initiate intersection *Pick any point ③*	Accepts modification
Select first element for extension *Pick point ④*	Highlights line
Select element for intersection *Pick point ⑤*	Highlights shape and extends line to meet
Accept - Initiate intersection *Pick any point ⑥*	Accepts modification

Figure 10.14

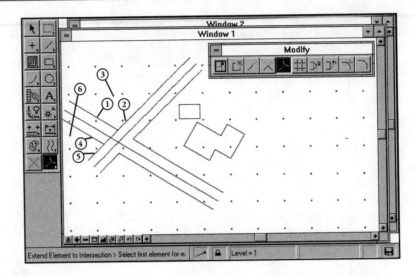

The Trim Element Command

The Trim Element tool is located on the Modify tool box. The Trim Element command combines two of the modify commands into one command. Like the Delete Part of Element command, this command partially deletes a closed shape. Like Extend Element to Intersection, it extends linear elements to intersect an element.

The Trim Element command requires you to identify two elements. The element you identify first is called the cutting element and the second element is the element that is to be trimmed.

Trimming Lines

The Trim Element command modifies linear elements, similar to the Extend Element to Intersection command. One difference between the Trim and Extend commands is that you can select the cutting edge once and then identify as many elements as necessary to trim to that edge. With Extend Element, however, you must reselect the element being extended to after you identify each element to extend.

In the next exercise, you will create a parking lot. This is easy to do with the parallel and trim tools. Zoom in once to get a little closer and create the elements that will begin your parking lot (see fig. 10.15).

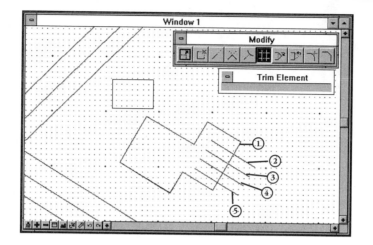

Figure 10.15

Parking in your site plan.

TRIMMING LINES

Continue from the preceding exercise with the CHAP10.DGN design file open.

Zoom in on the orthogonal shape in your site plan

Place a line similar to the line shown in figure 10.15

Use the Parallel command with the Make Copy toggle on to create the other three lines (see fig. 10.15)

Choose the Trim Element tool

`Select Cutting Element` *Pick point* ① *(see fig. 10.15)*	Highlights shape
`Accept, Identify Trim Element` `/ Reject` *Pick point* ②	Trims and highlights the line
`Accept, Identify Trim Element` `/ Reject` *Pick point* ③	Accepts the first trim and trims and highlights the next

Continue trimming the parking lines with the Trim Element command, then click the reset button.

Figure 10.16

*Trimmed parking
lines.*

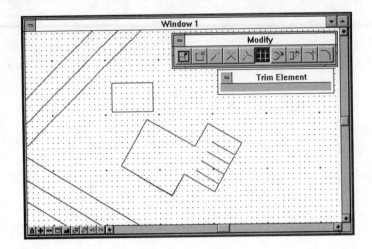

Another difference between the Trim Element command and the Extend Element to Intersection command is that the Trim command can be used to trim an element to multiple cutting edges. To trim an element to multiple elements in a single operation, first use the Element Selection tool to make a selection set with two cutting elements (see fig. 10.17). If you need help with the Element Selection tool, refer to Chapter 9.

Figure 10.17

*Selecting multiple
cutting elements.*

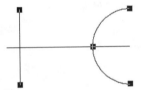

Next, choose the Trim Element command and identify the element to trim. Note that the command does not prompt you to identify the cutting element—it uses the selection set that was active when you executed the command for the cutting edge (see fig. 10.18).

Figure 10.18

*The completed
trim.*

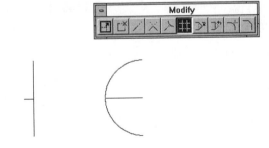

Trimming Shapes

The Trim Element command, when used on shapes or circles, is like an intelligent Delete Part of Element command. You select the cutting edge and identify the shape you want to trim, and the command partially deletes it at the cutting edge. The point that you pick on the element to be trimmed should be the portion of the element you want trimmed off (see fig. 10.19).

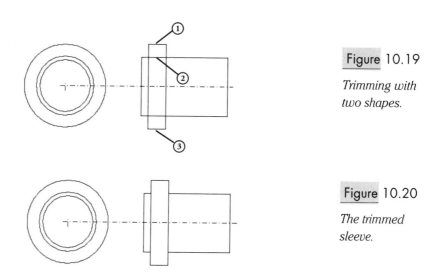

Figure 10.19

Trimming with two shapes.

Figure 10.20

The trimmed sleeve.

Inserting and Deleting Vertices

The Insert Vertex tool can be found on the Modify tool box along with the Delete Vertex tool. The Modify Element command only enables you to modify vertices, but what if you place the element with one too many or one too few vertices? If you use the Insert Vertex or Delete Vertex command, you do not have to start over to replace a line string or a shape that has 65 vertices just to add or delete one point or vertex.

Inserting a Vertex

The Insert Vertex command performs two functions: it adds a vertex and prompts you to accept the new vertex and position it at the same time. By identifying an element, a new vertex is displayed on your cursor. You then pick a second point to place and accept the vertex. You can add a vertex only on lines, line strings, and shapes.

Use the Insert Vertex to build an addition on to one of the buildings in the site plan.

INSERTING A VERTEX

Continue from the preceding exercise with the CHAP10.DGN design file open.

Zoom in on the block outline placed earlier (see fig. 10.21)

Choose Modify Element

Pick a point at ① (see fig. 10.21)

*Toggle off **O**rthogonal button in Tool settings box*

Pick a point at ②

Choose Insert Vertex

`Identify element` *Pick a point ①* (see fig. 10.22)	Highlights block
`Accept/Reject (select next input)` *Pick point at ②*	Places and accepts the vertex and modifies the shape (see fig. 10.22)
`Identify element` *Pick a point at ①* (see fig. 10.23)	Highlights shape
`Accept/Reject (select next input)` *Pick point at ②*	Places and accepts the vertex and modifies the shape (see fig. 10.23)

Figure 10.21

Modify the box.

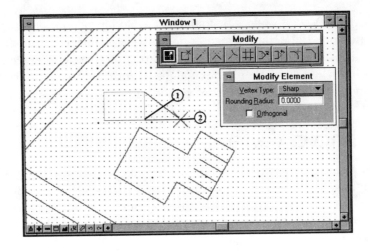

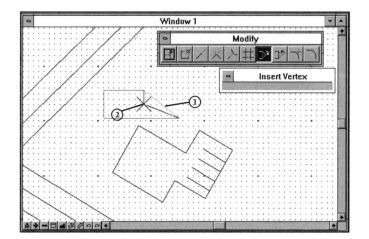

Figure 10.22

Insert one vertex.

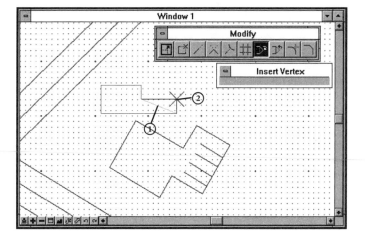

Figure 10.23

Insert second vertex.

Deleting a Vertex

The Delete Vertex command enables you to delete an unwanted vertex and modify the shape or line string by doing so. You can delete a vertex on a line, line string, or shape. The Delete Vertex command cannot be used on arcs or circles.

Deleting a vertex from a line creates a point or a line with no length. When you identify a line with the Delete Vertex command, the line seems to have disappeared but has actually been reduced to a dot or point on the screen. A point is actually a zero-length line or single-vertex element in MicroStation. Points have merit in some applications, and MicroStation supplies many special-purpose commands to place points. The commands for placing points are covered in the next chapter.

The Delete Vertex command has limitations because it does not change the element type. Each element type has a minimum number of allowable vertices. For example, lines can be reduced to one point, line strings can be reduced to two points, and shapes can be reduced to three points. The MicroStation Status Bar displays the error message `Minimum Element Size` if you attempt to delete a vertex on an element that currently has the minimum number of points for its element type.

Note   It is not good practice to modify an element and put two vertices on top of each other, giving the illusion that a vertex has been deleted. This makes future modification to the shape or line string confusing and unnecessarily difficult and the file larger than necessary.

In the next exercise, remove the vertices you added to the building outline. First, set Mark so you can undo the delete vertex commands.

DELETING A VERTEX

Continue from the preceding exercise with the CHAP10.DGN design file open.

Choose Set **M**ark *from the* **E**dit *pull-down*

Choose Delete Vertex

`Identify element` *Pick point on block*	Displays shape with removed vertex
`Accept/Reject (select next input)` *Pick point on next vertex*	Accepts the removal of previous vertex and displays the shape with the next vertex removed
`Accept/Reject (select next input)` *Pick a point anywhere to accept*	Removes second vertex
Choose Undo Ot**h**er, *then* **T**o Mark *from the* **E**dit *pull-down*	Shape is restored to the geometry you had before this exercise

---

Changing How Elements Look

Another way to modify an element, without modifying the endpoints or the geometry of the element, is to change the symbology or attributes. The attributes of an element are its line weight, color, line style, level, fill, and class. Tools for

changing symbology are on the Change Attributes tool box. You can open the
Change Attributes tool box (see fig. 10.24) by tearing it off the Main tool frame or by
choosing the Change Attributes from the Main pop-up menu under the Tools pull-
down menu.

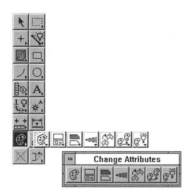

Figure 10.24

*The Change
Attributes tool
box.*

The Change Element Attribute Command

The first command on the Change Attributes tool box is the Change Element
Attributes command. The settings or constraints in the tool settings box indicate that
you can change any combination of the element attributes: Level, Color, Style,
Weight, and Class (see fig. 10.25). You also can change elements using all the
element grouping options: a selection set, a graphic group, or the contents of a
fence.

If you want to change a graphic group, make sure Graphic Group lock is turned
on. Then, when you identify an element in the graphic group, the whole group
highlights and is modified if you accept.

Tip

If you use a fence with the mode set to Clip, MicroStation breaks the elements
at the fence border and changes the different symbology.

Note

First you turn on the button for the attribute you want to change, and then you set
the value in the field or choose the setting from the pop-up menu. For example, to
change the color of an element, turn on the Color toggle. The field is activated, and

the color picker box is displayed. Choose the color or enter the color number into the field. Pick the element you want to change and the element highlights. Pick a point to accept the element or reset to reject. If a selection set or fence is active, the change is made to all the defined elements by picking one point.

Tip   Watch the Status Bar and the Primary tool box. The selections you make in the tool settings box with the Change Element Attributes command change the active attributes or symbology.

Before you place any new elements, make sure you determine whether the correct symbology is set after using the Change Element Attributes command.

In the following exercise change the symbology of the street rights-of-way and the centerline lines.

CHANGING ATTRIBUTES

Continue from the preceding exercise with the CHAP10.DGN design file open.

Tear off the Change Element tool box, then choose Change Element Attributes

*Turn on **W**eight, and enter **5** or choose from the pop-up list at the right of the **W**eight field*

*Turn on **C**olor, and change **C**olor to 1 or blue from the color picker*

Pick a point on each right-of-way line   Changes weight of rights-of-
(edges of roads), then pick any point to   way lines
accept on the last element to change

*Turn on **S**tyle and enter **4** or select Medium Dashed line in the pop-up list*

*Enter **2** in the **W**eight field*

Pick all the center lines and accept   Changes center lines to dot dashed
                                                    (see fig. 10.25)

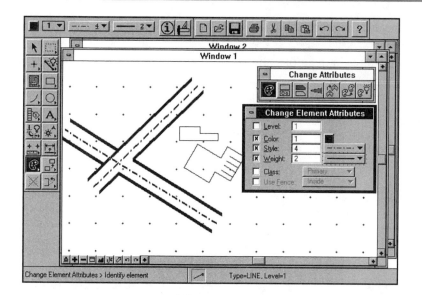

Figure 10.25

Symbology changed for streets.

The Match Element Attributes Command

Always picking the attributes before placing elements can be time-consuming and tedious if you do not have the symbology of all your different features memorized. To assist you in setting the active attributes or symbology, there is a tool for the command called Match Element Attributes on the Change Attributes tool box (see fig. 10.26). The command prompts you to identify an element in the view that already has the attributes you want. The command sets the active symbology to match the attributes of the element you identify. You can use this command to set the active symbology before you place new elements or before you use the Change Element Attributes command.

For convenience, the tool for the Match Element Attributes command is also located on the Match tool box (see fig. 10.26). You can activate this command by choosing Match from the Tools pull-down menu. This tool box also contains other match commands for text, multiines, dimensioning, patterning, and curves.

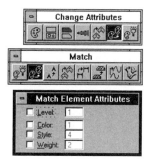

Figure 10.26

The Match Element Attributes command on both Change Attributes and Match tool boxes.

The Match Element Attributes command prompts you to identify an element in the view that is to be used as a template to set the active attributes. You can turn on the constraints in the tool settings dialog box to get an element's **L**evel, **C**olor, **S**tyle, and/or **W**eight. If you turn on all the buttons in the tool settings dialog box, the command reads the attributes from the selected element and changes the active attributes to reflect the attributes of the selected element. If you turn on just one button, the command only reads the one attribute from the element and sets the active settings accordingly.

Tip

If you are about to place an element that needs the same attributes as an element already displayed in the view, use the Match Element Attributes command to set the active attributes before placing your new element. Then you do not have to go back and change it later.

Want to make or match the active symbology to all the attributes from an element in the view? Choose the Match All Element Settings command from either the Change Attributes or Match tool box (see fig. 10.27).

Figure 10.27

The Match All Element Settings command.

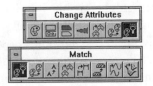

Selecting Elements by Attributes

Selecting elements by displaying the appropriate level and using the selection set or a fence might not always narrow the selection down to what you need. What if you place all the rights-of-way and center lines on the same level and then you want to change the symbology of the rights-of-way lines in your file? None of the grouping methods would work, and you would be forced to pick each right-of-way line to change.

This problem can be solved with the Select By settings box. Choose Select **B**y Attributes from the **E**dit pull-down menu and the Select By Attributes settings box is displayed (see fig. 10.28).

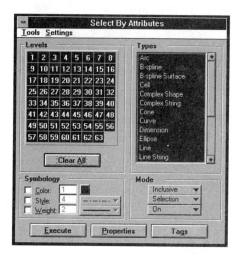

Figure 10.28

The Select By Attributes settings box.

The purpose of the Select By Attributes settings box is to enable you to identify just the elements you want. After you pick the attributes for the selection, the command searches the file for the elements that fit the criteria and puts them into a selection set. You can then use the selection set with the Change Element Attributes command or any of the manipulation commands covered in the previous chapter.

The Levels, Types, and Symbology settings defined in the settings box tell MicroStation what elements to search for. In addition, the **P**roperties button on the bottom of the settings box provides more selection criteria and displays another settings box for picking the Properties and **C**lass of elements (see fig. 10.29).

The Ta**g**s button on the bottom of the settings box provides selection criteria for database tags made to elements, and displays a settings box for choosing that information.

Tags can be used to store non-graphic data with elements in your design file. You can use tags to create a materials list or bill of materials. For even more sophisticated database applications, MicroStation has an interface to external relational databases.

Note

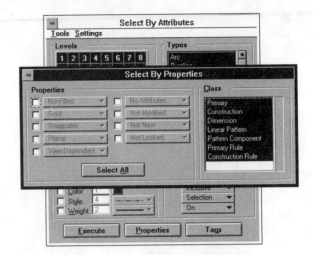

Figure 10.29

*The Select By
Properties settings
box.*

Additional options to define your search criteria can be found in the **S**ettings pull-down menu in the Select By Attributes settings box. You can identify a particular **C**ell or **S**hared Cell by selecting the name to search for. The **S**ettings pull-down also contains options for **T**ext and Text **N**ode and displays settings boxes for each to identify text elements by **F**ont, **H**eight, **W**idth, **J**ustification, and the characters or **S**tring contained in the text.

After setting the types of elements you want to select, you should turn your attention to the Mode section in the settings box. The three pop-up fields affect what happens when you choose the **E**xecute button. The first field has two choices, **I**nclusive and **E**xclusive. **I**nclusive selects all the elements that match the criteria set. **E**xclusive puts all the elements that do not meet the criteria into a selection set.

The second field defines how the elements are used. For your purposes, the field should be set to **S**election so that the **E**xecute button creates a selection set. Other options include **L**ocation and **D**isplay.

The third field should be set to **O**n for the selection criteria to become effective.

Tip   If nothing happens when you choose **E**xecute, the third field in the Mode section is probably set to off. Turn it on and try again.

In the next exercise, select all the rights-of-way lines and change the level to 2 with the Select By Attribute feature.

USING THE SELECT BY COMMAND

Continue from the preceding exercise with the CHAP10.DGN design file open.

Choose **E**dit, *then* Select **B**y Attributes	Opens settings box
Choose the Clear **A**ll *button in the Levels section*	Clears all levels from selection criteria
Choose Level 1 *(see fig. 10.30)*	Highlights 1
Select Line *in* Types *section*	Clears all and highlights line
Press Shift	
Pick Line String *in* Types *section*	Highlights Line String
Turn on St**y**le *button*	Sets style to solid or 0
Choose **O**n *in last* (**O**n/**O**ff) *field on* Mode *section*	Makes modes effective
Choose **E**xecute	Selects street rights-of-way
Check the selection set in view	

Use the Change Element Attribute tool to change the level of all the rights-of-way lines (choose the tool, set the level, and then pick any point). Make sure to deselect all buttons except level.

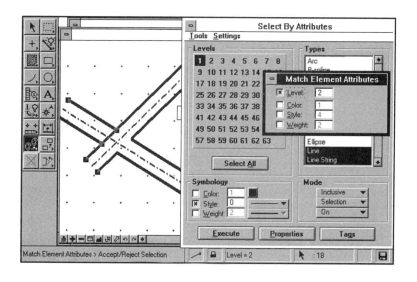

Figure 10.30

Changing the street rights-of-way to level 2.

Setting the Selector By an Existing Element

You can also identify an element in the design file to set the fields in the Select By Attributes settings box. Choose the **T**ools pull-down menu from the Select By Attributes settings box and choose Set Select By from **E**lement. The menu selection displays a settings box entitled Set Select By (see fig. 10.31).

*The Set Select By
settings box.*

Turn on the settings category that you want to select from an existing element. For example, turn on the toggle button for **S**ymbology and identify an element in your design file. After you have identified and accepted the element, the Symbology fields in the Select By settings box change to match the identified element.

You can use this option to quickly set up the fields of the Select By Attributes settings box. Using this option, the preceding exercise example could have been shortened to:

1. Choose **T**ools, then Set Select By from **E**lement

2. Turn on **L**evel and **S**ymbology

3. Pick the right-of-way line

4. Pick a point to accept

5. Choose **E**xecute

When you have finished with the Select By settings box, double-click on the upper left corner. An Alert box is displayed (see fig. 10.32). Choose Cancel to unload the Select By settings box. If you choose **O**K, the display or location of the elements might be altered if you select a mode other than **S**election.

*The Alert box
displayed when
closing the Select
By settings box.*

Changing Elements by Element Information

Another method you can use to display and change the attributes of an element is the Element Information settings box, which is opened by the **I**nformation item on the El̲ement pull-down menu. This menu selection first prompts you to identify an element and then displays the Element Information settings box on the screen (see fig. 10.33).

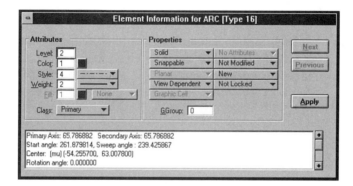

Figure 10.33

The Element Information settings box.

The settings box is full of valuable information about the element. The settings box header tells you what type of element it is, just as, for example, figure 10.33 shows "Element Information for ARC."

The Attributes section should look familiar to you. You can change any of the available attributes for the element. The **G**Group refers to the graphic group number associated with the element. If the **G**Group is set to 0, the element is not part of a graphic group.

The field across the bottom of the settings box displays other pertinent information about the element. The information in this field varies depending on the element type being displayed. In this example, the Start Angle and Sweep Angle are displayed because the element is an arc.

You can use the Element Information settings box to view or modify element information. To modify elements, change the appropriate fields, then choose the **A**pply button to modify any of the element's attributes or its geometry. An Alert box displays, prompting Are you sure you want to save changes to currently displayed element?. Choose the **O**K button, and the element is modified. Choose Cancel and no modification takes place.

To examine or modify a different element in the view, pick the element and the settings box information changes to reflect the selected element. To remove the settings box from the view, double-click the view icon in the upper left corner or choose any tool.

This method is certainly not the most efficient way to change element attributes, but it is worth mentioning. The other information in the display is useful as you become more familiar with MicroStation and how elements are stored.

Summary

As you have seen in this chapter, you can modify the geometry of an existing element or modify the symbology of an element. The methods and commands available for doing both are plentiful.

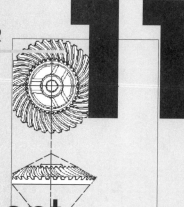

Advanced 2D Element Placement

*I*n this chapter, you learn some of the advanced element placement commands, which enable you to place elements with custom line styles, create your own custom line style, and construct curves and points. In this chapter, you build a subdivision by placing fence lines and tree lines with custom line styles, placing points for electric poles, and so on.

This chapter focuses on the following topics:

♦ *Using custom line styles*

♦ *Creating your own custom line styles*

♦ *Placing curves*

♦ *Placing points*

Many tools and settings boxes are covered in this chapter during the discussion of custom line styles. You activate the custom lines settings boxes by using the line style pop-up menu in the Primary tool box, which is just one more reason to have the Primary tool box docked in every design session.

Exploring Custom Line Styles

You can use and define custom line styles in MicroStation and store them in a line style resource file. Custom line styles provide a versatile way to place lines and symbols along a linear element.

A custom line style can contain line segments or strokes at any defined width or length, which gives you full flexibility to define any dash/dot line style. You also can add point data or symbols at different intervals within the style, giving you the capability to create any line pattern. An example of a custom line style might be a fence line for a mapper, an insulation pattern for an architect, or a special dash/dot pattern to depict phantom lines for a mechanical draftsman.

The line styles are stored in an external resource file. By default, a line style resource is automatically attached when you enter MicroStation. The configuration variable MS_SYMBRSC determines the name and directory of the default resource file.

You can change the default line style resource by modifying the settings for MS_SYMBRSC in the Configuration Variables dialog box. Chapter 17, "Boosting Your Performance," contains instructions on changing configuration variables.

You can activate a custom line style by choosing **C**ustom from the line style pop-up menu on the Primary tool box. The Line Styles dialog box is displayed with a list of line styles stored in the attached line style resource file (see fig. 11.1). Choose or activate the line style from the dialog box by double-clicking on the name.

Figure 11.1

The Line Styles dialog box.

The Primary tool box displays the currently active line code. Also in the Primary tool box, the last four custom line styles you select appear in the line style pop-up menu.

Tip

Options for Custom Line Styles

The Show **D**etails toggle button below the Names field expands the settings box and displays the style options, as shown in figure 11.2. With the details shown, you can change the way MicroStation applies the line style. You can change the width of the line style, scale, and shift for applying the style during placement of elements.

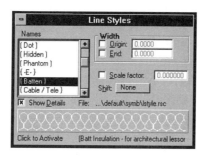

Figure 11.2

The Line Styles dialog box with Details visible.

Each toggle button or field shown in the dialog box enables you to further customize the line style to fit your needs. Review the parameters shown in the dialog box and the brief descriptions following.

♦ The Width settings enable you to supply a width to the beginning and end of the line style. This applies only to line styles composed of line segments. Width isn't applied to a line style that contains a symbol.

♦ Turn on **O**rigin or **E**nd Width and enter **2** to create an element with the current line style two master units thick. Turn on both **O**rigin and **E**nd and enter starting and ending widths in the fields to get a gradual increase or decrease of line style width over the length of the element (see fig. 11.3).

Figure 11.3

Applying a width to custom line style.

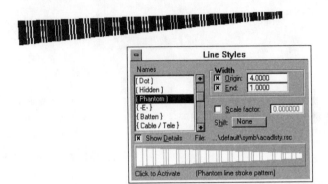

♦ *Tip*

> If turning on and changing the width option doesn't change the graphics display of the style in the bottom of the settings box, you cannot apply width to this line style. The style probably contains a symbol or point. You can only place stroke line styles with a width defined.
>
> If you want to thicken a line style that contains symbols or points, change the line weight in the conventional way by choosing a weight from the pop-up menu in the Primary tool box.

♦ Turn on the toggle for **S**cale factor and enter a number greater than 1 to scale up the line style, and a number smaller than 1 to scale down the line style. MicroStation applies the scale to the line length and any symbols in the line code.

♦ The **Sh**ift button invokes three options in the pop-up menu: None, Distance, and Fraction.

♦ A shift of None places the line style as designed.

♦ A shift of Distance displays a field in which you enter a value that represents the distance into the line style at which to begin placing. If you enter a distance of 4:0:0 or 4.0 when you use the line style, for example, the first point begins the line style four master units into the line style, possibly eliminating the first stroke or more.

♦ A shift of Fraction is a decimal value that defines the fraction of the first and last stroke in the stroke pattern of an element or element segment, thereby modifying all the strokes in the line style.

As you change the settings for the line style, the graphics display across the bottom of the settings box changes. With the details shown, you also can click on the graphics to activate the line style setting.

Note

The biggest advantage to custom line styles is that any primitive element (line, line string, arc, or shape) is placed with the custom line style. If you use multilines, you can use only the multiline tool to place linear (line string type) elements.

In the next exercise, you place a line string with the Railroad line style. To begin, you make a copy of CHAP10.DGN to start your design and scale the map to something more appropriate.

PLACING ELEMENTS WITH CUSTOM LINE STYLES

Open the CHAP10.DGN file.

Choose **F**ile, Save **A**s   Opens the Save Design As dialog box

Enter **CHAP11.DGN** *in the* F**i**les *field*

Choose OK   Closes dialog box and renames the
active design file to CHAP11.DGN

Place a fence block around the site plan

Scale the fence contents by **10**

Choose Fit View *from the*   Displays the entire site plan in the view
view controls

Continues

Choose Custom *from* the line style pop-up menu in the Primary tool box	Opens Select Line Style dialog box with all the styles
Double-click on {Rail Road}	Activates the style
Choose the Place Line *command and place a railroad in site plan (see fig. 11.4)*	

Figure 11.4

Placing a railroad.

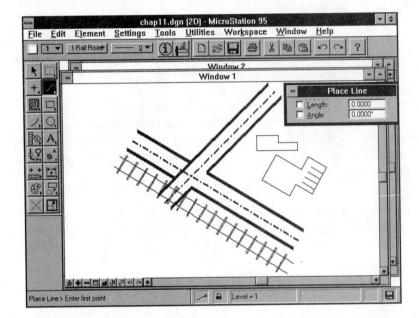

Notice that the Rail Road style places a symbol at a defined interval. Perhaps you would like the symbol at the origin and vertex of the element. To accomplish this, you would need to modify the line style point component. The next section discusses creating and/or modifying custom line styles.

Custom Line Styles and the Line Style Editor

To define your own custom line styles or modify existing custom line styles, choose Edit from the line style pop-up menu in the Primary tool box to open the Line Style Editor dialog box (see fig. 11.5). The Line Style Editor appears empty until you open a line style library for modification. Choose File, Open from the pull-down menu in the dialog box and select LSTYLE.RSC, the line style library resource file (see fig. 11.6).

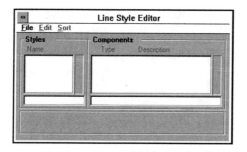

Figure 11.5

You can use the Line Style Editor dialog box to define or modify custom line styles.

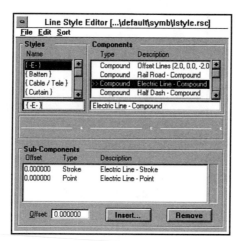

Figure 11.6

The Line Style Editor appears empty until you open a line style library, see?

> **Warning** Do not edit the delivered line style resource. You should make a copy before you begin any edits of the line style resource to maintain the delivered resource file. If you make a mistake editing the original, you must reload the MicroStation files to get it back.

Each line style name is linked to a compound component or is defined in the library as a stroke or a point pattern. For example, the line style name {-E-} is linked to a Compound Component called Electric Line - Compound. The Compound Component is created from two Sub-Components: a stroke that forms the lines and a point that supplies the E symbol.

To modify a stroke pattern, choose one from the Components list box or double-click on the one displayed in the Sub-Components list box. The settings for creating and modifying a stroke pattern are displayed (see fig. 11.7).

Figure 11.7

Choose a Stroke
type from the
Components list
to bring up the
settings in the Line
Style Editor dialog
box.

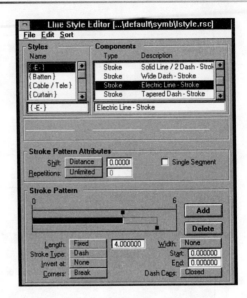

The stroke pattern sample shows the current definition as well as the changes you make to the attributes and pattern of the stroke while in this settings box. The stroke pattern itself appears and you can modify it by dragging on the handles to increase the dash or the gap between the strokes. The Add and Delete buttons add additional handles for dashes and gaps.

After you modify the stroke pattern, select a new item from the Components list.

To modify a point pattern, choose a point from the Components list box, or double-click on the one displayed in the Sub-Components list box. To redisplay the sub-components, click on the style name {-E-}. Doing so displays the settings for creating and modifying a point pattern.

The point pattern sample appears in the settings box and graphically shows the changes you make to the point component. MicroStation also displays the Base Stroke Pattern to help you define where to place the point symbols. You can choose to place a point symbol on the stroke pattern, at the origin of the element, at the vertex of the element, or at the end of the element. For example, pick a point on the gray portion of the stroke pattern (see fig. 11.8).

Click on the Select button to identify a different point symbol to place in the gap. The Select Point Symbol dialog box opens (see fig. 11.9).

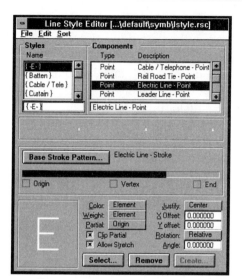

Figure 11.8

Pick a point on the gray portion of the stroke pattern.

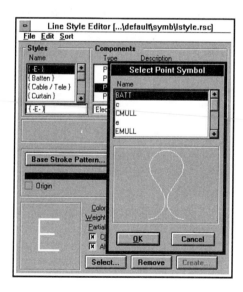

Figure 11.9

You use the Select Point Symbol dialog box to specify a different point symbol to place in the gap.

Choose the symbol you want to add to the point definition and choose **O**K. The Line Style Editor then shows the new symbol in the sample box. You can modify the Justify option to define where on that stroke or gap to place the pattern: **C**enter, **L**eft, or **R**ight. Other options for the point symbol include offset, rotation, and angle settings. In the Electric line style for example, the E symbol is selected for the gap portion of the stroke pattern, and **J**ustify is set to **C**enter. This places the point symbol in the center of every gap in the stroke pattern.

To create your own point symbol, create the geometry or draw the elements to represent the point in the design file at the appropriate size and place a fence around the elements. Then choose **E**dit, **C**reate, **P**oint from the pull-down menu in the Line Style Editor dialog box. Name the point in the Components section of the dialog box and click on the Create button in the lower right corner to open the Create Point Symbol dialog box (see fig. 11.10). After you enter the name of the new point symbol and choose OK, the Status Bar prompts you for the origin of the point symbol. Pick a point in the design file (see ① in fig. 11.10).

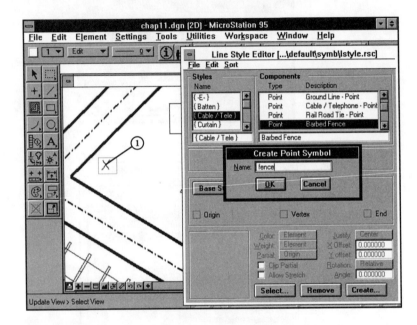

Figure 11.10

After you enter the name of the new point symbol and choose OK, the Status Bar prompts you for the origin of the point symbol.

In the following exercise, you try to create a fence line style called Barbed Fence from the existing {-E-} stroke, as well as a new point definition.

CREATING A CUSTOM FENCE LINE STYLE

Continue from the preceding exercise with the CHAP11.DGN design file open.

Zoom in and place two lines to represent fence symbol (refer to figure 11.10)

Place fence around elements

*Choose **E**dit from the line style pop-up menu*	Opens the Line Style Editor dialog box (refer to figure 11.5)

Choose **F**ile, **O**pen *from the Line Style Editor box*	Issues the Open Line Style Library dialog box
Select LSTYLE.RSC	
Choose **O**K *(refer to figure 11.6)*	Loads line styles in editor
Choose **F**ile, Save **A**s	Opens the Save Line Style Library As dialog box
Enter **ORIG.RSC**	
Choose **O**K	Saves copy of delivered resource file to file called ORIG.RSC
Select Electric Line - Stroke *from the Components list*	
Choose **E**dit, D**u**plicate	Copies line component
Enter **Fence Line - Stroke** *in key-in field below Components list*	
Modify the stroke gap Click and drag the handle displayed above where the stroke and gap meet (see fig. 11.11)	

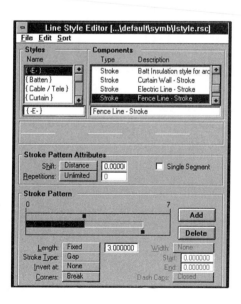

Figure 11.11

The new Fence Line Stroke component created and modified.

Continues

Choose **E**dit, **C**reate, **P**oint	Adds new point component
Enter **Barbed Fence** *in key-in field under Components list (refer to figure 11.10)*	
Choose Create *button*	Opens the Create Point Symbol dialog box
Enter **fence** *in the* **N**ame *field*	
Choose **O**K	
`Create symbol > Select Symbol Origin` ① *(refer to figure 11.10)*	
Choose Base Stroke Pattern	Opens the Base Stroke Pattern dialog box
Pick Fence Line-Stroke	
Pick a point in the gray gap portion of the stroke pattern display	
Click on the Select *button*	Opens the Select Point Symbol dialog box
Choose fence	
Choose **O**K	
Choose **E**dit, **C**reate, **N**ame	Adds new unnamed point component
Highlight the input field below the Name *list and type* **Fence**	
Press Tab	Changes Unnamed to the fence style name
Choose **E**dit, **C**reate, **C**ompound	Adds new compound component to Components list
Enter **Barbed Fence - Compound** *in input field*	
Choose **E**dit, **L**ink	Links new component to the style named fence
Choose Insert *button*	Opens the Select Component dialog box
Scroll down the list and select Point Barbed Fence	
Choose **O**K	Inserts internal default solid line to Sub-Components list

Choose Insert	Opens the Select Component dialog box
Select Stroke Fence Line *and choose* **O**K	
Choose **F**ile, **S**ave	Saves the new style to the resource file

Activate the fence custom line style and place a fence around the properties (see fig. 11.12).

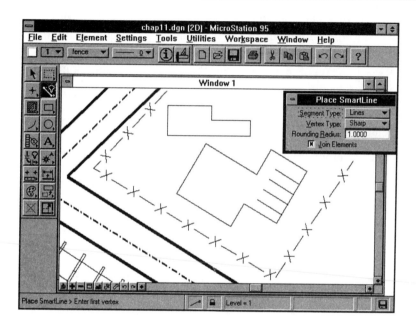

Figure 11.12

Placing fences in your site plan.

Placing Stream Curves

Placing curves is particularly important for a mapper. The curve command offers two methods: Point and Stream. A *point curve* is a calculated curve defined by the points given. More accurate methods of point curves can be found in the B-Spline curves. A *stream curve* is a freehand curve that might represent a contour line or a river. You have to place these types of elements by hand. You can find the Place Stream Curve tool on the Linear Elements tool box (see fig. 11.13).

Figure 11.13

The Place Stream Curve tool lets you draw a freehand line.

You place a stream curve by picking a point to start the curve and then just moving the cursor to place the curve. It acts similar to sketching. After you complete the curve, click the Reset button to terminate the curve. Picking a data point is like placing the pen down on paper, and resetting brings the pen up. The curve consists of short line segments.

The Place Stream Curve has four settings you use to determine the curve's smoothness: **D**elta, **To**lerance, **An**gle, and **A**rea. MicroStation uses all of these settings in a mathematical calculation of where and how often a point or vertex needs to be placed to define the curve. The Tolerance setting defines the distance between points or vertices on the curve. The Delta, Angle, and Area settings define maximum values that cannot be exceeded without recording more points.

If the stream curve doesn't look smooth, lower the Tolerance setting to place the vertices closer together, creating a smoother curve. Some general guidelines for stream settings are as follows:

♦ The Tolerance setting should be 5 to 10 times larger than the Delta setting.

♦ The Tolerance setting should be small enough that the curve doesn't appear choppy.

♦ The Angle setting should be set to 15° for the optimum curve.

In the following exercise, you review the Tool Settings window and place a creek in the site plan using the Place Stream Curve command.

PLACING A STREAM CURVE

Continue from the preceding exercise with the CHAP11.DGN design file open.

Choose the Place Stream Curve tool from the Linear Elements tool box	Displays Curve settings in the Tool Settings window
Choose the **M**ethod, Stream	
Enter **.1** *for the* **D**elta *setting*	
Enter **.5** *for the* T**o**lerance *setting*	
Enter **15** *for the* A**n**gle *setting*	
Set the line style to a solid line	
Pick a point ① *(see fig. 11.14)*	Defines starting point of curve

Move the cursor to define the river, *as shown in figure 11.14*	Draws the curve
Click the Reset button	Ends the curve

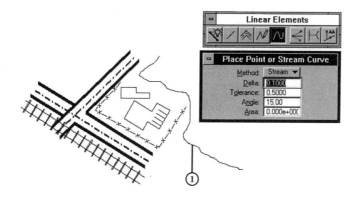

Figure 11.14

Use the curvy line shown here as a model for yours.

Using Points

Another way to place symbology along lines is to use point tools. The point tools provide several different ways to place points, characters, or cells. A *point* is a line element that has zero length, a *character* is a character or symbol in the font library, and a *cell* is any number of primitive elements grouped together. Chapter 16 focuses on cells and creating them.

Points can be useful for all applications. To a mapper, the point might represent the placement of a light pole or manhole. In other applications, a point might serve as a construction element, a reference marker, or a snap to for constructing other elements.

The Points tool box contains all the point tools. You can tear it off the Main tool frame or open it from the pull-down menu by choosing **T**ools, **M**ain, Po**i**nts (see fig. 11.15).

Figure 11.15

You can tear the
Points tool box off
the Main tool
frame.

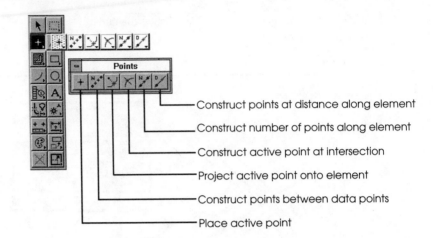

Construct points at distance along element

Construct number of points along element

Construct active point at intersection

Project active point onto element

Construct points between data points

Place active point

All the point tools shown in figure 11.15 provide different methods of placing a point. The following list gives a brief description of each command and the settings available.

♦ **Place Active Point.** Places a point, a character, or a cell at the point you pick in the view.

♦ **Construct Points between Data Points.** Places a defined number of points, characters, or cells equally spaced between two points you pick in the view.

♦ **Project Active Point onto Element.** Places a point, a character, or a cell on or along a element. Select an element to anchor the point on that element. Move the cursor to move the point along the element. Pick a point to accept the point location.

♦ **Construct Active Point at Intersection.** Places a point, a character, or a cell at the intersection of two elements. Identify each element to display the point at the intersection. Pick an accept point to place the point.

♦ **Construct Number of Points along Element.** Places a defined number of points, characters, or cells equally spaced on an element.

♦ **Construct Active Points at Distance Along Element.** Places a point, a character, or a cell along an element at a defined distance from the point you pick on the element.

Next, you test out some of the point commands in the following exercise. You place points that represent service poles near each property, then you use the point type Cell to place manhole symbols in the rights-of-way.

PLACING POINTS

Continue from the preceding exercise with the CHAP11.DGN design file open.

*Change the line weight to **6***

Open the Points tool box

Choose the Place Active Point tool

Pick a point at each building location
to indicate a pole (see fig. 11.16)

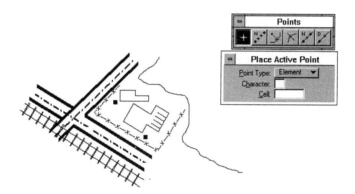

Figure 11.16

Placing points.

Summary

You have covered a great number of tools and concepts in this chapter.

Custom line styles are far improved over the older method of linear patterning. Custom line styles that you can create and modify offer flexible placement and modification options. If file translation or file sharing is an issue in your organization you can drop the custom line style or use the old method of linear patterning. The thing to remember about linear patterning is that it is not easily modified.

MicroStation has used curves and points for many years. Curves are used extensively in mapping applications for freehand drawing. This completes the explanation of the basic graphic element tools in MicroStation. The remaining chapters discuss dimensioning, text, and more advanced topics of MicroStation.

PART

3

Putting on the Final Touches

CHAPTER 12

Applying Patterns
and Fills

*Y*ou find patterned areas in every discipline. A patterned area might be a
hatched pattern that represents a solid piece of metal in a cross section, a
speckled pattern that represents a concrete slab, or a grass symbol pattern
that denotes the outline of a marshy area on a map. Filled areas can depict solid areas
of color on-screen and at plotting time. This chapter discusses MicroStation's
commands, procedures, and options for patterning and filling areas.

MicroStation requires a closed area before it can apply a pattern or fill. Sometimes a
closed shape as you know it (a block, circle, or polygon) isn't feasible. When
necessary, the pattern commands can create a closed shape from areas with
bounding elements. These closed shapes are called complex shapes. This chapter
explains how to use complex shapes for patterning, as well as how to create your own
complex shapes to fill elements.

In this chapter, you learn about the following:

♦ Placing patterns in a closed-element area

♦ Deleting a pattern

♦ Creating holes in a pattern

♦ Patterning linear elements

♦ Showing the pattern attributes

♦ Matching the pattern attributes

♦ Turning off pattern display

♦ Creating a single complex shape and complex chain from many linear elements

♦ Filling complex elements with color

♦ Dropping a closed complex shape and complex chain

This chapter primarily discusses the tools in the Patterns and Groups tool boxes (see figs. 12.1 and 12.2). You can open the Patterns and Groups tool boxes by choosing them from the Main tool frame or by choosing them from the **M**ain submenu from the **T**ools pull-down menu.

Figure 12.1

The Patterns tool box provides area patterning commands.

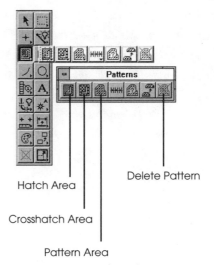

Hatch Area

Crosshatch Area

Pattern Area

Delete Pattern

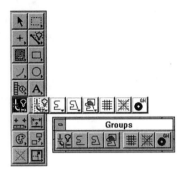

Figure 12.2

The Groups tool box.

Patterning an Area

To pattern an area, you have three options: hatching, crosshatching, or filling the area with an array of pattern cells. The Patterns tool box has three tools that correspond to these three options: the Hatch Area tool, the Crosshatch Area tool, and the Pattern Area tool (refer to figure 12.1). The section "Using Pattern Area," later in this chapter, briefly discusses cells and how they're used in the Pattern Area command.

Each of the three pattern tools has a setting for the method to be used, which you can select from the **M**ethod pop-up list in the Patterns tool box. The following list contains a brief description of each of the seven methods you can use for patterning.

♦ **Element.** Patterning an area by the Element method requires that you identify a shape and then accept the shape to initiate the pattern. With the Element method, if the area you want to pattern is not a closed element (a circle, block, or shape), you must first create a shape to enclose the area you want patterned. Read on for other methods that may save you the time and effort of creating a shape or complex shape if you don't need one (the Intersection, Union, Difference, and Flood methods create the complex shape for you).

♦ **Fence.** Patterning an area by the Fence method requires that you place a fence prior to executing the pattern command. If a fence is present in the design file, this menu item is available; otherwise, it's dimmed. Pick a point anywhere in the view to accept the fence area to be patterned.

♦ **Intersection.** Patterning an area by the Intersection method requires that you identify at least two shape elements. This option patterns the area common to all of the elements selected.

♦ **Union.** Patterning an area by the Union method requires that you identify at least two shape elements. This option patterns the total area that all of the selected elements occupy.

♦ **Difference.** Patterning an area by the Difference method requires that you identify at least two shape elements. The area contained by the element you select first will be patterned, minus the common area of the other elements you pick.

♦ **Flood.** Patterning an area by the Flood method requires that you pick a point in an area enclosed by elements. This option patterns an area without requiring a closed shape. For example, you may want to pattern one of the squares in an area having intersecting lines, such as a checkerboard. The square areas are not closed elements, but the area is bounded by four lines. The area defined by these elements can be patterned with the Flood method. When you pick a point inside the area, MicroStation automatically calculates the path and highlights it. If the highlighted area is correct, you pick a point in the view to accept and initiate the pattern.

The Max **G**ap field in the Patterns tool box is available with the Flood option. This field helps to determine the path that defines the area. The Max **G**ap value is the distance that MicroStation jumps in searching for the next element in the path. If this value is large, MicroStation searches a wider area for an element. If an element is found, the gap is closed between the two points and the command continues searching for the next available element to complete the closed area.

♦ **Points.** Patterning an area by the Point method requires that you pick points in the view to define an area. The command prompts you to pick the vertices for a temporary shape. After you place the vertices, click the Reset button to pattern the area.

The pattern commands have two option buttons: Associative Pattern and Snappable Pattern. Each of these buttons appears in the Patterning tool box when one of the area commands is activated.

♦ **Associative Pattern.** When you turn on the Associative Pattern button, you place pattern elements with an association to the original element. If a pattern was placed with the Associative Pattern button turned on, the pattern automatically gets modified when you modify the original element.

If the Associative Pattern toggle button is turned off, the pattern commands place the pattern components in a graphic group. Turn on the Graphic Group lock to manipulate all the pattern components; turn off the Graphic Group lock to manipulate individual pattern components.

If the Associative Pattern toggle button is turned on, the pattern commands include the pattern components with the primitive element or the complex shape, and there is no graphic group. A complex shape is always created with associative patterning on and Fence, Intersection, Union, Difference, Flood, or Points patterning method.

When you modify a shape that has associative patterning, the pattern changes too. If you modify the shape with one of the modify commands that change the element type, the pattern disappears. If you change the element type from a closed shape to a line string with the Delete Part of Element or the Trim command, for example, you lose the pattern components.

◆ **Snappable Pattern.** When you turn on the Snappable Pattern button, you create pattern elements that can be snapped to. If this button is turned on when you create the pattern, all the elements will be snappable. If your drawing is dense, however, you may want to turn off this toggle button. Turning it off can save time and reduce frustration later; otherwise, you may try to place a tentative point or to snap to an element and get the lines of the pattern rather than the element you want.

If you create associative patterns with any method other than the Element method, MicroStation creates a complex shape that defines the pattern area. The association is made to the complex shape, not to the original elements. The complex shape does not replace the original elements; rather, it is created to match them and is added to the design file. The symbology of the complex element is defined by the last element chosen.

Associative patterning creates a complex shape on top of the existing primitive element. To eliminate the duplicated elements in associative patterns, create a complex element yourself before issuing the pattern command. After you create the complex shape, use the Element method of patterning to place the associated pattern components. The section "Creating Complex Elements" later in this chapter furnishes more information about creating complex shapes.

Tip

Now that you have been introduced to the seven methods available for patterning and the two patterning toggle buttons, you can look at the settings that are associated with each pattern command.

Using Hatch Area

The first tool on the Patterns tool box is Hatch Area. The Hatch Area command places lines at a specified distance apart, at a specified angle, and at a specified tolerance. After you choose the Hatch Area tool, the Patterning tool box shows the following settings:

♦ **Spacing.** Enter the value in master units for the distance between the hatched lines. The format of this field depends on the format you have selected in the Coordinate Readout settings box.

♦ **Angle.** Enter the value as a whole number or a decimal number or both for the angle of the hatched lines.

♦ **Tolerance.** This setting determines how closely the pattern elements match a curved element. The smaller the tolerance setting, the closer the pattern elements match the curved element. A larger tolerance setting reduces the processing time required to pattern and creates a rougher approximation of a curve.

Tip   If you place a pattern that does not create pattern elements cleanly along a curve, lower the tolerance setting and try placing the pattern again.

In the following exercise, you use the Hatch Area command to pattern the areas that depict the solid surfaces in the cross section of the mechanical part. Because the elements that make up the area to be patterned are individual lines and arcs, the Flood patterning method is used.

Using the Hatch Area Command

Create a CHAP12.DGN design file.

Turn grid lock on and draw the simple machine part in figure 12.3 using the Place Line command

Open the Patterns tool box

Choose the Hatch Area tool   Displays settings for the Hatch Area command

Clear or highlight in the **S**pacing
field and enter .5

*Enter 45 in the **A**ngle field*

*Turn on the Ass**o**ciative Pattern button*

*Choose **F**lood from the **M**ethod pop-up list*   Issues Hatch Area Enclosing Point command

`Enter data point inside area` *Pick point ① (see fig. 12.3)*   Builds and highlights complex shape enclosing path of area that will be patterned

`Accept @pattern intersection point` *Pick any point in the view*   Accepts the path and patterns the area

`Enter data point inside area` *Pick point ②*   Builds and highlights complex shape enclosing area that will be patterned

`Accept @pattern intersection point` *Pick any point in the view*   Patterns the area

`Enter data point inside area`

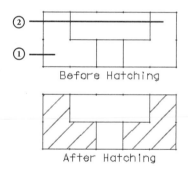

Before Hatching

After Hatching

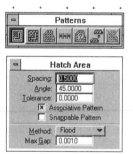

Figure 12.3

Patterned areas.

Deleting Area Patterns

A Delete Pattern tool is available on the Patterns tool box (refer to figure 12.1). The Delete Pattern tool is represented by the same icon as the Delete Element tool. When selected from this tool box, however, the tool activates the Delete Pattern command and deletes only patterns. The Delete Pattern tool differs from the Delete Element tool in that it deletes all the components of a pattern but leaves the original elements alone, regardless of the status of any of the locks or settings.

A complex shape is always created by placing an associative pattern using the Fence, Intersection, Union, Difference, Flood, or Points patterning method. When you use the Delete Pattern command to delete an associative pattern placed by any of these patterning methods, it deletes the pattern components and leaves the complex shape created by patterning. The Delete Element command, on the other hand, deletes both the pattern and the complex shape.

If an element was patterned with associative patterning by a method that did not create a new complex shape, the Delete Pattern command removes the pattern components from the element, whereas the Delete Element command deletes both the original element and the pattern components.

If an element was patterned without associative patterning, the Delete Pattern command deletes the entire pattern only, regardless of the status of Graphic Group lock. By contrast, the Delete Element command deletes all the pattern elements if the Graphic Group lock is on, and deletes selected individual pieces of the pattern if the Graphic Group lock is off. Review table 12.1 for all the possible options.

Table 12.1

Delete Pattern versus Delete Element

Command	Associative Patterning	Graphic Group Lock	Result
Delete Element	ON	ON or OFF	Deletes all pattern and original elements or complex shapes used in the patterning
Delete Pattern	ON	ON or OFF	Deletes all pattern elements
Delete Element	OFF	ON	Deletes all pattern elements
Delete Element	OFF	OFF	Deletes individual pattern elements
Delete Pattern	OFF	ON or OFF	Deletes all pattern elements

You try the Delete Pattern command in the following exercise. Note that in the preceding exercise you created a complex shape with the Flood method and associative patterning turned on. When you use the Delete Pattern command, you identify any pattern element and MicroStation removes all the pattern elements, leaving the complex element. You use the complex element to pattern the areas again in the exercise after this one.

Using Crosshatch Area

The second tool on the Patterns tool box is Crosshatch Area. The Crosshatch Area command has all the same settings as the Hatch Area command, but the tool box also has two additional fields to define the spacing and angle for the second hatch.

> If you leave second spacing and angle field at zero, MicroStation creates the crosshatching perpendicular to the angle set in the first angle field and uses the same spacing as the first spacing field.

Note

In the following exercise, you try crosshatching the same area in the cross section. First, remove the hatched pattern with the Delete Pattern tool. Then, you choose the Element method to place the crosshatch and identify the complex shape you created in the first exercise. You did not delete the complex shape with the Delete Pattern command in the last exercise, so it remains in the design file to be used again.

USING THE CROSSHATCH AREA COMMAND

Continue from the preceding exercise with the CHAP12.DGN design file open.

Choose the Delete Pattern tool

`Identify Element` *Pick point at* ① *(see fig. 12.4)* — Highlights pattern

`Identify Element` *Pick point* — Accepts and deletes pattern elements, then highlights second pattern

Pick any point to accept — Deletes pattern elements

Choose the Crosshatch Area tool — Displays settings for the Crosshatch Area command

Choose **E**lement *from* **M**ethod *pop-up list* — Issues Crosshatch Area command

`Identify Element` *Pick point at* ① *(see fig. 12.5)* — Highlights complex shape and identifies it as such in the Status Bar

`Accept @pattern intersection point` *Pick point at* ② — Accepts and patterns first area and highlights second complex shape

Continues

```
Accept @pattern intersection point          Patterns second area
```
Pick any point in the view

```
Identify element
```

Now remove the patterns again, but this time with the Delete Element tool from the Main tool frame. The patterns and the complex shapes are deleted, but the original elements remain intact. Be careful, however, not to delete the original elements that comprise the design (click the Reset button to cycle to the next element if you first pick the wrong element). After making the deletions, use the Update View tool to refresh the view.

Figure 12.4

Deleted patterns.

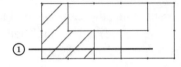 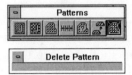

Figure 12.5

Crosshatched area.

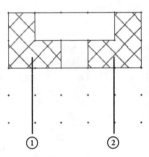 

Using Pattern Area

The third tool on the Patterns tool box is Pattern Area. The Pattern Area command enables you to place cells in an area to form a pattern. A *cell* is a collection of primitive elements grouped together and stored in a library. The library, called a cell library, is not saved in the design file but is saved as an external file with the CEL extension. The cell library can be attached to a design file, and any of the cells or elements stored in the cell library can be activated and placed in the design file as many times as you want.

In the case of area patterning, you can create a cell, store it in a cell library, and then use the cell to pattern an area. For example, a group of lines that represent a marsh symbol could be stored in a cell library under the name MARSH. For each design file that needs the marsh symbol, you simply attach the cell library in which the marsh cell was stored and activate the marsh symbol using the Pattern Area command. Shapes representing a concrete pattern or lines representing a brick pattern are other examples of using cells for area patterning. Chapter 16, "Building and Placing Standard Symbols," covers in more detail the topic of creating cells that can later be used to pattern an area.

After you choose the Pattern Area tool in the Patterns tool box, you must enter the cell name to be used in the **P**attern Cell field; for example, enter **SWAMP** to activate the swamp cell. The number of cells placed in the area is determined by the values entered in the Sc**a**le, **R**ow Spacing, and Co**l**umn Spacing fields. An **A**ngle setting also is available to rotate the elements as they are placed in the pattern.

Use cells with caution where the cell is comprised of many elements or using many cells over a large area. This will create a large design file and take a lot of disk space.

Warning

Figure 12.6 shows the Points patterning method being used to place swamp cells in the area. The row and column spacing has been set to 100 master units (in this case feet), which place a matrix of swamp cells 100 feet apart.

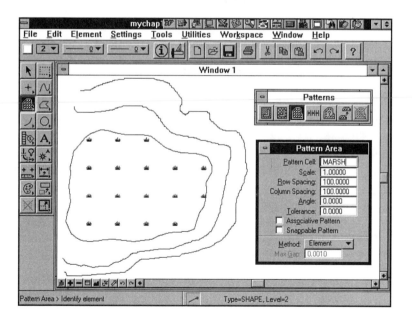

Figure 12.6

Patterning an area with swamp cells.

In figure 12.6, the Associative Pattern toggle button was turned off. Do you know why? Associative patterning would have created a complex shape in the design file with the points that were entered, which would not be acceptable for this application. The cells are not associated to any shape or element. You can move, copy, or delete the cells as a group by turning on the Graphic Group lock; or you can manipulate the individual marsh cells by turning off the Graphic Group lock.

Patterning Areas Containing Holes

Before you leave the pattern commands and move on to the next topic, you might be asking yourself how to make a hole in a patterned area. One way to create holes in a pattern might be to use the Difference method to pattern an area with holes. Another method might be to create the elements with hole mode. When you place elements as holes or change the element to a hole after placing it, some of the pattern commands recognize them as special elements.

Placing Hole Elements

Normally, you should always create elements in a design file using Solid mode. Solid mode is the default unless someone has changed it. To check the mode that is currently active, look at the Area setting in the Polygons, Circles and Ellipses, or Change Element tool boxes.

If you are about to place several holes in a solid surface and you know you will eventually want to pattern the solid portion, consider placing the hole elements using Hole mode. You can change the active setting from Solid to Hole mode by using the Area setting in the Polygons, Circles and Ellipses, or Change Elements tool boxes. After you activate an area mode, every element you place is in that mode.

Tip   If you change the active mode to Hole mode in a design file, it is a good practice to change it back to Solid mode after you have placed the hole elements. Do not create your entire design file in Hole mode. Hole elements cannot be patterned.

Changing Elements to Holes

If you have already placed the elements in the design file and later decide that the elements should be holes, you can change the mode on the existing elements by using the Change Element to Active Area (Solid/Hole) command. This command can be issued by choosing the tool from the Change Attributes tool box (see fig. 12.7).

Figure 12.7

The Change Element to Active Area (Solid/Hole) tool.

The Area setting displayed in the Change Attributes tool box indicates the active area mode. After you change the setting to the mode you want, you must identify the element and accept the highlighted element to effect the change.

The Area toggle button changes the active area mode. After using the Change Element to Active Area (Solid/Hole) command, be sure the Area setting is Solid before you continue drawing; otherwise, all the elements you subsequently place will be in Hole mode. Because holes are the exception, not the rule, always draw in Solid mode.

You can also check or change the mode of an element by using the Element Information dialog box. To open this dialog box choose Information from the Element pull-down menu or press Ctrl+I. Pick a point on the element you want to analyze and accept the highlighted element. When the Element Information settings box is displayed, review or change the first setting in the Properties section. The Apply button applies any changes you make.

Tip

Patterning Around Holes

After you have placed elements as holes or changed them to holes, you can choose the Hatch Area command, use the Element method, and pick the solid element to be patterned. The hatch pattern will be placed around all the elements defined as holes. Do not use associative patterning, however, unless they are grouped, because associative patterning does not recognize ungrouped hole elements.

In the following exercise you create a block that represents a metal plate, and you place several holes in the plate for bolt holes (see fig. 12.8). Pattern the solid element without associative patterning to see how the pattern commands respond to hole elements.

Figure 12.8

*Holes in a
patterned area.*

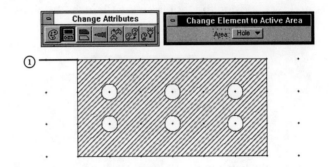

PLACING ELEMENTS AND PATTERNING AROUND HOLES

Continue from the preceding exercise with the CHAP12.DGN design file open.

Choose the Place Block tool

Choose the AccuDraw icon from the Primary tool box

`Enter first point` *Pick point at* ① *(refer to figure 12.8)*

Move cursor to the right of ① *and enter* **6**   Activates x field in AccuDraw box

Press Tab   Activates y field in AccuDraw box

Move cursor toward the top of the screen and enter **3**

`Enter opposite corner` *Pick a point*   Completes block

Choose the Place Circle command

*Choose **A**rea, **H**ole*

Choose Center Method from Tool Settings box

Turn on Diameter constraint and enter **.5**

Tentative point to lower left corner of box

Type **O**	Sets origin for AccuDraw
Move cursor right of tentative point	
Enter **1**	
Move cursor up and type **1**	
`Identify Center Point` *Pick a point*	Places circle
Choose the Construct Array tool (press and drag on the Copy tool to open the Manipulate Element tool box, then choose the last tool)	
Choose Array **T**ype, **R**ectangular	
Clear or highlight the Active **A**ngle field *and enter* **0**	
Enter **2** *in the* **R**ows *field*	
Enter **3** *in the* **C**olumns *field*	
Enter **1** *in the* Row **S**pacing *field*	
Enter **2** *in the* C**o**lumn Spacing *field*	
`Identify Element` *Pick a point on the circle*	
`Accept/Reject (select next input)` *Pick any point*	Places array

Pattern the block using the Hatch Area tool with the following settings: **S**pacing set to .1, **A**ngle set to 45. Use the Element method, and leave Ass**o**ciative Pattern off.

You must group hole elements with a solid element before you use the Associative Patterning option. First, choose the Group Holes tool from the Groups tool box (see fig. 12.9). The Group Holes command prompts you to identify the solid element and then to identify and accept each of the hole elements. After the solid and hole elements are grouped, they become a collection of elements called an *orphan cell*.

Figure 12.9

The Group Holes tool.

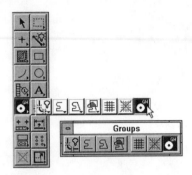

Warning   You cannot modify the individual elements of an orphan cell. Associative patterning can pattern the orphan cell appropriately; however, there is no advantage to grouping solids and holes because you cannot modify the individual components of an orphan cell to take advantage of the associative patterning feature.

The advantage to grouping solids and holes in a 2D design file is that the grouped elements can only be manipulated together. In other words, delete one element and you delete them all, copy one element and you copy them all, and so on.

If grouped elements are what you want, you could also use element selection groups or graphic groups to manipulate your solid and hole elements as one. See Chapter 9 on alternative methods of grouping elements.

Reviewing Patterning Hole Options

Looking at figure 12.10, consider the four options that give you the same graphic results.

Figure 12.10

Many holes in a solid.

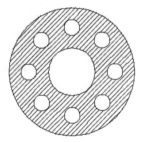

Option 1:

Using the Difference method, pattern the circle and leave the holes blank by identifying each of the holes. (This method does not require that the bolt holes be in Hole mode.)

Option 2:

1. Before placing the circles, set the active area mode to Hole in the tool settings box.

2. Place all the hole circles.

3. Before continuing any further, change the active area mode back to Solid.

4. Use the Pattern Area command with the Element method and no associative patterning to pattern the circle.

Option 3:

1. Use the Change Element to Active Area (Solid/Hole) command, and change all the existing (inside) circle elements to holes.

2. Use the Pattern Area command with the Element method and no associative patterning to pattern the circle.

Option 4:

1. Choose the Group Holes command, and identify the solid element and each of the holes. The command creates an orphan cell.

2. Use the Pattern Area command with the Element method and associative patterning to pattern the circle.

The approach you take depends on your drafting procedure. The previous illustrates that you can draw it with an area pattern in mind or if you later determine that an area pattern is required you don't have to redraw the elements. You have options and approaches to complete the task at hand without starting over.

Currently, the pattern commands do not recognize holes in the solid when you use the Flood method.

Note

Dropping Associative Patterning

In some cases, you may want to drop (disassociate) the associative patterning to modify the element without changing the pattern elements. You can choose the Drop Associative Pattern tool from the Drop tool box (see fig. 12.11). To open the Drop tool box, choose Drop from the Tools pull-down menu.

Figure 12.11

Dropping associative patterning.

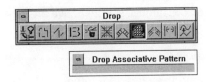

In the following exercise, you experiment with the effects of associative patterning and dropping an associative pattern.

DROPPING AN ASSOCIATIVE PATTERN

Continue from the preceding exercise with the CHAP12.DGN design file open.

Delete the patterned plate with holes

Place a simple block in the view making sure
A*r*ea *is set to* SOLID

Pattern the block with Hatch Area, Ass*o*ciative
Pattern *on, and the* **E**lement *method*

*Modify the block with the Modify Element
tool and see the patterning change*

Choose **T**ools, Dr**o**p   Opens the Drop tool box

*Choose the Drop Associative Pattern tool
(refer to figure 12.11)*

`Identify Element` *Pick a point on the*   Highlights the element and the pattern
pattern   components (see fig. 12.12)

`Accept/Reject (select next input)`   Accepts and drops association
Pick any point

Modify the element again. Use Reset to cycle the selection to identify the block. Observe that the pattern components do not get modified.

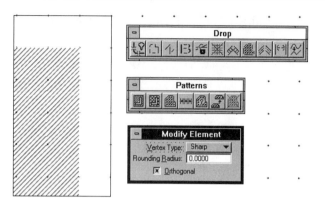

Figure 12.12

Modifying an element after dropping associative patterning.

Patterning Linear Elements

With the advent of custom line styles, linear patterning takes a step into history. As a matter of fact, the only reason MicroStation still has linear patterning on the menus is to make this version compatible with older versions. If you need to share files with users of MicroStation version 4 or older, linear patterning is your only option. Custom line styles will be lost if you open the file in older versions of MicroStation.

Custom line styles have two big advantages over linear patterning: flexibility and file space economy. See Chapter 11 for more details on creating and using custom line styles.

♦ **Flexibility.** A line style is part of an element's attributes and is therefore easily modified. When you modify the element, the line style is modified. On the other hand, linear patterning requires that you delete the pattern to modify the element and then reapply the pattern. Line-style definitions are stored externally in a style library. When you modify the line-style definition in the style library, the element immediately reflects the change.

♦ **File Space Economy.** Design files are smaller when you use custom line styles rather than linear patterns. The primitive elements that make up the style are not stored repeatedly in the design file as they are when you use linear patterning. Smaller-sized design files always mean improvements in speed.

When you use linear patterning on an element, a cell is placed in the file as many times as is necessary to complete the pattern. If you want to modify a line after it has been linear patterned, you have to run through the following steps:

1. Delete the pattern with the Delete Pattern command or the Delete Element command.

2. Turn off pattern display to see the original element. When a line is patterned, the primary element is modified to a linear pattern class element and can be viewed only if pattern display is off.

3. Change the element class back to primary so it can be viewed with pattern display on.

4. Modify the primary element.

5. Repattern the line.

To modify a patterned line with these steps is a lot of trouble, so whenever possible use custom line styles instead of linear patterning. Custom lines styles enable you to modify the line without any additional steps.

Showing Pattern Attributes

The tool for the Show Pattern Attributes command, on the Patterns tool box (see fig. 12.13), displays the pattern cell that was used or the word (Hatching), the pattern angle (PA=), and the pattern spacing or pattern delta (PD=) that were used in the Status Bar.

Figure 12.13

Showing pattern attributes.

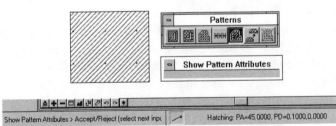

Matching Pattern Attributes

The Match Pattern Attributes tool can be activated from the Patterns tool box (see fig. 12.14). This command prompts you to identify a pattern on the screen to set the active patterning settings. The new settings are displayed in the status bar.

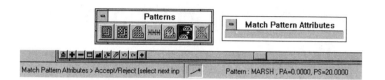

Figure 12.14

Matching pattern attributes.

Turning Off Pattern Display

You can turn off pattern display in any or all of the views by using the View Attributes settings box (see fig. 12.15). To open this settings box, choose **A**ttributes from the **S**ettings pull-down menu.

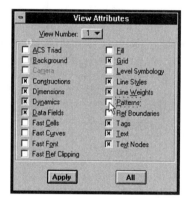

Figure 12.15

Turning pattern display on or off.

Turning off the display of the pattern elements does not remove the patterns; it only hides them from the view. In a dense design file, you may want to unclutter the view you are working in by turning off pattern display, or you may want to get a check plot with no patterns displayed.

> Pattern elements placed with the associative patterns option will be changed if the primary element is modified, regardless of the pattern display setting. Likewise, if Graphic Group lock is on, pattern elements are removed when you delete the primary element, regardless of whether or not you are displaying the pattern.

Warning

Defining and Filling Complex Elements

In the earlier chapters, you learned about fill for the shape and circle commands. These commands give you the option to fill the area of a shape with a color during placement. What if the area you want to fill cannot be drawn as a closed shape? The pattern commands create complex elements to generate a pattern of an area that is not bound by a single element. You can apply a fill to a complex element in the same manner, but first you have to create the complex shape yourself.

MicroStation has two different types of complex elements: complex chains and complex shapes. Both complex element types are made up of different linear elements (lines, arcs, line strings, and the like). These linear elements are grouped together to create a complex chain or a closed complex shape. The Groups tool box has three tools for creating complex elements (see fig. 12.16).

Figure 12.16

Tools for creating complex elements.

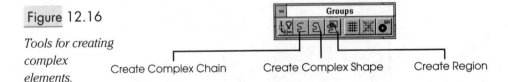

Create Complex Chain　　　Create Complex Shape　　　Create Region

Note　　The SmartLine tool creates a complex chain whenever you use the Join Element option. This combines the line and arc segment types into one element.

The second tool on the Groups tool box is Create Complex Chain. You can use the Create Complex Chain command to group together linear elements end to end. A complex chain never creates a closed shape. After a chain is created, you can modify the element attributes as if they were one element. For example, you could apply a custom line style to the chain, or you could change the attributes of all the elements at once.

The third and fourth tools on the Groups tool box are Create Complex Shape and Create Region. You have seen that some of the pattern commands can create complex shapes for you, but what if the pattern command with all its different methods does not create exactly what you want? You can create your own complex element and then pattern the defined area with the Element method. You can use the Create Complex Shape tool or the Create Region tool to accomplish this task.

> Besides using complex elements for patterning, you can use complex elements to make element manipulation easier and less troublesome by chaining elements or creating complex shapes. After the elements are chained or made into a complex shape, they can be manipulated as if they were a single element.

Note

Creating Complex Elements

The Create Complex Chain and Create Complex Shape tools have basically the same options. You first select the type of chain or complex shape tool you want in the **M**ethod field of the Groups tool box. You have two choices: **M**anual or **A**utomatic. If you choose Manual, the command prompts you to identify each piece of the complex element in order. If you choose Automatic, you pick the first element and MicroStation attempts to create the complex chain or shape. The Max **G**ap setting defines the distance that MicroStation looks for a connecting element. The chain or complex shape will jump the gap and place a line between the two points to make a continuous element. The create Automatic option will highlight the path and ask you to confirm each segment.

> If the design is complicated, the Automatic method may find many different paths to define the shape or chain. In this case, the Automatic method could be more trouble than picking the elements individually.

Note

> You must pick the elements in sequential order that defines the outside perimeter of the complex shape with the Manual method.

Warning

In the following exercise, you use the Automatic method to create the complex shape. Use the SmartLine tool to create the mechanical part shown in figure 12.17. Make sure the Join Element toggle is turned off.

CREATING A COMPLEX SHAPE AUTOMATICALLY

Continue from the preceding exercise with the CHAP12.DGN design file open.

Choose the Create Complex Shape tool

Choose **M**ethod, **A**utomatic	Issues the Automatic Create Complex Shape command
`Identify Element` *Pick point* *(see fig. 12.17)*	Highlights line element
`Accept/Reject (select next input)` *Pick any point*	Displays `Shape closed` in the status bar

Figure 12.17

Using the Automatic method to create a complex shape.

Use Automatic Method

After you choose any of the Create Complex Shape tools, the tool box displays options for filling the shape. These options should look familiar—they are the same options that appear with the Place Shape and Circle tools. To fill the complex shape automatically, choose **O**paque or Outl**i**ned from the **F**ill Type pop-up list and choose the Fill **C**olor.

After you have created the complex shape, if you determine that you need to fill the shape, choose the Change Element to Active Fill Type command from the Change Attributes tool box (see fig. 12.18). Choose the appropriate **F**ill type and Fill **C**olor and identify the shape or complex shape you want to change. Accept the highlighted element by clicking anywhere in the view.

Figure 12.18

The Change Element to Active Fill Type tool.

Now try using the manual method to create a complex shape. In the following exercise, you pick each element of the mechanical part to create the complex shape and then you apply a fill to it.

CREATING AND FILLING A COMPLEX SHAPE MANUALLY

Continue from the preceding exercise with the CHAP12.DGN design file open.

Choose **E**dit, **U**ndo create complex shape	
Turn on **F**ill *in the View Attributes dialog box*	
Choose the Create Complex Shape tool	
Choose **M**ethod, **M**anual	Issues the Create Complex Shape command
Choose **F**ill Type, **O**paque	
Choose Fill **C**olor *and select color*	
Identify Element *Pick point*	Highlights line element
Accept/Reject (select next input) *Pick points on each element that represent part outline in sequence*	Selects rest of elements in order
Accept/Reject (select next input) *Pick a point*	Accepts selections and displays Shape closed in status bar

---

Creating Complex Elements from a Region

The fourth tool on the Groups tool box is Create Region. The Create Region command creates a complex shape from two or more elements. The **M**ethod pop-up list contains four of the same options you have seen in the pattern commands: **I**ntersection, **U**nion, **D**ifference, and **F**lood. You could pattern the complex shape later, or you could use the Create Region command as another manipulation command for constructing elements. The **K**eep Original toggle button on the Groups tool box gives you the option of modifying the existing elements or creating a new element while leaving the original elements intact.

Dropping Complex Elements

When you drop a complex element, it reverts to its original components, namely lines, arcs, and line strings. The Drop Element tool is found on the Drop tool box (see fig. 12.19). You can activate this tool by choosing Drop from the **T**ools pull-down menu.

Figure 12.19

The Drop Element tool.

When the Drop Element tool is active it provides several selections in the tool settings box. Turn on the **C**omplex toggle button and identify an element, and then the complex element is highlighted. To drop the complex element, you must accept the highlighted element by picking a point anywhere in the view.

 Note   If you want to add an element to a complex chain, drop the old chain first, then re-create the chain, because you cannot add an element to an existing chain. You might consider adding a vertex and modifying the complex element as an alternative to dropping it and redefining the complex chain.

Summary

In this chapter, you have seen and tried many of the pattern commands. The different methods available for the pattern commands make patterning flexible and easy. To avoid repatterning after you modify elements, you should use associative patterning whenever possible. This procedure saves both time and money.

 Tip   With all the options and settings, remember to use the Undo command if you make a mistake while patterning and want to try again.

Complex chains and complex shapes are extremely useful features for many applications. Area patterning uses complex shapes to define an element for associative patterning. You can use complex elements to create and fill your own closed shapes, to modify attributes, or just to manipulate the elements as one piece.

Remember that patterning adds additional elements to your design file, so use patterns wisely. File sizes can become large and cumbersome to work with if you don't.

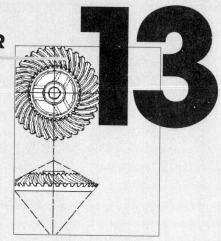

Placing Dimensions

U ntil now the emphasis has been on creating the elements or geometry
of a design in the design file. Often these graphic elements are not
enough to convey all the desired information; dimensioning needs to be
added to convey the size or measurement.

*This chapter discusses how to use MicroStation commands to add dimensions to
your design. This chapter helps you understand how dimensioning is handled in
MicroStation, what different types of dimensioning you have available, and then
how to modify the dimension settings.*

In this chapter, you learn:

♦ How to find and change the popular dimension settings

♦ What dimension component groups are

♦ How to dimension lengths

♦ How to dimension angles and arcs

♦ How to dimension diameters and radii

♦ How to change the way dimensions look

Understanding Dimensioning in MicroStation

Dimensions are complex elements made up of lines, arcs, text, and terminators. Each component of a dimension has a name, and each component can be customized (see fig. 13.1). The dimensioning commands covered in this chapter can be found on the Dimension tool box located in the Main tool frame (see fig. 13.2).

Figure 13.1

Dimension component names.

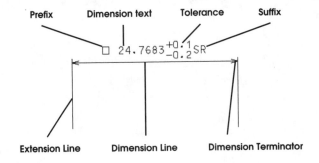

Figure 13.2

Activating the Dimensioning tool box from the Main tool frame.

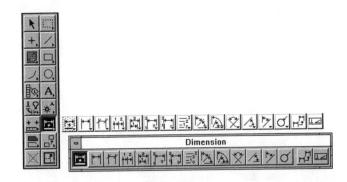

MicroStation Dimension elements have a number of advantages: they are easily modified; they use about 20 percent less space as using regular elements in the design file; their dimension text changes to reflect new working units; and they can be associated or connected to the graphic element they dimension.

If you need compatibility with 3.x versions of MicroStation, you should still use dimension elements but then drop them for compatibility. Dimension elements that have been dropped lose their associations and are reduced to primitive elements. After a dimension element has been dropped, it cannot be converted back to a dimension element. Another option is to freeze the dimension for downward compatibility. Freeze enables you to keep the association. Thaw returns the dimensions to the original state.

Dimensions are placed as primitive elements if the compatibility is set to 3.x. Choose User, then Preferences from the Application Window, then choose Category. Highlight Compatibility, and then choose 3.x from the Compatibility option list to change the compatibility. Dimension elements also can be reduced to primitive elements by using the Drop Dimension Element tool.

Basically, MicroStation contains three different types of dimensioning: length, arcs and angles, and diameters and radii. Each different type of dimension is addressed with several tools in MicroStation to get exactly what you want from your dimension. Each tool is looked at after a brief discussion on a general dimensioning tool called Dimension Element. The Dimension Element is very useful for the casual dimensioning user.

Dimensions are useless if your geometry is not placed accurately. Always use some means of placing them precisely. Usually this means snapping them to existing geometry with tentative points. Although the following exercises do not give specific tentative point instructions, you should use tentative points to snap to the existing geometry.

Warning

Working with the Dimension Element Tool

You use the Dimension Element tool to quickly dimension a line, circle, arc, or segment of a shape. Pick an element (or side of a shape) and MicroStation automatically computes the length of the line or element segment and places the dimension on your cursor. Pressing Enter on the keyboard will switch the dimension type from arrow, stroke, label, or the perpendicular type. Place an additional point to define the length of the extension line.

Try the Dimension Element command in the next exercise. Dimensioning requires an element, so place a shape similar to the ones shown in figure 13.3 to dimension later in the exercise.

DIMENSION ELEMENT

Create a design file called CHAP13.DGN.

Draw an element to dimension similar to the one shown in figure 13.3.

Choose the Dimension Element tool

`Select element to dimension` *Pick point at ① (see fig. 13.3)*	Dimension appears on the cursor
`Accept (Press return to Switch command)` *Pick point at ②*	Defines the length of the extension lines

---

Figure 13.3

Placing dimensions with the Dimension Element tool.

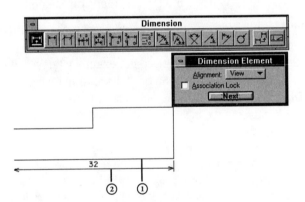

Associating Dimensions

Now that you have dimensioned your first element, what happens when one of the lines that represent the shape is modified? The dimension element that contains the witness lines, arrow, and text don't change. This might not be the desired result. Association Lock, located in the tool settings box when every dimension command is active, links a dimension element to the element you're dimensioning. When the element length is modified, the associated dimension is modified. Dimension elements can be associated with an element at the time the dimension element is placed by first turning on the Association Lock. An Association toggle button appears in the tool settings box for each of the dimension commands.

> *Tip*
>
> If a dimension element has been placed without an association, an association point can be added by turning on the Association lock and then using the Modify Element tool. The association is only made if you identify the dimension element and then snap to the element you want the dimension element to be associated to.

Try the Dimension Element again, but this time with Association Lock on. Modify the element and see how the two dimensions react.

CREATING ASSOCIATED DIMENSIONS

Continue from the preceding exercise with the CHAP13.DGN design file open and an element drawn similar to the one in figure 13.3.

Turn on the Association Lock toggle in the tool settings box.

Select element to dimension *Pick point at* ①   Dimension appears on the cursor

Accept (Press return to Switch command) *Pick point at* ②   Defines the length of the extension lines

Choose the Element Selection tool

Now modify the elements' segments of both dimensioned sides.

Dimensioning Lengths

The first several tools on the Dimension tool box (see fig. 13.4) are used to dimension linear distances in the design file. You open the Linear Dimensions tool box by choosing **M**ain, then **D**imension, from the **T**ools pull-down menu or by tearing this tool box off the Main tool frame. Figure 13.5 shows some examples of dimensions placed with linear dimensioning commands.

Figure 13.4

The Linear
Dimension tools.

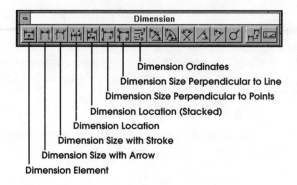

Dimension Ordinates
Dimension Size Perpendicular to Line
Dimension Size Perpendicular to Points
Dimension Location (Stacked)
Dimension Location
Dimension Size with Stroke
Dimension Size with Arrow
Dimension Element

Figure 13.5

Examples of linear
dimensions.

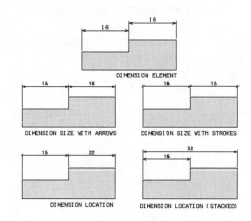

Dimension Size with Arrow or Stroke

You use the Dimension Size with Arrow tool or the Dimension Size with Stroke to place a dimension between two points. When multiple dimensions are placed, each is computed and placed from the end point of the previous dimension. Stroke line terminators typically are used by architectural drafters.

Note

Three points are required to place most linear dimensions, the exception being the Dimension Element command. The first point starts the dimension, the second defines the length of the extension line, and the third defines the end of the dimension. Press the reset button to reenter the last point. For example, after picking the second point that defines the length of the extension line, choose one reset to redefine the extension line length or choose two resets to back up to the starting point.

In the next exercise, place a dimension element with the Dimension Size with Arrow tool. Remember that this command will prompt you in the Status Bar for three points—watch the prompts for instructions.

DIMENSIONING SIZE WITH ARROW

Continue from the preceding exercise with the CHAP13.DGN design file open.

Choose the Dimension Size with Arrow tool

`Select start of dimension` *Pick point at* ① *(see fig. 13.6)*	Identifies the dimension origin
`Define length of extension line` *Pick point at* ②	Defines the length of the extension lines
`Select dimension endpoint` *Pick point at* ③	Defines the end point of the dimension
`Press Return to edit dimension text` `Select dimension endpoint` *Click the reset button*	Completes that dimension
`Define length of extension line` *Click the reset*	Completes the dimensioning command and you're ready to start a new dimension

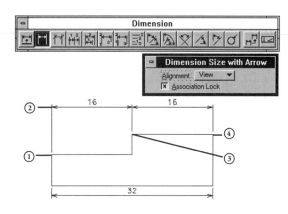

Figure 13.6

Using the Dimension Size with Arrow tool.

Consecutive dimensions like the two placed in the previous exercise are one dimension element. Delete one and they both get deleted from the drawing.

Dimension Location

You use the Dimension Location tool to place multiple dimensions from a common origin or datum. Each dimension is computed and placed from the dimension origin. The dimensions are chained.

Now try the Dimension Location command in the next exercise. Notice that the dimension text reflects a cumulative value.

DIMENSIONING THE LOCATION

Continue from the preceding exercise with the CHAP13.DGN design file open.

Delete the dimensions placed in the previous exercise.

Choose the Dimension Location tool

`Select start of dimension` *Pick point at* ① *(see fig. 13.7)*	Identifies the dimension origin
`Define length of extension line` *Pick point at* ②	Defines the extension line length
`Select dimension endpoint` *Pick point at* ③	Determines the dimension end point
`Press Return to edit dimension text`	
`Select dimension endpoint` *Pick point at* ④	Determines the end point for the next dimension
`Press Return to edit dimension text` `Select dimension endpoint` *Click the reset button*	Completes that dimension
`Define length of extension line` *Click the reset button*	Completes the dimensioning command and you're ready to start a new dimension

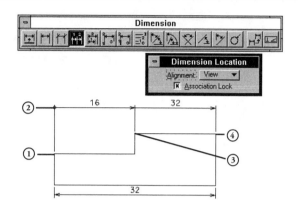

Figure 13.7

*Using the
Dimension
Location tool.*

Dimension Location (Stacked)

You use the Dimension Location (Stacked) tool to place multiple dimensions from a common origin or datum. Each dimension is computed and placed from the first dimension origin. The dimensions are stacked.

Try the Dimension Location (Stacked) command in the next exercise. The distance the second dimension is above the first is defined by the dimension text height.

DIMENSIONING THE LOCATION (STACKED)

Continue from the preceding exercise with the CHAP13.DGN design file open.

Delete the dimensions placed in the previous exercise.

*Choose the Dimension Location (Stacked)
tool*

`Select start of dimension` *Pick point at* ① *(see fig. 13.8)*	Identifies the dimension origin
`Define length of extension line` *Pick point at* ②	Defines the extension line length
`Select dimension endpoint` *Pick point at* ③	Determines the dimension end point
`Press Return to edit dimension text`	
`Select dimension endpoint` *Pick point at* ④	Determines the end point for the next dimension
`Press Return to edit dimension text` `Select dimension endpoint` *Click the reset button twice*	Completes the dimensioning command

Figure 13.8

*Using the
Dimension
Location
(Stacked) tool.*

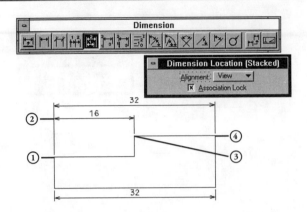

Dimensioning Arcs and Angles

To dimension arcs or angles, use the angular dimension tools in the Dimension tool box (see fig. 13.9). Each of the five tools is slightly different (see fig. 13.10).

Figure 13.9

*The angular
dimension tools.*

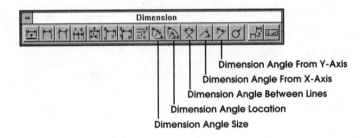

Dimension Angle From Y-Axis
Dimension Angle From X-Axis
Dimension Angle Between Lines
Dimension Angle Location
Dimension Angle Size

Figure 13.10

*Dimensions
placed with the
angular
dimensioning
tools.*

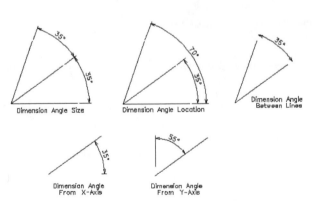

The next sections discuss the Dimension Angle and Arc tools in detail.

Dimension Angle Size

The Dimension Angle Size tool is used to dimension the angle between two lines or the sweep angle of an arc. If more than one dimension is placed, each successive dimension is computed and placed from the end point of the previous one. The dimension is measured in a counterclockwise direction from the dimension origin. After you enter the dimension end point, press Enter to edit the dimension text.

The key-in field must be the active window when you press Enter to edit the dimension text. If it is not, press Escape once to activate the key-in field.

Warning

After you place the first dimension, you can place another dimension by entering another end point, or you can press Enter to open a Dimension Text edit box, or you can click the reset button to complete the dimension command.

Try dimensioning an angle in the following exercise. Remember to snap with tentative points for accuracy.

DIMENSIONING THE ANGLE SIZE

Continue from the preceding exercise with the CHAP13.DGN design file open.

Place three lines like the ones shown in figure 13.22.

Choose the Dimension Angle Size tool

`Select start of dimension` *Pick point at* ① *(see fig. 13.11)*	Sets dimension origin
`Define length of extension line` *Pick point at* ②	Defines the length of the extension lines
`Enter point on axis` *Pick point at* ③	Defines the vertex of the angle
`Select dimension endpoint` *Pick point at* ④	Defines the end point of the dimension
`Press Return to edit dimension text` `Select dimension endpoint` *Pick point at* ⑤	
Click the reset button	Completes the dimensioning command

Figure 13.11

Using the
Dimension Angle
Size tool.

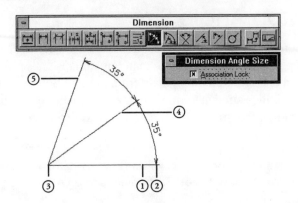

Note   You can change the number of digits past the decimal point in the Units
Category in the Dimension Settings box (see fig. 13.28).

Dimension Angle Location

The Dimension Angle Location tool (see fig. 13.12) is used to dimension the angle
between two lines using a datum. The first point defines the dimension origin
(datum). Angles are measured counterclockwise from this point. Multiple dimensions are stacked.

Figure 13.12

Using the
Dimension Angle
Location tool.

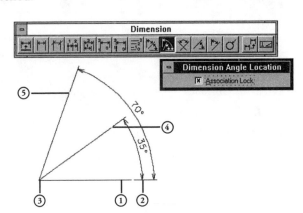

Dimension Angle Between Lines

The Dimension Angle Between Lines tool is used to place a dimension between two
lines, line strings, or two sides of a shape. Extension lines are not drawn. Select the
elements first, and then place a data point to define the radius of the dimension.

DIMENSIONING AN ANGLE BETWEEN LINES

Continue from the preceding exercise with the CHAP13.DGN design file open.

Delete the dimension placed in the previous exercise.

Choose the Dimension Angle Between Lines tool

`Select first line` *Pick point at* ① *(see fig. 13.13)*	Identifies the first element
`Select second line` *Pick point at* ②	Identifies the second element
`Accept/Reject (select next input)` *Pick point at* ③	Defines the radius of the dimension

Select first line

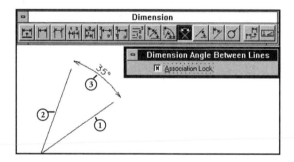

Figure 13.13

Using the Dimension Angle Between Lines tool.

Dimension Angle from X-Axis

The Dimension Angle From X-Axis tool dimensions angles between a line, line string, or the side of a shape and the X-axis of the active view. The first data point identifies the element to be dimensioned and defines the location of the dimension line. The second data point defines the direction of the dimension and the length of the extension line.

The next two exercises only require one line. Delete all but one line for the next exercise.

Dimensioning an Angle from the X-Axis

Continue from the preceding exercise with the CHAP13.DGN design file open.

Delete the dimension placed in the previous exercise.

Choose the Dimension Angle from
X-Axis tool

`Identify element` *Pick point at* ① *(see fig. 13.14)*	Identifies element and sets dimension line location
`Accept, define dimension axis` *Pick point at* ②	Defines location and direction of the dimension
`Identify element`	

Figure 13.14

Using the Dimension Angle From X-Axis tool.

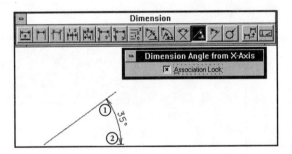

Dimension Angle From Y-Axis

The Dimension Angle From Y-Axis tool dimensions angles between a line, line string, or the side of a shape and the Y-axis of the active view. The first data point identifies the element to be dimensioned and defines the location of the dimension line. The second data point defines the direction of the dimension and the length of the extension line.

Dimensioning an Angle from the Y-Axis

Continue from the preceding exercise with the CHAP13.DGN design file open.

Delete the dimension placed in the previous exercise.

Choose the Dimension Angle From
Y-Axis tool

`Identify element` *Pick point at* ① *(see fig. 13.15)*	Identifies element and sets dimension line location
`Accept, define dimension axis` *Pick point at* ②	Defines location and direction of the dimension
`Identify element`	

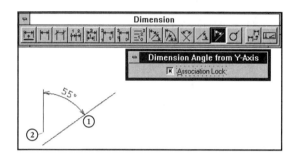

Figure 13.15

Using the Dimension Angle From Y-Axis tool.

Dimensioning Diameters and Radii

The Radial Dimensions tool is used to dimension the radius and diameter of circles and arcs. There are five different modes of this tool, effectively giving you five different commands. Figure 13.16 shows several examples of dimensions placed using the radial dimensioning tool.

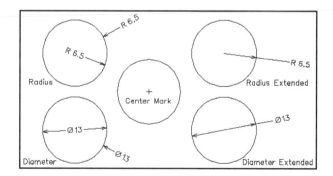

Figure 13.16

Examples of radial dimensions.

The way the text is placed when you are using this tool is based on the dimension settings. For example, if the text **O**rientation is set to In-line or Above the dimension follows the leader lines (inside or out of the circle or arc) as shown in figure 13.16. If you desire a bent or shoulder leader line, change the dimension text **O**rientation to Horizontal in the Text category of the Dimension settings box. To place multi-segment leader lines, set the dimension text **L**ocation to manual, which can be found in the Placement category of the Dimension Settings box.

Note   Remember the dimension element tool for quick and easy linear dimensioning? This command also works with diameter and radius dimensions. MicroStation is smart enough to recognize an arc or circle element and the space bar lets you toggle through all the radial dimension options.

Center Mark Mode

You use the Place Center Mark mode to place a center mark in a circle or an arc, as shown previously in figure 13.16. The first data point identifies the arc or circle, and the second data point accepts placement of the center mark. You can change the size of the center mark by entering a different value in the Center Size field.

Note   The Center Mark is a dimension element. Make sure to place the Center Mark with association lock if you want it to move, copy, and so on with the circle or arc.

Radius Mode

The Dimension Radial tool is used to dimension an arc or circle. The first data point identifies the arc, and the second data point identifies the rotation and position of the leader and text. If a data point is entered inside the circle, a dimension line is placed from the center with the dimension line terminator pointing outward. A data point outside the circle places a leader and dimension text. Dimensions are dynamically dragged. Identify the circle, and then move the pointer. The dimension will change its orientation until a second data point is placed to anchor the dimension.

DIMENSIONING THE RADIUS

Continue from the preceding exercise with the CHAP13.DGN design file open.

Place an arc in the view

Choose the Dimension Radial tool

*Choose the **R**adius from the **M**ode pop-up menu*

Identify element *Pick point at* ① Identifies the arc to be dimensioned
(see fig. 13.17)

Select dimension endpoint *Pick point at* ② Places dimension

Identify element

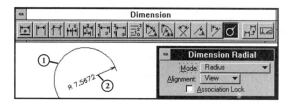

Figure 13.17

*Using the
Dimension Radial
tool.*

Dimension Radial (Extended Leader)

The Dimension Radial (Extended Leader) tool (see fig 13.18) places a dimension with a radial leader through the center of the arc. A leader and dimension text are placed inside or outside the arc.

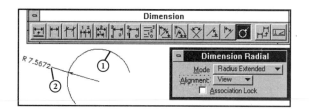

Figure 13.18

*Using the
Dimension Radial
(Extended Leader)
tool.*

Dimension Diameter

The Dimension Diameter tool (see fig 13.19) is used to dimension the diameter of circles or arcs. The first data point identifies the element to be dimensioned. The second data point determines the location and orientation of the leader or dimension line. If a data point is entered inside the circle, a dimension line is placed through the center with dimension line terminators pointing outward. A data point outside the circle places the leader and dimension text.

If the text and leaders are too large to place inside the circle or arc, MicroStation will force the arrows and leader line outside the circle pointing inward.

Note

Figure 13.19

*Using the
Dimension
Diameter tool.*

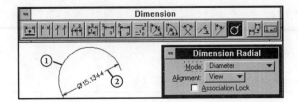

Dimension Diameter (Extended Leader)

The Dimension Diameter (Extended Leader) tool is the same as the Dimension Diameter tool with one exception. A dimension line with terminators is placed inside the circle when the second data point is entered outside the circle.

DIMENSIONING THE DIAMETER (EXTENDED LEADER)

Continue from the preceding exercise with the CHAP13.DGN design file open.

Delete the dimension placed in previous exercise

Choose the Dimension Radial tool

*Choose the D**i**ameter Extended from the **M**ode pop-up menu*

Identify element *Pick point at* ① *(see fig. 13.20)*   Identifies the circle to be dimensioned

Press Return to edit dimension text

Select dimension endpoint *Pick point at* ②   Places the dimension inside the circle

Identify element

Figure 13.20

Using the Dimension Diameter (Extended Leader) tool.

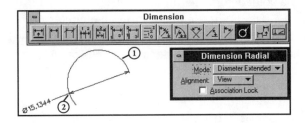

Creating and Using Dimension Components Groups

If you need to customize the dimension settings for different applications, you will want to use dimension components groups to help manage the dimension settings. You use the Settings Manager to manage sets of dimension settings as dimension components groups. To activate the Settings Manager, choose **M**anage from the **S**ettings pull-down menu and the Select Settings box is displayed. See Chapter 20 for detailed information about creating settings groups for dimensioning as well as other settings.

After you have made appropriate dimensioning settings (saving or selecting them as a dimension component group if they are standard settings you will use repeatedly), you are ready to place dimensions with the dimensioning tools.

Choosing the Settings

Dimensioning is useless unless you can make it conform to your office's or industry's dimensioning standards. In MicroStation, you use dimension settings to control the appearance of dimensions. Dimension settings can be controlled by using settings boxes (see fig. 13.21). To activate this settings box choose **D**imensions from the E**l**ement pull-down menu. Several of the categories listed on the left side of the settings box will be reviewed in the following sections.

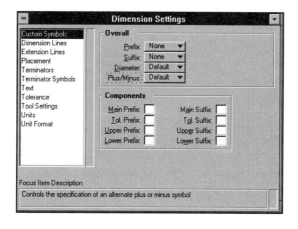

Figure 13.21

The Dimension Settings settings box.

Dimension Placement Settings

Choose Placement from the Category list in the settings box to display the Dimension Placement settings (see fig. 13.22). The Placement options in the settings box contain buttons for turning on or off Adjust **D**imension Line, **R**eference File Units, and R**e**lative Dimension Line. The Placement settings also have two pop-up list boxes for **A**lignment and **L**ocation controls.

Figure 13.22

The Dimension Placement settings.

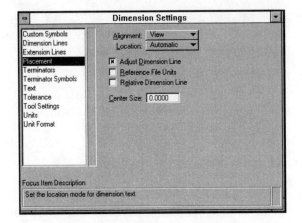

The **A**lignment control changes the orientation of the dimension line. This control has four menu options: **V**iew, **D**rawing, **T**rue, and **A**rbitrary. The **V**iew option draws the dimension horizontally with respect to the active view. If the view has been rotated, the **D**rawing option draws the dimension line, using the view rotation angle. The **T**rue option draws the dimension line parallel to the entity being dimensioned. The **A**rbitrary option draws dimensions with a fixed extension line length (see fig. 13.23).

Figure 13.23

Alignment options.

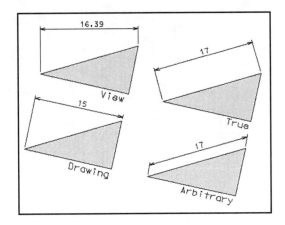

Choose **A**utomatic, **S**emi-Automatic, or **M**anual from the **L**ocation pop-up menu to control the location or placement of dimension text.

If the Adjust **D**imension Line button is turned on, the dimension command will take action if the text does not fit without overwriting existing dimension text. The dimension line and text are dynamically moved, and the extension lines are dynamically extended.

The **R**eference File Units button enables you to choose between using the active design file units or a reference file's units while dimensioning.

> Turn on the **R**eference File Units lock when dimensioning reference file elements that have been attached with a scale that is not 1:1 or the dimension text will be in your active design file units.

Tip

The R**e**lative Dimension Line button is used when modifying dimension elements. When it is turned off, the location of the dimension line remains the same, and the extension lines are allowed to change. When it is turned on, the dimension line length is allowed to vary, and the extension line length remains the same.

Dimension Terminators Settings

The Terminators control changes the way dimension line terminators are displayed. To review and set the terminator settings choose Terminators from the Category list (see fig. 13.24). This control has four menu options: **A**utomatic, **I**nside, **O**utside, and **R**eversed. If you choose **A**utomatic, MicroStation decides where to place the dimension line terminators. The **I**nside and **O**utside selections force the terminators to draw either on the inside or outside of the extension line. The **R**eversed option is a combination of the Inside and Outside options. The terminators are placed on the outside of the extension line while the dimension text and line appear inside the extension line.

The Attributes section of the settings box indicates whether the terminator should be placed at the active symbology or a predefined setting. You will see similar settings in the Dimension Lines, Extension Lines, and Text Categories. If a button is turned off, the active settings are used for that item. To override the active color, style, or weight when MicroStation places the terminators, turn on the toggle button and set the symbology.

Figure 13.24

*The Dimension
Terminators
settings.*

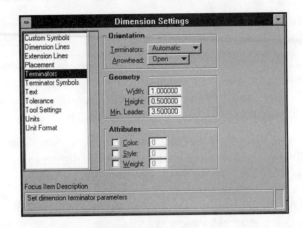

Dimension Text Settings

Another important part of every dimension is the text; therefore, the settings box
contains four controls to change the way dimension text is displayed: **O**rientation,
Justification, **T**ext Frame, and **M**argin (see fig. 13.25). Text can be oriented in three
ways: **I**n-line, **A**bove, or **H**orizontal. In-line text is placed on the dimension line,
which is then broken to fit the text. Dimension text placed above the dimension line
is normally oriented with the dimension line. If the dimension line is vertical, the
text is oriented vertically. Choosing horizontal text forces the text to be oriented
horizontally. You can justify dimension text in three ways: **L**eft, **C**enter, and **R**ight.

Figure 13.25

*The Dimension
Text settings.*

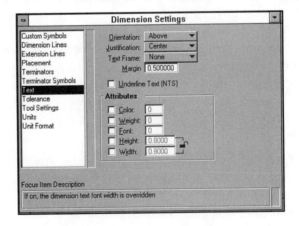

The toggle button, **U**nderline Text, is used to indicate when the dimension is not to
scale (NTS), by placing a line under the dimension text.

The Attributes section gives you the capability to set symbology for the text other
than the active symbology. For example, change the text size for the dimension text.
This does not change or affect the current text settings for the design file.

Dimension Extension Lines Settings

You use the Dimension Extension Lines settings (see fig. 13.26) to define the extension line symbology to something other than the default dimension symbology. In other words, the extension lines can be defined with different symbology—color, weight, and style—than the dimension lines. Turn off the **E**xtension Lines toggle button if you do not want extension lines to be placed.

The Geometry offset is expressed relative to the active text height. The **E**xtension Lines field contains a value of 0.5, which means that the extension line will be offset from the part geometry by half of the text height. If the text height is 1/8", then the offset is equal to 1/16".

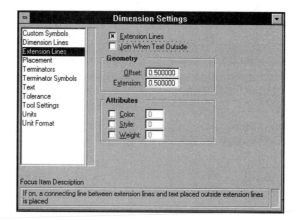

Figure 13.26

The Dimension Extension Lines settings.

Tolerance Settings

The Tolerance settings add tolerance information to mechanical drawings. Tolerance is expressed either as plus/minus or limit (see fig. 13.27).

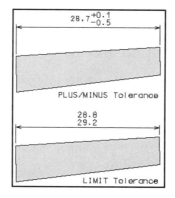

Figure 13.27

Tolerance examples.

Dimension Units Settings

The Dimension Units settings (see fig. 13.28) is used to format the dimension text.

Figure 13.28

The Dimension Units settings.

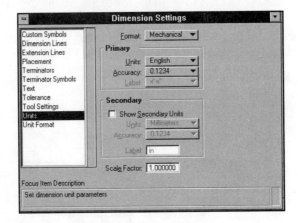

You can use the Units settings box to set units and accuracy. The **F**ormat setting controls whether the settings apply to mechanical or architectural (AEC) dimensions. Architectural dimensions have an additional **L**abel list box to format how feet and inches are displayed. The format for dual dimensioning is set in the Secondary section by turning on the Show **S**econdary Units button and changing the appropriate fields. See the Unit Format category to change dimension text output for angular and radial dimensioning.

Warning

Always make sure the Scal**e** Factor field is set to 1 when dimensioning a design that is drawn full-scale.

When dimensioning a cell or referenced drawing that is attached at a scale other than 1:1, set the Scal**e** Factor before dimensioning.

Custom Symbols Settings

The Custom Symbols settings (see fig. 13.29) are used to add special prefixes or suffixes, including plus/minus and diameter symbols, to dimension text and tolerance text. The prefixes and suffixes you set are automatically added to the text when you place dimensions. You can also control prefixes and suffixes with the Tool Settings category to assign prefixes or suffixes to specific tools.

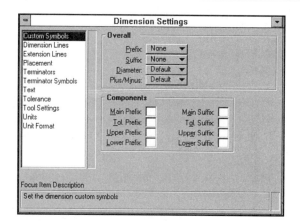

Figure 13.29

The Custom Symbols settings.

Terminator Symbols Settings

The Terminator Symbols category (see fig. 13.30) enables you to customize four types of dimension line terminators: **A**rrow, **S**troke, **O**rigin, and **D**ot. Each can be customized by replacing the default terminator with a cell or a font symbol (font 102 contains line terminators for MicroStation).

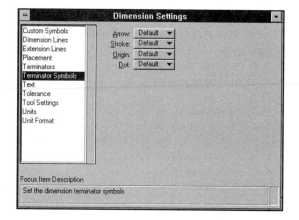

Figure 13.30

The Custom Terminators settings.

To change the dimension line terminator, click on one of the four buttons and an option list appears. Click on one of the items (**D**efault, **S**ymbol, or **C**ell), and fill in the field that appears to the right. You can also use the Tool Settings box to control terminators, assigning different terminators to specific types of dimensions.

Tool Settings

The Tool Settings box (see fig. 13.31) controls settings associated with individual dimensioning tools.

Figure 13.31

The Tool Settings box.

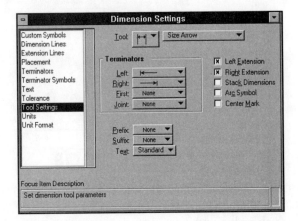

The previous settings change the dimension settings globally. The Tool Settings category changes dimension settings for individual tools. The buttons and option buttons displayed in the Tool Settings are dependent on the tool selected in the first two option fields. The tool is selected by choosing an icon from the first option field or by choosing a written description from the second option field. After selecting a tool, you can customize it by turning buttons on or off, choosing items from the option lists, and filling in the fields.

Changing the Way Existing Dimensions Look

Drafting standards often change during a project. This usually requires changes in the way a dimension looks. Levels, line weights, line styles, and colors can all change. Use the Change Dimension to Active Settings tool to change the way your dimensions look (see fig. 13.32).

To change an existing dimension's attributes, you can make the changes in the Dimension Settings box to change the active settings. Then you use the Change Dimension tool to apply the active settings to the dimension element. Another approach would be to use the Match Dimension tool found in the Match tool box to set the active settings from an existing dimension element, then use the Change Dimension to Active Settings tool to modify a dimension.

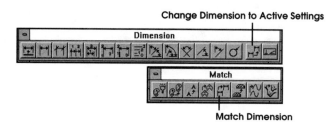

Change Dimension to Active Settings

Match Dimension

Figure 13.32

Match and Change Dimension settings tools.

Summary

In this chapter, you have learned some of the many ways to improve the appearance of your drawing by using dimensions. Dimensioning has many settings and controls for getting the standards that you desire or are accustomed to. Experience and studying the Dimension Settings box will give you a good understanding of all the options available with the dimensioning tools. Consider using Settings Groups if you have many different dimension setting requirements in a single design file. You will find more information about the functions and features of Settings Groups in Chapter 20.

CHAPTER

Working with Text

*T*ext or annotation appears on every drawing, whether the drawing is a representation of an architectural floor plan, an electrical schematic, or a map. In this chapter, you learn the fundamentals of placing, changing, and manipulating text in a design file. The first half of the chapter discusses the text settings and the features of placing and manipulating text. The second half covers more advanced text options and their idiosyncrasies.

MicroStation has three different varieties of text: text strings, enter data fields, and text nodes. This chapter discusses text strings and enter data fields at length, devoting particular attention to the situations to which each method might be best suited. You could place a regular text string, for example, for a title block; you might use an enter data field for a character inside a circle, such as the bubbles used in the figures in this book. To take full advantage of MicroStation's features, you should use different text placement methods in different situations. The final product, the plot, looks the same regardless of the method you use to place the text. MicroStation offers these different methods of text placement to enhance productivity.

In this chapter, you learn about doing the following actions:

♦ Placing text

♦ Placing text with graphics

♦ Editing existing text

♦ Finding and changing text in your design file

♦ Copying and incrementing the numbers in a text string

♦ Manipulating and changing the way text looks

♦ Creating placeholders for text to be filled in later, using advanced text features such as enter data fields

♦ Placing leader notes

♦ Creating and using a glossary to place commonly used text strings

Placing Text

You have waited long enough, so try placing some text in your design file. Open the Text tool box by tearing it off the Main tool frame, as shown in figure 14.1. You also can open the Text tool box from the pull-down menu by choosing **T**ools, **M**ain, Te**x**t.

Figure 14.1

The Text tool box.

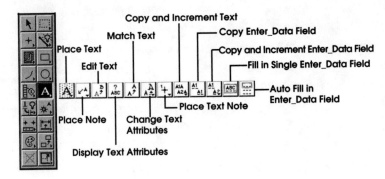

The tool for the Place Text command, denoted by a capital A, is on the Text tool box. After you choose the Place Text tool, several options appear in the tool settings box and a Text Editor window appears on your screen. The Text Editor window opens and the flashing cursor tells you where to begin typing.

To place the first piece of text, choose the Place Text tool, using the default selection type of By **O**rigin, and enter your name in the Text Editor window. After you enter the text, move the cursor into your design file area; you should see the text floating on the cursor. After you position the text correctly, pick a point. Note that after you place the text once, the text still floats on the cursor. You can pick more data points to place additional text as often as you want, or you can click the Reset button to clear the cursor.

When you place text, your cursor changes from a "+" to an "x." If your cursor appears as an "x" and you cannot see the text, your window might be too small or too large to see the text.

Tip

Placing Text

Create a design file called CHAP14.DGN.

Tear off the Text tool box from
the Main tool frame

Choose the Place Text tool from the   Opens the Text Editor window
Text tool box

`Enter text` *Type your first name*   Enters text in the Text Editor window and
                                            displays text at the x drawing cursor

Move cursor and pick a point at   Places your text
① *(see fig. 14.2)*

You could pick additional points to place the same text elsewhere.

`Enter more chars or position text`   Clears cursor and the Text
Click the Reset button   Editor window

`Enter text` *Close the Text Editor window*

Figure 14.2

Placing text.

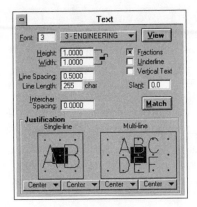

Choosing a command other than the text commands dismisses the Text Editor window.

Note

MicroStation places text with the active symbology just like other element placements (color, weight, level, and linecode). MicroStation also places text at the active angle setting. If you have your active angle set to 45 degrees, MicroStation automatically places your text at that angle. Read on for the other types of default settings, such as font, size, and so on.

Choosing and Changing Text Settings

MicroStation places text with the active text setting. You can change the text defaults to fit your drawing needs. These settings include defaults for text font, size, line spacing, line length, intercharacter spacing, fractions, underline, vertical text, slant, and justification. You can access the Text settings box (refer to figure 14.3) by choosing Element, Text. The Text settings box shows the current default text characteristics, which MicroStation applies each time you place text in the design file.

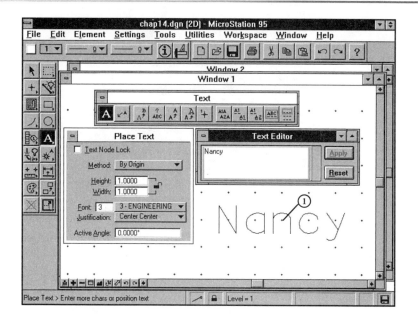

Figure 14.3

The Text settings box.

Changing the Font

The *font* is the style of text used when you place text. MicroStation comes with several fonts—fancy, simple, italic, bold, and so on—which should suffice for most applications.

> Some of the fonts might look identical. Look closely, however; the differences could be subtle. Often the numbers in the font distinguish one from another; for example, the way a zero appears (0 or ø).

Note

To review the different MicroStation fonts, choose the **V**iew button from the Text settings box, which opens the Fonts settings box (see fig. 14.4). To view a font, select one of the fonts in the list. The font character set then appears in the lower portion of the settings box. This procedure enables you to have a clear look at the upper- and lowercase characters and the numeric and fractional characters of the font.

Figure 14.4

*Reviewing fonts
from the Text
settings box.*

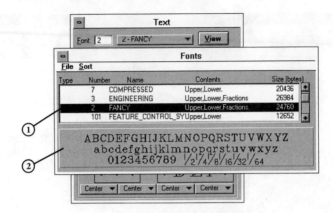

To activate the selected font, click in the preview area of the Fonts settings box (see fig. 14.4). After you activate the font, any text you place has that font.

CHANGING THE ACTIVE FONT

Continue from the preceding exercise with the CHAP14.DGN design file open.

Choose Element, Text	Opens the Text settings box
Click on the View button	Opens the Fonts settings box
*Click on the Fancy font at ①
in figure 14.4*	Highlights the selected font
Click in the preview area at ②	Sets active font to the displayed font

You don't have to view the font. If you know the font number, enter it in the Font field in the Text settings box or click in the pop-up field to select the font. Notice that the pop-up menu shows the font number and name to help you select the appropriate font (see fig. 14.5).

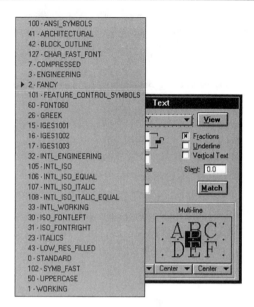

Figure 14.5

*Changing the
active font.*

Changing Text Size

The first two fields in the Text settings box control the active font selection. In the preceding section, you saw how to view and change the active font. The next two fields, **H**eight and **W**idth, enable you to set the active text size. The size of the text is defined by the number of working units. The active text size default is set to 1 master unit.

Note

The text size might appear different in your company's custom environment. Text size is a function of the coordinate readout's setup. If you see a 1.0000 in the text Height and Width field, for example, your coordinate readout format is set to Master Units with an accuracy of 4 places past the decimal point. See Chapter 7, "Drawing with Accuracy," for a complete discussion on the Coordinate Readout settings box and what it contains.

You use the lock icon, which appears to the right of the text size parameters, to determine whether the text has equal height and width. If the lock is open, you can change height independently of width (for example, height=1.5, width=2). If the lock is closed, any change you make to height or width automatically changes both to the same size. Simply click on the lock icon to open or close it. Locking the size provides a quick way to make the same changes to your text height and width without entering both numbers.

Tip

If you just want to change text size, you also can do so in the tool settings box during the Place Text command (refer to figure 14.3).

The next two fields, **L**ine Spacing and Line Length, affect the way MicroStation places multiple lines of text. When you enter text in the Text Editor window, you can enter a whole paragraph and place it as one text element. Line spacing defines the spacing between lines of text, and line length defines the number of characters placed per line when placed as multiple lines of text. The advantage of entering the text as a group is that you can manipulate all the text as one element.

The **I**nterchar Spacing field affects the distance between each character of the text string. Enter 0.0000 to place the text using the default character spacing inherent in the font's design. Enter 1.0000 to place the text with one blank space (the width of a character) between each letter in the text string. Enter a negative number to move the characters closer to each other. Be careful about using negative numbers—MicroStation does allow you to bunch the characters on top of each other.

The F**r**actions toggle button appears on the top right of the Text settings box; its status indicates whether MicroStation should interpret text you enter as a fraction or as regular text (see fig. 14.6).

Figure 14.6

Effects of turning Fractions on and off.

Fractions turned on, gives you ¹/₄

Fractions turned off, gives you 1/4

Note

Some MicroStation fonts do not allow for fractions. Check the Content column in the Fonts settings box to determine if the font you have active supports fractions.

If you turn on the **U**nderline feature in the Text settings box, all the text you place is underlined, including not only the characters, but also the spaces between them. The default distance between the characters and the line is 20 percent of the text height. You can change this setting by choosing Wor**k**space, **P**references to open the Preferences dialog box, then choosing Text from the **C**ategory field. The settings fields for text appear on the right. Other text preferences are discussed in Chapter 19, "Changing the Way MicroStation Looks."

In the Text settings box, turn on the Ver**t**ical Text option to place one character per line.

The Sla**n**t field in the Text settings box enables you to italicize any font, slanting the characters relative to the baseline; just enter the angle (between 0 and 89) for the slant you want.

Finally, the lower portion of the Text settings box enables you to control text justification. The justification determines how MicroStation places the text relative to the data point in the view. The Text settings box demonstrates the relationship between the cursor and the text placement. To change the current justification setting, click on the dots that show around the text.

You also can change the current justification by choosing one of the four pop-up menu options across the bottom of the settings box. If you choose a justification, the pop-up menus reflect the change. Selecting the correct justification before you place text often means the difference between placing the text accurately the first time and having to move the text to the proper location afterward. The exercise, "Placing Text on an Element," later in this chapter, provides an example of how justification can help you in text placement.

The changes you make in the settings box are reflected in the display of the text in the Justification section. Notice that the text changes if you turn on **U**nderline or enter a Sla**n**t value.

The justification also determines the snap point of the text for future manipulations.

Note

CHANGING TEXT ATTRIBUTES

Continue from the preceding exercise with the CHAP14.DGN design file open and text setting box displayed.

Double-click on the **H**eight *field and enter* **.5**	Replaces setting with .5 and highlights the Width field
Enter **.8** *in the* **W**idth *field*	Sets width to .8

Place some text with the new settings. Note the changes in the text font and size (see fig. 14.7).

Figure 14.7

*Changing the
active text
attributes.*

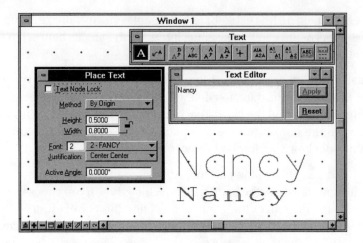

The term *text node,* in the scope of this book, refers to text that contains multiple lines of text. The Text settings box calls text nodes "Multiline Text." If you choose Element, Information or the Analyze Element command, MicroStation lists the element type for multiple lines of text as a text node. The Analyze Element command lists a single line of text as a text string.

Using Text Placement Options

MicroStation offers eight options for placing text. The options appear in the Method pop-up list in the tool settings box. The default option of By Origin was covered in a previous section. The option you choose determines the variation of the Place Text command to issue.

♦ **Fitted.** The Place Fitted Text command enables you to dynamically determine the text size. After you enter text in the Text Editor window, you pick a point for the left edge of the text and then a point for the right edge. MicroStation automatically sizes the text to fit between the two points.

A use for fitted text might be a map title in which you would have the freedom to place the text at a size that fits into a specific area. Rather than guess what size the title should be in working units, you could just place fitted text.

♦ **View Ind.** The Place View Independent Text command acts exactly like the By Origin option; the only difference being that the text has special properties. Text placed as view-independent does not rotate with a view rotation. A piece of text you place by origin appears rotated when you rotate the view, whereas a piece of text you place as view-independent always appears at the same angle, regardless of the view rotation.

A use for view-independent text might be a note on a mechanical drawing in which the text should remain at 0 degrees (right reading) regardless of the view's rotation.

♦ **Fitted VI.** The Place Fitted View Independent Text command is a combination of the previous two options. You enter two data points to determine the text size and the text does not rotate when you rotate the view.

You use the final four methods, Above Element, Below Element, On Element, and Along Element of text placement when you place text relative to a graphics element; for example, text above or below a line, text on an arc, or text along a curve. Each of these commands requires you to identify a graphics element; MicroStation places the text at the appropriate angle and distance from that element.

♦ **Above Ele.** The Place Text Above Element command enables you to place text above an element. The spacing above the element is determined by the line spacing defined in the Text settings box. You also need to consider the justification of the text before you use this option to place text. MicroStation places the text from the data point you give on the graphics element with the current justification.

PLACING TEXT ABOVE AN ELEMENT

Continue from the preceding exercise with the CHAP14.DGN design file open.

Place a line in your design file like the one shown in figure 14.8

Choose the Place Text tool from the Text tool box

Click on the **M***ethod button and choose* **A***bove Ele*	Issues the Place Text Above Element command and sets default method
Enter Text *Type your street name*	
Identify element *Pick a point at* ① *(see fig. 14.8)*	Defines element placement and displays text
Accept/Reject (select next input) *Pick any point* ②	Places the text
Identify element *Click the reset button*	Starts the process over again to enter new text

Figure 14.8

Placing text above an element.

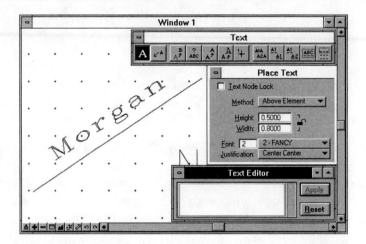

- **Below Ele.** The Place Text Below Element command enables you to place text below an element. Identify a graphics element and the MicroStation places the text below, offset by the line spacing setting, and at the angle of the element. This command prompts and acts just like the Above Element option you tried in the most recent exercise.

- **On Ele.** The Place Text On Element command enables you to place text on an element. This command places the text on the element and automatically deletes the portion of the element that otherwise would cut through the text.

Before you place the text on an element in the following exercise, delete or undo the street name you place above the line in the previous exercise.

PLACING TEXT ON AN ELEMENT

Continue from the preceding exercise with the CHAP14.DGN design file and Text tool box open.

Choose the Place Text tool from the Text tool box

*Click on the **M**ethod button and choose **O**n Ele*   Issues the Place Text On Element command

Enter Text *In the Text Editor window, type your street name again and press Enter*

Identify element *Pick a point at* ① *(see fig. 14.9)*	Defines element placement and displays text
Accept/Reject (select next input) *Pick any point* ②	Places the text
Identify element *Click the Reset button*	Starts process over again to enter new text

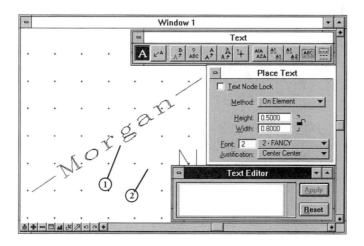

Figure 14.9

Placing text on an element.

♦ **Along Ele.** The Place Text Along Element command enables you to place text along any element. This option is similar to placing text above or below an element, with one exception—the text follows along the element. For example, the text along an arc curves along with the arc, whereas the text above or below an arc is placed at one angle. Each letter becomes a text string of its own, and you can no longer edit the text string as a unit.

Editing Text

Now that you have successfully placed text in your design file, you might need to change or edit the text you've already placed. Editing gives you the flexibility to change existing text without deleting and replacing it. Imagine the effort involved in replacing text and establishing the correct settings (size, font, justification, line spacing, and so on) just to correct a typing or spelling error. The Edit Text tool is found on the Text tool box.

Editing text recalls the characters into the Text Editor window, where you can quickly make the necessary changes. MicroStation offers many different ways to select and change text in the Text Editor window. The simplest way is to select text using a data point, position the cursor in the Text Editor, and then use the Delete or Backspace keys to remove characters or type new characters to input.

For quicker editing, you can select or highlight groups of characters in the Text Editor to edit all at once. After you highlight a group, you can remove all the characters by pressing any key, or you can start typing to delete and insert in one step. Review table 14.1 for other editing and selection options.

Table 14.1

Text Selection Options

Action	Results
Arrow keys	Position flashing input cursor
Click	Positions flashing input cursor
Double-click	Highlights the word
Press and drag	Highlights selected text
Shift-click	Highlights from previous to new input cursor position

After you edit the text in the Text Editor window, choose the **A**pply button to make the change to the text in the design file. If you mess up the change in the Text Editor window, choose the **R**eset button. The text in the Text Editor window reverts to the way it was before you began editing or if you change your mind and decide to not edit at all, simply close the editor box.

EDITING TEXT

Continue from the preceding exercise with the CHAP14.DGN design file open and with the previously entered text.

Choose the Edit Text tool from the Text tool box (see fig. 14.10)

`Identify element` *Pick a point on the text you want to edit*   Highlights text to modify

`Accept/Reject(select next input)` *Pick any point*   Accepts selection and displays in the Text Editor window

Delete the street name from the Text
Editor box and enter your address using any
method covered in the preceding
section (see table 14.1)

*Click on the **A**pply button*   Applies the edit to the text

Identify Element   Prompts you to identify another
                                    piece of text to edit

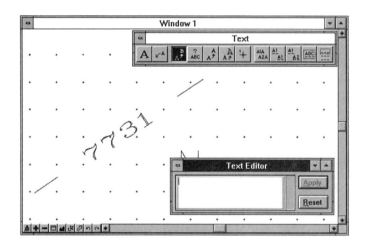

Figure 14.10

Editing text.

Note that when you use the Edit text, MicroStation doesn't modify the line that
you partially deleted to fit the first piece of text. In this example, you might have
been better off to choose the **U**ndo command and replace the text.

If Undo isn't available, you can use the Extend Line commands to close up the
gap between the line and the text.

Tip

Replacing Text

Editing text in a design file can be tedious if you need to make major changes.
Choose **E**dit, Replace Te**x**t to invoke the Replace Text settings box (see fig. 14.11),
which provides a way to edit text using a global or design file search and replace.

Figure 14.11

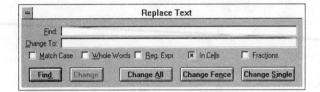

The Replace Text
settings box.

You enter the text for which to search in the **F**ind field, and then you enter the text
with which to replace it in the **C**hange To field. The four buttons below the fields
enable you to narrow your search of the find. The **M**atch Case button enables you
to find only the text case as entered in the Find field (for example, enter A, and
MicroStation searches only for uppercase As). The **W**hole Words button searches
only for text surrounded by spaces. The **R**eg. Expr. button enables you to find text
that meets certain criteria (see table 14.2). Finally, the In Ce**l**ls and Frac**t**ions toggle
buttons let you search for text contained within a cell or fraction and then changes
it appropriately.

Table 14.2

Regular Expressions and Examples for the Replace Text Command

Regular Expression	Find	Change To	Result
^	^The	Their	Finds text beginning with **The**, and then changes to **Their**
$	.$	?	Finds text that ends with **.**, and then changes to **?**
.	.h.	the	Finds all occurrences of **h** with any single character before and after it, and then changes to **the**
:<space>	:	/	Finds all occurrences of a space, and then changes to **/**
:a	:a	xxx	Finds all occurrences of alpha characters, and then changes to **xxx**
:d	:d	yyy	Finds all occurrences of digits, and then changes to **yyy**
:n	:n	zzz	Finds all occurrences of digits and alpha characters, and then changes to **zzz**

Regular Expression	Find	Change To	Result
(...)	(a-e)	1	Finds all occurrences of the single characters **a**, **b**, **c**, **d**, or **e**, and then changes to **1**
(A...)	(Aa-e)	1	Finds all occurrences of a single character that is not **a**, **b**, **c**, **d**, or **e**, and then changes to **1**

Copying and Incrementing Text

The last text placement command to cover stands alone because it enables you to place and modify text simultaneously. You can find the Copy and Increment Text tool in the Text tool box (see fig. 14.12). This command requires you to identify an existing piece of text from your design file and then enter a point for the placement of the new text. The Copy and Increment Text command works only with text strings that contain a number, not with text nodes and fractions. You can change the number increment (called the tag), default 1, from the Text tool box.

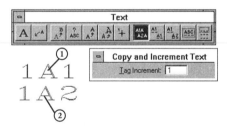

Figure 14.12

The Copy and Increment Text tool and incremented text.

The Copy and Increment Text command increments only the last number found in the text string. If you were to copy and increment the string "This is 1 of 4 text strings," for example, the outcome would be "This is 1 of 5 text strings."

Tip

Electrical diagrams are an excellent application for the Copy and Increment Text command in situations with (numbers) text appearing many times in a drawing. Another example would be a floor plan in which rooms are numbered consecutively. In the following exercise, you place the text once and use the Copy and Increment Text command to place all the remaining room numbers.

Copying and Incrementing Text

Continue from the preceding exercise with the CHAP14.DGN design file open. Before you use the Copy and Increment Text command, you place incremented text that contains numbers, such as in figure 14.12.

Make level 2 the active level

Turn off level 1   Turns off display of previous exercise elements

Choose the Place Text tool from the Text tool box and set the method to By Origin

`Enter Text` *In the Text Editor, type* **1A1** *and press Enter*

`Enter more chars or position text`   Places text

Pick a point at ① *(refer to figure 14.12)*

Choose the Copy and Increment Text tool from the Text tool box

`Identify element` *Pick a point at* ①

`Accept/Reject (select next input)`   Places copied and incremented text
Pick ② *(refer to figure 14.12)*   (refer to figure 14.12) and prompts for point to place next copy

`Accept/Reject (select next input)`   Prompts for new text to copy and
Click the Reset button   increment

`Identify element`

Matching Text in the Drawing

Initially, you need to set up all the text settings as you place each piece of text. MicroStation furnishes three commands that save you the steps of setting text defaults later in the design process: Display Text Attributes, Match Text Attributes, and Change Text to Active Attributes. The combination of these three commands is quite powerful and can save you a great deal of time redefining active settings.

You can find the tools for these text attribute commands in the Text tool box (refer to figure 14.1). The Display Text Attribute command prompts you to identify a piece of text in the design file and displays the text settings that apply to that piece of text in the Status Bar. If you select a text string, the command displays text height, width, level, and font. If you select a text node, the command displays node number, line length, line spacing, level, and font.

You find the Match Text Attributes tool in the Text tool box (refer to figure 14.1), and it also appears as a button in the Text settings box. It enables you to set the active settings by selecting an existing piece of text. After you select and accept the text, the active settings change and appear in the left field of the Status Bar, which shows text height, text weight, font number, and line spacing as: TH=1.000, TW=1.000, FT=2, LS=0.5000.

You find the Change Text to Active Attributes tool in the Text tool box (refer to figure 14.1). It enables you to change existing text attributes easily. You can use the Change Text to Active Attributes command in conjunction with the Match Text Attributes command to quickly make two different text strings look identical.

When you choose Change Text to Active Attributes, the tool settings box displays all the different features you can change about a piece of text. Toggle on only the text settings you want to apply to the text. In the following exercise, for example, you toggle on Font in the tool settings box to change the font, and the height and weight settings do not change.

MATCHING AND CHANGING TEXT ATTRIBUTES

Continue from the preceding exercise with the CHAP14.DGN design file open.

Make level 1 the active level	Displays name and street text
Choose the Match Text Attributes tool from the Text tool box	
`Identify text element` *Pick name text at* ①	Highlights text
`Accept/Reject (select next input)` *Pick accept point*	Sets the active text attribute settings and displays in the Status Bar
Choose the Change Text to Active Attributes tool from the Text tool box	
Toggle on **F**ont	
`Identify text element` *Pick text at* ② *(see fig. 14.13)*	Highlights element
`Accept/Reject (select next input)` *Pick any point*	Changes selected text to current active font
`Identify text element`	Prompts to change more text

Figure 14.13

*Matching and
changing text
attributes.*

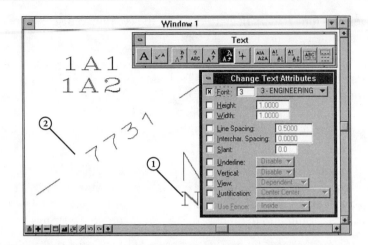

Using Advanced Text Placement Types and Features

Two advanced text placement features enable you to place a text holder and enter the text at a later date. The text holder is an enter data field or a text node that you place with the active text settings. The advantage afforded by placing enter data fields is that when you fill in the text later, MicroStation automatically applies the attributes you define by placing the enter data field to the text.

Placing Enter Data Fields

You can think of an *enter data field* as a template or holder for text you want to complete later. One good use for enter data fields might be in a case in which you have many text strings that contain both common and unique characters; for example, Page `_` of `_`. If this text string appeared in your drawing multiple times, you could create a template text string with blanks in the page number locations. Later you can fill in the blanks when you assign page numbers, rather than less efficiently copy and edit each string. Another advantage is that if you overlook a number when you fill in the enter data field, your plot prints blanks rather than the incorrect numbers you forgot to edit. Missing data are easier to spot than incorrect data.

Creating an enter data field is as easy as placing text. Enter data fields are just what they sound like—text with the enter data field character. The default character for an enter data field is the underscore character (_). You should place each enter data field character with an underscore. The preceding example would be placed as text like this: Page _ of _, or Page __ of __ if you expect two-digit page numbers.

> You can change the default enter data field character in the text preferences if it conflicts with your application. Be careful, however, not to use characters that might be common display characters, such as a period or slash.

Note

Filling Enter Data Fields

Later during the design process, you can return to the enter data fields and fill in individual enter data fields with the Fill in Single Enter Data Field command (see fig. 14.14) or automatically fill in each enter data field with the Auto Fill in Enter_Data Fields command (see fig. 14.15). The enter data field holds the text attributes that were active when you placed it. The fill-in process places the text as you intended when you placed the enter data field.

In the next exercise, you try placing several enter data fields and use the Fill in Single Enter_Data Field command to enter some of the missing page numbers.

PLACING AND FILLING ENTER DATA FIELDS

Continue from the preceding exercise with the CHAP14.DGN design file open.

Choose the Place Text tool from
the Text tool box

Enter Text *In the Text Editor,*
type **Page _ of _**

Pick four points to place   Places text
four times (see fig. 14.14)

Choose the Fill in Single Enter_Data   Opens the Text Editor window
Field tool from the Text tool box

Identify element *Pick underscore*   Displays a box around the
at ① *(see fig. 14.14)*   underscore character

Enter text or to fill in field   Clears the Text Editor and
Choose **R**eset, *then type* **1** *and press Enter*   enters 1 in the enter data field

Identify element   Prompts to select another field

Figure 14.14

Figure 14.14

*Placing and filling
in enter data
fields.*

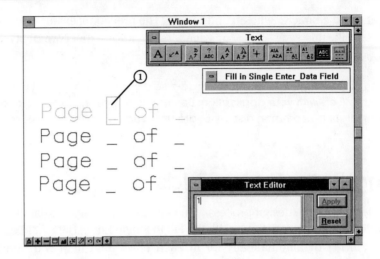

You probably have noticed that the text appears on-screen with the underscore. You can suppress the underscore display by turning off the enter data field display from the View Attributes settings box. You can fill in enter data fields even if you do not have them showing; however, this procedure makes finding them harder, so leave the display on for the duration of these exercises.

What if you want to make sure you address every empty enter data field? Use the Auto Fill in Enter_Data Fields command to have MicroStation pick each enter data field that is empty in the view. In this method, you enter the text, and MicroStation automatically selects the next field. You never have to leave the keyboard. Try this in the next exercise. Do not fill them all in—you work with two more commands yet after this exercise.

Note   The Auto Fill in command finds only the enter data fields visible in the view.

USING AUTO FILL IN ENTER_DATA FIELDS

Continue from the preceding exercise with the CHAP14.DGN design file open.

Choose the Auto Fill in Enter_Data Fields tool from the Text tool box	Opens the Text Editor window
`Select view` *Pick any point in view 1*	Displays a box around first blank enter data field

↵ to fill in or DATA for next field *Type **4** and press Enter*	Enters 4 in enter data field, and displays box around next blank enter data field
↵ to fill in or DATA for next field *Type **2** and press Enter*	Enters 2 in enter data field, and displays box around next blank enter data field (see fig. 14.15)
↵ to fill in or DATA for next field *Click the Reset button*	Ends fill-in command

Select view

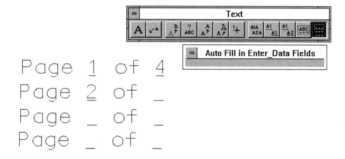

Page 1 of 4
Page 2 of _
Page _ of _
Page _ of _

Figure 14.15

Using the Auto Fill in Enter_Data Fields command.

Copy Enter Data Fields

In this section, you use the Copy Enter_Data Field command and the Copy and Increment Enter_Data Field command. These commands are self-explanatory: one command copies the contents of one enter data field to another enter data field, and the other command increments and copies the contents from one field to another.

USING COPY ENTER_DATA FIELD

Continue from the preceding exercise with the CHAP14.DGN design file open.

*Choose the Copy Enter_Data Field
tool from the Text tool box*

Select enter data field to copy *Pick a point at ① (see fig. 14.16)*	Displays a box around 4 in the enter data field
Select destination enter data field *Pick a point at ②*	Copies 4 to selected enter data field

Continues

Select destination enter data field *Pick a point at ③*	Copies 4 to enter data field
Select destination enter data field *Pick a point at ④*	Copies 4 to enter data field
Select destination enter data field *Click the Reset button*	Ends the fill-in copy command
Select enter data field to copy	

Figure 14.16

*Using the Copy
Enter_Data Field
command.*

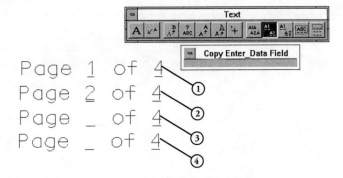

USING COPY AND INCREMENT ENTER_DATA FIELD

Continue from the preceding exercise with the CHAP14.DGN design file open.

*Choose the Copy and Increment
Enter_Data Field tool from the
Text tool box*

Select enter data field to copy *Pick a point at ① (see fig. 14.17)*	Displays a box around 2 in the enter data field
Select destination enter data field *Pick a point at ②*	Copies and increments to enter 3 in enter data field
Select destination enter data field *Pick a point at ③*	Enters 4 in enter data field
Select destination enter data field *Click the Reset button*	Ends fill-in copy command
Select enter data field to copy	

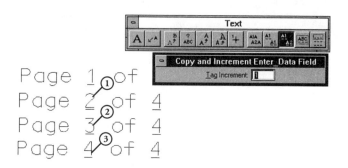

Figure 14.17

Using the Copy and Increment Enter_Data Field command.

Placing Notes

You find the Place Note tool in the Text tool box (see fig. 14.18). Place Note is a simple command you use to place text that has a leader line. The Place Note command requires you to enter text, pick a starting point for the leader line, and pick an end point.

You can place notes with single lines of text or with text nodes or multilines of text. Choose the Multiline type from the tool settings box and several other settings appear. Some of these settings should seem familiar, including **F**ont, **J**ustification, and **A**ssociation Lock. The others are unique to the Multiline type Place Note command. T**e**xt Frame contains a pop-up list with None, Line, and Box options for customizing the node text. **G**enerate leader enables you to generate a shoulder or bent leader line when placing the note.

Try using the Place Note command to place text in the next exercise.

PLACING A NOTE

Continue from the preceding exercise with the CHAP14.DGN design file open.

Choose the Place Note tool from
the Text tool box (see fig. 14.18)

Enter text in the Text Editor window

Enter start point ①   Displays beginning of leader line

Enter end point ②   Completes command

Enter start point

Figure 14.18

The Place Note tool.

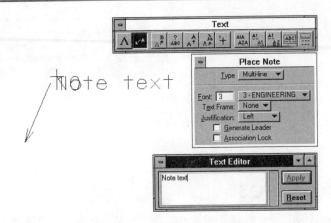

 Note   The text (cross and number) that appears over your text in figure 14.18 is the text node origin and number. To turn this display off, toggle off Text Node in the View Attributes settings box.

 Note   Changing your dimension Location setting to Manual will allow you to place additional leader lines with the note.

Creating and Using Glossaries

Some of the text you place in your design file appears again and again. For example, the word "easement" appears many times in a civil or mapping application, and the word "relay" appears repeatedly in an electrical application. You can put these words in a glossary and place them quickly without having to enter the text over and over.

Building a Glossary of Common Text Strings

You create a glossary in a text editor or word processor. Each glossary entry is two lines in an ASCII file: the first line contains an alias for the text string, and the second line contains the exact text to substitute for the alias.

The following is an example of a glossary ASCII file:

EASE

Easement

XYZ

XYZ Company, Inc.

REV

Revised Date:

Window Note

Split Steel Bucks are shown in these details for the purpose of positioning window in wall forms. Sash and screen must be removed from frame when using split bucks in order to bolt assembly together and to drive nails into wall form.

The default glossary file is located in the \ustation\wsmod\default\data directory under the file name `example.gls`. You can change this default and the MS_GLOSSARY variable by choosing Wor**k**space, **C**onfiguration. Chapter 17 offers more information about modifying configuration variables. If you can't find the glossary file defined in the MS_GLOSSARY variable, MicroStation prompts you to choose a glossary file from the Open Glossary dialog box.

Using a Glossary

To use a glossary, choose **U**tilities, Text **G**lossary from the Application window, which opens the Glossary settings box (see fig. 14.19).

The alias you entered in the ASCII file appears in the Glossary settings box. Click on an alias, and the text associated with that alias appears in the field below. To place a glossary item, click on the Build button. The text appears in the Text Editor or the third field of the Glossary settings box. Move the cursor into the view, and pick a point to place the text.

USING A GLOSSARY

Choose **U**tilities, Text **G**lossary	Opens the Glossary settings box
Click on ab	Displays associated text
Click on the Build *button*	Displays and activates the text edit field
Pick a point	Places glossary text

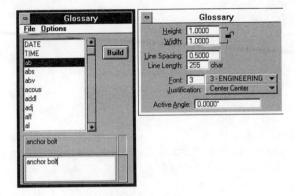

Figure 14.19

The Glossary settings box.

Editing the Glossary Item

You can edit or add to the glossary text as you place it. After you choose the alias and click on the Build button, the text appears in the Text Editor window of the Glossary settings box, where you can modify it.

You can put glossary items together in one text string by choosing each alias and clicking on the Build button. If you have a glossary item for Revised by: and a glossary item with your name, you can put the two items together and place one piece of text without ever touching the keyboard.

Note

To make any permanent changes to the glossary, you must use a text editor or word processor to work in the ASCII file.

Placing Glossary Text in Different Ways

The text you place using the glossary feature you place with the active text settings. The tool settings box provides the standard text settings and the Options menu in the Glossary settings box allows modification with the **C**ase item. The **C**ase option enables you to place the text as it was entered in the ASCII file (default) or to change the text to all uppercase or lowercase.

Summary

You have completed all the basic text functions MicroStation has to offer. The things to remember are that you place text with the active text settings, which include the text style or font, the height and width measured in design file units, justification of the text, line spacing and intercharacter spacing. After you place text, MicroStation provides several methods for changing both the settings and the characters. MicroStation doesn't replace a good word processor, but it does have tools you can use to annotate a drawing quickly and efficiently.

CHAPTER 15

Plotting Your Drawing

*P*lotting with MicroStation involves three basic steps: specifying the area of your file for plotting, selecting the proper driver file for your plotter, and generating the plot. This chapter explains and illustrates how to generate a plot of your MicroStation design file.

Before you proceed to plot, you should consider a number of factors. The scale you use and your plotting standards (line weights, line-style pattern spacing) affect your plot's appearance. Drawing composition also is important, for no matter how high a given plot's quality, it can be useless if the information is organized poorly in the design file. The settings for features such as fast cells, curves, fonts, data fields, and text nodes, as well as level symbology, line styles, and line weights, can have a dramatic impact on your plot's appearance.

In this chapter, you learn:

- ◆ *Selecting a plotter*

- ◆ *Plotting a design file*

- ◆ *Plotting full-scale drawings*

- ◆ *Composing drawings for plotting*

- ◆ *Using the Plot settings box*

- ◆ *Plot resymbolization*

- ◆ *Saving your plot reconfiguration file*

Creating Your First Plot

The best way to begin learning about plotting is to jump right in and make a plot. Before you can plot, however, you need to know how to select your plotter.

Selecting Your Plotter

Plotting in MicroStation varies based on the operating system (such as DOS, Windows, Unix, and so on). When you plot in Windows 3.1, Windows NT, or Windows 95, MicroStation plots to the default Windows printer set in the Windows Print Manager. When you plot in DOS, you must tell MicroStation what plotter or printer you are using. The MicroStation Plot settings box offers a list of supported plotter driver files from which to choose; you select the one that matches your plotter or printer model. Most of these driver file names are abbreviations of plotter model names, such as: CAL104X.PLT for a Calcomp 1041, 1042, or any other model in the 1040 series; HP7585B.PLT for the Hewlett-Packard 7585B; or HPDJET for the Hewlett-Packard Design Jet. The HPGL2.PLT file is a general driver file for any HPGL-compatible plotter. The PSCRIPT.PLT file is for any PostScript-compatible printer or plotter. If you have an unlisted dot-matrix printer, try one of the EPSON files with your printer set for Epson compatibility.

 Note

> MicroStation's plotting treats printers and plotters the same. The rest of this chapter refers to both as plotters. If you have a supported printer, you should be able to follow the exercises, but your sheet sizes and scales might vary. Likewise, if your plotter is smaller than the exercise examples, your sheet sizes and scales vary.

The first exercise assumes that you have a supported plotter connected to one of your computer's ports or through a network. If you don't, give the exercise a try anyway—you just won't have a hard copy afterward.

Furthermore, the exercise assumes that your plotter is connected to the LPT1 parallel port in DOS operations or is the default Windows plotter. If you run the DOS version of MicroStation and your plotter is connected through LPT2, 3, 4, or COM1, 2, 3, or 4, substitute the correct port name for LPT1 in the exercise. If connected to a serial port such as COM1, you probably need to use the DOS MODE command to set the port's communication parameters—*before* plotting. See your plotter's manual for the settings and a DOS manual for the MODE command syntax. Do this before you start MicroStation.

Plotting the Design File

The following exercise uses the design file FLOOR.DGN in the ustation/dgn/ learning directory. If you use a pen plotter, it might take a long time to plot. You can substitute any other less complex design file for this exercise.

CREATING A QUICK PLOT

Open the FLOOR.DGN design file.

Close views 2,3, and 4

Maximize view 1

Choose Fit View   Fits the entire drawing for
from the view 1 border   plotting

Choose **F**ile, **P**rint/Plot   Opens the Plot settings box (see fig. 15.1)

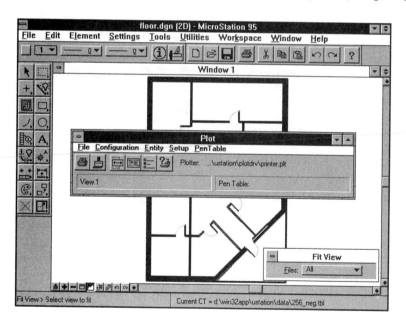

Figure 15.1

The Plot settings box.

Choose **S**etup, **D**river   Opens the Select Plotter Driver
                                         File dialog box (see fig. 15.2)

Continues

Figure 15.2

The Select Plotter Driver File dialog box.

If you run MicroStation under Windows, you need to be sure to select the printer.plt driver. If you run in DOS, scroll through the list of files on the left until you find the driver file for your type of plotter.

Choose **O**K   Selects the plotter driver
                                   file and closes the dialog box

Choose **F**ile, **P**review   Expands the settings box to display
                                   the Plot Preview (see fig. 15.3)

Figure 15.3

The Preview in the Plot settings box.

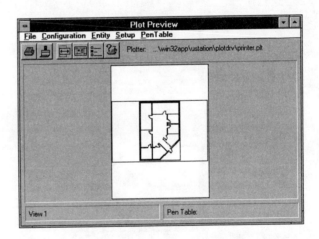

Make sure your plotter is turned on and ready.

Choose **F**ile, **P**lot   Sets the plot to the Print Manager
                                   (in Windows), or opens the Save
                                   Plot As dialog box (in DOS), as
                                   shown in figure 15.4

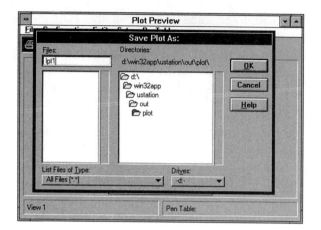

Figure 15.4

The Save Plot As dialog box, as seen by DOS users of MicroStation.

If you use DOS, you need to follow these additional steps, substituting your port name for LPT1.

Type **LPT1** *in the* Files *text field of the Save Plot As dialog box*	Tells MicroStation where to send the plot file
Choose **O**K	Sends the plot information to your plotter and closes the Save Plot As dialog box

Your plot should begin in a moment.

Note

If no plot was generated, you might have used an incompatible port, driver file, or serial port settings.

Congratulations—you have just made your first plot. While you admire your plot, a brief overview of what just happened is in order.

Understanding the Plotting Process

The elements shown in view 1 were sent to your plotter directly through the computer's port or network. The screen information was translated through a plotter driver file (such as the hpljet.plt or printer.plt file) so that your output device could interpret the plot information. MicroStation used the default settings for line weight, sheet size, and a variety of other variables, and scaled the plot to fit the sheet. With any luck, your plot came out looking pretty good. The rest of this chapter explains how to get that plot from pretty good to perfect.

One of MicroStation's strengths is its capability to plot elements in the design file based on element criteria such as color, weight, level, or type. You should establish office, project, and/or user standards so that when you are ready to plot, you can tell the plotter which design file elements to plot light or thin and which ones to plot dark or thick. You could use different standards for different clients and store these settings in different configuration variable files.

The Preview option in the Plot settings box enables you to check the plot before sending it to the plotter. When you choose **P**review, MicroStation emulates the plotter you have selected, using the settings in that plotter's driver file and possibly the pen table if attached. The image on your monitor is a scaled version of the plot's final appearance. Showing the preview can point out possible errors such as incorrect level, reference file attachments, or symbology and can save wasted plotting time as well as paper.

Computers were supposed to eliminate or at least reduce the amount of paper used for creating traditional hand-drawn documents—according to the "Myth of the Paperless Office." When you view computer drawings on a monitor, you can lose a sense of proportion. Constantly zooming in and out leaves you uncertain of anything's actual size. Looking at a plotted image of your entire design can help you regain your sense of proportion. Until that day arrives in which everyone in construction, manufacturing, or other industries involved with CAD uses computers to view and create the objects you design, paper output will continue to be necessary.

Plotting devices now are so fast that computers actually *increase* the amount of paper used in an office. After you make even minor changes to a file, you tend to want a plot. You quickly have several paper copies of each file, and you can easily lose track of which one is the most current. Plot management is an art as well as a skill, and learning it does take time. Remember, use the **P**review option. Maybe you'll save a tree.

 Note

MicroStation also enables you to plot to a file on your local or network hard disk. Choose the driver that matches your plotter and then choose Plot to open the Save Plot As dialog box. MicroStation has entered the default file name FLOOR.000 in the **N**ame text field. MicroStation creates a plot file and stores it in the subdirectory \ustation\out\plot\.

You can generate plot files from as many design files as your hard disk can hold. After you create all the plot files you need to print, you can send these files directly to your plotter from the operating system by using the PLOTUTIL.EXE program supplied with MicroStation. Check the delivered documentation for more information about batch plotting with MicroStation.

Plotting Full-Scale Drawings

One of the most difficult concepts for new MicroStation users is making the transition from drawing at a specific scale to the concept of full-scale drawing. When you draw at a specific scale, you begin with a fixed area in which you can draw and you scale your objects to fit into that area. A 30" × 42" sheet limits the size of objects you can draw based on their scale.

When you use MicroStation to draw real objects (such as buildings, site plans, or circuit boards), you draw those objects at their real (full) sizes and then you scale them down (or up) to fit the plot sheet. You set this plot scale in the Plot settings box; it doesn't change anything in the design file. If you need a border or title block to be plotted along with the design, however, you attach it in the design file as a reference drawing (see Chapter 18).

Because you are drawing real objects at full size, the concept of scaling the design comes into play only at plotting time. When you want a 1/8"=1'-0" plot of your design file, you tell the plotter to plot everything that is 1' long as if it were only 1/8" long. You could just as easily tell the plotter to make that same 1'-long element 1/4", 1/2", or 6" long. The real objects remain full size. They are scaled by the plotter when you specify the output scale you want.

Scaling Symbology for Plotting

Symbology includes non-real objects, such as text, dimensions, annotation, graphics symbols, and patterning. Because these elements are not real, the concept of scale is critical when you create them. If you want all the text in your design file to plot at a scale of 1/8"=1'-0", then you must make it 1'-0" high in the design file. That same file plotted at 1'-0" to 1/4", however, would require the text to be only 6" high. This same logic carries through to all non-real elements. You must decide a design's plotting scale *before* you start adding notes, dimensions, symbols, and hatching to it.

The best way to handle symbols, such as section bubbles, door number bubbles, fence posts, power poles, electrical outlets, valves, or schematic logic symbols, is to create them at a one-unit scale as cells in a cell library file, and attach them at the necessary height in the design file. A valve symbol to be plotted 1" high in a design plotted at 10':1", for example, would be created in the cell library as 10' tall. If the valve cell were to be placed in a design file intended to eventually be plotted at 1"=30'. You can set the scale to 3 at the time of placement. See Chapter 16 for details on cells.

Note

In addition to attaching and placing correctly scaled symbology, hatch patterns, and text, you often might need to combine other elements (including bills-of-materials, schedules, specifications, sections, details, and blow ups such as plans) to compose a plot. You often combine these elements at various scales, usually by creating them as separate design files and attaching them as references. You also can attach part of a drawing to itself, and clip the reference, change the view attributes, or turn layers on and off to show exactly what you want. You attach these references in the master drawing, using appropriate scales, to compose the desired drawing for plotting. See Chapter 18 for details on reference drawings.

Using the Plot Settings Box

The Plot settings box contains five pull-down menus and six icons. The icons are a quick way to activate the commonly used features of plotting in MicroStation. You can send the plot to your printer, for example, by choosing **F**ile, **P**lot in the Plot settings box or by choosing the first icon. See figure 15.5 for functions of the icons.

Figure 15.5

Plot settings box icons.

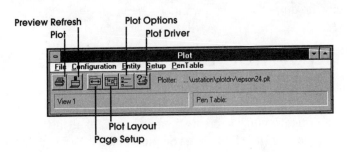

Plotting to a File by View

The following exercise reconfigures your plot driver to HPGL/2, and then generates a plot file based on view 1. Use the HPGL2.PLT driver (see fig. 15.6), even if your plotter isn't HPGL/2-compatible, so that your settings match those in the following exercises.

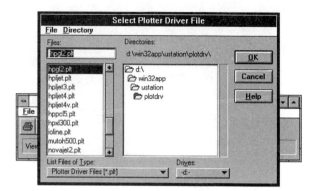

Figure 15.6

Selecting the HPGL2.PLT driver.

USING A VIEW TO PLOT

Choose Plot Driver icon   Opens the Select Plotter Driver File dialog box

Scroll the list of files on the left until you find HPGL2.PLT.

Select hpgl2.plt, *and then choose*   Selects the HPGL/2 plotter
OK, *or double-click* hpgl2.plt   driver file and closes the dialog box

Continue with the next few exercises with the hpgl2.plt driver activated.

Plotting to a File by Fence

The plot file you created in the first exercise was based on view 1. What happened to the scale? By default, MicroStation maximizes your view to fit on the selected paper size. To get only a portion of the view or a selected area of your design file, you can place a fence in the view before you activate the Plot settings box.

The next section includes a more detailed review of the Plot settings box features.

Setting the Page Size

The Page setup button opens the Page Setup dialog box (see fig. 15.7). Notice that the Page Size pop-up menu is set to E. The pop-up menu displays different options available for the selected plot driver. The hpgl2.plt driver has A, B, C, D, and E options; choosing any of which will automatically adjust the height and width of your plot area to that sheet size.

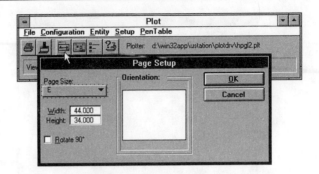

Figure 15.7

*Page Setup dialog
box defaults for
hpgl2.plt driver.*

Setting the Plot Layout

Clicking on the Plot Layout icon opens the Plot Layout dialog box (see fig. 15.8). Again, the defaults you see in this dialog box vary according to the active plot driver.

Figure 15.8

*Plot Layout
defaults for the
hpgl2.plt driver.*

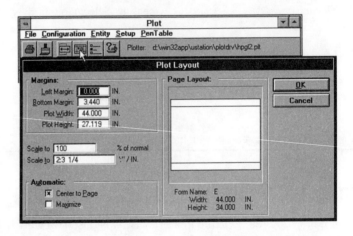

The Scale to ':"/IN field indicates how many Master Units per Inch one plotted inch represents in this plot. The blue rectangle in the Page Layout section indicates the area of the plot within the page. Try some different settings and watch how the blue rectangle moves around inside the Printable Area black rectangle. Two buttons on the bottom left of the Plot Layout settings box have different effects on your plot file. The Center button retains your current drawing settings of width, height, and scale and places your plot in the center of the printable area. The Maximize button takes neither your current View nor Fence area, retains either the Width or Height from your current Page Settings (depending on the shape of your Fence or View to be plotted), and recalculates the Scale and Width/Height to fit the largest plot possible onto the printable page area.

Setting Plot Options

The final icon to review is Plot Options. Clicking on the Plot Options icon opens the Options dialog box (see fig. 15.9). The only buttons available might be for drawing a border around your plot (based on the Border record in the plotter driver file) and for plotting the fence outline (if you used a fence). The remaining buttons show what the current display settings of the view or fence are.

The Option dialog box can force the display settings of the file when used in conjunction with plot configuration files.

Note

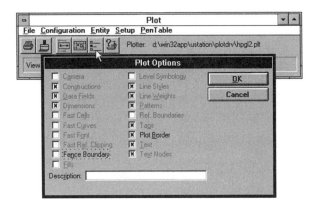

Figure 15.9

The Plot Options dialog box.

Plot Resymbolization with Pen Tables

Plot resymbolization enables you to modify the way elements look on the plotted output without changing the element symbology in the design file. You can find and resymbolize elements from the active file and/or the reference files. Pen tables serve to help you locate elements by the level or symbology in the design file, and then to manipulate the way MicroStation plots those elements.

Pen tables are particularly useful with reference files; because you might not own the reference, you have little control over the file's element symbology. Consider a mapping example in which your job is to place the water infrastructure on top of a base map already drawn and maintained by another person or group in your organization. You naturally would use the base map so you wouldn't have to redraw all the streets, alleys, easements, and so on, contained in the base map files. You would create a new series of files that contain the water mains, hydrants, valves, and so forth. To plot your maps, you would attach the base map as a reference file.

Because the base map was drawn to display and plot the engineer's specifications, you might want to change the symbology of the elements in the base map to de-emphasize some of the features to make your water data distinctly visible. A pen table can do this for you.

Note   Another use of pen tables might be to create check plots to smaller output devices. Lighten up the line weights for easy reading on smaller pages; or to plot reference files as screened images if your plotter is capable, to make your overlay stand out.

Although the preceding examples are very practical ones, why don't you start by creating a pen table that resymbolizes the active design file.

To create a pen table, choose **P**enTable, **N**ew in the Plot settings box, which opens a Create Pen Table dialog box. Enter a name for the pen table in the F**i**les field. MicroStation creates a pen table file by default in the ustation\tables\pen directory, and gives it a .tbl extension. Choose OK and the Modify Pen Table settings box appears (see fig. 15.10).

Figure 15.10

The Modify Pen Table settings box.

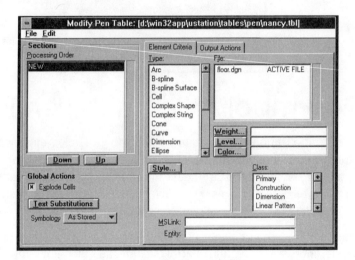

The Modify Pen Table settings box contains four major areas: Sections, Global Actions, Element Criteria, and Output Actions.

1. The Sections area enables you to name and prioritize each set of element manipulations you plan to do in this pen table. For example, the first section you create in the floor.dgn file might resymbolize the slab to a dotted line

style. You might create another section to resymbolize the drywall or exterior wall lines in the file.

2. After you create a section name, the next step is to define the criteria to find the element you want to resymbolize. You can define the element(s) you want to resymbolize by using the **T**ype, F**i**le, **W**eight, **L**evel, C**o**lor, **S**tyle, **C**lass, **M**SLink, and E**n**tity options. Use as many of these element criteria as necessary to get just the elements you want.

3. The next step is to define how it should resymbolize the elements it finds. Choose the Output Actions tab in the Modify Pen Table settings box and the right side displays the available output actions (see fig. 15.11). The **M**aster Control pop-up menu contains four options: **A**llow Additional Processing, **N**o Additional Processing, Don't Display Element, and Call BASIC Macro Function. To resymbolize the elements found by the criteria set choose **A**llow Additional Processing and choose the symbology changes displayed by the toggle buttons.

Tip

The P**r**iority button enables you to define the order the elements will be plotted. This is of particular significance when plotting shaded or color plots. Valid entries in the priority field are -2147483648 to 2147483647. The elements that are not prioritized are plotted first, then the lowest to highest. Priority settings require more processing time, so don't use priority unless necessary.

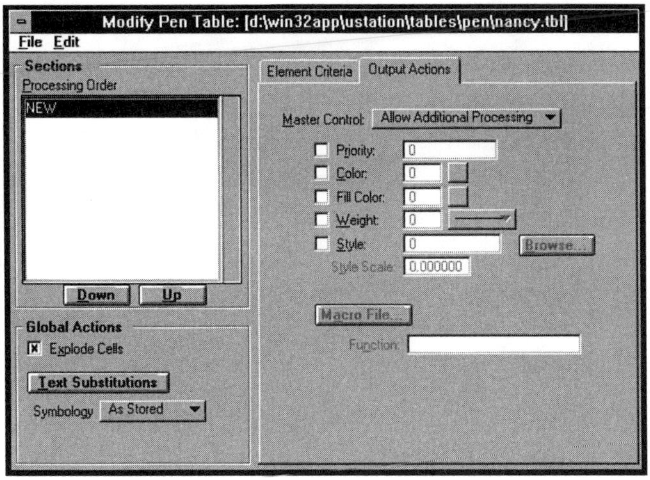

Figure 15.11

The Modify Pen Table settings box displaying Output Actions.

In the next exercise, you create a pen table to resymbolize the slab elements contained on level 3. The plot you created in the first exercise of this chapter should resemble figure 15.12. Work through the exercise and see figure 15.14 for the resymbolized plot.

Figure 15.12

Floor plan plot without resymbolization.

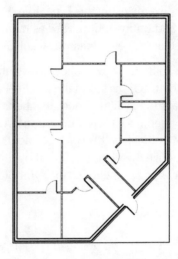

CREATING A PEN TABLE

Continue from the preceding exercise with the FLOOR.DGN design file open and the Plot settings box open.

Choose **P**enTable, **N**ew	Opens the Create Pen Table file dialog box
Enter **your name** *in the* F**i**les *field and choose* **O**K	Creates a file with the name given and a .tbl extension in the \ustation\tables\pen directory, then opens the Modify Pen Table settings box
Choose **E**dit, **R**ename Section	Opens the Rename Section dialog box
Enter **Slab**	
Choose **O**K	Dismisses the Rename Section dialog box and new name appears in the Sections area of the Modify Pen Table settings box
Enter **3** *in the field immediately to the right of the* **L**evel *button in the Element Criteria section of the settings box*	See figure 15.13

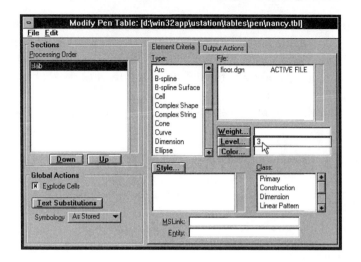

Figure 15.13

Element Criteria set to resymbolize the slab.

Choose the Output Actions *tab in the Modify Pen Table settings box*	Opens the Output Actions dialog box
Turn on the **S**tyle *toggle button*	
Enter **1** *in the field*	Defines dotted line style for slab
Choose **F**ile, **S**ave *in the Modify Pen Table settings box*	
Double-click on the minus sign in the upper left corner of the settings box	Closes the Modify Pen Table settings box

Now, replot your design file (see fig. 5.14).

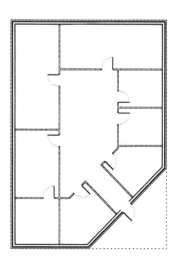

Figure 15.14

The floor plan with the slab resymbolized.

The previous exercise walks you through only one element selection. To continue, you would create another section for this pen table and define the next element criteria and the output action you want. You might ask yourself why not just change the element symbology for the slab and skip the whole pen table thing. The answer might be that the file contains the company standards and you can't change the floor plan slab, or this is just one of the plots that the customer will receive.

Saving the Configuration

Now that you have set up and defined all these parameters for your plot, you might want to save the settings to use again later for plotting this design file. The plot configuration file enables you to save the following:

♦ Plot area (view or fence location)

♦ Plot options

♦ Levels shown in the plotted view

♦ Page size, margins, and scale

♦ Pen table attachment

After you save the plot configuration file, you can recall it anytime to get the same results.

You save the configuration by choosing **C**onfiguration, **N**ew from the Plot settings box, which opens the Plot Configuration File dialog box. Enter the name you want the configuration file to have and choose **O**K. MicroStation creates a file in the \ustation\data\ directory and gives it an .ini file extension. The next time you want to plot this view again choose **C**onfiguration, **O**pen and select the configuration file you saved. The configuration file sets up the plot with the same file area, levels, options, and the pen table defined during creation of the configuration file.

Summary

Plotting is a major part of many CAD projects and MicroStation provides plenty of functionality and flexibility for creating the paper output. Pen tables enable you to customize how the elements are plotted and enable you to use the same graphic design files with many different effects. Configuration files give you a way to save your plotting specifications so that after you initially set up the plot you can recall the settings in future design sessions.

PART

4

Sharpening Your Skills

CHAPTER  16

Building and Placing Standard Symbols

I *n this chapter, you learn how to create cells or commonly used symbols and how to store them for future use. A cell can represent a sofa, directional arrows, a top or side view of a nut, or any group of elements that commonly appears in your drawings.*

The elements that make up the cell are stored in a cell library. The cell library is an external file attached to your design file. You can activate a cell from the library and place the elements in the design file as many times as necessary. This chapter reviews how to create a cell library, how to create cells, how to place and manipulate cells, and how to perform cell library maintenance functions.

In addition, it includes a short discussion on advanced cell placement of shared cells and dimension-driven cells. Shared cells provide a space-saving technique for multiple copies of cells in a design file. Dimension-driven cells are special intelligent cells placed by defining key dimensions and constraints on the elements that make up the cell.

In this chapter, you learn about doing the following:

♦ Creating a cell library to store cells

♦ Attaching a cell library to your design file

♦ Creating a cell and storing it in your cell library

♦ Activating a cell

♦ Placing a cell and using relative, interactive, and absolute cell placement methods

♦ Deleting a cell from your cell library

♦ Dropping the cell status so you can manipulate the elements of the cell individually

♦ Placing and dropping shared cells

♦ Using the Cell Selector utility

Creating and placing cells primarily involves the Cells tool box and the Cell Library settings box. You can tear off the Cells tool box from the Main tool frame, or you can open it by choosing **T**ools, **M**ain, **C**ells (see fig. 16.1).

Figure 16.1

The Cells tool box.

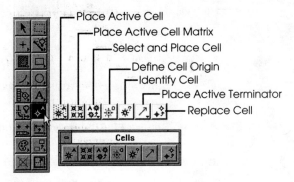

Place Active Cell
Place Active Cell Matrix
Select and Place Cell
Define Cell Origin
Identify Cell
Place Active Terminator
Replace Cell

Cells

You can open the Cell Library settings box (see fig. 16.2) by choosing E**l**ement, C**e**lls. The Cell Library settings box's menu bar shows the attached cell library's name and path. Here, [none] shows because no cell library is attached.

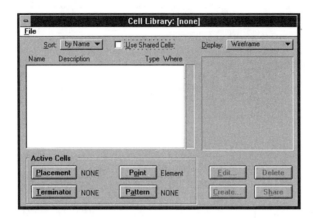

Figure 16.2

The Cell Library settings box.

Understanding Cell Libraries

A *cell library* is a file that stores the cells you have defined. Because a cell library is an external file, you can attach it to as many design files as you want. A cell library is a special file (not a design file) that has a CEL filename extension.

Note

If you share your cell library with other MicroStation users, you can copy the file from workstation to workstation or share it over a network, thus eliminating the need for everyone to create the same cells. Chapter 20, "Creating Drawing Standards," provides more information on sharing files.

The next section discusses how to create a new cell library. After it has been created, you will attach and view a cell library in your design file.

Creating a Cell Library

You can create a cell library by entering the appropriate information in the Create Cell Library dialog box (see fig. 16.3). You can open this dialog box from the Cell Library settings box by choosing **F**ile, **N**ew.

You create a cell library in the same way you create a design file. You enter a name in the Create Cell Library dialog box's Name field, and you define the directory and a seed file for the cell library in the respective fields. The seed file defines an existing cell library to use (copy) during creation. After you create the cell library, MicroStation automatically attaches it to the design file. The Status Bar displays the path and file name, such as the following:

```
Cell
Library=c:\win32apps\ustation\msmod\default\cell\chap16.cel.
```

Cell libraries have the CEL extension by default.

Note   You must use an existing cell library as a cell library seed file. MicroStation copies the file to the new name. If cells exist in the seed cell library, the new cell library contains copies of those cells. You can find empty cell library seed files in the MicroStation subdirectory wsmod\<workspace>\seed.

In the following exercise, you create a cell library.

CREATING A CELL LIBRARY

Create a design file called CHAP16.DGN.

Choose Element, **C**ells   Activates the Cell library settings box

Choose **F**ile, **N**ew   Activates the Create Cell Library dialog box

The directory defined for the cell library should be \ustation\wsmod\default\cell.

Type **CHAP16** *in the* **N**ame *field*
(see fig. 16.3)

Choose **O**K   Creates CHAP16.CEL and attaches the new
                cell library

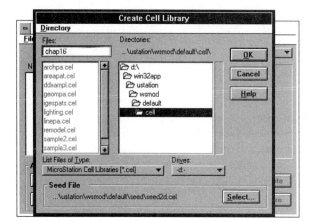

Figure 16.3

Creating the CHAP16.CEL cell library.

The seed file defines whether the cell library contains 2D or 3D cells. You can attach a 2D cell library to a 2D or a 3D design file; however, you can use a 3D cell library only in a 3D design file.

Note

Attaching Existing Cell Libraries

After you create a cell library and populate it with cells, you can attach it to any design file in MicroStation. As soon as the cell library is attached, you can place the cells in your active design file. You can choose File, Attach in the Cell Library settings box to open the Attach Cell Library dialog box (see fig. 16.4), which you can use to attach a cell library.

MicroStation enables you to activate and place cells from multiple cell libraries without redefining the active cell library each time. In your user configuration variable (MS_CELLLIST), you can define a list of cell libraries to search if the desired cell isn't found in the current cell library.

You still must attach a cell library for the purpose of creating and reviewing cells. The cell libraries defined in the MS_CELLLIST can be used only for placing cells. All modifications are done to the attached cell library.

Note

You can save the cell library attachment to your design file by choosing **F**ile, Sa**v**e Settings. If you then exit and reenter the design file, the cell library attachment is still there.

Tip
You attach a cell library to your design seed file in the same way you attach it to your active design file. You open the design seed file as you open any other graphics file, then you attach the cell library and save the settings by choosing **F**ile, Sa**v**e Settings. From that point on, every newly created design file automatically has the cell library attached. Chapter 17, "Boosting Your Performance," provides more information about default settings in seed files.

Viewing a Cell Library

The Cell Library settings box displays the currently attached cell library in the title bar and the name of the cells contained in this library in the list box. Figure 16.5 displays the currently attached cell library as c:\ustation\wsmod\mapping\cell\mapping.cel. If you select one of the cells in the list box, the cell appears in the box to the right.

Tip
Programs that document and print your cell library are available as shareware and from third-party software vendors. See your local dealer for more details.

In the following exercise, you try attaching an existing cell library to your design file. Note that attaching this cell library detaches CHAP16.CEL. Then, review your current cell library and the cells in that library.

ATTACHING AN EXISTING CELL LIBRARY AND REVIEWING ITS CONTENTS

Continue from the preceding exercise with the CHAP16.DGN design file open and the Cell library settings box still open.

Choose **F**ile, **A**ttach	Opens the Attach Cell Library dialog box

Change to the \ustation\wsmod\mapping\cell directory.

Select mapping.cel *in the* **F**iles *list box (see fig. 16.4)*	Sets Name field to mapping cell
Choose **O**K	Displays attached file in the Status Bar

Select the ELEXL cell (see fig. 16.5)   Displays cell

Now attach the cell library you created, called CHAP16.CEL. Look back at the previous exercise for help on attaching an existing cell library.

Close the Cell Library settings box

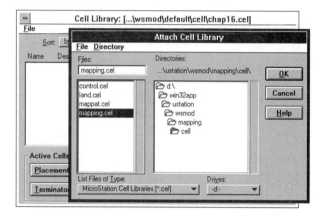

Figure 16.4

Attaching MAPPING.CEL with the Attach Cell Library dialog box.

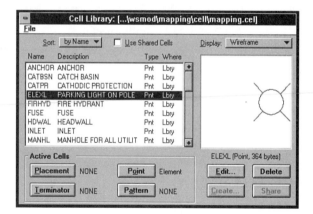

Figure 16.5

The parking lot light pole cell.

Building Your First Cell

Four steps are required to build a cell and store the elements in a cell library:

1. Create the elements in a design file.

2. Select the elements that make up the cell.

3. Define the point to use for placing the cell (origin).

4. Specify the name of the cell and description.

Placing and Selecting Elements

You can draw the elements you define for the contents of the cell in any design file. Consider the following items as you draw the elements that will make up your cells:

♦ Define the appropriate level for the cell elements. Cells can contain elements on one or more levels. Determine the level standard for the cell.

♦ Draw the element to scale in a design file with the same working units as your production files. Elements drawn to scale or full size are placed at an active scale of 1 for quick and accurate placement. Other types of cells might lend themselves to a unit size that can be scaled during the placement of the cell; for example, a 1×1 block with an X through it representing a cross section of a piece of lumber in an architectural plan. The cell can be scaled when placed to represent 2×4 by changing the X (2) and Y (4) scale.

♦ Take special care in creating the elements of a cell. Snap wherever appropriate. Remember that the cell will be placed multiple times—so make it look good.

♦ Draw the symbol or cell with as few elements as possible for the most efficiency; for example, place a line string rather than multiple line elements, or place a block or shape rather than multiple lines. The fewer elements a cell contains, the smaller and more efficient the cell.

♦ You also can place text in a cell. Consider using enter data fields for text that changes inside the cell. Enter data fields enable you to create a text holder that maintains the text size, font, and justification. The enter data field can easily be filled after the cell is placed. Chapter 14, "Working with Text," provides more information on enter data fields.

 Warning

You cannot edit text that is not a data field inside a cell unless the cell status is dropped. The section on modifying cells later in this chapter discusses the implications of dropping cells. You should use enter data fields wherever you might expect text modification. In a civil application, for example, you could use a cell at the station locations. The station cell would contain enter data fields to enter the station number after cell placement. A similar example might be room number symbols in an architectural floorplan.

After you draw the elements for the cell to contain, you must select the elements with a fence or by using the Element Selection tool. If you use the fence option for selecting the elements, remember to set the fence mode selection. If you need help with element selection or fence modes, refer to Chapter 9, "Manipulating 2D Elements."

Defining a Cell Origin

You must define the cell origin for each cell you create. The origin determines how the cell is placed relative to the point you enter on-screen. You should determine the placement of the origin point with cell placement in mind.

> If you find yourself moving the cell after placement, you might reconsider the origin that was defined during creation of the cell. An appropriate cell origin can preclude moving the cell each time you use it.

Tip

When you choose the Define Cell Origin tool from the Cells tool box and pick a point in the view for the cell origin, an O appears, indicating the point that will be used for the cell creation and later for cell placement. The O is for display purposes only and will not be part of the cell. The O appears bottom left justified from the point given.

The O disappears when you update the view. MicroStation still remembers the origin you defined, regardless of whether the temporary O appears in the view.

Use the tentative snap feature to place the cell origin accurately.

> You must define an origin before creating a cell. If you have defined a cell earlier, MicroStation uses the previous origin point, thus giving you unpredictable results. If no origin has been defined previously, an error message `No cell origin defined` appears in the Status Bar when you attempt to create the cell.

Warning

In the following exercise, you draw the elements that represent a marsh symbol, use the Element Selection tool to select all the elements, and then define a cell origin.

DEFINING THE CELL CONTENTS AND ORIGIN

Continue from the preceding exercise with the CHAP16.DGN design file open.

Place the elements of the marsh symbol (see fig. 16.6)	
Choose the Element Selection tool	
Press and drag from ① to ②, then release (see fig. 16.6)	Displays handles on selected elements
Tear off the Cells tool box (refer to figure 16.2) and choose the Define Cell Origin tool	
Pick a point at ③	Displays O at the cell origin location

Figure 16.6

Creating a marsh cell and defining an origin.

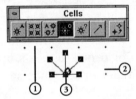

Creating the Cell Information

With the elements selected and the origin defined, you are ready to store the cell in the cell library. The cell is stored in the cell library with a name, a description (optional, but recommended), and a cell type.

Cell Names

A cell name must be unique in the cell library and can be a maximum of six characters.

Tip   MicroStation uses the name later to activate and place the cell, so try to make your cell names meaningful.

Cell Descriptions

A cell description is optional but recommended. The six-character name doesn't always give the user enough information about the cell. With a maximum of 32 characters, a description can help you determine the cell's purpose. For example, a utility application might have many different symbols for pole purposes and material types. You might have a cell for wood poles with electrical services, wood poles with TV cable services, and wood poles with or without lights. A description can easily help you determine which cell to activate for placement.

Cell Types

MicroStation offers four different types of cells: graphic, point, menu, and tutorial. You can use graphic and point cells for placing elements in a design file for the purposes described in this chapter. *Menu and tutorial cells* are special nongraphic cells used to create screen and tablet menus. Graphic and point cells react differently when placed in the design file.

Graphic and point cells have two primary differences. A graphic cell places the elements of the cell with the symbology used in creating each element. For example, if the marsh cell is created with a color of purple, line weight of 1, and style of 0, then the cell is placed with that symbology if it is stored as a graphic cell. A point cell, on the other hand, is placed with the active symbology, regardless of the symbology of the original elements.

Point cells are shown in the Cell Library settings box with the active symbology. Also, the type appears in the list box as Pnt.

Note

The other difference between graphic and point cells is the effect on cells when you rotate a view. A graphic cell rotates with the view, whereas a point cell doesn't. For example, the north arrow is created as a graphic cell and the map scale symbol is created as a point cell. The map scale cell doesn't rotate as the north arrow does when the view rotates. The map scale always appears right-reading, regardless of the view's rotation.

Storing the Cell

The Cell Library settings box provides a method for creating your cells. If the elements are selected in the design file and an origin is defined, the **C**reate button in the settings box becomes available.

Tip If the **C**reate button is not available, you have not fulfilled the requirements for defining the cell. Check to make sure that either the elements are selected with the Element Selection tool method or a fence is present. Verify that the origin has been defined.

After you choose the **C**reate button in the Cell Library settings box, a Create New Cell dialog box appears (see fig. 16.7). You enter a name and a description and then choose the **C**reate button.

Figure 16.7

*The Create New
Cell dialog box.*

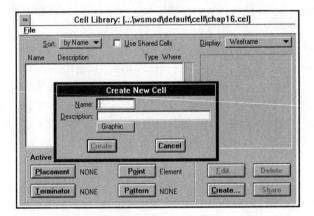

The following exercise stores the marsh cell in your active cell library. The elements of the marsh should be selected and the origin defined from the previous exercises.

Creating the Cell

Continue from the preceding exercise with the CHAP16.DGN design file open, the elements selected, and the origin defined.

*Choose **S**ettings, then **C**ells*   Opens the Cell Library settings box

*Choose the **C**reate button*   Opens the Create New Cell dialog box

Type **marsh** *in the* **N**ame *field and press Tab or click in the* **D**escription *field*

Type **Marsh for area patterning** *in the* **D**escription *field*	Removes dialog box and displays `Cell added to library` in the Status Bar
Choose **C**reate	Creates cell and closes the Create New Cell dialog box displays `Cell added to library` in the Status Bar
Choose the marsh cell in the list box	Displays the elements in the box to the right (see fig. 16.8)

Close the Cell Library settings box

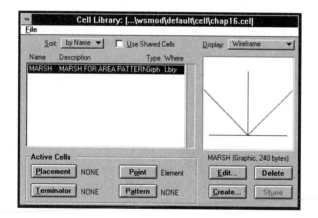

Figure 16.8

Marsh cell created and displayed in the Cell Library settings box.

To be certain that you created the cell you think you created, always place the cell you just created before you delete the original elements.

Tip

Using Your First Cell

You can place cells in several different ways: by using the cell placement tools, or by placing the cells as terminators, as points, or as a pattern. Whichever method you choose, the first step of every cell placement command is to identify the name of the cell you want to place.

Note   Chapter 11, "Advanced 2D Element Placement," discusses placing cells as points, and Chapter 12, "Applying Patterns and Fills," covers placing cells in a pattern area. This chapter concentrates on placing cells with the cell placement tools.

Activating a Cell

You can activate a cell for placement in the Cell Library settings box or in the Cells tool box. Choosing a cell from the Cell Library settings box is useful when you don't know the exact name of the cell. This settings box enables you to view each cell and to choose it for placement (**P**lacement) or use as a terminator (**T**erminator), a point (P**o**int), or a pattern (P**a**ttern). You identify the cell in the list box, and then you choose the **P**lacement button in the Active Cells area of the settings box.

The other option for activating a cell is to enter the cell name in the Active **C**ell field in the Tool Settings window while a cell placement command is active. Of course, this option requires that you know the cell names.

Placing the Active Cell

The first tool on the Cells tool box is Place Active Cell. Choosing it displays several settings for placement in the tool box: Active **C**ell, Active **A**ngle, **X** Scale, **Y** Scale, and toggle buttons for **R**elative and **I**nteractive.

You enter the name of the cell you want to place in the Active **C**ell field of the Tool Settings box, or you can activate the cell by using the Cell Library settings box techniques discussed earlier. The Active **A**ngle, **X** Scale, and **Y** Scale fields display the active settings. To eliminate any need to scale or rotate the cell after placement, you should change the settings in the fields before you place the cell.

Note   After you change the settings for Active **A**ngle, **X** Scale, and **Y** Scale in the Cells tool box, your active settings change and are reflected in other tool boxes and element placement commands.

PLACING A CELL

Continue from the preceding exercise with the CHAP16.DGN design file open.

Choose the Place Active Cell tool

Type **marsh** *in the* Active **C**ell *field*

Move the cursor into the design area	Cell is attached to cursor
Enter cell origin *Pick point at* ① *(see fig. 16.9)*	Places marsh cell

Click the Reset button

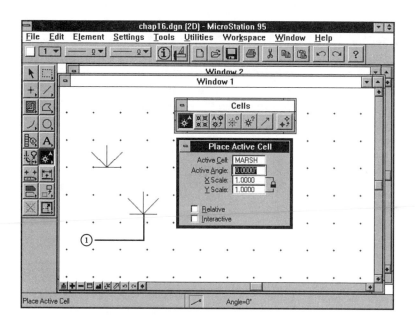

Figure 16.9

The marsh cell after placement.

Relative Cell Placement

The preceding exercise placed the marsh cell by using the absolute method of cell placement. The cell elements are placed on the level defined as the active level when you created the elements of the cell. Another method of cell placement is the relative method. You can turn on the relative method of cell placement by choosing the **R**elative toggle button in the Cells tool box. The relative method places the cell relative to the currently active level. In other words, even if the components of the cell were created on level 2, the cell would be placed on the active level if you used the relative method. As an example, if the active level is 30 and the cell is placed with the relative method, the cell is placed on level 30. The same cell placed with the absolute method is placed on level 2, regardless of the active level.

Note

Cells can contain elements on different levels. A cell created with elements on levels 2, 4, and 5 would be placed with the relative method on levels 30, 32, and 33 when the active level is 30. Notice that the relationship between the levels remains unchanged.

Interactive Cell Placement

The interactive method of cell placement enables you to dynamically define the scale and angle of the cell. This command requires three points for placing the cell. The first point anchors the cell at the origin point defined for the cell. As you move the cursor, you see the cell display and change orientation and shape. The second point defines the size of the cell. The third point defines the cell's rotation (see fig. 16.10).

Figure 16.10

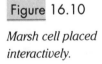

*Marsh cell placed
interactively.*

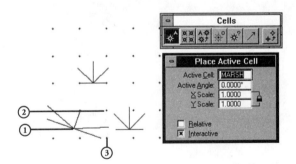

Using Other Special-Purpose Cell Commands

You find two other tools for cell placement on the Cells tool box: Place Active Cell Matrix, and Select and Place Cell. In addition, you use the Identify Cell tool to determine the name of a previously placed cell.

Place Active Cell Matrix

The Place Active Cell Matrix tool is similar to the Rectangular Array command covered in Chapter 8, "Placing More 2D Elements." The matrix is created from the number of rows (**R**ows) and columns (**C**olumns) and from the row spacing (Row **S**pacing) and column spacing (C**o**lumn Spacing). The Place Active Cell Matrix command prompts you to enter the lower left corner of matrix. You identify a point, and the first cell is placed at its origin. MicroStation places the remaining cells according to the row and column settings, relative to the placement of the first cell, to form the matrix.

> You could achieve the same effect by placing the cell and using the Rectangular Array command. This command creates the matrix in one step.

Note

Identify Cell

Another tool on the Cells tool box is Identify Cell. This command prompts you to identify a cell in the view; it then displays the name of the cell and the levels with which it was created in the Status Bar. The Identify Cell command is useful for identification purposes and doesn't modify or change any of the active settings.

Select and Place Cell

The Select and Place Cell command eliminates the need for you to activate the cell before you place it. If a cell you want to place shows in the view, this command enables you to identify the cell and activate it for placement. You identify an existing cell in the view with one point, making it the active cell, and pick another point to place the active cell by its origin.

> The Select and Place Cell command works only if the cell you identify in the view is in the current cell library or in the list of cell libraries defined by the MS_CELLLIST configuration variable. If the cell is not in any of these libraries, MicroStation displays the message Cell not found in the Status Bar.

Warning

The Select and Place Cell command differs from the Copy Element command in that the cell scale and angle are not duplicated from the cell you identify. The Select and Place Cell command uses the active scale and angle. If you use the Copy Element command, the cell scale and angle are duplicated.

Working with Cells

The cell that has been placed in your design file is a special grouping of elements. You can manipulate the cell as a single element or you can drop the complex status, enabling you to manipulate the individual elements that make up the cell. Along with cells and cell libraries comes the maintenance of the cell library and its contents.

Deleting a Cell from the Library

You can delete a cell from the cell library by using the Cell Library settings box. From the Cell Library settings box, you identify the name of the cell in the list box and then choose the Delete button. MicroStation displays an Alert box asking, Are you sure you want to delete the cell <cellname>? You can choose **O**K or Cancel.

 Note

Deleting a cell from the cell library doesn't affect any of the cells placed in the design file. The cells in the design file remain intact because placing a cell from the cell library copies the information into the design file.

You can delete cells only from the active cell library. You cannot delete cells from the cell libraries defined in the MS_CELLLIST configuration variable.

The only cell information you can modify or edit is the name and description. You can modify cell information from the Cell Library settings box by choosing the cell from the list box and then clicking on the **E**dit button. The Edit Cell Information dialog box appears, containing the current name and description (see fig. 16.11). After you make the changes, choose the **M**odify button.

Figure 16.11

The Edit Cell Information dialog box.

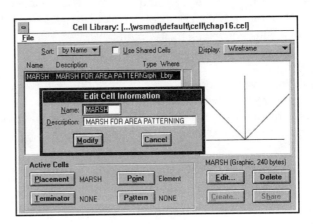

Manipulating Cells in the Design File

You can manipulate cells by using many of the tools from the Element Manipulation tool box, such as Copy, Move, Scale, Rotate, Mirror, and Array. You can modify cell symbology (color, weight, line style, or level) by using the Change Element Attributes command. You can use the Element Selection tool on cells for scaling and moving the cell.

If any modification to an individual element in a cell is required, the cell status must be dropped. After the cell status has been dropped, you can modify the original elements independently.

The cell status can be dropped with the Drop Element tool located on the Groups tool box (see fig. 16.12). You identify the cell to be dropped and accept the highlighted cell with another point anywhere in the view. Chapter 12 discusses other uses of the Drop Complex Status tool.

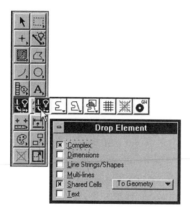

Figure 16.12

The Drop Element tool.

> After the cell status has been dropped, you no longer can manipulate the cell as a whole, and the elements no longer are grouped together. To manipulate the pieces of the cell as a group, you need to use one of the element grouping techniques discussed in Chapter 9, "Manipulating 2D Elements."

Warning

Changing the Cell Contents in the Cell Library

The only way to change the contents of the cell or the cell type is to re-create the cell. You can place the cell in your design file, drop the cell status on the cell, make the necessary modifications, delete the cell from the cell library, and re-create the cell.

Warning   Do not unnecessarily create a cell from a cell (called a *nested cell*). You should always drop the cell status on a cell before you use it to create another cell. For example, suppose that you have a cell for a desk and another cell for a chair. To combine the two cells, you would place each cell in a design file, drop the complex status on each, and create a new cell that contains the table and chair elements.

In the following exercise, you modify the marsh cell by placing the cell, dropping the complex status, modifying the elements, deleting the original, and creating a new marsh cell (see fig. 16.13).

Changing a Cell

Continue from the preceding exercise with the CHAP16.DGN design file open.

Choose the Place Active Cell tool

Move the cursor into the design area

Enter cell origin *Pick a point*   Places marsh cell

Choose the Drop Element tool

Identify element *Pick a point on*   Highlights cell
marsh cell

Pick a point anywhere in the view   Accepts and drops complex (cell) status

Modify the elements of the marsh elements by changing the color, symbology, weight, and/or level (see fig. 16.13).

*Choose the Place Fence tool from the Main
tool frame*

*Pick two points to place fence around the
elements*

*Choose the Define Cell Origin tool from the
Cells tool box*

Pick a point to define the origin point   Displays O in the view at the origin

*Open the Cell Library dialog box
by choosing E*lement, **C**ells *from the
pull-down menu*

Select the stored marsh symbol	Shows cell contents on the right side
Choose the Delete *button*	Alert box is displayed
Choose **O**K *from the Alert dialog box*	Deletes the stored cell
Choose the **C**reate *button*	Opens the Create New Cell dialog box
Type **marsh** *in the* **N**ame *field and press Tab or click in the* **D**escription *field*	
Type **Marsh for area patterning** *in the* **D**escription *field*	Removes dialog box and displays Cell added to library in the Status Bar
Choose **C**reate	Creates cell and closes the Create New Cell dialog box
Choose the marsh cell in the list box	Displays the elements in the box to the right
Close the Cell Library settings box	

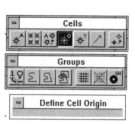

Figure 16.13

The new marsh cell.

Replacing a Cell

The Replace Cell command enables you to replace the existing cells in the design file with a newly designed cell. For example, now that you have modified the marsh cell, the other marsh cells in the design file need to be replaced with the new one. You can delete each of the old marsh cells and replace them by using the Place Active Cell command, or you can use the Replace Cell command. You simply identify the cell to be replaced, and MicroStation does the rest. The old cell is deleted, and the new cell is placed from the cell library.

Note

> The Replace Cell command places the new cell at the origin of the old cell. If the new and old origin are not at the same point on the cell, you might need to move the new cell to align properly.
>
> You can replace only cells that have the same cell name. You have to remove the old cell from the cell library and create the new cell with the same name.

Using Shared Cells

The term *shared cells* refers to the way the cells are stored in your design file. You can use shared cells in your design file to save disk space, keeping your design file size small and easy to manage.

Each time you place an unshared cell in a design file, MicroStation copies the cell header and each element contained in the cell into the design file. Therefore, if you place a cell 12 times and it contains 10 elements, the design file contains 12×11 elements (10 elements and 1 cell header) = 132 elements.

A shared cell saves space in the design file because each of the elements contained in the cell is not repeated multiple times in the design file. The elements of the cell are placed once when the first cell is placed. Additional shared cell instances place only an additional cell header and point to or share the elements of the original. In the example, placing the 12 cells as shared cells results in 12 cell headers + 10 elements = 22 elements. Placing the cell as shared reduces the file size from 132 elements to 22 elements.

Placing Shared Cells

You use a toggle switch to control placement of shared cells versus unshared cells and can turn it off and on from the Cell Library settings box. After you determine the method of placement (using the toggle button), you place the cells using the same cell placement tools as for unshared cells: Place Active Cell Absolute, Place Active Cell Relative, and Place Active Cell Matrix.

The Cell Library settings box shows the Use Shared Cells toggle button (see fig. 16.14) above the list box. If you turn on the toggle button, each cell you place from then on is placed as a shared cell instance. If you turn off the toggle button, the cells are placed as unshared cells.

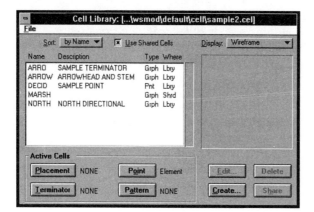

Figure 16.14

Use Shared Cell toggle on.

If you turn on the **U**se Shared Cells toggle, the design file in a sense acts as a cell library itself. You can activate and place cells currently placed in the design file, even if they're not contained in the currently attached cell library.

Note

If the **U**se Shared Cell toggle is on, the list box displays cells that are placed in the design file and are denoted by Shrd in the Where column in the Cell Library settings box. Cells contained in the cell library are displayed in the list box and are denoted by Lbry in the Where column.

You cannot fill in enter data fields on a shared cell. Place all cells that contain enter data field as unshared cells.

You save the shared cell setting (on or off) with your design file by choosing **F**ile, Sa**v**e Settings.

Dropping Shared Cells

The cell header is unique to each cell, regardless of whether the cell is placed as shared or unshared. The header contains information (such as origin, scale, and rotation) that enables each shared cell to exist in different locations, sizes, and angles and still share the bulk of the element data.

In some cases, a shared cell might need to be dropped to an unshared status (for example, if a cell containing an enter data field is placed as a shared cell). Because the enter data field is an element of the shared portion of the cell, you cannot fill in the text until the shared status is dropped.

Note Compatibility with versions of MicroStation earlier than 4.0 requires that you drop all the shared cells. Or, check out the Freeze and Thaw commands provided with MicroStation for downward compatibility.

Drop the shared status in the Drop tool box. Notice the toggle button in the tool settings box, which includes a pop-up list box that contains To **G**eometry and To **N**ormal Cell.

Replacing Shared Cells

The Replace Cell command has added functionality with shared cells. After you change the cell in the cell library, choose the Replace Cell tool and identify one of the shared cells. After you accept the cell with a point in the view, MicroStation replaces all instances of the shared cell.

Cell Selector

To assist in activating cells, MicroStation offers a utility that dynamically creates a tool box (of sorts) of the cells in your cell library. Choose Cell **S**elector from the **U**tilities menu in the Application window. The Cell Selector box appears with buttons assigned for each cell in your cell library (see fig. 16.15).

Figure 16.15

Your custom cell selector box.

Note The Cell Selector utility prompts you to identify a cell library by displaying a Select Cell Library to Load dialog box if no cell library is attached when the utility is executed.

The File pull-down menu in the Cell Selector enables you to include more cells from other cell libraries, save the configuration you have created so it can be used in other design files, or create a new or open existing cell selector files.

The Edit pull-down menu gives you some customization tools such as changing the button size, changing the color of the cells in the button, displaying cell names rather than icons of the cells, inserting individual cells from existing cell libraries, or deleting individual buttons.

> Dimension-driven cells are created from elements placed with an advanced set of tools. These tools define associations, constraints, and constructions between the elements of the design. Modifying or changing a dimension recalculates the constraints and constructions, often changing the entire design.

Note

Summary

Symbols, regardless of the method you use to create and place them, are an integral part of every design file. A well-designed cell with the correct origin can be an asset to any production environment. A library of commonly used cells is one of the most powerful advantages over manual drafting. Many drawings are just different combinations of your cells.

MicroStation beginners usually do see the power of cells and use the features extensively. But if you are a beginner, don't underestimate the powerful features of reference files (see Chapter 18) or glossary files (refer to Chapter 14).

Boosting Your Performance

T *he purpose of this chapter is to consolidate and elaborate on some of MicroStation's tips and production hints, which give valuable advice on working productively in the MicroStation environment. You should not stop with this chapter, however, because the next three chapters—"Referencing Other Drawings," "Changing the Way MicroStation Looks," and "Creating Drawing Standards"—also provide valuable production tips and techniques.*

The major topics this chapter covers are workspaces and configuration variables and how to change them. Configuration variables tell MicroStation where to begin looking for files and resources. What the default path is for design files and where to find the glossary file are a few of the items of information stored in configuration variables.

Besides the major topics, this chapter covers many small tips and tricks that can make your life easier in a normal production environment.

This chapter covers the following topics:

♦ Understanding workspaces and how they affect the default settings, available tools, and general look and feel of MicroStation

♦ Changing the default environment settings for directories and files stored in the configuration variables

♦ Customizing the keyboard function keys

♦ Using the Key-in Browser to find the key-in equivalents for all the MicroStation commands

♦ Setting up and modifying seed files

♦ Changing cursor-button assignments

♦ Creating and executing macros

 Warning

Be careful about modifying any files or settings. Check with your system manager or project coordinator for project and site standards before you modify the current settings. For example, seed files may be firmly established and changes to that file might affect other people at your company.

Defining a Workspace

The term *workspace* refers to the MicroStation environment, which is divided into three components: module, user interface, and user preferences.

♦ **Module.** The module component encompasses all the data defined as part of the workspace. The module might consist of paths to seed files, symbology resources, cell libraries, and any other project- or task-specific data. Find out more about the module or workspace settings in the following discussion of configuration files.

♦ **User interface.** The user interface component comprises the tools and commands on the tool boxes and pull-down menus in the workspace. You can customize the user interface by removing the tools you don't use. Chapter 19, "Changing the Way MicroStation Looks," provides more information on the user interface.

♦ **User preferences.** The user preference component enables you to customize default settings for tools and the GUI. User preferences determine the size of the tool boxes, the dialog boxes, and the screen cursor, for example. Preferences are another way to customize the MicroStation environment. Again, Chapter 19 provides more information on this topic.

The user configuration file ties these three components together. This chapter covers the functions and settings of the configuration files in detail.

Understanding Configuration Variables

Configuration variables tell MicroStation where to find the directories and files necessary to run MicroStation. Configuration variables also are commonly referred to as *environment variables* because they define the environment for MicroStation. Two configuration variables are defined for plotting, for example: MS_PENTABLE and MS_PLTR. These variables tell MicroStation where to find the plotting pentable files (MS_PENTABLE) and how to identify the default plot driver file (MS_PLTR). In this example, MS_PENTABLE is defined as ustation\tables\pen, and MS_PLTR may be defined as ustation\plotdrv\print.plt. Configuration variables can be multiple paths separated by a semicolon, a directory, a filename, a keyword, or a keywords list.

MicroStation has five levels at which these configuration variables can be set: system, application, site, project, and user.

♦ **System.** System variables are the first level of configuration variables. System variables are set by the system configuration file, which is created when you load MicroStation. This level of configuration variables should not be modified—it is reserved for system upgrades. Any changes to this level will be removed if you upgrade or reinstall MicroStation.

♦ **Application.** Application variables are the second level of configuration variables. Application variables are set by third-party developers to MicroStation and generally are required for their applications.

♦ **Site.** Site variables are the third level of configuration variables. Site variables generally are set by the system to set some standards for your site or company.

♦ **Project.** Project variables are the fourth level of configuration variables. Project variables can be defined for a particular project or discipline at your site.

♦ **User.** User variables are the fifth level of configuration variables. After getting all the configuration from the files mentioned above, the user can add to or change the variables to meet his or her personal needs.

How would these five configuration files be used at your site? As an example, imagine that you work for a city government, with many different disciplines and projects being developed simultaneously. The system configuration file would be the starting point for every project and user within the organization. Application variables would be added for third-party applications such as plotting. Site configuration variables would be established by the site CAD manager added for all commonly used directories and files in the organization. A project manager in the engineering department would then define configuration variables for each group or discipline in the department or bureau. As examples, the paving engineers would have a project configuration file defining directory and default files for their application, and the water engineers would likewise have a project configuration file pointing them to different directories and defaults. A project configuration file might contain definitions for the cell library, the seed file, the symbology files, and other data unique to this project or discipline. Finally, each person in the paving department would use the system and project configuration files and further define user-specific variables.

 Note

All the configuration files are stored as ASCII or text files in a delivered MicroStation directory. See table 17.1 for the directory location and the file extensions. Each file can be modified by your favorite text editor.

Level	File location	Extension
System	ustation\config\system	.CFG
Application	ustation\config\appl	.CFG
Site	ustation\config\site	.CFG
Project	ustation\config\project	.PCF
User	ustation\config\user	.UCF

Configuration files and workspaces are not stored with each design file. They are activated when you enter a graphic design session at the MicroStation Manager dialog box.

Creating a Workspace and Assigning Workspace Components

Your user configuration file combines the configuration files and a default preference file to create the workspace. For all intents and purposes, the user configuration file is your workspace.

The user interface defined for the workspace determines what items appear in the pull-down menus and what tools appear on the palettes. Delivered interfaces included with MicroStation are arch, autocad, civil, learning, mapping, mde, and mechdrft. These other interfaces restrict the tools to those germane to that particular discipline or application; for example, the learning workspace provides only the basic tools. Chapter 19, "Changing the Way MicroStation Looks," discusses how to customize a user interface.

The preference file controls many of the display defaults, such as tool size, dialog box text size, and so on. Chapter 19 covers several of the preference file settings in detail.

In the city government example previously cited, individuals would each create their own user configuration file. As an example, Paul would have a user configuration file, PAUL.UCF, with the appropriate project configuration file, user interface, and user preference file attached; and Bryan would have a user configuration file, BRYAN.UCF, which might have the same project configuration file attached but a different preference file.

You must create a workspace before you enter MicroStation from the MicroStation Manager dialog box. Create a workspace by choosing **W**orkspace, **N**ew to open the Create Workspace dialog box, in which you can provide a name for your new workspace. Choosing **O**K opens a second dialog box, also called the Create Workspace dialog box (see fig. 17.1). The default Project and User Interface is selected automatically and MicroStation creates and then selects a preference file with the same name as the workspace.

Create your own workspace in the next exercise.

CREATING A WORKSPACE

From the MicroStation Manager dialog box choose **N**ew *from the Workspace pop-up menu*	Create Workspace dialog box appears
Enter your name in the **N**ame *field*	

Continues

Choose **O**K	Closes that Create Workspace dialog box and opens another (see fig. 17.1)
Enter **Book Exercise Workspace** *in the Description field*	
Choose **O**K	Closes that Create Workspace dialog box

Figure 17.1

Creating your very own workspace.

In summary, workspaces serve as a way to organize projects and share settings with all users and at the same time give individuals the flexibility to customize MicroStation as they please.

Reviewing and Changing Configuration Variables

You can use the Configuration : User dialog box during a design session to review and change the configuration variables defined in the user configuration file (see fig. 17.2). To open this dialog box, choose **W**orkspace, **C**onfiguration.

The **C**ategory list box on the left side of the Configuration : User dialog box displays all the different types of configuration variables available for the user to define. The **C**ategory list box includes configuration variables that define directories and defaults for cells, data files, plotting, and so on. When you choose an item in the **C**ategory list box, the variables for that item appear in the list box at the top right of the dialog box.

The All (By Level) item in the **C**ategory list box displays all variables, with the user-defined variables first, then the project-defined variables, and then the system-defined variables.

Note

When you choose Data Files from the **C**ategory list box, four Data File variables appear in the list box to the right (see fig. 17.2). The list box also shows you at what level the configuration variable was set. In this example, all the variables are set by the system-level configuration file. You might also see the word "Appl," "Site," "Project," or "User" in this list box when variables are defined by these levels.

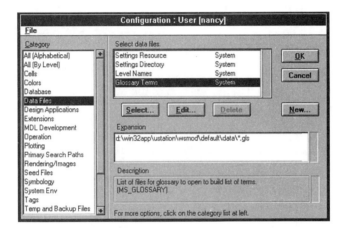

Figure 17.2

The data file variables in the Configuration : User dialog box.

After you choose one of these variables, such as Glossary Terms, the list box displays further information: the E**x**pansion field gives the current definition, and the Descri**p**tion field gives an explanation of the setting. If you want to use a custom- or project-specific glossary, or use multiple glossary files, you need to modify the Glossary Data (MS_GLOSSARY) variable to the new name and/or directory. The **S**elect, **E**dit, and **D**elete buttons are available for changing the definitions.

♦ The **S**elect button opens a Select File dialog box, which is similar to the file dialog boxes you see throughout MicroStation (see fig. 17.3). You identify the new directory in the Directories list box and the default glossary file in the F**i**les list box. To set the variable, choose D**o**ne.

Figure 17.3

The Select File dialog box.

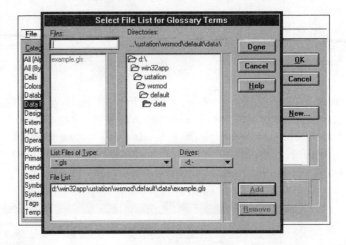

♦ The **E**dit button opens an Edit Configuration Variable dialog box (see fig. 17.4), which you can use instead of the Select button to define the variable. In this dialog box, you enter the full path and glossary filename in the New Value field. To set the variable, choose **O**K.

Figure 17.4

The Edit Configuration Variable dialog box.

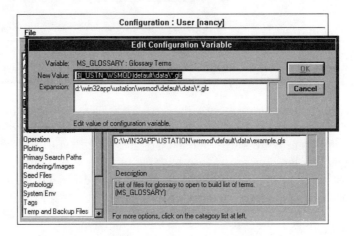

♦ The **D**elete button removes the selected user-defined variables. After you delete a user variable, MicroStation reads the definition from the next level up that had defined the variable.

Note

You can delete only user definitions in the Configuration : User dialog box. You cannot delete any other level configuration variables from a graphics session. Project and Site level configuration variables can only be modified using a text editor—outside a graphic session. Think twice before changing these variables, you might be affecting more people than just yourself if the file is on a network or if several people use the same machine.

The next section gives you an opportunity to try to change a configuration variable.

To dismiss the Configuration : User dialog box, you can choose the **O**K or the Cancel button. The Cancel button dismisses the dialog box and disregards any changes you have made. The **O**K button opens an Alert box (see fig. 17.5). If you choose the **Y**es button in this Alert box, you save the changes permanently by writing the changes to the .UCF file. If you choose the **N**o button from this Alert box, you save the changes only for the current design session. After you exit MicroStation, your changes are lost. If you choose the Cancel button from this Alert box, you return to the Configuration : User dialog box, in which you can choose Cancel again to exit without changing the variable settings.

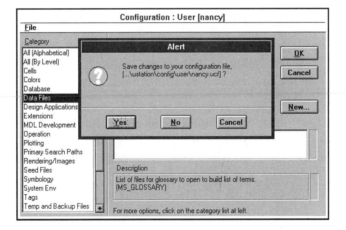

Figure 17.5

The Alert box for saving changes.

Working with Function Keys

Function keys are the keys labeled with F and then a number (such as, F8), usually located above the standard character keys on your keyboard. MicroStation enables you to define each of these keys with tools or key-ins that you would normally choose from the tool boxes or menus. As an example, suppose that you often need to change the active angle to 90° and then back to 0°. You could assign the key-ins for setting the active angle to a function key; then simply by pressing a key, the active angle becomes 90° and pressing another key changes the active angle back to 0°.

Function keys can facilitate many MicroStation procedures. Another example might involve placing a command or tool you routinely use on a function key. But first you need to know the key-in commands.

Using the Key-in Browser

You can use a utility called the Key-in Browser to find and learn the key-in commands for MicroStation. The Key-in Browser is particularly useful for determining key-ins to use in function key definitions.

The Key-in Browser settings box provides a method for you to determine the key-in equivalents for all the commands that you activate from the tool boxes and pull-down menus. After you determine the key-in equivalent, you then can use it on a function key to activate the command. If you want to activate the command for Place Circle By Diameter on a function key, for example, the Key-in Browser assists you by indicating that the key-in command name is Place Circle Diameter.

To open the Key-in Browser settings box, choose **K**ey-in Browser from the **H**elp pull-down menu in the Application Window. This settings box has three major parts: the key-in field, the command section, and the history section (see fig. 17.6).

The command section contains the four list boxes and two buttons. The first list box represents all the first-level MicroStation commands. Because the MicroStation key-in command names are hierarchical in nature, selecting a command in the first list box often activates more choices in the second list box. The hierarchical command structure can be a maximum of four commands long, although many commands have only two or three levels in the command name. For example, if you choose "place" from the first list box, the Key-in Browser settings box displays available options for commands that begin with the word place in the second list box. In turn, if you choose "circle" from the second list box, six options appear in the third list box.

As you choose items from each of the list boxes, the command name is being built in the key-in field. You choose the Key in button to issue the command shown.

> If you choose the Key in button before choosing a unique command string, the Status Bar displays the error message `Insufficient Arguments`.

Note

In the following exercise, you use the Key-in Browser to find the key-in for the circle commands.

USING THE KEY-IN BROWSER

Create a design file called CHAP17.DGN and enter MicroStation with your workspace.

Choose **H**elp, **K**ey-in Browser	Opens the Key-in Browser settings box
Locate and select `place` *from the first list box (see fig. 17.6)*	Displays place in the key-in field of the Command window

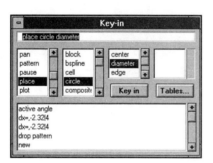

Figure 17.6

The Key-in Browser settings box.

Select `circle` *from the second list box*	Adds circle to the key-in field of the Command window
Choose `diameter` *from the third list box*	Adds diameter to the key-in field of the Command window
Choose the Key in *button*	Activates the Place Circle By Diameter command

> Click on any entries in the history list to recall a previous key-in, then choose the Key in button or press Enter.

Tip

You can activate all the tool boxes and dialog boxes using a key-in; therefore, you can assign a function key to activate any tool box or dialog box. You could add a function key that enters **DIALOG CMDBROWSE**, for example, and pressing that function key would invoke the Key-in Browser.

Copying a Function Key

Function keys are stored and saved in a menu file. By default, the function key menu attached when you enter MicroStation is defined in your configuration file. To start the next series of exercises, you copy the current function key menu to a new name and location, and then you change the configuration variable for MS_FKEYMNU.

To save the current function key menu with a new name, you must first choose Wor**k**space, **F**unction Keys to open the Function Keys dialog box (see fig. 17.7).

Figure 17.7

*The Function Keys
dialog box.*

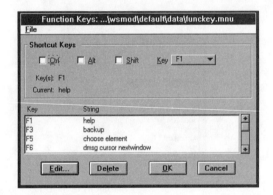

When you choose the **F**ile pull-down menu in the Function Keys dialog box and then choose Save **A**s, the Save Function Key Menu As dialog box opens (see fig. 17.8). You enter a filename and choose **O**K to save the function key menu with the new name. MicroStation adds the default extension of MNU for menu files. After you copy the function key menu, you need to change the user variable to point to your new function key menu.

In the following exercise, you create your own function key menu by copying the attached one and modify your configuration variable to point to the new function key menu.

Copying a Function Key Menu and Attaching It

Continue from the preceding exercise with the CHAP17.DGN design file open.

Choose Wor**k**space, **F**unction Keys	Opens the Function Keys dialog box
Choose **F**ile, Save **A**s	Opens the Save Function Key Menu As dialog box (see fig. 17.8)

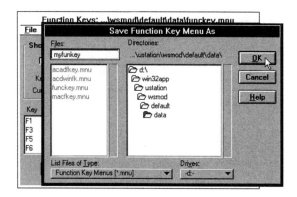

Figure 17.8

The Save Function Key Menu As dialog box.

Type **myfunkey** *in the* **N**ame *field and choose* **O**K	Specifies file, closes the dialog box, and makes the copy
Choose Cancel *from the* Function Keys *dialog box*	
Choose Wor**k**space, **C**onfiguration	Opens the Configuration : User dialog box
Choose Operation *from the* **C**ategory *list box*	Displays five variables in the top center list box
Select Function Key Menu	Displays definition in the E**x**pansion field and text in the Descri**p**tion field
Choose **S**elect	Opens the Select File dialog box
Select the file MYFUNKEY.MNU	
Choose **O**K *from the Select File dialog box*	Modifies MS_FKEYMNU variable
Choose **O**K *from the Configuration Variables dialog box*	Invokes the Alert box
Choose **Y**es	Saves changes to the *<your name>*.UCF file

Note   The Save As operation simply copies the menu file to a new name and directory. You could achieve the same results by copying the file from the operating system.

Modifying a Function Key

To modify function keys in the menu, you must use the Function Keys dialog box (refer to figure 17.7). The lower portion of this dialog box shows what is currently defined in this function key menu. The F5 key on your keyboard, for example, currently is defined with the Choose Element command. Pressing the F5 key (when the function key dialog box is closed) immediately activates the Element selection tool or Choose Element command.

The top portion of the Function Keys dialog box, Shortcut Keys, is used to define new function key assignments or to change existing function keys. To add a key-in to the function key F2, for example, choose the **K**ey field and select F2 from the pop-up menu. Clicking on the **E**dit button at the bottom of the dialog box opens the Edit Key Definition dialog box (see fig. 17.9).

Figure 17.9

The Edit Key Definition dialog box.

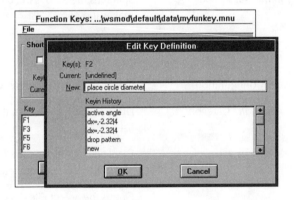

The Edit Key Definition dialog box contains three fields: the Key(s) field designates a function key; the Current field shows the current definition of that function key; and the **N**ew field enables you to enter the new definition of that function key. You can enter any key you find in the Key-in Browser in the **N**ew field.

After you enter the key-in (such as **place circle diameter**) in the **N**ew field and choose **O**K, the Edit Key Definition dialog box disappears and the added key is listed in the Key list box of the Function Keys dialog box. You can make more additions or change the existing function key assignments in the same manner.

After you complete all the necessary changes to the function key menu, choose the **O**K button in the Function Keys dialog box. An Alert box appears containing the usual three button options: **Y**es, **N**o, or Cancel.

If you respond to this Alert dialog box by choosing **Y**es, the changes you have made are permanently written to the function key menu file stored on the hard drive. If you respond with **N**o, the changes you have made are effective only until you exit MicroStation.

In the following exercise, you add the F2 function key to the menu, and assign place circle diameter to it.

ADDING FUNCTION KEY DEFINITIONS

Continue from the preceding exercise with the CHAP17.DGN design file open.

Choose Wor**k**space, **F**unction Keys	Opens the Function Keys dialog box
Choose F2 *from the* **K**ey *pop-up list in the Function Keys dialog box*	
Choose **E**dit	Opens the Edit Key Definition dialog box (refer to figure 17.9) for key F2, the default
Type **place circle diameter** *in the* **N**ew *field and choose* **O**K	Defines F2 key
Choose **O**K	Displays an alert box
Choose **Y**es	

Now try the F2 function key. Watch the active command change in the Status Bar as you press the key.

Putting Multiple Key-ins on a Function Key

You can put multiple key-ins on one function key by entering a semicolon (;) between the key-ins. Setting the symbology for a particular feature in your design could serve as a good example of this concept. Consider the following: If the correct symbology for the circle is level 20 and the color of blue, you could enter all this information on a function key. When you press the function key, you activate the correct symbology for the circle and activate the command. Thus function keys provide a great time-saving technique for setting symbology.

Note   Function keys are limited to definitions of 55 characters or less.

In the following exercise, you edit the function key F2 and add the setting for level and color.

ASSIGNING MULTIPLE KEY-INS TO A FUNCTION KEY

Continue from the preceding exercise with the CHAP17.DGN design file open.

Choose Wor**k**space, **F**unction Keys	Opens the Function Keys dialog box
Choose F2 *from the* **K**ey *pop-up list*	
Choose **E**dit	Displays the Edit Key Definition dialog box for Key(s): F2
Type **active level 20;active color blue;** *in the* **N**ew *field before the place circle diameter key-in and choose* **O**K	Defines F2 key
Choose **O**K	Displays the Alert box
Choose **Y**es	

Now try the function key F2. Note that the changes are reflected in the Status Bar's message field when you press the function key.

Tip   You can send messages to the Status Bar fields on a function key by prefacing them with "m," in the function key definition, as in the following line:

```
m,cfSetting Level 20;active level 20
```

The "m" tells MicroStation that the following is a message. The "cf" tells MicroStation to send the message to the command field of the Status Bar. See the documentation for a complete listing of field abbreviations.

These ideas introduce you to the facilitating role of function keys in MicroStation. Chapter 20, "Creating Drawing Standards," expands on this discussion in its presentation of the Settings Manager.

Setting Up and Modifying Seed Files

As promised in the first few chapters, a more detailed discussion of seed files is warranted after you have examined the features of MicroStation. A *seed file* typically is an empty design file that contains design file defaults for working units, views, and file settings, such as active level. In the process of creating a new design file, the first step MicroStation takes is to copy the seed file. You should define the defaults and settings in the seed file so that you do not need to spend time setting up each individual design file.

To modify or set up a seed file for your project and personal needs, you can open and modify the seed file just as you do any other design file. You should consider defining or setting the following items:

♦ **Working units.** Define the working units and precision. See Chapter 3 for details on working units.

♦ **Global origin.** In most cases, the global origin defined in the center of the design plane should be sufficient. Do not redefine that global origin often, however, or you might have problems when referencing files later. Chapter 18, "Referencing Other Drawings," covers the topic of reference files.

♦ **Coordinate readout.** Define the way that the coordinate data are displayed in the fields of the tool boxes. This setting also affects the way that the measurement commands display the results.

♦ **Tables and structures.** Attach the default color table used for your application and the default level structure used at your site.

♦ **Active settings.** Set the active settings, such as angle and scale, level, color, weight, style, and so on.

♦ **Libraries and references.** Attach the appropriate cell libraries and any commonly used reference files, such as borders. The files created with this seed file automatically get the reference attachment.

♦ **Grid.** If a grid or a grid lock or both are commonly used for your application, define the appropriate grid settings.

♦ **Default symbology.** Set the default element attributes, which include level, weight, color, and line style. Do not forget default settings for text attributes, such as text size, font, line spacing, line length, fractions, slant, and so on.

- **Level symbology.** Define the default level symbology. Level symbology is not saved as an external file; therefore, it must be set up in each design file or copied from the seed file when the design file is created.

- **Default lock settings.** Turn on the appropriate locks typically used for your application. If the Unit and Axis locks are not relevant to your application, be sure that they are not on. Also, define the default snap mode and Fence mode.

- **Default display settings.** Set up the views and the area defined in each view. Define the view attributes for each view, such as grid display, area fill display, and so on.

- **Default dimension settings.** Set the default dimension attributes, such as geometry, tolerance, units, and so on.

After you have the seed file the way you would like all the new files to look, choose File, Save Settings. The settings saved to the seed file are the settings with which you begin every new design file you use that seed file to create.

You can change these settings in a newly created design file. The seed file settings give you only a known starting point from which to work. If you find yourself changing settings and displays each time you create a new design file, you should rethink your seed file.

Changing Button Assignments

Chapter 1, "Getting Started," introduced the tablet-cursor or mouse-button default assignments. You have the flexibility to change the function for each tablet-cursor or mouse button to meet your individual needs. You can rearrange the button assignments for the Data, Reset, Tentative, and Command buttons. To open the Button Assignments dialog box (see fig. 17.10), choose Workspace, Button Assignments.

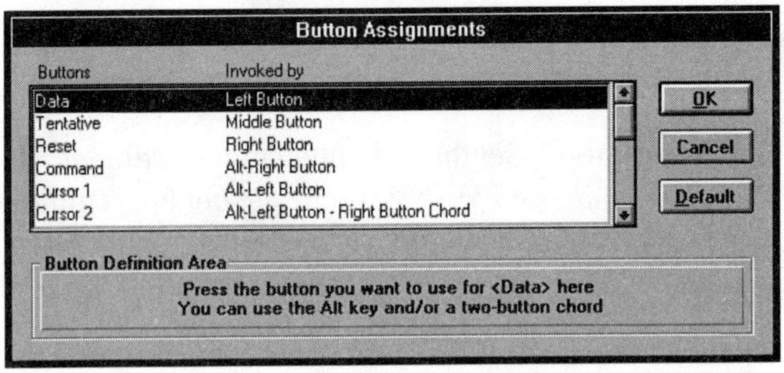

Figure 17.10

The Button Assignments dialog box.

Users of a two-button mouse don't have a great deal of flexibility. Users of tablet cursors, however, can use the Button Assignments dialog box to define the additional 12 buttons. If you select the Data line from the MicroStation Buttons list in the dialog box, for example, a large message button appears below the list in the Button Definition Area, instructing you to press the button you want to use for Data. To assign another button or button/key combination, place the screen cursor on this large message button and press the mouse or tablet-cursor button or button/key combination.

If you have a tablet cursor, you can assign key-ins and commands to extra cursor buttons, much as you assign them to function keys on your keyboard. A cursor-button menu is created as a cell, placed in the cell library, and attached with the key-in **AM=*name*,CB**. Check the delivered documents for the procedure for creating cursor-button menus.

If you have a three-button mouse, you can utilitize all the buttons by assigning data, tentative, and reset to each of the buttons. *Tip*

Attaching Menus

Many different kinds of menus are available in MicroStation. The screen-driven tool boxes and pull-down menus are only two ways to issue commands. Other menu types include:

♦ **Command menus.** A *command menu* (paper menu or tablet menu) is an alternative to using the tool box. This type of menu requires a digitizing tablet to which you attach a paper menu.

♦ **Matrix menus.** A *matrix menu* is a paper menu you create. You can attach a maximum of three matrix menus at one time by using the menu type of m1, m2, and m3. The location of each matrix menu is defined by the origin and size of the menu.

♦ **Sidebar menus.** A *sidebar menu* is the old text-only hierarchical screen menu.

You can create your own matrix menus and sidebar menus, but Chapter 19 introduces you to creating your own tool boxes. You can read more about alternative menus in the delivered documentation. *Note*

Macros

A macro is a BASIC language program that you create and run in MicroStation to perform a sequence of commands or tasks. An example of a macro might be setting a series of text parameters and issuing the place text command. You then can place this macro on a function key to facilitate execution.

Creating Macros

Creating a macro is easy and dialog box driven. Choose **U**tilities, **C**reate Macro in the Application Window to open the Create Macro dialog box (see fig. 17.11). Enter the name of your new macro in the **N**ame field. Enter a description that might include your name and the purpose of this macro in the **D**escription field and choose **O**K. After you choose the **O**K button, the recording box opens (see fig. 17.12) with three icons for play, pause, and end. The name that appears in the title bar of this box is the name you gave the macro and the play button is pressed, ready to record.

Figure 17.11

*Create Macro
dialog box.*

Figure 17.12

*Record macro
box.*

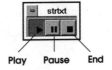

In the following exercise, you create a macro to set some active symbology and issue the Place SmartLine command. You call the macro "strsym" to indicate that the symbology is for street placement.

CREATING A STREET SYMBOLOGY MACRO

Continue from the preceding exercise with the CHAP17.DGN design file open.

Choose **U**tilities, **C**reate Macro   Opens the Create Macro dialog box

Type **strsym** *in the* **N**ame *field*	Defines the name for this macro
Type **Street parameter by ,<your name>** *in the* **D**escription *field*	Describes the purpose and records the author's name with the macro (refer to figure 17.11)
Choose **O**K	Displays the record box (refer to figure 17.12) Records everything you do from this point on as the strsym macro

Change the active symbology from the primary tool box and choose the Place SmartLine tool from the Main tool frame.

Choose the End button	Completes recording and closes record box

Running Macros

After you record a macro, you can run the macro from the Macro dialog box (see fig. 17.13) or from a key-in. Activate the Macro dialog box by choosing Ma**c**ros from the **U**tilities pull-down menu.

Figure 17.13

Running a macro from the Macros dialog box.

You can enter the key-in, macro *<macro name>* from the key-in field, place it on a function key, or place it on a personal tool box. Chapter 19 offers more information about personal tool boxes.

In the next exercise, you run the macro you created in the last exercise. You change the settings again before you run the macro to verify that the macro runs correctly.

RUNNING THE STREET SYMBOLOGY MACRO

Continue from the preceding exercise with the CHAP17.DGN design file open.

Change the active symbology from the primary tool box and choose a tool other than the Place SmartLine tool from the Main tool frame.

Choose Utilities, Key-in	Opens the Key-in dialog box
Type **macro strsym** *and press* Enter	Activates the macro

Summary

You have seen several time-saving techniques in this chapter. None of these techniques are necessary to work with MicroStation, but they do make you more efficient.

Workspaces and the configuration variables defined give you the freedom to create your own custom environment. Chapter 19, "Changing the Way MicroStation Looks," provides more information about the other components of the user workspace.

Function keys and macros are all easy ways to help you work more efficiently with MicroStation.

CHAPTER 18

Referencing Other Drawings

*H*ave you ever run out of disk space? Have you ever worked on a project with people who promise no forthcoming changes, but after completing your part of the project, discovered that last-minute changes were made after all? Perhaps you need to see multiple drawings at the same time on the display screen or on the same hard copy plot. Did you ever pull a part drawing and its details from the flat files only to find out someone had updated the part drawing but forgot to revise the details? MicroStation's reference file capability overcomes all these problems and more, if used with good forethought and some planning.

Chapter 18 first examines the different ways you might use MicroStation's reference file capability. A reference file *is a design file attached to an active design file. After you attach the reference file, you can view the design file and its attached reference files together. You can use any design file as a reference file. After a short tour on the use of reference files, the chapter shifts to teaching you how you can take advantage of this powerful MicroStation feature in your drawings. You learn how to attach, display, and detach reference files. Then you learn the techniques for moving, scaling, rotating, and mirroring what you see. Other exercises in this chapter take you through defining "clipping boundaries" to show a particular portion of a reference file and the techniques of copying graphics from a reference file into the active design file.*

An important feature of reference files is that they are secure against accidental change when you are working in the active file to which they are attached. You can see the information in the reference file, but you cannot modify, move, change the color of, or delete any element in a reference file. Reference files are attached for display purposes only. You can, however, turn the display of levels on and off, snap to elements in a reference file, and copy information from a reference file into an active design file. To change a reference file, you must open it as an active design file.

In this chapter, you learn about the following:

♦ Advantages to using reference files

♦ Attaching a reference file

♦ Hiding or showing only certain reference information

♦ Keeping track of details by referencing a drawing to itself

♦ Attaching and detaching reference files

♦ Moving, scaling, mirroring, and rotating reference files

♦ Copying graphics from a reference file into the active design file

The Reference Files tool box (see fig. 18.1) and the Reference Files settings box (see fig. 18.2) make up the tools you use to reference other design files. To activate the Reference Files tool box, you choose **T**ools, **R**eference Files in the Application Window. You activate the Reference Files settings box by choosing **F**ile, **R**eference.

Figure 18.1

The Reference Files tool box.

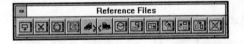

Figure 18.2

The Reference Files settings box.

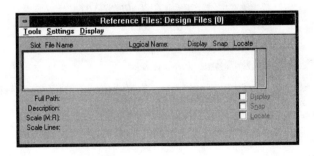

Benefits of Using Reference Files

There are several advantages to using reference files in MicroStation. Before we discuss how to use reference files, let's review some techniques and applications. Using reference files can save disk space and eliminate duplicate data. Attaching multiple reference files provides a way to improve communications between work groups by referencing each other work, and cropping reference files to show only the part you want.

Saving Disk Space

Reference files save disk space, freeing your system from having the same graphics in every design file. A good example of a reference file is a company's border file with its outline, title block, company logo, text, and notations. Suppose that all these border graphics add up to 400 KB. Having the same border graphics in all 10,000 company drawings would add up to 4 MB of disk space—4 MB of the same information.

Suppose you create a single design file with the border information in it and attach that file to every new design file. Now all 10,000 design files reference the one border file for their graphics. You would never use more than the initial 400 KB of disk space that the border file occupies.

Another advantage is when the border file needs to be modified—you only have to do it once.

Note

When you need to display the same information in several design files, use MicroStation's reference file capability to display the data.

Watching Someone Else Work

Reference files enable workgroups to share design files while the drawings are still under construction. Think about being given the task of laying out the HVAC (heating, ventilating, and air conditioning) in newly constructed office space. To create the HVAC design, you would begin by referencing the floorplan. If anyone makes changes to the floorplan, those changes immediately reflect in your HVAC design files. You don't have any unpleasant surprises at the end of the project, because you have been working on the correct copy of the floorplan.

Reference files reduce the need for communication in a workgroup by enabling people to view each other's work in progress. Because reference files are attached to the active design file, it is like having multiple design files open at the same time. You can change the active design file, but you cannot change the attached reference file information. Each time you refresh or reload the reference file information, you can see the changes taking place in your neighbor's design file. With the floorplan referenced to the HVAC layout, the fact that a door had been moved would be spotted easily.

Note

> Remember, MicroStation furnishes the capability to store the active design file and any attached reference files in main memory for faster display. You would do this by changing the Max. Element Cache setting (8,000 KB, by default). If you notice a good deal of disk activity when you refresh the display screen, you might need to raise the value. You can view and change this setting by choosing Workspace, Preferences, then selecting Memory Usage from the Category field.

Referencing Multiple Design Files

The need to see more than one CAD drawing at the same time can occur in several situations. The task at hand might be to build a mosaic of quarter-section maps, or perhaps the need arises to display several water maps to verify that the ends of the water pipes match. Maybe the need arises to display several details together or to build a quick assembly drawing by referencing several subassemblies. Not one of these feats is too difficult for reference files.

MicroStation enables you to attach up to 255 reference files to a single design file. After the reference files have been attached, MicroStation treats each reference file as a separate connection, which means you can display certain levels of information and hide others. You also can rotate, mirror, clip, and scale any reference file independently of the other reference file attachments.

Cropping Reference Files

Think of reference file "clipping" and "masking" as tools to use when creating details or sections. *Clipping* enables you to "clip out" pieces of a reference file. *Masking* enables you to hide those pieces of a reference file that you have no need to see.

You could, for example, clip the boundary of a floorplan reference file to display only one office. The Define Reference File Clipping Boundary command enables you to place a fence around the office and clip away the rest of the floorplan to hide it from view. In figure 18.3, the full office plan is attached to the active design file, and a second attachment illustrates the clip boundary. Enlarging Ray's office consists of referencing the floorplan again, scaling, and clipping out only Ray's office.

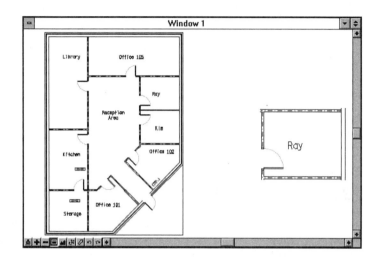

Figure 18.3

Clipping a reference file. (Office.dgn courtesy of Bentley.)

Reference File Clipping Mask handles the opposite circumstance. Suppose that you want to view the outside walls of the office plan but don't need to see the inside features. Reference File Clipping Mask enables you to define a border along the outside walls. Now the outside walls are visible, and the inside of the floorplan appears vacant. Figures 18.4 and 18.5 show a before and after picture of two desks cut out of the reference file.

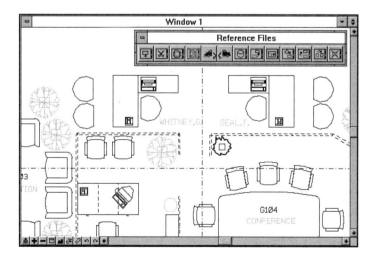

Figure 18.4

Before the Clip Mask.

Figure 18.5

*After the Clip
Mask.*

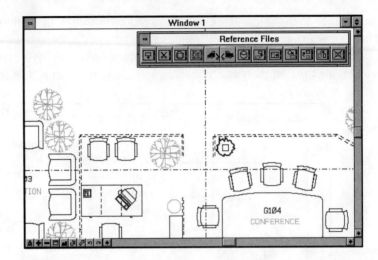

Referencing the Active Drawing to Itself

Inaccurate drawings make construction, modification, and updating costly, time-consuming, and nerve-racking. Referencing a drawing back to itself to show additional detail makes sense.

If you had a utility map showing the gas and electric lines running down Broadway in the city of New York, for example, the information on the connections in the manholes would be lost at a plotted scale of 1":100'. You might create a detail or blowout to clarify the connections and features. You do not have to draw the connections twice, though; draw the utilities in the street where appropriate and reference the design file to itself for the detail or blowout. After you make the reference, you can clip the boundary of the reference file, scale the reference file, and move the detail to show the field crews exactly what connections and equipment are contained in the street intersection. Each time the map needs changes, you change the information in the street intersection, and MicroStation automatically changes the detail or blowout. Remember, it's actually the same drawing, and the detail always reflects a scaled version of what's in the intersection.

Attaching a Border File

Probably the most redundant data in a design file is the border information. Accompanying the border outline are the title block graphics, the company logo, and maybe an address. Some borders also include a lengthy area for notes or revisions. The information in the note or revision area differs from file to file, but the lines that make up those shapes remain the same. So, the first use of reference files in your shop should be to create a set of border files: one file for A-size drawings, one for B-size, and so on.

You should place any elements unique to the design file, such as drawing number, date drawn, and so on, as elements in the active design file. To improve productivity, consider using cells with enter data fields to place the text of your title block.

The first thing you would do in a newly created design would be to attach the border design file as a reference file. You could attach the border design file to the appropriate seed file. When you create a design file that needs a B-size border, for example, use the BSEED.DGN file as the seed file to automatically have the B-size border attached as a reference.

> *Warning*
>
> If MicroStation displays the message `Incompatible dimensions`, you have attempted to reference a 3D design file to a 2D file. MicroStation doesn't enable you to attach a 3D design file to a 2D design file; however, you can reference 2D design files to 3D design files.

Making the Connection

Connecting a reference file to an active design file is simple. Choose **T**ools, **A**ttach in the Reference Files settings box to open the Attach Reference File dialog box (see fig. 18.6). If you prefer, you can pick the first icon in the Reference Files tool box to activate the Attach Reference File dialog box. This is a typical "file open" dialog box. Skim through the directories selection until you locate the file name you want, choose the file for the attachment and a third dialog box opens (see fig. 18.7). This dialog box lets you set a logical name, a description, and an attachment mode. The reference file's file name shows in the title bar of this dialog box.

MicroStation enables you to attach 255 reference files to a single active design file. After you attach them, you can treat each reference file separately. You can display certain levels of information while hiding others. You can rotate, mirror, clip, or scale any reference file independently.

Figure 18.6

Figure 18.6

*The Attach
Reference File
dialog box.*

Figure 18.7

*The Reference
Files attachment
dialog box.*

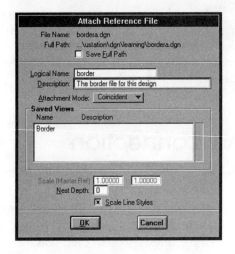

Using Common Names

You can refer to an attached reference file in one of three ways: by the file name,
by the logical name, or by picking an element in the reference file.

Referring to reference files by their file names could be a laborious process. The
reference file's directory path and file name might look like this:
f:\CITY\WATER\BORDERS\CBORDER.DGN. It could test your patience to enter this
path and file name. What if the file attached was a D-size border sheet for the
Hewlett-Packard pen plotter? The file name could be DBRDRHP.DGN, which might
not be easy to remember. Instead, give the border file a short and easier to
remember name when you attach it as a reference file; for example, BRD.

Using Helpful Descriptions

With a good memory and a little luck, you might be able to differentiate between reference files by file name. The logical name and description field, however, could be a better choice for remembering which file is which.

The description field is 42 characters long. The reference file description makes sense when sharing files with others in your office or with clients. You can never give people enough information about a file.

Always enter a description of some sort to further describe the file you attach or the purpose of attaching it.

Tip

Deciding on the Attachment Mode

The default attachment mode coincides on the same coordinates as the active design file. The two files you intend to overlay must have the same global origin; otherwise, they can't match up. Also, if the active design file has a window origin of 0,0 and the reference file was drawn near the coordinate of 1000,1000, you could attach the files, but you might not see all the data immediately. Use the Fit View and the All option from the tool settings box to fit the view to display both the active design and the reference files.

If two files don't match, you can use Reference Move to shift the position of the reference file to match the active design file. Reference Move is studied in detail later in this chapter under the section titled "Lining Up the Files."

MicroStation has a second attachment mode, called *saved view*, for attaching saved views of the target reference file. The section "Keeping Track of Details," later in this chapter, covers attaching saved views as reference files. For now, you can leave the attachment mode at the default attachment mode—Coincident.

Adjusting the Scale Factor

The last choice you have to make when attaching a reference file is whether to adjust its scale. You might want to show a 2X enlargement of a part's detail, or you might want to show a 1/2-scale view of a street intersection. A practical exercise on changing a reference file's scale is covered in detail later in this chapter. For now, leave the reference scale default at 9600:1.

Attaching the Drawing Border

To recap, you attach a reference file by choosing File, Reference, then choosing Tools, Attach from the Reference File settings box or clicking on the first icon in the Reference Files tool box.

In the following exercise, you create a design file named CHAP18.DGN. Next, you attach a border file called bordera.dgn from the /ustation/dgn/learning directory. The logical name is *border* in this exercise (refer to figure 18.7).

ATTACHING THE BORDER

Create a design file called CHAP18.DGN.

Choose Tools, Reference Files	Opens the Attach Reference File dialog box
Choose the Attach Reference tool (first button)	
Change the directory to .. \dgn\learning	
Choose the BORDERA.DGN file, then choose OK	Opens the Characteristics dialog box
*Type **border** in the Logical Name input box*	
Type a description, and then click on OK	Attaches file with the reference name border
Fit All files in View 1	Adjusts view to show entire border (see fig. 18.8)

After you attach the border file, you can look at how to change a reference file's display, how to snap to elements in the reference file, and how to copy data from the reference file into the active design file.

Choosing the Settings

The Display, Snap, and Locate toggle buttons shown in the Reference Files settings box indicate the default attachment and define how you can manipulate this reference file data (see fig. 18.9).

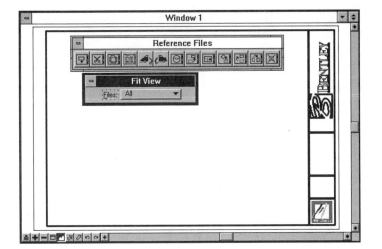

Figure 18.8

Reference file after Fit All is executed.

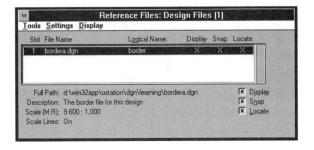

Figure 18.9

The Reference Files Settings dialog box.

You can leave a reference file attached to the active design file and not view it by turning off the Reference Display. Turning on Reference Snap enables you to snap to elements in the reference file. Turning on Reference Locate enables you to locate and copy information from the reference file into the active design file. You can change these three button settings separately for each reference file attached.

Reference Display

MicroStation plots what you see. Turning off Reference Display comes in handy if you don't want to plot the drawing border information; for example, when you check-plot. Just turn off the display of border reference file attached to the active design file. To illustrate Reference Display, leave the border file attached but turn off its display. MicroStation updates the views automatically. Notice how the reference file is hidden from view. The reference file still is attached to the active design file; it is just out of sight for now.

You can turn on and off the display of entire reference files or separate levels of the file. You turn off levels in a reference file in much the same way you turn off levels in the active design file. MicroStation has a Reference Levels settings box (see fig. 18.10) similar to the View Levels settings box for turning on and off drawing levels of a reference file. Invoke the Reference Levels settings box by choosing **S**ettings, **L**evels.

Figure 18.10

The Reference Levels settings box.

Why turn off some levels in a reference file? You might want to attach a map file and display only street right-of-ways and center lines. How you build your design files in regard to level layout dictates their flexibility when you attach them as reference files later in the process.

Note

When you have multiple reference files attached to your active design file, select the reference file so that it appears highlighted in the Reference File settings box before you manipulate the settings to tell MicroStation the file for which you want to change the attachment.

The next exercise attaches another design file of an office floorplan (see fig. 18.11) to the active design file and turns off the display of your work area (see fig. 18.12). The office perimeter is on levels 1–8, the furniture is on levels 15 and 16.

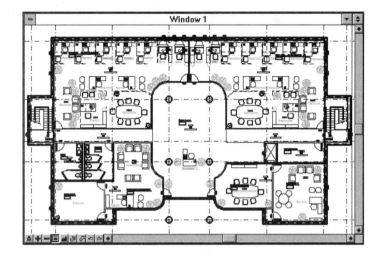

Figure 18.11

The complete view of the office floor-plan.

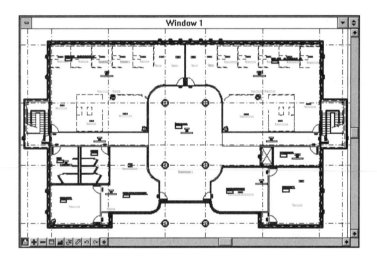

Figure 18.12

Turning off your office furniture.

TURNING OFF REFERENCE DISPLAY LEVELS

Continue from the preceding exercise with CHAP18.DGN still open and BORDERA.DGN still attached as a border file.

*Choose **T**ools, **A**ttach*   Opens the Attach Reference File dialog box

Select OFFICE.DGN, *then choose **O**K*

*Type **FLOOR** in the **L**ogical Name field*

Continues

Type **Office Floor Plan** *in the* **D**escription *field and click on* **O**K	Attaches file with the reference name FLOOR (refer to figure 18.11)
Fit All files in View 1	Shows the floor plan in the lower half of the view
Window Area around the floor plan	Brings the floor plan closer in the view
Choose **S**ettings, **L**evels	Opens the Reference Levels settings box
Click on 15 *and* 16, *then choose* **A**pply	Turns off the furniture on levels 15 and 16
Click on level 30, *then choose* **A**pply	Hides the office plants on level 30
Close the Reference Levels settings box	

Reference Snap

Use Reference Snap to snap to elements in the reference file. With Reference Snap turned on, you snap to the existing elements in the reference file and add elements accurately. You cannot modify the lines that make up the office perimeter.

You can turn on Reference Snap in one file, or you can turn it on in all reference files attached. Toggle on and off the Reference Snap from the Reference File Settings dialog box.

Note   The preference file automatically turns on the display, snap, and locate locks when you attach a reference file. To change these default settings choose Workspace, Preferences from the Application Window to open the Preferences dialog box, then select Reference File from the Category list box (see fig. 18.13).

Reference Locate

Using Reference Locate enables you to get information, copy, use the dimension element command, and measure along elements in a reference file.

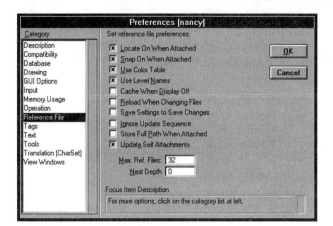

Figure 18.13

*Changing your
default Reference
File preferences.*

If you leave Reference Locate on and do a Fence Copy operation, MicroStation copies all the reference file data within the fence's border into the active design file. Turn on Reference Locate only if you want to copy something from the reference file into the active design file. After MicroStation finishes copying, turn off Reference Locate.

Warning

Other Ways to Manipulate Reference Files

All the other manipulation commands (scale, rotate, and mirror) are similar to the element manipulation, with one exception: You must always tell MicroStation what reference file you want to manipulate. The following list discusses reference file manipulation options:

♦ **Scaling.** You also can scale a reference file after you make the attachment. Alternatively, if you know you will have to scale the reference file, you can scale during the attach process. Each reference file can be scaled independently. Remember that scaling does not affect the contents of the reference file itself, only the display of the reference data.

♦ **Rotating.** Rotating a reference file works in much the same way as Rotate Fence works. To rotate the reference file, you define an angle and a pivot point. You might want to rotate a blowup of a street intersection or a part detail for space considerations or for determining available room on a drawing sheet.

♦ **Mirroring.** MicroStation provides a horizontal and a vertical tool to mirror reference file data. Mirroring reference file information works in the same way element mirroring does. You choose the Mirror tool, identify the reference file for mirroring, and then enter an input point to define the horizontal or vertical axis.

Breaking the Reference Connection

MicroStation provides two ways to detach the reference file. You can detach a reference file by using the Detach Reference File command on the Reference Files tool box or by choosing **T**ools, **D**etach in the Reference Files settings box.

If you use the Detach Reference File command from the tool box, you must identify the reference file to detach. If you use the **T**ools, **D**etach menu option in the References Files settings box, you must first highlight the file you want to detach.

Note Remember, if you do not want to use the reference file anymore, detach it. If you think you will want the reference file again later, consider turning off Reference Display instead of detaching it.

Using the Tool Box to Detach a Reference File

This exercise steps you through detaching a reference file using the Detach Reference File tool on the Reference Files tool box (see fig. 18.14). You select the tool and then identify the file.

Figure 18.14

Detach Reference File tool activated.

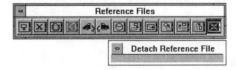

After you choose the Detach Reference File tool, MicroStation prompts you to identify the reference file you want to disconnect from the active design file. You can identify the reference file in question in three ways: enter the reference file's file name or its logical name in the key-in field, or use the pointer to identify an element in the reference file. After you identify the reference file, MicroStation detaches it from the active design file.

USING THE TOOL BOX TO DETACH A REFERENCE FILE

Choose **T**ools, **R**eference Files   Opens the Reference Files tool box

Choose Detach Reference File
(refer to figure 18.14)

`Identify (or key in) Ref File`   Prompts you for a decision
Pick a point on any element of the
reference file

`Accept/Reject (select next input)` *Pick*
another point in the View to accept
element selection

`>Reference file detached`   Confirms success

You're not done using this reference file, so reattach it using the Reference File tool box. *Note:*
Undo does not work using this detach command.

Using the Settings Box to Detach a Reference File

Detaching a reference file using the Reference Files settings box differs slightly from
picking the tool from the Reference Files tool box.

After you open the Reference Files settings box, you highlight the file you want to
disconnect, then choose **T**ools, **D**etach. At this point, an alert box opens, asking you
to confirm the detach action. Click on **O**K to complete the detachment (see fig.
18.15).

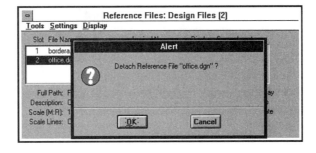

Figure 18.15

An alert box
asking for
confirmation.

Lining Up the Files

Sometimes you need to move reference files. You can use the Move Reference File command to align reference files to the active design file. The Move Reference File command acts much like the Move Element command, the difference being that you move only the display of the information on your screen. You don't move the information in the reference file; you choose the Move Reference File tool, identify the reference file to move, and pick a new location.

Try the following exercise to move the office floorplan reference file into the border.

Moving a Reference File

Continue from the preceding exercise with CHAP18.DGN open and the border and office floorplan file still referenced.

Fit All Files in View 1   Displays both reference files (see fig. 18.16)

Figure 18.16

Locations of your reference file before the move.

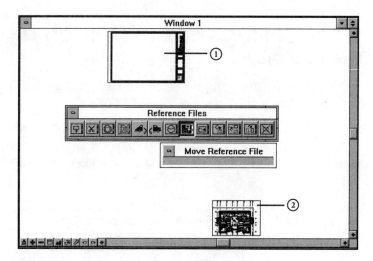

Choose Move Reference File tool from the Reference Files tool box

`Identify (or key in) Ref File` *Pick an*   Highlights the element
element of the border file

`Accept/Reject (select next input)` *Pick*
a point in the view to accept reference
file selection

`Enter point to move from`
Pick a point at ① (see fig. 18.16)

`Enter point to move to`
Pick a point at ② (see fig. 18.16)

Fit All Files in View 1
(see fig. 18.17)

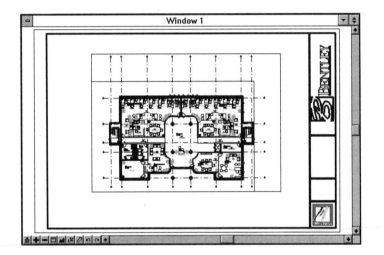

Figure 18.17

A moved reference file.

Keeping the Reference File Information Fresh

You do not have to restart the design session to freshen the reference file display. You can use the Reload Reference File tool (see fig. 18.18).

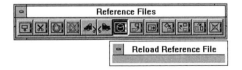

Figure 18.18

The Reload Reference File tool activated.

Reload Reference File freshens or reloads the reference file attached to the active design file. MicroStation sets some of the computer's memory aside to cache or store the active design file and its attached reference files. Storing these images in memory rather than on the hard disk speeds up the display screen functions. If a second user changes the reference file, however, the copy cached in the computer's memory becomes outdated. Reloading the reference file information ensures that the cached copy is as up-to-date as possible. Reload Reference File prompts you to enter the name of the reference file or to identify some element in the drawing.

Note   The reference file information also reloads in the computer's memory when you end and restart a drawing session.

Keeping Track of Details

Details of a floorplan usually are drawn in separate files or are redrawn as redundant graphics on the same drawing sheet. These redundant graphics could cause problems—someone might change one part of the floorplan but forget to change the corresponding detail. Using MicroStation's reference file feature, you could represent both the main floorplan and its individual details with the same graphics. This method has the following advantages: you have fewer files to manage and fewer graphics to draw, and you never have to remember to update the detail.

How do you accomplish this feat? You can reference the active drawing to itself. You know how to attach, move, and scale a reference file. You can set the clipping boundary by placing a regular fence. The following list reviews the necessary steps:

1. Attach an active design file to itself. Set the scale to 1:0.5. Remember, the graphics in both files overlay each other exactly if the scale is 1:1 and then you cannot tell the files apart.

2. Next, use the Move Reference File command to shift the reference file to a new location on the drawing sheet.

3. Place a fence around the area you want to display.

4. Last, choose Define Reference File Clipping Boundary, to hide the area outside the clipping boundary.

All right, Ray is out of his office. Now is the perfect time to move in. If you use the Edit Text tool to change Ray's name to your name on the main floorplan, the detail identifying Ray's office changes as well, because there really is only one text string element. Now anytime changes are made to the main floorplan, Ray's detail instantly reflects the change. That could be Ray coming down the hall. You need to put Ray's name back on the floorplan.

How MicroStation Finds the Reference Files

A common problem when you use reference files is that when you re-enter the design file, the reference file doesn't appear. If you look at the Reference File settings box, the attachment appears in the list but the path to the file has been lost.

It helps to know how MicroStation finds or looks for the attached reference files. MicroStation looks for reference files in the following places in the following order.

1. **Configuration variable (used when the file was attached).** Create a configuration variable for your commonly used reference files. For example, a configuration variable called borders would be set to define the path f:\borders. The border reference files would then be attached by choosing **D**irectory, **S**elect Configuration Variable in the Attach Reference dialog box. The configuration variable then becomes a permanent record with the reference file name.

2. **Directory of the active design file.** If the reference file is located in the same directory as the active design file the reference file will be displayed. This does not, however, give you license to copy the borders into each subdirectory that contains design files.

3. **Directories defined in the MS_RFDIR variable.** Define MicroStation's MS_RFDIR variable to point to the directory that contains the reference files. Choose Wor**k**space, **C**onfiguration to set the reference file path. You can assign multiple directories to a single MS variable by putting ";" between directory names. MicroStation looks in the order in which the paths are defined.

The first reference file it finds is the one displayed (in the above order), so you might not get the file you think you attached.

Warning

4. The last, and probably the least flexible, is to store the full path name with the reference file attachment. You can choose this option in the Save Full

Path button on the Attach Reference File dialog box when you attach the reference file. What happens if the file is moved or the system administrator changes the location of the commonly used files? The path name breaks. This time, you'll need to reattach all reference files. Using the full path name option when you attach a reference file means MicroStation won't look anywhere but in the store path or directory.

Although reference file paths take some thought to implement, they do pay off in the long run, so determine an approach to finding reference files early in your design process.

Refer to the appropriate system documentation on each computer to assign names to directory paths.

Summary

The reference file capability probably is one of MicroStation's most important features. Use MicroStation's reference file feature when you need to do one of the following:

♦ Save disk space

♦ Speed up sharing drawings within or outside a workgroup

♦ Create custom drawings by displaying different levels of multiple reference files or by cropping and masking

♦ Keep track of details

CHAPTER

19

Changing the Way MicroStation Looks

*T*his chapter discusses how to change the way MicroStation looks by modifying the tools, windows, tool boxes, dialog boxes, and other MicroStation features. The concept is similar to that of organizing your desk. The purpose of changing MicroStation's looks is not merely to add variety, however, but to create an environment that best meets your individual needs and preferences.

The chapter begins by examining the workspace environment. The key to customizing MicroStation is the workspace. The two components of the workspace this chapter discusses at length are user preferences and the user interface.

The first half of the chapter examines the user preference file and some of what that resource contains. The user preferences that modify tool sizes and dialog box text sizes might be an easy place to start changing the way MicroStation looks. Other user preferences include those that modify where the tools are located, how they are organized, what they look like, and how they act (for example, setting the defaults for reference file attachments).

The second half of the chapter examines the user interface and how you can further change MicroStation's look.

In this chapter, you learn about the following:

♦ Modifying user preferences to change the size and functionality of the tools, windows, and commands

♦ Creating a personal user interface

♦ Creating a custom tool box

♦ Changing the pull-down menus

♦ Changing the view borders

Warning

You shouldn't modify an existing workspace that other people might be using. Chapter 17 included instructions for creating your own personal workspace and modifying your personal components.

To prevent accidentally modifying originally delivered workspaces, you should follow the exercises and information in the order in which they occur.

Examining the Workspace Components

The *MicroStation environment* is the workspace you have chosen in the MicroStation Manager dialog box. Chapter 17, "Boosting Your Performance," provides an in-depth discussion of the configuration variables or the User Configuration and Project components of the workspace. This chapter concentrates on the second and third components of the workspace—user preferences and the user interface.

To understand what you affect when you modify MicroStation's appearance, you should review the current workspace components before you go any further. Choosing **A**bout Workspace from the Wor**k**space pull-down menu opens a window that shows the components of the current workspace (see fig. 19.1).

The user interface and the preference file are the components of the workspace that modify the way MicroStation looks. Before you modify the existing workspace, you need to ask yourself if anyone else uses the workspace; if so, you should create a new workspace to modify. Most of the topics this chapter covers are individual preferences and should not be imposed on others.

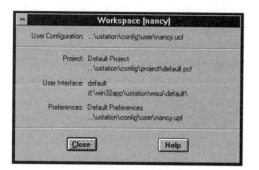

Figure 19.1

The Information window after choosing About Workspace.

Creating a new workspace creates a user preference file, which has a filename that consists of the workspace name and an extension of UPF. This file is located in the \ustation\config\user directory by default.

Setting User Preferences

The first half of this chapter discusses how you can change the way MicroStation looks by modifying user preferences. Before you begin modifying the preference settings, create a design file called CHAP19.DGN and enter MicroStation with the workspace you created in Chapter 17.

To open the Preferences dialog box, you choose Wor**k**space, **P**references. The Preferences dialog box appears with your workspace name in brackets in the title bar (see fig. 19.2).

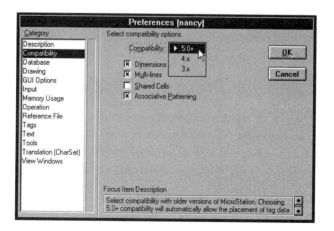

Figure 19.2

Compatibility preferences.

Note
You can activate the appropriate workspace when starting MicroStation by adding -wuworkspace to the command line. Microsoft Windows users can copy and modify the MicroStation icon and include the -wu<*yourname*> switch.

If your name doesn't appear in brackets in the title bar, you didn't successfully execute your workspace. If you continue, you will affect a workspace other than your personal workspace. You should exit the design file and try again.

You can verify that the workspace was created by getting a directory of the files in \ustation\config\user. If you don't see a UCF and PCF file with your name, you know you didn't actually create a personal workspace. You should repeat the exercise in Chapter 17 on creating a workspace.

The **C**ategory list box displays the types of settings that you can modify and save in the Preferences dialog box. The next sections describe in detail some of these preference settings. As you read through the sections, try the preferences that interest you. Specific exercises aren't provided, but the workspace you created contains your personal preference file, so feel free to experiment—you won't affect other users.

After experimenting, you can choose **O**K to save any changes you made in the Preferences dialog box or Cancel to exit the dialog box without saving any changes. Or, if you want to return to the default settings, choose the **D**efaults button.

Note   Some of the preference settings take effect only after you exit and reenter MicroStation. These preferences are noted where appropriate.

Compatibility Preferences

Compatibility is one of the first preference categories in the **C**ategory list box. When you choose the Compatibility item, its settings options appear to the right (see fig. 19.2). These settings determine which MicroStation features are available in this workspace. Choosing the Co**m**patibility pop-up list enables you to select settings for version 5.0, 4.0, or 3.0.

If you choose 4.0 compatibility, the Associative **P**atterning option is dimmed because associative patterning was new in MicroStation 5.0. If you want to create a version 4.0 compatible file, you can't place any associative patterning. Likewise, if you choose 3.0 compatibility, all the option buttons are dimmed because

MicroStation 3.0 lacked dimensions, multilines, shared cells, and associative patterning.

This setting guarantees that your design file won't contain elements the older versions cannot read. You still can use the tools MicroStation 5.0 has to offer; the Compatibility setting affects only the placement of the elements in the design file. The Dimensions button, for example, indicates whether the Dimension tools place dimension elements or line and text elements graphically grouped.

Turning options on and off doesn't affect elements you have previously placed in the design file; however, you should set the compatibility version and options before you place any advanced element types.

Warning

Drawing Preferences

The Drawing preference category provides options for changing the way MicroStation displays some of the drawing features and settings. Chapter 7 told you that the grid display (dots and crosses) disappears from the view when a maximum number is in the view. You can customize these numbers in the Drawing preferences (see Max. **G**rid Pts/View and Max. Grid **R**efs/View in figure 19.3).

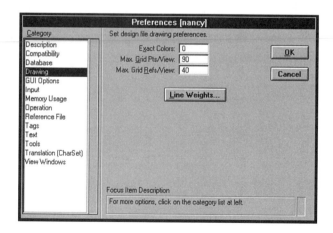

Figure 19.3

Drawing preferences.

The **L**ine Weights button in the Preferences dialog box is of particular interest. Click on it to open a Line Weight Translation dialog box (see fig. 19.4), which lets you specify the relationship of the display line weights to the design line weights. Valid display sizes fall between 0 and 63.

Figure 19.4

*The Line Weight
Translation dialog
box.*

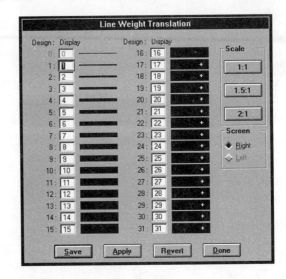

GUI Options Preferences

The GUI Options preference category (see fig. 19.5) enables you to change the size of the text in dialog boxes and the border. The choices for font sizes are 10, 12, 14, 18, and 24 points for both dialog and menu text. After you make a change to the Dialog **F**ont settings, you must exit and reenter MicroStation before you can see the effect of the change.

Figure 19.5

*The GUI Options
preference
category.*

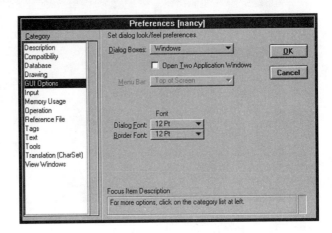

You also can change the tool sizes that appear in the tool frames and tool boxes. The section entitled "Tool Palette Preferences" covers this topic.

Note

Operation Preferences

The Operation preference category (see fig. 19.6) includes a miscellaneous group of settings that affect the display and default actions of the screen cursor and design session functions.

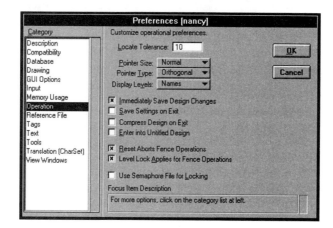

Figure 19.6

Operation preferences.

The **L**ocate Tolerance setting determines the distance that MicroStation searches for an element from the point you enter during element manipulation commands. You probably have noticed that you do not have to pick directly on the element to select it—this is a function of the **L**ocate Tolerance setting. When you change the number in this field, the circle that appears on the arrow selection tool is larger (as is the circle on the modify cursor), indicating a larger area for locating elements. The default **L**ocate Tolerance setting is 10, but the value can range from 1 to 100. The value is unitless.

The **P**ointer Size and Pointer **T**ype settings enable you to customize the screen cursor. The **P**ointer Size options are **N**ormal or **F**ull View. The **N**ormal setting is the setting you have used throughout the exercises; the **F**ull View setting provides a crosshair screen cursor composed of two lines that span the full view. The Pointer **T**ype options are **O**rthogonal or **I**sometric. The **O**rthogonal setting displays the cursor lines horizontally and vertically, and the **I**sometric setting displays the cursor lines with an isometric alignment.

The Display Levels setting determines whether MicroStation displays level names (**N**ames) or level numbers (N**u**mbers) in the Status Bar. **N**ames is the default setting.

The toggle buttons in the Operation preference category are defined as follows:

♦ **Immediately Save Design Changes.** Turn this toggle off and MicroStation reacts much like other applications—you must save your changes when you exit the session or lose all. The default is on..

♦ **Save Settings on Exit.** Turn this toggle on and MicroStation automatically saves the settings when a design session is closed.

♦ **Compress Design on Exit.** Turn this toggle on and MicroStation automatically compresses the design (permanently removing all deleted elements) when you close a design file.

♦ **Enter into Untitled Design.** Turn this toggle on and MicroStation enters into an untitled design file and does not display any MicroStation Manager dialog box.

♦ **Reset Aborts Fence Operations.** Use this toggle to determine whether clicking on the Reset button during a fence command stops the process. For example, if you click the Reset button during a Delete Fence Contents command, the operation aborts and only a portion of the elements are deleted.

♦ **Level Lock Applies for Fence Operations.** This toggle, when on, directs MicroStation to process only the active level within the fence.

Reference File Preferences

The Reference File preference category (see fig. 19.7) enables you to customize how reference files are attached and how they behave in your design file.

The first two buttons are **L**ocate On When Attached and **S**nap On When Attached. If you turn them on, the Snap and Locate locks are turned on automatically when you reference a design file. For more information on the locate and snap features, refer to Chapter 18.

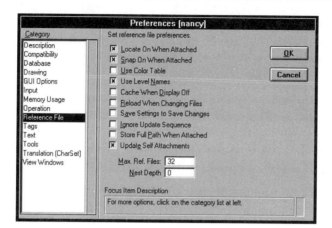

Figure 19.7

Reference File preferences.

The **U**se Color Table button determines whether the elements of a reference file appear in the colors defined by its color table or in the colors defined by the active design file's color table. If this button is turned on, MicroStation displays the reference file elements in the colors of the reference file's color table. Consider this example: If the **U**se Color Table button is turned off and color number 1 in the active design file color table is black, the elements of the reference file that are defined as color number 1 display in black. If the **U**se Color Table button is turned on, the elements display in the color assigned to color number 1 in the reference file's attached color table.

The Use Level **N**ames toggle enables you to determine whether you see the level name when you identify an element of the reference file for manipulation in the Status Bar.

The next two buttons (Cache When **D**isplay Off and **R**eload When Changing Files) let you determine what reference file data are stored in memory. Both setting options attempt to save the reference file data in memory when the reference file display is turned off and when you change design files. You can turn on these buttons to save time when reloading reference files. The limitation and productivity results are determined by the amount of available physical memory in your computer.

If the S**a**ve Settings to Save Changes button is on, MicroStation does not immediately save changes you make to the attached reference file (such as levels, attachment settings, and the reference file manipulation functions) to the design file. You must save the changes yourself by choosing **F**ile, Sa**v**e Settings. The default for the S**a**ve Settings to Save Changes setting is off.

The next noteworthy toggle is the Store Full **P**ath When Attached button. Turn this button on and the button Save Full Path in the Attach Reference dialog box appears on by default. See Chapter 18 for more information about saving the full path name with a reference file attachment.

The **M**ax. Ref. Files setting is defined with a number between 16 and 255 (default is 32). You should change this setting only when necessary, because approximately .5 KB of memory is reserved for each reference file when you execute MicroStation. Therefore, setting this variable higher than necessary needlessly reserves available memory.

The **N**est Depth setting allows you to attach a reference file to your active design and also attach the reference files. For example, if you set this field to 1, attaching a plan that has a border reference file attached automatically displays the plan and its border reference file.

Note Making a change to the Reference File settings requires that you exit and reenter MicroStation for the changes to take effect.

Text Preferences

The Text preference category (see fig. 19.8) offers a wide range of settings and defaults for text. The settings in this category affect the way text appears, how the text commands function, and the default settings or text attributes.

Figure 19.8

Text preferences.

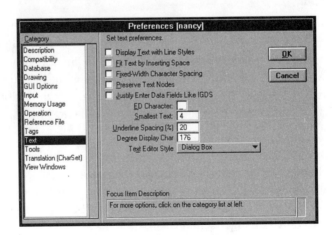

♦ **Display Text with Line Styles.** If the Display Text with Line Styles setting is turned on, MicroStation displays text in the assigned line style. If this setting is turned off, all text is displayed in a solid line style.

♦ **Fit Text by Inserting Space.** If the Fit Text by Inserting Space setting is turned on, the Place Fitted Text command places the text without changing the text size by inserting spaces between characters to fit the text between two points.

♦ **Fixed-Width Character Spacing.** If the Fixed-Width Character Spacing setting is turned on, MicroStation places each character a fixed (equal) distance apart. Fixed-width character spacing has little effect on fonts designed with equal-size character spacing (for example, the standard font). On the other hand, fixed-width character spacing has a profound effect on fonts designed with proportional spacing (for example, the working font).

♦ **Preserve Text Nodes.** If the Preserve Text Nodes setting is turned on, the text node element type is not modified to a text string when a text node is reduced to one line of text.

♦ **Justify Enter Data Fields Like IGDS.** If the Justify Enter Data Fields Like IGDS setting is turned on, an enter data field that is center-justified places the odd number of blank spaces at the end; for example, _1234567__. If this setting is turned off, MicroStation places the odd number of blank spaces at the beginning; for example, __1234567_.

♦ **ED Character.** In the ED Character field, you enter the character you want to designate as the enter data field character. The default is the underscore (_) character. You might choose this setting option if you want to use the enter data field commands and you also need to display an underscore in the text. As an example, change the ED Character to *, and place a piece of text: **Filename * is 12345_A.dgn**. Incidentally, turning off the Data Fields display in the View Attributes settings box does not turn off the underscore used in the filename.

♦ **Smallest Text.** In the Smallest Text field, you enter the value (in screen pixels) that MicroStation uses as the smallest readable text. When you zoom out in the view and the text size drops below this value, MicroStation then displays the text as a rectangle with an X through it. The rectangle represents the beginning and end point of the text string. You can enter values between 0 and 100 in this field. If you enter a 0, MicroStation displays the individual characters no matter how small they appear in the view.

Note   Making MicroStation display individual characters for text that is too small for you to read is pointless and slows down display update processing.

♦ **Underline Spacing (%).** The value in the **U**nderline Spacing (%) field defines the space between the text and the underline when using the Underline option in the Text settings box. You enter a percentage (between 0 and 100) of the text height for the distance.

Tools Palette Preferences

The Tools palette preference category (see fig. 19.9) offers a variety of ways to change the look and feel of the tool boxes.

Figure 19.9

Tools palette preferences.

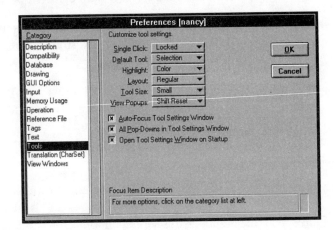

♦ **Single Click.** The **S**ingle Click setting has two options: **L**ocked or **S**ingle-shot. **L**ocked is the default setting and the one you have been using throughout the exercises in this book. With the **L**ocked setting, the tool you choose remains active until you choose another tool. With the **S**ingle-shot setting, the default tool is activated after you use the selected tool once (see D**e**fault Tool).

♦ **Default Tool.** The D**e**fault Tool setting has two options: **N**one or **S**election. The default tool is activated when you enter MicroStation or when you perform a one-time function, such as the **S**ingle-shot option selected from the **S**ingle Click field. The **S**election setting automatically chooses the Selection Tool after a single operation. The **N**one setting issues a null command, and no tool is activated.

- **Highlight.** The Highlight setting has three options: **B**lack, **G**ray or **C**olor. These settings determine the highlight color of the active tool.

- **Layout.** The **L**ayout setting has three options: **N**arrow, **R**egular, or **W**ide. This setting affects the 3D look of the tools on the tool boxes. You can choose **N**arrow to save space on your screen. Only the tool boxes opened after making changes to the **L**ayout setting are affected.

- **Tool Size.** The **T**ool Size setting has two options: **S**mall or **L**arge. This setting affects the size of the tools on the tool boxes. The **S**mall setting saves space on your screen and is the default. Only new tool boxes opened after changing the **T**ool Size setting are affected.

- **View Popups.** The **V**iew Popups setting has two options: **N**one and **S**hift Reset. You can hold the **S**hift Button down on your keyboard and click the reset to activate a pop-up menu for view controls (see fig. 19.10). If you change the **V**iew Popups setting to **N**one, you disable the pop-up menus.

Figure 19.10

The View pop-up menu.

Holding the Shift key down on your keyboard and choosing a tentative button activates a pop-up menu for tentative modes (see fig. 19.11).

Tip

Figure 19.11

The tentative mode pop-up menu.

The Tools palette preference category includes the following buttons:

- **Auto-Focus Tool Settings Window.** If this button is turned on, the Tool Settings window (if displayed) is automatically activated each time you choose a tool from a tool box that has constraints or settings.

♦ **All Pop-Downs in Tool Settings Window.** If this button is turned on, the Tool Settings window displays the constraints and settings for the command, regardless of the presence of the tool box. The default for this option is off; in other words, the constraints and settings display in the Tool Settings window only if the tool box is not displayed.

♦ **Open Tool Settings Window on Startup.** If this button is turned on, the Tool Settings window is activated each time you enter MicroStation with this workspace or preference file.

Configuring the User Interface

The second half of this chapter discusses how you can change the way MicroStation looks by modifying the user interface.

Remember that you created your personal workspace without defining a personal user interface. You don't want to modify a user interface that others might be using. Therefore, before going any further, you need to create a personal user interface.

Creating Your Personal User Interface

You create your own personal user interface at the MicroStation Manager box by choosing **I**nterface, **N**ew to open the Create User Interface dialog box (see fig. 19.12), which prompts you to enter a name and description.

Figure 19.12

The Create User Interface dialog box.

> Do not modify the default workspace! If you destroy the default workspace, you must reload MicroStation to retrieve another copy.

Warning

In the following exercise, you create your personal user interface.

CREATING A PERSONAL USER INTERFACE

Continue from the preceding exercise with the CHAP19.DGN design file open.

Choose **F**ile, **C**lose	Closes the CHAP19.DGN file and opens the MicroStation Manager dialog box
Choose I**n**terface, **N**ew	Opens the Create User Interface dialog box (refer to figure 19.12)
Enter your name in the **N**ame *field*	
Enter **Book Exercise** *in the* **D**escription *field*	
Choose **O**K	Closes the dialog box and activates your new interface
Open the CHAP19.DGN *design file*	Enters MicroStation

Now you're ready to modify your user interface. Choose Wor**k**space, Customi**z**e in the Application window to open the Customize settings box (see fig. 19.13). With your personal workspace and your personal user interface, you can feel free to modify the Application window menu or the tool boxes without affecting the original default interface or other users. If your user interface functions well, you can always share it with the other users.

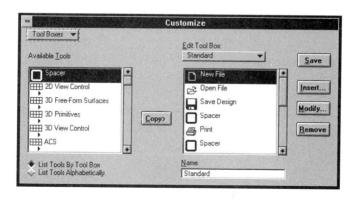

Figure 19.13

The Customize settings box.

Entire books have been written on the subject of the user interface. This chapter provides only an introduction to the configuration tools and a glimpse at some of the possibilities.

Changing the Tool Boxes

To access existing tool boxes, you choose the **E**dit Tool Box pop-up menu. The contents of the tool box are shown below with icon representation and command names. The Customize settings box opens with the Standard tool box selected and the New File, Open File, Save Design, and so on, displayed (refer to figure 19.13). You can add tools, delete tools, rearrange tools, or modify the icons of the tools on a new or existing tool box.

As well as modifying existing tool boxes, you also can create your own tool boxes. To create a custom tool box, choose **E**dit Tool Box, **C**reate Tool Box to open the Create Tool Box dialog box, in which MicroStation prompts you to enter a name.

You can create custom tool boxes with your favorite and most frequently used tools by using the Available **T**ools list box to the left. You can choose any command from the existing tool boxes by double-clicking on the tool box listed in the Available **T**ools to display the tools of that box. Then double-click on the tool you want in your personal tool box or click once and choose the **C**opy button. In the following exercise, you create a new tool box and populate your personal tool box with several commands.

CREATING A CUSTOM TOOL BOX

Continue from the preceding exercise with the CHAP19.DGN design file.

Choose Wor**k**space, **C**ustomize	Opens a Customize settings box
Click and hold on the **E**dit Tool Box *pop-up menu*	Opens pop-up menu
Choose **C**reate Tool Box *item*	Opens the Create Tool Box dialog box
Enter a name for the tool box	
Choose **O**K	Closes the Create Tool Box dialog box
Double-click on 2D View Control *in the* Available **T**ools *list box*	Displays icons and tool names for all cell tools contained in the Cells tool box
Double-click on Update View *in the* Available **T**ools *list box*	Copies icons and tool names your personal tool box (see fig. 19.14)

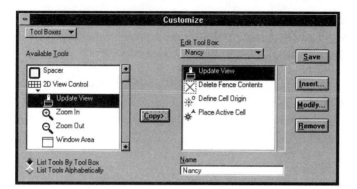

Figure 19.14

Your custom tool box.

Continue selecting your most popular tools.

In addition to creating custom tool boxes, you can create your own tools by defining the key-in that should be entered when the tool is chosen. You also can create your own icon for the new tool by choosing the **I**nsert button, which opens the Insert Tool dialog box (see fig. 19.15). A quick review of the Update View tool should illustrate the function and features of the dialog box.

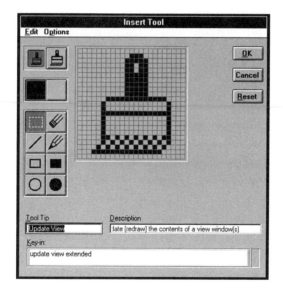

Figure 19.15

The Insert Tool dialog box showing the Update View tool.

You can change or view any icon in your palette by double-clicking on it in the list box, which brings up the Insert Tool dialog box with the tool and its settings.

Note

The icon area is represented by the grid. The top two boxes on the left show the icon as a small and a large representation. You can draw each icon individually, or you can draw them simultaneously by choosing Options, Draw **B**oth Icons.

Warning

You must have both small and large icons when you create new tool boxes. If you display small icons (a preference setting) and no small icon was drawn, the tool appears blank.

The second two boxes show the color as being on or off. The active color is displayed with a depressed button. Icons are drawn with a series of pixels, and each pixel is either on or off. To fill in a pixel, you choose the colored button and pick a square in the grid area; the pixel is turned on. To erase a pixel, you choose the off button and pick a square in the grid area; the pixel then is turned off.

The drawing tools provide four ways to manipulate the pixels of the icon.

♦ The selection tool enables you to select groups of pixels and move them to another location by dragging the marquee.

♦ The Eraser tool erases pixels.

♦ The Line tool draws a line by pressing and dragging the pointer (with active color).

♦ The Pencil tool enables you to pick individual pixels, turned on or off depending on the current active color selection.

You can even create colored icons by choosing Options, Icon **C**olor to select the color. An icon can have only one color, however.

Tip

After you add the tools to your custom tool box, you can rearrange them by clicking and dragging the items in the list.

To save the tool box changes, choose the **S**ave button. Your new tool box appears on-screen as soon as you save it. You can test it and do any redesigning before you exit the Customize settings box.

Changing the Pull-Down Menus

By choosing Menu Bar from the pop-up menu in the upper left corner of the Customize settings box, you can change the Application Window pull-down menus by adding, deleting, or modifying the items. You might modify the items on the Application Window pull-down menus by adding a hot key or an accelerator key or by rearranging or renaming the items.

You can perform the following tasks from the Modify Menus settings box:

♦ Modify the menu bar name that appears on the pull-down menu

♦ Modify the item name that appears in the pull-down menu

♦ Modify or add accelerator keys to items on a menu

♦ Delete a whole pull-down menu or an item from a pull-down menu

♦ Rearrange the pull-down menus or the items on the pull-down menus

♦ Create your own menu bar pull-down menus and items

Deleting and Moving Menu Items

You might not use all Application Window menu items in your application. You can delete any unneeded menu items from the pull-down menu. You could, for example, remove the 3D items to streamline your workspace for 2D. You also can rearrange the items in the Application Window menu to group commonly used items together.

The dash in the list box indicates the lines dividing the pull-down menu into sections. You can delete the dividing lines, cut and move them with **P**aste, or use **C**opy from the **A**vailable Menu list box to add additional dashed lines to divide the menu.

Tip

Adding Menus and Menu Items

Another way to modify the user interface is to add pull-down menus and menu items to the Application Window pull-down menu. Chapter 17, "Boosting Your Performance" includes a discussion of function keys and scripts. You can add the same key-ins to a menu-bar item. You could create a new pull-down menu in the Application Window called Myproject, for example, and add a menu item for executing a macro with the key-in macro strsym.

Changing the View Borders

The third and last customization tool option is to change the view border, by choosing View Border from the pop-up menu in the upper left corner of the **C**ustomize settings box. Several additional commands that you can add to the existing view border appear in the Available Tools list box.

Summary

You have seen many different ways to customize the way MicroStation looks and functions in this chapter. All modifications require that you create a personal workspace. The workspace concept gives you personal freedom to modify the interface and preferences without affecting the default files or any of your colleagues' files.

The user preferences are a good place to start customizing MicroStation. The choices offer an easy way to start your customization of MicroStation.

You must become comfortable with the menus and tool boxes in MicroStation before you start modifying the interface. As a beginner to MicroStation, you probably should work with the defaults first and discover what you like and do not like before you jump in and modify the menus and tool boxes.

Creating Drawing Standards

*W*hat this whole book has been leading up to is that first production job. You have practiced with the tools, you have read through the concepts, and you have received many suggestions, tips, and hints. Now you are ready to start production. Stop—before you dive into your first production drawing, you need to fill the pool.

What are your drawing standards? Is everyone working on the project going by the same rules? What should the final product look like? And what are the best ways to achieve those results? It is critical to a successful MicroStation project to spend the time up front with these issues before creating the first file.

In this chapter, you will learn:

♦ Approaching drawing standards

♦ Using standards for design and directory names

♦ Sharing files within your organization

♦ Establishing working units

♦ Defining design-file features

♦ Standardizing cells, shared cells, and symbols

♦ Applying custom linestyles

♦ Using reference files

♦ Archiving and backups

Approaching Drawing Standards

You might be tempted to just jump in to your first design file and get your feet wet. Drawing standards, however, can make your transition from the manual drawing method to the automated CAD method easier and more productive by considering the following topics:

♦ **File-naming conventions.** Standards for naming the design files and directories.

♦ **Sharing files.** Specifications for sharing the design file and resource files.

♦ **Working units.** Precision requirements for placing and measuring your design.

♦ **Element or feature symbology.** Means for assigning each element or type of feature in the design file a level, weight, line style, and color.

♦ **Cells and symbols.** Choice of cells, shared cells, or font symbols.

♦ **Resources.** Resource files (such as linestyle libraries, level structures for level names, glossary files, and so on), for defining and sharing among the users of the system.

♦ **Reference files.** Files for determining the elements to be active in each design and the elements to be referenced.

♦ **Archiving and backups.** Specifications for copying and storing the files.

If your CAD project involves several different people, everybody will have his or her own ideas. If you don't set the standard and conventions, you end up with a mishmash of files, data, resources, and elements by the time the project ends. Each user will have a unique approach to the problem, and every file will look and act a little different. Imagine going back later and trying to use these files again—all kinds of problems might turn up.

MicroStation reads resource files, for example, such as linestyle libraries, to display and plot linestyles. What happens if the original style library is gone or lost? The file appears without any linestyles. This type of problem can arise if you have no standards. You can eliminate such problems before they show up by setting linestyle library standards.

Using Standards for Design and Directory Names

File-name standards can be a major problem if you haven't thought out the potential pitfalls. Try to define design meaningful file-naming conventions, such as the project or billing number associated with the job. File names such as FLOOR.DGN and SITE.DGN are meaningful only in a learning situation, and can prove confusing and dangerous in a production environment.

Multiple design files called SITE.DGN in different directories can be overwritten or misunderstood. Refer to Chapter 18 and consider how MicroStation will look for a file called site.dgn. Can you realistically expect to achieve the site plan you intend if multiple files have the same name in different directories?

The manual method of filing and storing design files is a good place to start for ideas on how files are typically retrieved or referenced. Each design or drawing probably has a number, name, or code associated with it in the manual method. Will this work for your computer designs?

The names of the directories in which the files are stored should also contribute to your file-naming conventions. A directory can help you divide the project files into meaningful groups. You can, for example, have a directory for the project design files and a directory for resource files.

Tip   Directories that contain many files (hundreds) can slow down the dialog boxes that display the contents of directories in MicroStation. This is especially true for large directories that are stored on a network server.

Along with defining standards for file- and directory-naming conventions, you must also consider issues associated with operating systems and file extensions.

Operating Systems

Each operating system has a maximum number of allowable characters for a file name. In DOS, the file-name maximum is eight characters plus a three-character extension. A file name like MYSITE10.DGN, for example, is the maximum length for a DOS and Windows 3.1 file name. In Unix, the maximum is 14 characters, including the file extension. The Unix operating system also does not require an extension, and allows file names such as aldermanicdist. Likewise the long file names in Windows NT and Windows 95 can be problematic in a mixed operating system environment.

If you have multiple operating systems in your workplace, define the file-naming conventions with the requirements and limitations of each in mind. Unix can distinguish between upper- and lowercase characters, for example, whereas DOS cannot. If your site includes both operating systems, define your file conventions to only lowercase characters.

Warning   Stay away from special characters like *, ?, -. In many operating systems, these characters have special meanings. Stick with alphanumeric characters. If you must use a special character, try an underscore (_) for file names like ALD_12.DGN.

File Extensions

In addition to a file name's eight characters, MicroStation requires a file extension. In MicroStation, the default file extension is DGN, but you don't have to use only that extension.

Note   If you don't enter an extension in key-in commands, MicroStation assumes an extension of DGN. You must specify the extension in MicroStation if it isn't DGN. Enter the file extension, such as **12345.SIT** or **12345.WAT**.

File extensions can be a good way to indicate the kind of design the file contains. XXX.FLR indicates a design of the floor plan for the project. A file name of XXX.HAC indicates a design of the heating and cooling portion of the project. You can use any three characters for a file extension. You might, however, want to stay away from any extensions that MicroStation or your operating system uses for resources and other support files. See table 20.1 for a list of some of the file extensions MicroStation uses.

Table 20.1

MicroStation File Extensions

Extension	Purpose in MicroStation
CEL	Cell-library files
CDX	Cell-library index files
RSC	Resource files
CFG	System, Application, and Site configuration files
UCF	User-configuration files
UPF	User-preferences files
PCF	Project-configuration files
TBL	Color-table files
LVL	Level-structure files
STG	Settings-group files
UCM	User-command files
MKE	MDL make files
MA	MDL-executable files
MNU	Function-key menu files
GLS	Glossary files
SHT	Sheet files
TXT	Text files
PLT	Plotting-configuration files
INI	Plot configuration files

Sharing Files

Sharing files is an important concept in MicroStation and most CAD packages. File sharing is one of the ways CAD can increase productivity. If file sharing is not a concept instituted in your organization, the chances are that CAD will offer little productivity improvement over the manual drafting methods. File sharing can offer the following advantages:

♦ You can copy and modify similar designs to create new drawings.

♦ Multiple disciplines can work on their respective portions of the project at the same time. By using reference files, the different workgroups can display each other's progress and view the current design changes.

♦ Resource files can be created once and used by everyone on the project.

Which Files to Share

Design files are the obvious files to share, including seed files and common border-design files. Some not-so-obvious files are the supporting files that go along with the design files and their projects. Cell libraries, glossary files, and settings group files, for example, are common support files. Other files include resource files; for example, linestyle resource files, font files, color tables, and so on.

File sharing can be accomplished through servers on a network or by copying the files to all the machines running MicroStation.

Support Files

You can share cell libraries, glossary files, and settings-group files so that everyone doesn't have to re-create the files and their contents. Because these files are used in the construction of your design file, you don't have to share them. For productivity reasons, however, you should share them. Why should everyone create a north arrow? Otherwise, every north arrow will probably look different.

One approach to cell libraries is to have a master copy for making changes and additions. When a change takes place, the cell library is passed around to everyone in that project or discipline. Then everyone uses the same north arrow, but only one person had to take the time to create it.

> If you subscribe to this method of sharing files, make sure everyone knows it. If people add or change their copies of the cell library, you could destroy their work when you copy the master cell library to their system.

Warning

You also can approach glossary files and settings groups in the same manner as cell libraries.

Resource Files

Resource files, such as color tables, font libraries, and linestyle libraries, are discussed separately because they affect file sharing differently. Resource files are not just supporting files you use to create your design; they must always be available to the design file if you want to fulfill your original intent. If you create and use a custom linestyle in your design, for example, what happens if you give the design file to another user without giving him the linestyle library resource? The linestyle definition is stored in the resource, not in the design file itself. When the person in the next office views your design, the linestyles don't look the way you intended unless you also give him—or he has access to—the linestyle resource file.

Another example is the font library. What if you create your design file with font 13, and you share the file with someone who doesn't have font 13 or has assigned a completely different-looking font to the number 13? The file won't look as you intended, or worse, the text might overlap or misalign.

You should always share resource files with the people who are sharing design files with you by using network access or by copying and updating the files regularly.

How to Share Files

Depending on your workplace, file sharing can prove to be a simple matter or a maintenance nightmare.

If your machines are not networked, you have to copy the files manually. You must copy the file to a disk, walk to each machine, and copy the file to the hard drive. This situation is less desirable. Files quickly become outdated, and the effort of sharing files becomes tedious and time-consuming.

If your machines are networked, you can pass files around relatively easily with copy utilities supplied by the network software. For example, Unix or DOS machines that are networked and have the TCP/IP (Transmission Control Protocol/ Internet Protocol) software can copy files between machines with a wide range of commands supplied with the software, such as ftp (file-transfer protocol) or rcp (remote copy).

Better yet, if your network has file-sharing capability across nodes or machines, you do not need to copy the files at all. Products such as NFS (Network File Sharing) and Novell NetWare provide ways for you to treat a remote hard drive like your own. Dedicate a machine to be the server for support files, and keep all the files centrally located. You don't need to copy the files because you can all access the same file from a server. Define the configuration variables on each machine to point to the server or remote machine's hard drive for the resource files.

Warning   Make sure you have good backups of your resource files. If the server experiences a hardware failure, you do not want to lose your only copies of fonts, line styles, and so on.

Establishing Working Units

The concept of working units is always a hard one for MicroStation beginners to grasp. Struggle through the chapter on working units, define your needs, and then relax. You should not have to change or rethink your working units often. Perhaps you could use one of the delivered seed files to get you started.

Selecting a Delivered Seed File

MicroStation provides several seed files to illustrate and get you started with seed files. See table 20.2 for the directory and file names of some of the delivered seed files and their defined working units. If you need help interpreting the working units, refer to Chapter 3, "Building a Solid Foundation."

Table 20.2
Delivered Seed Files

Directory\File Name	Working Units
\win32apps\ustation\wsmod\arch\seed\seed.dgn	1:12:8000
\win32apps\ustation\wsmod\civil\seed\civ2d.dgn	1:10:100
\win32apps\ustation\wsmod\mapping\seed\sdmap2d.dgn	1:10:100
\win32apps\ustation\wsmod\mapping\seed\sdmapm2.dgn	1:1000:10
\win32apps\ustation\wsmod\mechdrft\seed\sdmech2d.dgn	1:1000:254
\win32apps\ustation\wsmod\mechdrft\seed\mechdetm.dgn	1:1000:100

Table 20.2 shows the directory path on a Window 3.1, NT, or 95 system, and it assumes that MicroStation was delivered to the \ustation directory.

Changing Your Working Units

Consider the implications if you change working units midstream during a project. Elements are drawn and stored in the design file in UORs (Units of Resolution). When you change the working units in a design file that contains active elements, the measurement reading of each element changes proportionally to the change in working units. See Chapter 3 for additional information on working units.

Files drawn in one set of working units might reference smaller or larger than you want. When reference files are attached, they display UOR to UOR. A right-of-way drawn at 60' in a design file with working units of 1:10:1000 references to a design with working units of 1:10:100 as a 600' right-of-way. You can scale the reference file after or during the attachment, but doing so just adds a needless step.

Everyone working on the *same* project should use the *same* working units!   *Tip*

What about changing the global origin during the course of a project? This would really disturb your capability to reference other files. If you see the message Off the Design Plane in the MicroStation Status Bar while referencing one file to another, chances are that you have two files with different global origins. Refer to Chapter 3 for the information on the global origin.

Note   Chapter 17, "Boosting Your Performance," covers other considerations for seed files.

Defining Design-File Features

Each feature in your design file should have element standards. Everything you place on the drawing needs a standard. The symbology of an exterior wall, for example, should look slightly different than an interior wall. Or perhaps an element that represents concrete should look different than an element that represents gypsum. Each feature should have a standard symbology so all your files look the same.

Weights and Styles

The line weight and line style of the element probably already are determined by the manual drafting methods. Now, you convert them to CAD standards and add level and color to complete the element symbology standards.

Levels

Level definitions are important for printing and reference file use. For example, if you have drawn a floor plan with all the elements on level 1, the design might not be very useful as a reference file. If you try to use the floor plan as a base for a design, you must display all the elements on level 1 as reference file data. You really only want selective features of the floor plan. A better design of the original floor plan is to put the border annotation on level 1, the exterior walls on level 2, interior walls on level 3, doors on level 4, and so on. Then the design lends itself to being used efficiently as a reference file.

> You can use named levels to facilitate many different levels in your design—see Chapter 3.   *Note*

Define your levels and symbology down to the letter. The best scenario is to put all unique features on their own level. In a mapping application, this means putting major rights-of-way on one level, major right-of-way center lines on another, secondary rights-of-way on another, and so on.

Interview the potential users of your design file for their wants and needs to use your files as reference files. Do not have a "Who cares?" attitude about the other guy. The usefulness of your design reflects on your ability to create a product that is useful for the whole organization.

Review your plotting requirements for issues reflected in level requirements. The more diversely you define your levels, the greater the variety of plotting products you can produce. To use the mapping example, you could produce maps of only the primary streets or primary and secondary or secondary only. This method enhances your flexibility, and when a unique request comes along, you can fill it easily.

Look into the future for other possible uses for your designs. You might be able to offer suggestions for things not previously possible. In a water-utility application, for example, you can supply a map of water hydrant locations for fire department inspection if the water hydrants are on a level of their own.

Color

Colors can help distinguish features in your design file. With the technology improving rapidly, color plotters and color copy machines might be commonplace in the office in a few years.

Define a level, color, weight, and line style for each feature in your design file. After you define those standards, you can use settings groups to help you adhere to them.

Settings Groups

Settings groups help you set and adhere to your drawing standards. You can assign a name to each feature that appears in your drawings; and you can set the level, weight, color, and style associated with it. In addition to the symbology, you can also define a default command for each feature.

The first level of organization is the group; for example, a settings group name for a mapping application could be "contours." Within the settings group of contours, you could have settings components for major contour lines, minor contour lines, major contour annotation, and minor contour annotation. A group example for an architect might be doors with components of various sizes of doors, such as 3' doors and 2'6" doors.

By using settings group components that make both settings and issue commands, you can ensure that the correct standard settings are made before the command is used.

Settings groups are saved as an external file, not as part of the design file. The external resource file gives you the capability to attach the same settings file to any design file you want. The default settings groups resource file is defined in the configuration variable labeled Settings Resource, or MS_SETTINGS.

Selecting a Settings Group

To activate an existing settings group, you need to open the Select Settings window. Open the Select Settings window by choosing **S**ettings, **M**anage. When you choose the group item from the **G**roup list box, the components of that group appear in the Com**p**onent list box. You activate a setting by selecting one of the items in the Com**p**onent list box. The settings behind this component might set all or some of the active symbology: level, line weight, line code, and color. After you select a component, the primary tool box shows a new active level, line weight, line style, and color. If the setting doesn't explicitly set one of the attributes, MicroStation doesn't change the current attribute.

In the following exercise, you select and place tree lines in the site plan. Make sure that the mapping workspace is active. Enter MicroStation with the mapping workspace selected in the MicroStation Manager dialog box.

SELECTING SETTINGS GROUPS

Start MicroStation and select the mapping workspace, then copy the design file called mapland.dgn to CHAP20.DGN.

Choose **S**ettings, **M**anage	Opens the Select Settings window
Select Fences	Displays seven components (see fig. 20.1)
Select Barbed Wire Fence	Activates barbed wire fence (level, line code and color; line weight does not change)

Choose the Place Line tool

Place a fence on the map.

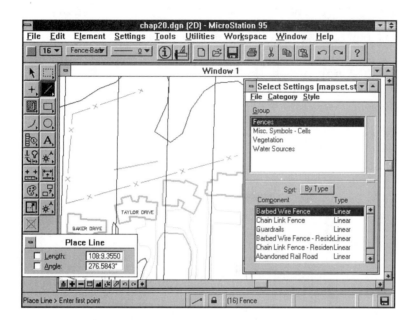

Figure 20.1

The Barbed Wire Fence settings group selected.

Creating and Editing Settings Groups

You use the Edit Settings box (see fig. 20.2) to edit or create new settings groups. To open the settings box, choose **F**ile, **E**dit in the Settings Group settings box.

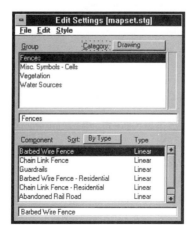

Figure 20.2

The Edit Settings box.

The Edit Settings box displays two list boxes: **G**roup and Com**p**onent. You can use this dialog box to add components to an existing group, modify existing components, or create a new group. A group has no function other than to organize the settings. You can define as many groups as you find necessary.

To modify an existing setting, double-click on the component to open the Modify settings box. The contents of this settings box vary, depending on the type of component you create. The settings in the Modify settings box, as shown in figure 20.3, are common to all the component types and are the settings for a linear type element.

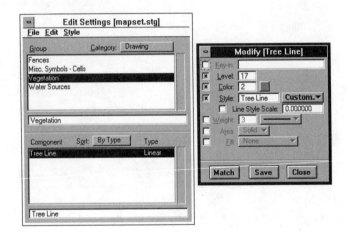

Figure 20.3

The Modify settings box.

You turn on all the buttons for the symbology for which you want to set the selected component. The buttons not turned on do not affect any settings (the defaults are used instead). In this example (see fig. 20.3), selecting the Tree Line component sets the level, color, and style attributes without changing the line weight.

The **K**ey-in button enables you to set any additional setting using standard MicroStation key-ins. You can enter anything you can find in the Key-in Browser, much like defining function keys, as discussed in Chapter 17. You can issue the Place Shape command, for example, by entering **PLACE SHAPE** in the **K**ey-in field.

You close the Modify settings box and return to the Edit Settings box by choosing the SAVE button or the Close button. Choosing Close does not save any of the modifications you just made.

You create component settings by choosing **E**dit, **C**reate, and then one of the following: **A**ctive Point, Area **P**attern, **C**ell, **D**imension, **L**inear, **M**ulti-Line, or **T**ext. An Unnamed component is created in the currently selected group.

Change the name of the Unnamed component by entering the name in the field below the Component list box. To modify the settings for the component, double-click on the component name in the list box or select the item and choose Edit, Modify to open the Modify settings box (refer to fig. 20.3).

In the following exercise, you modify the Tree Line component to add a key-in that issues the Place SmartLine command.

MODIFYING COMPONENT SETTINGS

Continue from the preceding exercise, with the CHAP20.DGN design file open.

Choose File, Edit *from the*   Opens the Edit Settings box
Select Setting opened in previous exercise

Select Vegetation *from the* Group *list box*

Double-click on Tree Line

Turn on the Key-in *button*

Enter **place smartline** *(see fig. 20.4)*

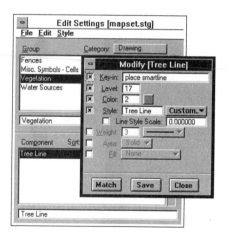

Figure 20.4

The modified Tree Line settings.

Choose Save   Closes Modify setting box

Choose File, Exit *from the Edit settings box*   Closes Edit settings box

Now, if you select Tree Line from the Select Settings window, it sets the active attributes and issues the Place SmartLine command.

In the next exercise, you create a new group called Street Annotation and add two components—one to place text for the primary street text. These components issue the Place Text On Element command. You also add another key-in (dialog textedit) to each component to open the Text Editor window.

Creating Component Settings

Continue from the preceding exercise, with the CHAP20.DGN design file and the Edit Settings box open.

Choose **F**ile, **E**dit *from the Select Setting opened in previous exercise*	Displays Edit settings Box
In the Edit Settings box, choose **E**dit, **C**reate, **G**roup	Creates Unnamed group
Double-click on Unnamed *in the field below the* **G**roup *list box*	
Enter **Street Annotation**	Changes Unnamed to Street Annotation Group
Choose **E**dit, **C**reate, **T**ext	Creates Unnamed component
Double-click on Unnamed *in the field below the* Com**p**onent *list box*	
Enter **Primary Street**	Changes Unnamed to Primary Street
Double-click on Primary Street *in the* Com**p**onent *list box*	Displays Modify settings box for text type (see fig. 20.5)

Figure 20.5

The Modify settings box for Text type.

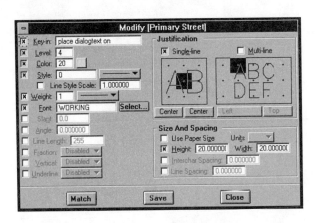

Turn on **K**ey-in *button*

Enter **Place Text on** *in* **K**ey-in *field*

Turn on **L**evel, *and enter* **4**

Turn on **C**olor *and select a color by dragging on the button to the right of the* **C**olor *field*

Turn on **S**tyle, *and enter* **0**

Turn on **W**eight, *and enter* **1**

Turn on **F**ont, *and enter* **1**

Turn on the Singl**e**-line *button in the Justification section and set both of the buttons below the example box to* Center, Center

Turn on **H**eight *button in the Size and Spacing section, and enter* **20** *in* the **H**eight *field and* **20** *in the* Wi**d**th *field*

Close the Modify settings box	Initiates an Alert box
Choose **S**ave	Updates Primary Street component
Choose **F**ile, **E**xit *from the Edit settings box*	Closes the Edit settings box

In the following steps, you use the new Street Annotation components to label the streets in the site plan.

Select Street Annotation *from the* **G**roup *list box in the Select Settings window*	Displays street components
Select Primary Streets	Sets active symbology, issues Place Text On Element command

Enter **Center Blvd.**

Pick a point on center line (see fig. 20.6)	Places highlighted text

Continues

Figure 20.6

*The annotated
streets.*

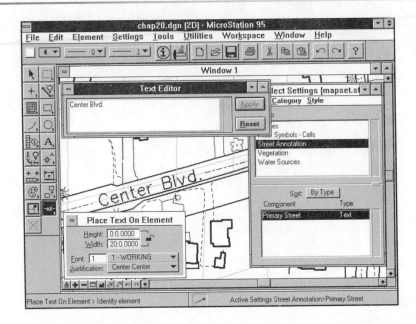

Pick any point   Accepts placement

Note   You also can call macros by using a settings group component.

Utilizing Cells, Shared Cells, and Symbols

Cells and symbols appear on nearly every drawing, whether the cell is a tree, an electrical symbol, a bolt, or a table and chair. For consistent drawings, standardizing cells and symbols is extremely important.

You should consider what cells you need and create a library that contains the common cells. Pass the cell library around to all the users so everyone isn't re-creating the same cells.

Pay close attention to the details when you create a cell because it might be plotted several times on a design file. A poorly created cell, placed dozens of times in a drawing, degrades a drawing's appearance. Be sure to snap elements together to make neat edges and corners.

> Use the fewest possible number of elements to create cells. Use line strings or shapes rather than multiple lines, if possible. The fewer the number of elements in the cell, the faster and more efficient that cell.

Tip

Consider the origin of the cell in relationship to the way the cell will be placed or used. If you place the cell and then must move it, reconsider the origin. Redefining the cell with a different origin can eliminate the extra step of moving it after placing it.

Shared Cells

A cell is a group of elements. When you place a cell, you place the primitive elements in the design with a cell header. Multiple cells in a design file mean multiple copies of the cell header and the primitive elements.

Shared cells eliminate some of the redundancy you see in conventional cell placement. Shared cells place a cell header in the design file with a pointer back to one copy of the cell's primitive elements. Multiple occurrences of shared cells mean multiple cell headers, but only one copy of the elements that make up the cell. Figure 20.7 shows a representation of a design file that uses cells versus a design file that uses shared cells. The cell in this figure consists of a shape and two lines. The diagrams show the way those elements are stored three times in the design file that placed the cell normally. The second diagram shows the way the elements are stored when the cells have been placed as shared.

Cell Header
Shape
Line
Line
Cell Header
Shape
Line
Line
Cell Header
Shape
Line
Line

Shared Cell Definition
Shape
Line
Line
Shared Cell Instance
Shared Cell Instance

Figure 20.7

Elements stored as cells versus shared cells.

Shared cells do not limit cell placement. Each instance of a shared cell places a cell header in the design file. The cell header stores the instance's unique settings of rotation, scale, and X,Y location.

You should use shared cells whenever possible to save disk space.

Symbol Fonts

What is a *symbol font*? An example of a symbol font is the font 102 (see fig. 20.8), which the dimensioning tools use. Using symbol fonts rather than conventional cells serves two major advantages: smaller design files for disk space savings and external symbol definition for easy updates.

Figure 20.8

Symbol Font 102.

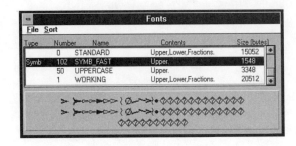

Note   Shared cells offer disk space savings, but they are not as efficient as symbol fonts. Shared cells do not offer the advantage of global updates that the symbol fonts do.

Symbols are placed in the design file as font characters or pieces of text. You can, for example, activate font 102 and place a piece of text by typing the letter *a*. An arrowhead symbol is placed. MicroStation displays the text with the symbol found in the font resource for font 102, character a.

The elements that make up the symbol are stored in the font library, not in the design file. You can get information on the symbol by choosing **E**dit, **I**nformation. MicroStation displays the element type as text.

You can create your own symbol fonts and add them to the font resource. A symbol font might be landuse symbols, for example, like churches, houses, and so on.

The font-resource file is external to the design file, thus facilitating global changes to symbols. If you change the symbols in the font resource, MicroStation automatically reflects that change in each design file that uses that resource.

Share your font library with anyone with whom you share design files. A symbol or character is stored in the design file with a font number. The library tells MicroStation how to display that font. If you reference a design file that has a custom font number 99, the symbol or character won't display correctly unless you have the same font assigned to font 99.

> Someone needs to coordinate the font assignments in your organization. Consider assigning number ranges to groups of users to eliminate use of duplicate numbers.
>
> As an example, look at what could happen in a facility mapping environment. The sewer department creates a custom font and assigns it number 104. The water department also creates a custom font and assigns it number 104. When each group attempts to reference the other's maps, the symbols of the reference files display incorrectly. The water department sees its symbols on the sewer map, and vice versa.

Tip

Using Reference Files

Reference files are just ordinary design files attached to your design file as a reference. Chapter 18 includes details about reference files.

You can and should use reference files for standard graphics, such as drawing borders. Do not repeat the elements that make up a border in each design file—they waste disk space. Create a design file, and place the border information that is common to every design. Reference the border design file to each design file that needs it. This method keeps your design files smaller and more consistent. You cannot accidentally delete or modify the elements of the reference file border, so every border you plot is complete and accurate. If a change is necessary, you make the change in one design file and all the designs that reference the border file are automatically changed.

You also should use reference files to eliminate redundant project data. In an architectural application, if you are responsible for supplying the heating and cooling for the building project, reference the floor plan instead of copying it. If you copy the data, the floor plan could change and you wouldn't know it. If you reference it, it automatically updates your file. Besides, you don't want to be responsible for that data anyway.

> If the floor plan design needs symbology changes to fit your needs, use reference file level symbology to make the reference file look the way you want. By using reference file level symbology, you can emphasize or deemphasize reference file data for your discipline. For example, the floor plan may have the wall in a heavier line weight for emphasis. That might interfere with your lines that represent the heating duct work. Create reference level symbology to deemphasize the walls and display them in a thinner line weight.

Tip

File ownership and data maintenance responsibility often are determining factors for dividing data into multiple files. If server technology is available at your site, design files can be protected. Write privileges or modify privileges can be given to people in a specific group, and everyone outside the group can use the files only for reference.

Archiving and Backups

Nobody likes to back up files. If you have had the experience of suddenly finding your file corrupted when you were about to complete a major project with a deadline of yesterday, you understand why you need to implement a backup strategy.

A backup strategy can be as simple as copying the files you have worked on to disk at the end of the day. In the worst-case scenario, you start over from yesterday. If your machine is on a network, you can invest in more sophisticated methods that store files on tape or CDs. You can purchase software programs that enable you to schedule backups as often as you need to, once at midnight or periodically during the course of the day.

The backup method you choose depends on the amount of data you are backing up and how much money you have. In any case, do not test your fate. Back up your files to something other than the machine on which you are working. Both new and old machines can have hardware and software problems that will destroy your data!

Summary

You have a lot to think about when you are setting up a project, and being new to MicroStation does not make it any easier. This chapter does not give you all the answers, but it may start you thinking. You have decisions to make about file names, working units, element symbology, cells, line styles, reference files, and more.

The details on how to implement standards can be found in many resource books and manuals. This chapter attempted to explain what you should consider, why, the potential pitfalls, and some real-world situations.

MicroStation is a great tool, but a tool is good only if you use it correctly. This book is not the end, but the beginning of your learning process. The real learning situation occurs when you try to apply the knowledge you have to your production.

INDEX

Symbols

; (semicolon), multiple key-ins, 471

A

AccuDraw, 187-195
  compass, 188-189
  placing elements, 191-193
  polar coordinate system, 190-191
  rectangular coordinate system, 190
  tentative points, 193-195
accuracy/precision
  coordinate data formats, 185-187
  design plane, 83
  measurement commands, 196-205
ACS Triad (View Attribute setting), 159
activating cells, 444
active cells
  Place Active Cell Matrix tool, 447
  Place Active Cell tool, 444-446
active level, 65-67
  changing, 66, 126
  placing elements on, 67
  turning off, 71
active symbology, 125-126
  Element Attributes settings box, 128-129
  Primary tool box, 126-128
Add to Graphic Group tool, 253-255
adding elements
  to graphic groups, 253-255
  to selection sets, 245-246
Along Element option (Measure Distance tool),
  197-199

angles
  constraints, drawing lines, 48, 121
  coordinate angle formats, 186-187
  dimensions, 364-369
    Dimension Angle Between Lines tool,
    366-367
    Dimension Angle From X-Axis tool,
    367-368
    Dimension Angle From Y-Axis tool,
    368-369
    Dimension Angle Location tool, 366
    Dimension Angle Size tool, 365-366
  Measure Angle tool, 201
  Modify Arc Angle tool, 223
application variables, 459
Application Window, 19
  menus, 20-22
arcs
  Construct Circular Fillet tool, 228-232
  dimensions, 364-369
    Dimension Angle Between Lines tool,
    366-367
    Dimension Angle From X-Axis tool,
    367-368
    Dimension Angle From Y-Axis tool,
    368-369
    Dimension Angle Location tool, 366
    Dimension Angle Size tool, 365-366
  drawing, 217-221
    Place Arc By Center tool, 218-220
    Place Arc By Edge tool, 220-221

modifying
Element Selection tool, 225-226
Modify Arc tools, 222-224
Arcs tool box, 217
modifying arcs/partial ellipses, 222-224
areas, patterning, 329-338
Crosshatch Area tool, 335-336
Delete Pattern tool, 333-334
Hatch Area tool, 332-333
Pattern Area tool, 336-338
Arrange command (Window menu), 147
arrays, 233-238
polar, 235-238
rectangular, 234
arrows, sizing linear dimensions, 360-362
Association Lock (dimensions), 358-359
Associative Patterning option
Drop Associative Pattern tool, 344
hole elements, 341-342
Patterns tool box, 330-331
Attach Cell Library dialog box, 435-436
Attach Reference File dialog box, 485-487
attaching color tables to design files, 162
attachment modes (reference files), 487
attributes
Change Element Attributes tool, 297-298
Element Information settings box, 305-306
Match Element Attributes tool, 299-300
selecting elements by, 300-304
text, 400-401
see also symbology
Auto Fill in Enter_Data Fields tool, 404-405
automatically saving design files, 86
axes
ellipses, 215
Modify Arc Axis tool, 224
axis lock, 183

B

Background (View Attribute setting), 159
backing up files, 542

base maps, flexibility of levels, 72
Between Points option (Measure Distance tool), 197-198
beveled edges, creating, 232
Bisector (Snap Mode setting), 176
blocks
drawing (Place Block tool), 50-51, 132-137
of levels, turning on, 70
modifying (Modify Element tool), 280
bookmarks, setting, 243-244
border files, 484-494
Attach Reference File dialog box, 485-487
settings, 488-494
Button Assignments command (Workspaces menu), 14, 474-475

Camera (View Attribute setting), 159
Cartesian coordinate systems
global origin point, 80
polar (AccuDraw), 190-191
rectangular (AccuDraw), 190
Cascade command (Window menu), 146
cell libraries, 336, 433-437
Attach Cell Library dialog box, 435-436
Create Cell Library dialog box, 433-435
deleting cells, 448
sharing, 526-527
storing cells, 442-443
viewing, 436-437
Cell Library settings box, 433
activating cells, 444
Cell Selector utility, 454-455
cells, 336
activating, 444
Cell Selector utility, 454-455
defining origin, 439-440
deleting from cell library, 448
descriptions, 441
drawing standards, 538-539
elements, drawing, 438-439

Identify Cell tool, 447
modifying, 449-451
names, 440
Place Active Cell Matrix tool, 447
Place Active Cell tool, 444-446
Replace Cell tool, 451-452
Select and Place Cell tool, 447
shared cells
    drawing standards, 539
    dropping, 453-454
    placing, 452-453
    replacing, 454
storing, 442-443
types of, 441
Cells tool box, 432
center, placing elements by
arcs, 218-220
circles, 209-211
ellipses, 215
Center (Snap Mode setting), 176
center marks (Place Center Mark tool), 370
Chamfered vertex type, 124
chamfers (Construct Chamfer tool), 232
Change Attributes tool box, 297
Change Dimension to Active Settings tool, 380
Change Element Attributes tool, 297-298
Change Element to Active Area (Solid/Hole)
  tool, 339
Change Text to Active Attributes tool, 401
circles
deleting part of, 285-286
dimensions, 369-372
    Dimension Diameter (Extended Leader)
      tool, 372
    Dimension Diameter tool, 371
    Dimension Radius (Extended Leader)
      tool, 371
    Dimension Radius tool, 370-371
    Place Center Mark tool, 370
drawing, 208-214
    Place Circle By Center tool, 209-211
    Place Circle By Diameter tool, 213-214
    Place Circle By Edge tool, 211-213

modifying via Element Selection tool,
  226-227
trimming, 293
circumscribed polygons, 141
classes of elements, 130
clipping reference files, 482-483
Close command (File menu), 61, 107
Close Tool Boxes command (Tools menu), 29
closing
design files, 61, 107
settings boxes, 23
tool frames/boxes, 29-30
views, 145-146
Color Table dialog box, 160-162
color tables, 160-162
attaching to design files, 162
colors
active color, changing, 126
copying, 161
drawing standards, 531
fill color (blocks), 136-137
highlight color, changing, 172
modifying on color palette, 161-162
command line
activating workspaces, 95
opening design files, 108
command menus, 475
command points (tablets), 13
commands
Directory menu
    Compress, 113
    Copy, 112
    New, 112
Edit menu
    Copy, 264
    Group, 250-251
    Lock, 206
    Paste, 264
    Redo, 243
    Set Mark, 243-244
    To Mark, 243-244
    Undo, 58-59, 242-243

Ungroup, 250-251
Unlock, 206
File menu
  Close, 61, 107
  Compress, 60, 112
  Copy, 109
  Delete, 110
  Exit, 61, 107
  Info, 110
  Merge, 111
  Rename, 109
  Save As, 86
  Save Settings, 44, 79, 103
measurement commands, 196-205
  Measure Angle, 201
  Measure Area, 203-205
  Measure Distance, 196-200
  Measure Length, 202-203
  Measure Radius, 201
terminating, 12-13
Tools menu (Close Tool Boxes), 29
Window menu
  Arrange, 147
  Cascade, 146
  Open/Close, 145
  Tile, 146
Workspaces menu
  Button Assignments, 14, 474-475
  Preference, 86
  see also tools
compass (AccuDraw), 188-189
Compatibility option (Preferences dialog box), 504-505
complex elements, 348-352
  chains, 348
    Create Complex Chain tool, 348-351
  Create Region tool, 348, 351
  creating, 349-351
  Drop Element tool, 352
  shapes, 348
    Create Complex Shape tool, 348-351

Compress command
  Directory menu, 113
  File menu, 60, 112
compressing design files, 60, 104
Configuration : User dialog box, reviewing configuration variables, 462-465
configuration files (plots), saving, 428
configuration variables, 459-465
  application variables, 459
  creating workspaces, 461-462
  project variables, 460
  reference file directory paths, 499
  reviewing/changing, 462-465
  site variables, 459
  system variables, 459
  user variables, 460
constraints, drawing lines, 47-50, 119-121
Construct Chamfer tool, 232
Construct Circular Fillet tool, 228-232
Construct Parabolic Fillet tool, 232
Construction (View Attribute setting), 159
construction element class, 130
Coordinate Readings settings box, 185-187
coordinate systems
  global origin point, 80
  polar (AccuDraw), 190-191
  rectangular (AccuDraw), 190
Copy and Increment Enter_Data Field tool, 406
Copy and Increment Text tool, 399-400
Copy command
  Directory menu, 112
  Edit menu, 264
  File menu, 109
Copy Element tool, 55-56, 262-264
Copy Enter_Data Field tool, 405-406
copying
  colors, 161
  elements, 55-56, 262-264
  enter_data fields, 405-406
  function keys, 468-470
  text, 399-400
corners, rounding, 228-233

corrupted files, repairing, 103
Create Cell Library dialog box, 433-435
Create Complex Chain tool, 348-351
Create Complex Shape tool, 348-351
Create Design File dialog box, 97-102
    default destination directory, 98
    file name extensions, 100-102
    seed files, 99
    selecting directories, 98
Create Macro dialog box, 476-477
Create Pen Table dialog box, 424
Create Region tool, 348, 351
Create User Interface dialog box, 514-516
Create Workspace dialog box, 461-462
creating
    cell libraries, 433-435
    complex elements, 348-351
    custom tool boxes, 516-518
    design files, 17-19, 97-102
        default destination directory, 98
        naming conventions, 100-102
        seed files, 99
        selecting directories, 98
    macros, 476-477
    menus/menu items, 519-520
    named levels, 75-76
    pen tables, 424
    personal user interfaces, 514-516
    regions, 348, 351
    settings groups, 533-538
    user interfaces, 514-516
    workspaces, 461-462
Crosshatch Area tool, 335-336
cursors, 35
    locking to grid, 41-43
    opening menus, 20
    tablet cursors
        Button Assignments dialog box, 474-475
        default settings, 14-15
curves, drawing stream, 319-321
custom line styles, 308-319
    compared to linear patterning, 345-346
    Line Style Editor dialog box, 312-319

Line Styles dialog box, 309-312
Custom Symbols settings (dimensions), 378
custom tool boxes, creating, 516-518

D

Data Fields (View Attribute setting), 159
data points, 12
default destination directory, creating design
    files, 98
default mouse button settings, 14
default tablet cursor settings, 14-15
Define Cell Origin tool, 439-440
defining
    cell origins, 439-440
    display grid, 180-182
    scale of working units, 80-81
    working units, 84-86
Delete command (File menu), 110
Delete Element tool, 57-58, 241
Delete Part of Element tool, 283-286
Delete Pattern tool, 333-334
Delete Vertex tool, 295-296
deleting
    associative patterns, 344
    cells from cell library, 448
    elements, 57-58, 240-242
        complex elements, 352
        Element Selection tool, 242
        from graphic groups, 255
        in design files, 60, 104
        undoing deletions, 58-59, 242-243
    fence contents, 258-261
    menu items, 519
    part of lines/line strings, 283-284
    part of shapes/circles, 285-286
    patterns, 333-334
    shared cells, 453-454
    vertices, 295-296
    views, 167-168
descriptions
    cells, 441
    reference files, 487

deselecting selection sets, 250
Design File Settings dialog box, 84-86, 180
design files
    border files, attaching, 484-494
        Attach Reference File dialog box, 485-487
        settings, 488-494
    cell libraries, attaching, 435-436
    closing, 61, 107
    color tables, 160-162
        attaching, 162
    compressing, 60, 104
    coordinate systems
        global origin point, 80
        polar (AccuDraw), 190-191
        rectangular (AccuDraw), 190
    creating, 17-19, 97-102
        default destination directory, 98
        naming conventions, 100-102
        seed files, 99, 473-474
        selecting directories, 98
    drawing standards, 530-538
    ending sessions, 59-60
    levels, 64-79
        active level, 65-67
        advantages, 65
        display levels, 67-71
        flexibility, 72
        groups, 74
        named levels, 72-79
        symbology, 163-165
    naming conventions, 523-525
    opening, 102-106
        at command line, 108
    panning views, 153-154
    plotting, 415-417
    reference file directory paths, 499
    referencing back on themselves, 484,
     498-499
    saving, 86
        settings, 43-45, 103
    sharing (reference file advantage), 481-482
    working units, setting, 84-86

design plane, 79
    accuracy/precision, 83
    working units, 82-83
destination directory, creating design files, 98
Detach Reference File tool, 494-495
detaching reference files
    Reference Files settings box, 495
dialog boxes, 22-25
    Attach Cell Library, 435-436
    Attach Reference File, 485-487
    Button Assignments, 474-475
    Color Table, 160-162
    Configuration : User, reviewing configuration
     variables, 462-465
    Copy Directory, 112
    Copy File, 109
    Create Cell Library, 433-435
    Create Design File, 97-102
        default destination directory, 98
        file name extensions, 100-102
        seed files, 99
        selecting directories, 98
    Create Macro, 476-477
    Create Pen Table, 424
    Create User Interface, 514-516
    Create Workspace, 461-462
    Design File Settings, 84-86, 180
    Edit Key Definition, 470
    File Information, 110
    Function Keys, 468
    Insert Tool, 517
    Level Names, 72-79
    Line Style Editor, 312-319
    Line Styles, 309-312
    Macro, executing macros, 477-478
    Make Directory, 112
    Merge, 111
    MicroStation Manager, 95-96
        directory maintenance, 112-113
        file maintenance, 108-112
        opening design files, 102-103

Open Design File, 105
Options, plotting options, 423
Page Setup, plotting, 421
Plot Layout, 422
Preferences, 86, 503-514
  Compatibility option, 504-505
  Drawing option, 505
  GUI Options option, 506-507
  Operation option, 507-508
  Reference File option, 508-510
  Text option, 510-512
  Tools Palette option, 512-514
Rename File, 109
Save Function Key Menu As dialog box, 468
Select Files to Merge, 111
Select Seed File, 99
Set Active Level, 66
diameters
  dimensions, 369-372
    *Dimension Diameter (Extended Leader)
      tool, 372*
    Dimension Diameter tool, 371
    Place Center Mark tool, 370
  placing circles by, 213-214
Difference option (Patterns tool box), 330
dimension components groups, 373
Dimension Size with Arrows tool, 360-362
Dimension Size with Strokes tool, 360-362
dimensions, 356-358
  arcs/angles, 364-369
    *Dimension Angle Between Lines tool,
      366-367*
    *Dimension Angle From X-Axis tool,
      367-368*
    *Dimension Angle From Y-Axis tool,
      368-369*
    Dimension Angle Location tool, 366
    Dimension Angle Size tool, 365-366
  Association Lock, 358-359
  Change Dimension to Active Settings
    tool, 380

diameters/radii, 369-372
  *Dimension Diameter (Extended Leader)
    tool, 372*
  Dimension Diameter tool, 371
  *Dimension Radius (Extended Leader)
    tool, 371*
  Dimension Radius tool, 370-371
  Place Center Mark tool, 370
Dimension Element tool, 357-358
linear distances, 359-363
  Dimension Location (Stacked) tool, 363
  Dimension Location tool, 362
  sizing with arrows/strokes, 360-362
settings, 373-380
  Custom Symbols, 378
  Extension Lines, 377
  Placement, 374-375
  Terminator Symbols, 379
  Terminators, 375
  Text, 376
  Tolerance, 377
  Tool, 380
  Units, 378
Dimensions (View Attribute setting), 159
directories
  destination directory, creating design
    files, 98
  maintenance (MicroStation Manager dialog
    box), 112-113
  naming conventions, 523-525
  paths (reference files), 499-500
  selecting when creating design files, 98
  switching, 96
Directory menu commands
  Compress, 113
  Copy, 112
  MicroStation Manager dialog box, 96
  New, 112
disabling automatic saving, 86
disk space, saving (reference files), 481
display grid, 41-45
  defining, 180-182
  design plane, 79

grid lock, 41-43, 180
saving settings, 43-45
View Attributes settings box, 159, 178-180
display levels, 67-71
display settings, Reference Display option
(Reference Files settings box), 489-492
Display Text Attribute tool, 400
divisors, snap lock, 177-178
docking tool frames/boxes, 28
drawing
    arcs, 217-221
        Place Arc By Center tool, 218-220
        Place Arc By Edge tool, 220-221
    blocks, Place Block tool, 50-51, 132-137
    circles, 208-214
        Place Circle By Center tool, 209-211
        Place Circle By Diameter tool, 213-214
        Place Circle By Edge tool, 211-213
    elements
        AccuDraw, 191-193
        for cells, 438-439
    ellipses
        Place Ellipse By Center and Edge tool, 215
        Place Ellipse By Edge Points tool, 216
    lines, 45-50, 117-124
        constraints, 47-50, 119-121
        Place Line tool, 45, 118-119
        Place SmartLine tool, 45, 122-124,
          232-233
        selecting tools, 45-47
    orthogonal shapes, Place Orthogonal Shape
      tool, 139
    partial ellipses, 221-222
    polygons, Place Polygon tool, 139-142
    shapes, Place Shape tool, 137-139
    stream curves, 319-321
Drawing option (Preferences dialog box), 505
drawing standards, 522-523
    backing up files, 542
    cells, 538-539
    colors, 531
    levels, 530-531
    line weights/styles, 530

naming conventions, 523-525
reference files, 541-542
settings groups, 531-538
sharing
    cells, 539
    files, 526-528
symbol fonts, 540-541
working units, 528-530
Drop Associative Pattern tool, 344
Drop Element tool
    complex elements, 352
    shared cells, 453-454
Drop from Graphic Group tool, 255
Dynamics (View Attribute setting), 159

E

EdG (Edit Graphics Utility), 103
edges, placing by
    arcs, 220-221
    circles, 211-213
    ellipses, 215-216
    polygons, 141
Edit Key Definition dialog box, 470
Edit menu commands, 20
    Copy, 264
    Group, 250-251
    Lock, 206
    Paste, 264
    Redo, 243
    Set Mark, 243-244
    To Mark, 243-244
    Undo, 58-59, 242-243
    Ungroup, 250-251
    Unlock, 206
Edit Text tool, 395-397
editing
    custom line styles, 312-319
    function keys, 470-471
    glossaries, 410
    settings groups, 533-538
    text, 395-397

Element Attributes settings box, changing
  active symbology, 128-129
Element Information settings box, 305-306
Element Manipulation tool box, modifying
  cells, 449-451
Element menu, 21
Element option (Patterns tool box), 329
Element Selection tool, 224-227
  deleting elements, 242
  grouping elements, 244-251
  modifying
    arcs, 225-226
    circles/ellipses, 226-227
    elements, 281
elements
  AccuDraw, 187-195
    compass, 188-189
    placing elements, 191-193
    polar coordinate system, 190-191
    rectangular coordinate system, 190
    tentative points, 193-195
  active symbology, 125-126
    Element Attributes settings box, 128-129
    Primary tool box, 126-128
  adding to selection sets, 245-246
  arrays, 233-238
    polar, 235-238
    rectangular, 234
  Change Element Attributes tool, 297-298
  classes, 130
  complex elements, 348-352
    creating, 349-351
    Drop Element tool, 352
  copying, 55-56, 262-264
  deleting, 57-58, 240-242
    complex elements, 352
    Element Selection tool, 242
    from graphic groups, 255
    in design files, 60, 104
    parts of elements, 283-286
    undoing deletions, 58-59, 242-243
    vertices, 295-296

deselecting selection sets, 250
dimensions, 356-358
  Association Lock, 358-359
  *Change Dimension to Active Settings
    tool, 380*
  Custom Symbols settings, 378
  Dimension Element tool, 357-358
  Extension Lines settings, 377
  linear distances, 359-363
  Placement settings, 374-375
  Terminator Symbols settings, 379
  Terminators settings, 375
  Text settings, 376
  Tolerance settings, 377
  Tool settings, 380
  Units settings, 378
drawing
  blocks, 50-51
  for cells, 438-439
Element Information settings box, 305-306
Extend 2 Elements to Intersection tool,
  286-287
Extend Element to Intersection tool, 288-289
extending lines, 281-283
grouping
  Element Selection tool, 244-251
  fences, 244, 255-261
  Graphic Groups, 244, 252-255
Hole mode, 338
  changing to, 339
Insert Vertex tool, 293-294
linear patterning, 345-346
locking/unlocking, 206, 247
Match Element Attributes tool, 299-300
measurement commands, 196-205
  Measure Angle, 201
  Measure Area, 203-205
  Measure Distance, 196-200
  Measure Length, 202-203
  Measure Radius, 201
mirroring, 272-273

modifying
   Element Selection tool, 281
   Modify Element tool, 276-280
moving, 52-55, 264-266
Parallel tool, 266-267
patterning
   around holes, 339-343
   hiding pattern display, 347
   Solid/Hole modes, 134
plotting with pen tables, 423-428
rotating/spinning, 270-272
rounding corners, 228-233
scaling, 268-269
selecting by attributes, 300-304
selection rectangles, 247-249
snap locks, 170-178
   divisors, 177-178
   mode settings, 174-177
text placement
   Place Text Above Element tool, 393
   Place Text Along Element tool, 395
   Place Text Below Element tool, 394
   Place Text On Element tool, 394-395
Trim Element tool, 290-293
ellipses, 208
   drawing, 215-216
      Place Ellipse By Center and Edge tool, 215
      Place Ellipse By Edge Points tool, 216
   modifying via Element Selection tool, 226-227
   partial ellipses
      drawing, 221-222
      modifying, 222-224
Ellipses tool box, 208
End Width setting (Line Styles dialog box), 310
ending design sessions, 59-60
English working units (seed files), 99
enter_data fields, 402-403
   Copy and Increment Enter_Data Field tool, 406
   Copy Enter_Data Field tool, 405-406
   Fill in Single Enter_Data Field tool, 403-405

environment variables, 459-465
   application variables, 459
   creating workspaces, 461-462
   project variables, 460
   reference file directory paths, 499
   reviewing/changing, 462-465
   site variables, 459
   system variables, 459
   user variables, 460
executing macros, 477-478
Exit command (File menu), 61, 107
exiting MicroStation, 61, 107
Extend 2 Elements to Intersection tool, 286-287
Extend Element to Intersection tool, 288-289
extending
   elements
      Extend 2 Elements to Intersection tool, 286-287
      Extend Element to Intersection tool, 288-289
   lines, 281-283
Extension Lines settings (dimensions), 377
extensions, 524-525
   creating design files, 100-102

F

Fast Cells (View Attribute setting), 159
Fast Curves (View Attribute setting), 159
Fast Font (View Attribute setting), 159
Fast Ref Clipping (View Attribute setting), 159
Fence option (Patterns tool box), 329
Fence tool box, 255
fences, 244, 255-261
   creating custom line styles, 316-319
   moving elements, 265-266
   plotting by, 421
File Information dialog box, 110
file maintenance (MicroStation Manager dialog box), 108-112
File menu commands, 20
   Close, 61, 107
   Compress, 60, 112

Copy, 109
Delete, 110
Exit, 61, 107
Info, 110
Merge, 111
MicroStation Manager dialog box, 95
Rename, 109
Save As, 86
Save Settings, 44, 79, 103
file sharing, 526-528
file name extensions, 524-525
    creating design files, 100-102
Fill (View Attribute setting), 159
fill color (blocks), 136-137
Fill in Single Enter_Data Field tool, 403-405
fill type (blocks), 135
fillets (Construct Circular Fillet tool), 228-232
fitting
    text
        Place Fitted Text tool, 392
        Place Fitted View Independent Text
            tool, 393
    views, 148-149
flexibility of levels, 72
Flood option (Patterns tool box), 330
fonts, symbol (drawing standards), 540-541
Fonts settings box, 387-388
Fractions option (Text settings box), 390
full-scale drawings, plotting, 419-420
function keys, 465-472
    copying menus, 468-470
    editing, 470-471
    Key-in Browser settings box, 466-468
    multiple key-ins, 471-472
Function Keys dialog box, 468

G

global origin point, 80
glossaries, 408-410
    creating, 408-409
    editing, 410
    Glossary settings box, 409-410
    sharing, 526-527

Glossary settings box, 409-410
graphic cells, 441
Graphic Groups, 244, 252-255
graphical user interface, *see* GUI
grayed out menu items, 22
grid lock, 41-43, 180
grid, 41-45
    defining, 180-182
    design plane, 79
    grid lock, 41-43, 180
    saving settings, 43-45
    View Attributes settings box, 159, 178-180
Group command (Edit menu), 250-251
grouping elements
    dimension components groups, 373
    Element Selection tool, 244-251
    fences, 244, 255-261
    Graphic Groups, 244, 252-255
    hole elements, associative patterning,
        341-342
    levels, 74
Groups tool box, complex elements, 348-349
GUI (graphical user interface)
    Application Window, 19
        menus, 20-22
    cursors, 35
    dialog boxes, 22-25
    settings boxes, 22-25
    Status Bar, 19
    tool boxes, 25-30
    tool frames, 25-30
        opening tool boxes from, 31-33
    tools, selecting, 30-31
    views, 33-34
GUI Options option (Preferences dialog box),
    506-507

H

half ellipses (Place Half Ellipse tool), 221
Hatch Area tool, 332-333
Help menu, 21, 35
hiding pattern display, 347
highlight colors, changing, 172

Hole mode, 338
  blocks, 134
  changing elements to, 339
  patterning around, 339-343

I

icons, creating for tools, 517-518
Identify Cell tool, 447
incrementing text (Copy and Increment Text tool), 399-400
Info command (File menu), 110
input devices, 12-15
  button actions (mouse), 15
    default settings, 14
  command points (tablets), 13
  data points, 12
  reset button (mouse), 12-13
  tablet cursors, default settings, 14-15
  tentative points, 13, 170-178
    AccuDraw, 193-195
    snap lock divisors, 177-178
    snap mode settings, 174-177
inscribed polygons, 140
Insert Tool dialog box, 517
Insert Vertex tool, 293-294
interactive cell placement, 446
Interchar Spacing option (Text settings box), 390
interfaces, 92-95, 458, 514-520
  changing view borders, 520
  creating
    custom tool boxes, 516-518
    personal user interfaces, 514-516
  Modify Menus settings box, 519-520
Intersection option
  Patterns tool box, 329
  Snap Mode setting, 177
intersections, extending elements to, 286-289

J-K

justification (text), 391
Key-in Browser settings box, 466-468
key-ins (multiple), adding to function keys, 471-472
keyboard accelerators, 22
keyboard shortcuts
  function keys, 465-472
    copying menus, 468-470
    editing, 470-471
    Key-in Browser settings box, 466-468
    multiple key-ins, 471-472
  opening menus, 20
Keypoint (Snap Mode setting), 176
  snap lock divisors, 177-178

L

layers, *see* levels
left mouse button, data points, 12
length constraints, drawing lines, 48, 120-121
level lock, 41
Level Names dialog box, 72-79
Level Symbology (View Attribute setting), 159
levels, 64-79
  active level, 65-67
    changing, 66, 126
    placing elements on, 67
    turning off, 71
  advantages, 65
  display levels, 67-71
  drawing standards, 530-531
  flexibility, 72
  groups, 74
  named levels, 72-79
    creating, 75-76
    turning on/off, 77-79
  opening existing structures, 73-74

reference file levels, displaying, 489-492
saving level structures, 76, 79
symbology, 159, 163-165
Line Length option (Text settings box), 390
Line Spacing option (Text settings box), 390
line strings, 122-124
    deleting part of, 283-284
Line Style Editor dialog box, 312-319
line styles
    changing active, 127
    custom, 308-319
        compared to linear patterning, 345-346
        editing, 312-319
        Line Styles dialog box, 309-312
    drawing standards, 530
    views, 159
Line Styles (View Attribute setting), 159
Line Styles dialog box, 309-312
line weights
    changing active, 128
    drawing standards, 530
    views, 159
Line Weights (View Attribute setting), 159
Linear Dimensions tool box, 359
linear patterning, 345-346
lines
    deleting part of, 283-284
    dimensions, 359-363
        Dimension Angle Between Lines tool,
            366-367
        Dimension Location (Stacked) tool, 363
        Dimension Location tool, 362
        sizing with arrows/strokes, 360-362
    drawing, 45-50, 117-124
        constraints, 47-50, 119-121
        Place Line tool, 45, 118-119
        Place SmartLine tool, 45, 122-124,
            232-233
        selecting tools, 45-47
    extending, 281-283
        Extend 2 Elements to Intersection tool,
            286-287
        Extend Element to Intersection tool,
            288-289

modifying, 278-279
    symbology (Points tool box), 321-323
    trimming, 290-292
Lock command (Edit menu), 206
Lock Toggles settings box, 171
locking/unlocking
    elements, 206, 247
    tool selections, 54
locks, 41
    Association Lock (dimensions), 358-359
    axis lock, 183
    Graphic Group lock setting, 252
    grid lock, 41-43, 180
    level lock, 41
    snap locks, 41, 170-178
        divisors, 177-178
        mode settings, 174-177
        toggling on/off, 171
    text sizing, 389
    unit lock, 184-185
Locks settings box, 174

M

Macro dialog box, 477-478
macros
    creating, 476-477
    executing, 477-478
Main tool frame
    opening, 39
    selecting tools, 45-47
Make Directory dialog box, 112
Manipulate tool box
    arrays, 233
    Copy Element tool, 262-264
    Mirror Element tool, 272-273
    Move Element tool, 264-266
    Parallel tool, 266-267
    Rotate/Spin tool, 270-272
    Scale Element tool, 268-269
master units, 81
Match Element Attributes tool, 299-300
Match Pattern Attributes tool, 346

Match Text Attributes tool, 401
matrix
    menus, 475
    Place Active Cell Matrix tool, 447
maximizing views, 34
maximum window, 151
Measure Angle tool, 201
Measure Area tool, 203-205
Measure Distance tool, 196-200
Measure Length tool, 202-203
Measure Radius tool, 201
measurement
    commands, 196-205
        Measure Angle, 201
        Measure Area, 203-205
        Measure Distance, 196-200
        Measure Length, 202-203
        Measure Radius, 201
    coordinate data formats, 185-187
    working units, 81-82
        accuracy/precision, 83
        defining scale, 80-81
        design plane, 82-83
        drawing standards, 528-530
        English working units (seed files), 99
        master units, 81
        metric working units (seed files), 99
        positional units, 81-82
        setting, 84-86
        subunits, 81
menu cells, 441
menus, 20-22
    command menus, 475
    copying function key menus, 468-470
    dialog/settings boxes, 22-25
    matrix menus, 475
    Modify Menus settings box, 519-520
    sidebar menus, 475
Merge command (File menu), 111
metric working units (seed files), 99
MicroStation
    exiting, 61, 107

input devices, 12-13
    setting, 13-15
    starting, 16-19
MicroStation Manager dialog box, 95-96
    directory maintenance, 112-113
    file maintenance, 108-112
    opening design files, 102-103
Midpoint (Snap Mode setting), 176
minimizing views, 33
Minimum Between option (Measure Distance
    tool), 197, 200
minimum window, 151
Mirror Element tool, 272-273
mirroring
    elements, 272-273
    reference files, 494
Modify Arc Angle tool, 223
Modify Arc Axis tool, 224
Modify Arc Radius tool, 222-223
Modify Element tool, 276-280
Modify Menus settings box, 519-520
Modify Pen Table settings box, 424-425
Modify tool box
    Delete Part of Element tool, 283-286
    Trim Element tool, 290-293
modules (workspaces), 458
mouse
    button actions, 15
    Button Assignments dialog box, 474-475
    data points, 12
    default button settings, 14
    reset button, 12-13
    tentative points, 13
Move Element tool, 52, 264-266
Move Reference File tool, 496-497
moving
    elements, 52-55, 264-266
    menu items, 519
    reference files, 496-497
    tool frames/boxes, 26-27
multiple key-ins, adding to function keys,
    471-472
multiple reference files, 482

N

naming
    cells, 440
    conventions, 523-525
        creating design files, 100-102
    levels, 72-79
        creating, 75-76
        turning on/off, 77-79
    reference files, 486
    views
        deleting, 167-168
        recalling, 167
        saving, 165-167
Nearest (Snap Mode setting), 176
nested cells, 450
networks, sharing files, 527-528
New command (Directory menu), 112
notes (Place Note tool), 407-408

O

online help, 21, 35
Open Design File dialog box, 105
Open/Close command (Window menu), 145
opening
    design files, 102-106
        at command line, 108
    level structures, 73-74
    menus, 20
    tool boxes, 31-33, 39-40
    toolframes, 39-40
    views, 145-146
operating systems, naming conventions, 524
Operation option (Preferences dialog box), 507-508
Options dialog box, plotting options, 423
Origin setting
    Line Styles dialog box, 310
    Snap Mode setting, 176
origins, defining for cells, 439-440
orthogonal blocks, drawing, 132-133
orthogonal shapes, drawing, 139
overlays, *see* levels

P

Page Setup dialog box, plotting, 421
panning views, 153-154
Parallel (Snap Mode setting), 177
Parallel tool, 266-267
partial ellipses
    drawing, 221-222
    modifying via Modify Arc tools, 222-224
Paste command (Edit menu), 264
Pattern Area tool, 336-338
patterning
    areas, 329-338
        Crosshatch Area tool, 335-336
        Delete Pattern tool, 333-334
        Hatch Area tool, 332-333
        Pattern Area tool, 336-338
        Solid/Hole modes, 134
    around holes, 339-343
    Drop Associative Pattern tool, 344
    hiding pattern display, 347
    linear, 345-346
Patterns (View Attribute setting), 160
Patterns tool box, 329-338
    Crosshatch Area tool, 335-336
    Delete Pattern tool, 333-334
    Hatch Area tool, 332-333
    Match Pattern Attributes tool, 346
    Pattern Area tool, 336-338
    Show Pattern Attributes tool, 346
pen tables, 423-428
Perp From (Snap Mode setting), 177
Perpendicular option
    Measure Distance tool, 197, 199-200
    Snap Mode setting, 177
personal user interfaces, creating, 514-516
Place Active Cell Matrix tool, 447
Place Active Cell tool, 444-446
Place Arc By Center tool, 218-220
Place Arc By Edge tool, 220-221
Place Block tool, 50-51, 132-137
    fill color, 136-137
    fill type, 135
    orthogonal blocks, 132-133
    rotated blocks, 133-134

Place Center Mark tool, 370
Place Circle By Center tool, 209-211
Place Circle By Diameter tool, 213-214
Place Circle By Edge tool, 211-213
Place Ellipse By Center and Edge tool, 215
Place Ellipse By Edge Points tool, 216
Place Fence tool, 255
Place Fitted Text tool, 392
Place Fitted View Independent Text tool, 393
Place Half Ellipse tool, 221
Place Line tool, 45, 118-119
    constraints, 47-50, 119-121
Place Note tool, 407-408
Place Orthogonal Shape tool, 139
Place Polygon tool, 139-142
Place Quarter Ellipse tool, 222
Place Shape tool, 137-139
Place SmartLine tool, 45, 122-124
    rounding corners, 232-233
Place Stream Curve tool, 319-321
Place Text Above Element tool, 393
Place Text Along Element tool, 395
Place Text Below Element tool, 394
Place Text On Element tool, 394-395
Place Text tool, 384-386
Place View Independent Text tool, 392-393
Placement settings (dimensions), 374-375
Plot Layout dialog box, 422
Plot settings box, 420-423
plotters, selecting, 414
plotting
    by fences, 421
    by views, 420-421
    design files, 415-417
    full-scale drawings, 419-420
    Options dialog box, 423
    Page Setup dialog box, 421
    pen tables (symbology), 423-428
    previewing plots, 417-418
    saving configuration file, 428
    scaling symbology for, 419-420

point cells, 441
Point On (Snap Mode setting), 177
point patterns, modifying, 314-316
points, measuring distance between, 197-198
Points option (Patterns tool box), 330
Points tool box, 321-323
polar arrays, 235-238
polar coordinate system (AccuDraw), 190-191
polygons, drawing, 139-142
Polygons tool box, 131
positional units, 81-82
    setting, 84
precision/accuracy
    coordinate data formats, 185-187
    design plane, 83
    measurement commands, 196-205
Preference command (Workspaces menu), 86
Preferences dialog box, 86, 503-514
    Compatibility option, 504-505
    Drawing option, 505
    GUI Options option, 506-507
    Operation option, 507-508
    Reference File option, 508-510
    Text option, 510-512
    Tools palette option, 512-514
preferences, 459, 503-514
    compatibility, 504-505
    drawing, 505
    GUI options, 506-507
    operation, 507-508
    reference file, 508-510
    text, 510-512
    Tools palette, 512-514
previewing plots, 417-418
primary element class, 130
Primary tool box, active symbology, 125-126
    changing, 126-128
project variables, 460

Q-R

quarter ellipses (Place Quarter Ellipse tool), 222

Radial Dimensions tool, 369-370
radius
    dimensions, 369-372
        Dimension Radius (Extended Leader) tool, 371
        Dimension Radius tool, 370-371
        Place Center Mark tool, 370
    Measure Radius tool, 201
    Modify Arc Radius tool, 222-223
Radius option, placing polygons, 141-142
recalling views, 167
rectangles, selection (grouping elements), 247-249
rectangular arrays, 234
rectangular coordinate system (AccuDraw), 190
Redo command (Edit menu), 243
Ref Boundaries (View Attribute setting), 160
Reference Display option (Reference Files settings box), 489-492
Reference File option (Preferences dialog box), 508-510
reference files
    advantages, 481-484
    attaching border files, 484-494
        Attach Reference File dialog box, 485-487
        settings, 488-494
    attachment modes, 487
    clipping files, 482-483
    description field, 487
    design files, referencing back on themselves, 484, 498-499
    detaching
        Detach Reference File tool, 494-495
        Reference Files settings box, 495
    directory paths, 499-500

drawing standards, 541-542
mirroring, 494
Move Reference File tool, 496-497
multiple files, referencing, 482
naming, 486
Reload Reference File tool, 497-498
rotating, 493
saving disk space, 481
scaling, 487, 493
sharing design files, 481-482
Reference Files settings box, 480, 488-494
    detaching reference files, 495
Reference Files tool box, 480
Reference Locate option (Reference Files settings box), 492-493
Reference Snap option (Reference Files settings box), 492
regions (Create Region tool), 348, 351
relative cell placement, 445-446
Reload Reference File tool, 497-498
Rename command (File menu), 109
repainting views, 147-148
repairing corrupted files, 103
Replace Cell tool, 451-452
    shared cells, 454
Replace Text settings box, 397-399
reset button (mouse), 12-13
resizing views, 34
resource files, sharing, 527
right mouse button, 12-13
Rotate View tool, 156-157
Rotate/Spin tool, 270-272
rotating
    blocks, 133-134
    elements, 270-272
    reference files, 493
    views, 156-157
Rounded vertex type, 124
rounding corners, 228-233

S

Save As command (File menu), 86
Save Function Key Menu As dialog box, 468
Save Settings command (File menu), 44, 79, 103
Saved Views settings box, 165-168
saving
   design files, 86
     settings, 103
   disk space (reference files), 481
   display grid settings, 43-45
   function key menus, 468
   level structures, 76, 79
   plot configuration files, 428
   views, 165-167
   workspace settings, 104
scale
   defining display grid, 180-182
   elements, 268-269
   plotting full-scale drawings, 419-420
   reference files, 487, 493
   symbology scales for plotting, 419-420
   working units, defining, 80-81
Scale Element tool, 268-269
Scale factor setting (Line Styles dialog box), 310
screen cursors, 35
   locking to grid, 41-43
   opening menus, 20
seed files, 92, 528-529
   creating design files, 99
   settings, 473-474
Select and Place Cell tool, 447
Select By Attributes settings box, 301-304
Select By settings box, 301
Select Files to Merge dialog box, 111
Select Seed File dialog box, 99
selecting
   cells
     Cell Selector utility, 454-455
     Select and Place Cell tool, 447
   directories, creating design files, 98

   elements, 247-249
     by attributes, 300-304
     for cells, 438-439
   files to merge, 111
   plotters, 414
   seed files, 99
   settings groups, 532-533
   text, 396
   tools, 30-31, 45-47
selection rectangles, 247-249
selection sets, 244-251
   adding elements to, 245-246
   deselecting, 250
   moving elements, 264-265
semicolon (;), multiple key-ins, 471
Set Active Level dialog box, 66
Set Mark command (Edit menu), 243-244
Set Select By settings box, 304
settings boxes, 22-25
   Cell Library, 433
     activating cells, 444
   closing, 23
   Coordinate Readings, 185-187
   Dimensions, 373-380
     Custom Symbols settings, 378
     Extension Lines settings, 377
     Placement settings, 374-375
     Terminator Symbols settings, 379
     Terminators settings, 375
     Text settings, 376
     Tolerance settings, 377
     Tool settings, 380
     Units settings, 378
   Element Attribute, changing active symbology, 128-129
   Element Information, 305-306
   Glossary, 409-410
   Key-in Browser, 466-468
   Lock Toggles, 171
   Locks, 174
   Modify Menus, 519-520
   Modify Pen Table, 424-425
   Plot, 420-423

Reference Files, 480, 488-494
  detaching reference files, 495
Replace Text, 397-399
Saved Views, 165-168
Select By, 301
Select By Attributes, 301-304
Set Select By, 304
Text, 386-392
  fonts, 387-388
  text size, 389-392
Tool, 116-117
View Attributes, 144, 158-160
  display grids, 178-180
  hiding pattern display, 347
View Levels, 67-71
settings groups, drawing standards, 531-538
Settings menu, 21
settings-group files, sharing, 526-527
shapes, 131
  deleting part of, 285-286
  drawing
    Place Orthogonal Shape tool, 139
    Place Shape tool, 137-139
  trimming, 293
sharing
  cells, 452-454
    drawing standards, 539
    dropping, 453-454
    placing, 452-453
    replacing, 454
  design files (reference file advantage),
    481-482
  files, 526-528
Shift button (Line Styles dialog box), 310-311
Show Pattern Attributes tool, 346
sidebar menus, 475
single-shot tool selections, 54
site variables, 459
sizing
  linear dimensions, 360-362
  text, 389-392
Slant option (Text settings box), 391

snap, Reference Snap option (Reference Files
  settings box), 492
snap locks, 41, 170-178
  divisors, 177-178
  mode settings, 174-177
  toggling on/off, 171
Snap Mode tool box, 174
Snappable Pattern option (Patterns tool box),
  331
Solid mode (blocks), 134
spinning elements, 270-272
standards (drawing), 522-523
  backing up files, 542
  cells, 538-539
  colors, 531
  levels, 530-531
  line weights/styles, 530
  naming conventions, 523-525
  reference files, 541-542
  settings groups, 531-538
  sharing
    cells, 539
    files, 526-528
  symbol fonts, 540-541
  working units, 528-530
starting Microstation, 16-19
Status Bar, 19
  displaying levels, 65
storing cells, 442-443
stream curves, drawing, 319-321
stroke patterns, modifying, 313
strokes, sizing linear dimensions, 360-362
subunits, 81
  setting, 84
switching directories, 96
symbol fonts, drawing standards, 540-541
symbology
  active, 125-126
    Element Attributes settings box, 128-129
    Primary tool box, 126-128
  levels, 163-165
  lines (Points tool box), 321-323
  modifying cells, 449-451

of plots, changing with pen tables, 423-428
    scaling for plotting, 419-420
    see also attributes
symbols (dimensions)
    Custom Symbols settings, 378
    Terminator Symbols settings, 379
system variables, 459

T

tablet cursors
    Button Assignments dialog box, 474-475
    default settings, 14-15
tablets, command points, 13
Tags (View Attribute setting), 160
Tangent (Snap Mode setting), 177
Tangent From (Snap Mode setting), 177
tearing off tool boxes, 53
tentative points, 13, 170-178
    AccuDraw, 193-195
    snap lock divisors, 177-178
    snap mode settings, 174-177
terminating commands, 12-13
Terminator Symbols settings (dimensions), 379
Terminators settings (dimensions), 375
text
    attribute settings, 400-401
    Copy and Increment Text tool, 399-400
    Edit Text tool, 395-397
    enter_data fields, 402-403
        *Copy and Increment Enter_Data Field
        tool, 406*
        Copy Enter_Data Field tool, 405-406
        *Fill in Single Enter_Data Field tool,
        403-405*
    fonts, changing, 387-388
    glossaries, 408-410
        creating, 408-409
        editing, 410
        Glossary settings box, 409-410
        sharing, 526-527

placement tools
        Place Fitted Text, 392
        Place Fitted View Independent Text, 393
        Place Note, 407-408
        Place Text Above Element, 393
        Place Text Along Element, 395
        Place Text Below Element, 394
        Place Text On Element, 394-395
        Place Text, 384-386
        Place View Independent Text, 392-393
    Replace Text settings box, 397-399
    selecting, 396
    sizing, 389-392
Text Nodes (View Attribute setting), 160
Text option
    dimensions, 376
    Preferences dialog box, 510-512
    View Attribute setting, 160
Text settings box, 386-392
    fonts, 387-388
    text size, 389-392
three-dimensional seed files, 99
Through Point (Snap Mode setting), 177
Tile command (Window menu), 146
To Mark command (Edit menu), 243-244
Tolerance settings (dimensions), 377
tool boxes, 25-33
    Arcs, 217
        modifying arcs/partial ellipses, 222-224
    Cells, 432
    Change Attributes, 297
    closing, 29-30
    creating custom, 516-518
    docking, 28
    Element Manipulation, modifying cells,
     449-451
    Ellipses, 208
    Fence, 255
    Groups (complex elements), 348-349
    Linear Dimensions, 359
    Manipulate
        arrays, 233
        Copy Element tool, 262-264
        Mirror Element tool, 272-273

Move Element tool, 264-266
Parallel tool, 266-267
Rotate/Spin tool, 270-272
Scale Element tool, 268-269
Modify
    Delete Part of Element tool, 283-286
    Trim Element tool, 290-293
moving, 26-27
opening, 39-40
Patterns, 329-338
    Crosshatch Area tool, 335-336
    Delete Pattern tool, 333-334
    Hatch Area tool, 332-333
    Match Pattern Attributes tool, 346
    Pattern Area tool, 336-338
    Show Pattern Attributes tool, 346
Points, 321-323
Polygons, 131
Primary
    active symbology, 125-126
    changing active symbology, 126-128
Reference Files, 480
Snap Mode, 174
tearing off, 53
undocking, 29
View Control, 144
tool frames, 25-30
closing, 29-30
docking, 28
moving, 26-27
opening, 39-40
    tool boxes from tool frames, 31-33
undocking, 29
Tool settings (dimensions), 380
Tool Settings box, 116-117
tools
    Add to Graphic Group, 253-255
    Auto Fill in Enter_Data Fields, 404-405
    Change Element Attributes, 297-298
    Change Element to Active Area (Solid/Hole), 339
    Change Text to Active Attributes, 401
    Construct Chamfer, 232

Construct Circular Fillet, 228-232
Construct Parabolic Fillet, 232
Copy and Increment Enter_Data Field, 406
Copy and Increment Text, 399-400
Copy Element, 55-56, 262-264
Copy Enter_Data Field, 405-406
Create Complex Chain, 348-351
Create Complex Shape, 348-351
Create Region, 348, 351
creating custom, 517-518
Crosshatch Area, 335-336
Define Cell Origin, 439-440
Delete Element, 57-58, 241
Delete Part of Element, 283-286
Delete Pattern, 333-334
Delete Vertex, 295-296
Detach Reference File, 494-495
Dimension Angle Between Lines, 366-367
Dimension Angle From X-Axis, 367-368
Dimension Angle From Y-Axis, 368-369
Dimension Angle Location, 366
Dimension Angle Size, 365-366
Dimension Diameter (Extended Leader), 372
Dimension Diameter, 371
Dimension Element, 357-358
Dimension Location (Stacked), 363
Dimension Location, 362
Dimension Radius (Extended Leader), 371
Dimension Radius, 370-371
Dimension Size with Arrows, 360-362
Dimension Size with Strokes, 360-362
Display Text Attribute, 400
Drop Associative Pattern, 344
Drop Element
    complex elements, 352
    shared cells, 453-454
Drop from Graphic Group, 255
Edit Text, 395-397
Extend Element to Intersection, 288-289
Element Selection, 224-227
    arcs, modifying, 225-226
    circles/ellipses, modifying, 226-227
    deleting elements, 242

grouping elements, 244-251
modifying elements, 281
Extend 2 Elements to Intersection, 286-287
Fill in Single Enter_Data Field, 403-405
Hatch Area, 332-333
Identify Cell, 447
Insert Vertex, 293-294
Match Element Attributes, 299-300
Match Pattern Attributes, 346
Match Text Attributes, 401
Mirror Element, 272-273
Modify Arc Angle, 223
Modify Arc Axis, 224
Modify Arc Radius, 222-223
Modify Element, 276-280
Move Element, 52, 264-266
Move Reference File, 496-497
Parallel, 266-267
Pattern Area, 336-338
Place Active Cell Matrix, 447
Place Active Cell, 444-446
Place Arc By Center, 218-220
Place Arc By Edge, 220-221
Place Block, 50-51, 132-137
    fill color, 136-137
    fill type, 135
    orthogonal blocks, 132-133
    rotated blocks, 133-134
Place Center Mark, 370
Place Circle By Center, 209-211
Place Circle By Diameter, 213-214
Place Circle By Edge, 211-213
Place Ellipse By Center and Edge, 215
Place Ellipse By Edge Points, 216
Place Fence, 255
Place Half Ellipse, 221
Place Line, 45, 118-119
    constraints, 47-50, 119-121
Place Note, 407-408
Place Orthogonal Shape, 139
Place Polygon, 139-142
Place Quarter Ellipse, 222

Place Shape, 137-139
Place SmartLine, 45, 122-124
    rounding corners, 232-233
Place Stream Curve, 319-321
Place Text Above Element, 393
Place Text Along Element, 395
Place Text Below Element, 394
Place Text On Element, 394-395
Place Text, 384-386
Radial Dimensions, 369-370
Reload Reference File, 497-498
Replace Cell, 451-452
    shared cells, 454
Rotate/Spin, 270-272
Rotate View, 156-157
Scale Element, 268-269
Select and Place Cell, 447
selecting, 30-31, 45-47
Show Pattern Attributes, 346
Trim Element, 290-293
Update View, 147-148
View Next, 155-156
View Previous, 155-156
Window Area, 151-152
Tools menu commands, 21
    Close Tool Boxes, 29
Tools palette option (Preferences dialog box),
    512-514
Trim Element tool, 290-293
tutorial cells, 441
two-dimensional seed files, 99

U

Underline option (Text settings box), 390
Undo command (Edit menu), 58-59, 242-243
undocking tool frames/boxes, 29
undoing view operations, 155-156
Ungroup command (Edit menu), 250-251
Union option (Patterns tool box), 330
unit lock, 184-185

units, 81-82
    defining scale, 80-81
    design plane, 82-83
        accuracy/precision, 83
    drawing standards, 528-530
    English working units (seed files), 99
    master units, 81
    metric working units (seed files), 99
    positional units, 81-82
    setting, 84-86
    subunits, 81
Units settings (dimensions), 378
Unlock command (Edit menu), 206
unlocking/locking elements, 206, 247
UORs (Units of Resolution), 79, 82-83
Update View tool, 147-148
user interfaces, 92-95, 458, 514-520
    changing view borders, 520
    creating
        custom tool boxes, 516-518
        personal user interfaces, 514-516
    Modify Menus settings box, 519-520
user preferences, 459, 503-514
    compatibility, 504-505
    drawing preferences, 505
    GUI options preferences, 506-507
    operation preferences, 507-508
    reference file preferences, 508-510
    text preferences, 510-512
    Tools palette preferences, 512-514
user variables, 460
utilities
    Cell Selector, 454-455
    EdG (Edit Graphics Utility), 103
Utilities menu, 21

V

Vertex Type (Tool Settings box), 124
Vertical Text option (Text settings box), 390
vertices
    Delete Vertex tool, 295-296

Insert Vertex tool, 293-294
    Vertex Type (Tool Settings box), 124
View Attributes settings box, 144, 158-160
    display grids, 178-180
    hiding pattern display, 347
view borders, changing, 520
View Control tool box, 144
View Levels settings box, 67-71
View Next tool, 155-156
View Previous tool, 155-156
viewing cell libraries, 436-437
views, 33-34
    deleting, 167-168
    display grids, 178-180
    fitting, 148-149
    Identify Cell tool, 447
    level symbology, 163-165
    maximizing, 34
    minimizing, 33
    opening/closing, 145-146
    panning, 153-154
    Place Fitted View Independent Text tool, 393
    Place View Independent Text tool, 392-393
    plotting by, 420-421
    recalling, 167
    repainting, 147-148
    resizing, 34
    rotating, 156-157
    saving, 165-167
    undoing view operations, 155-156
    Window Area tool, 151-152
    zooming, 149-151

W

Width settings (Line Styles dialog box), 310
Window Area tool, 151-152
Window menu commands, 21
    Arrange, 147
    Cascade, 146
    Open/Close, 145
    Tile, 146

working units, 81-82
  defining scale, 80-81
  design plane, 82-83
    accuracy/precision, 83
  drawing standards, 528-530
  English working units (seed files), 99
  master units, 81
  metric working units (seed files), 99
  positional units, 81-82
  setting, 84-86
  subunits, 81
workspaces, 92-95
  configuration variables, 459-465
    application variables, 459
    project variables, 460
    reviewing/changing, 462-465
    site variables, 459
    system variables, 459
    user variables, 460
  creating, 461-462
  overview, 458-459
  reviewing components, 502-503
  saving settings, 104
  user interfaces, 514-520
    custom tool boxes, creating, 516-518
    Modify Menus settings box, 519-520
    personal user interfaces, creating, 514-516
    view borders, changing, 520
  user preferences, 503-514
    compatibility, 504-505
    drawing preferences, 505
    GUI options preferences, 506-507
    operation preferences, 507-508
    reference file preferences, 508-510
    text preferences, 510-512
    Tools palette preferences, 512-514
Workspaces menu commands, 21
  Button Assignments, 14, 474-475
  Preference, 86

X-Y-Z

x-axis (Dimension Angle From X-Axis tool), 367-368

y-axis (Dimension Angle From Y-Axis tool), 368-369

zooming views, 149-151